For

UNCONSCIOUS DOMINIONS

with
best wishes,

Rick

UNCONSCIOUS
DOMINIONS

Psychoanalysis,

Colonial Trauma, and

Global Sovereignties

Edited by

WARWICK ANDERSON,

DEBORAH JENSON, AND

RICHARD C. KELLER

Duke University Press | Durham and London | 2011

© 2011 Duke University Press

All rights reserved.

Printed in the United States of America on acid-free paper ∞

Designed by Heather Hensley

Typeset in Warnock Pro by Keystone Typesetting, Inc.

Library of Congress Cataloging-in-Publication Data appear
on the last printed page of this book.

CONTENTS

ACKNOWLEDGMENTS

Like most collective efforts, this book has acquired countless debts, far too many to acquit adequately here. We are grateful to the Division of International Studies and the Department of Medical History and Bioethics of the University of Wisconsin for supporting our workshop on "Unconscious Dominions: Comparing Histories of Psychoanalysis, Empire, and Citizenship" (2005), from which most of these essays derive. Lucienne Loh and Michitake Aso provided the necessary research assistance, along with counsel and advice. At Duke University Press, Ken Wissoker has nudged this project forward into new and surprising territories, with the help of comments from two anonymous reviewers. The editors especially appreciate the support and patience of their families and friends, sustained even when those closest to us came to wonder about our strange enthusiasm for this topic.

WARWICK ANDERSON, DEBORAH JENSON,
AND RICHARD C. KELLER

Introduction | **Globalizing the Unconscious**

In *Globalization and Its Discontents*, the economist Joseph Stiglitz chose to echo Sigmund Freud's *Civilization and Its Discontents*. In this volume, we explore in a more deliberative mode the globalization of the unconscious as a mediating discourse of modern civilization, its discontents, and its others. We ask how psychoanalysis and colonialism together forged the conflicted cosmopolitan figure of the universalized, psychoanalyzable subject—a figure that has withstood the removal of the formal psychoanalytic scaffolding that once buttressed it. That is, we seek to gauge the extent to which the psychoanalytic subject, that figment of European high modernism, is constitutively a colonial creature. Embedded in this project are other pressing questions. How did people around the world come to recognize this hybrid and cathectic configuration of unconscious, ego, and sometimes even superego in themselves and others? How, indeed, did the modern psychoanalytic subject—a distinctive style of imagining one's subjectivity or psychic makeup—go global? Further, does charting the generalization of a particular sort of psychological subject offer a means of retrieving and imagining other "possible selves" in globalization?

From the 1920s, psychoanalysis was a mobile technology of both the late colonial state and anti-imperialism. Insights from psychoanalysis shaped European and North American ideas about the colonial world, the character and potential of "native" cultures, and the anxieties and alienation of displaced white colonizers and sojourners. Moreover, intense and intimate engagement with empire came to shape the apparently generic psychoanalytic subjectivities that emerged in the twentieth century—whether European or non-European. Our understandings of culture, citizenship, and self thus have a history that is both colonial and psychoanalytic—yet the character of this intersection has been scarcely explored and never examined in comparative perspective.

We have heard plenty about global capitalism, global warming, and the globalization of religion, education, science, and the English language. We recognize global disease threats, develop global organizations to manage them, and manufacture global pharmaceuticals to contain them. We know perhaps even more about global terrorism and policing. Then, there are global environmental movements, global feminisms, global financial crises, global food shortages, and the World Wide Web. Cosmopolitan figures are everywhere on the move, and everywhere as well are the traces of diaspora. Here, though, we want to draw attention particularly to the colonial emergence and global dispersal of the psychoanalytic subject. In the following chapters, we reveal the multiple relations of psychoanalysis with the colonial state, the nation, and the modern citizen, charting the *specificity* of the relations of psychology and globalization.

Like psychoanalysis and the discourses of scientific rationalism, biomedicine, and Enlightenment republicanism in which it finds its roots, cultural globalization assumes a universal and cosmopolitan subject as prerequisite for its possibility. Globalization's aqueous metaphors (flows of information, the fluidity of capital exchange, floods of refugees) tap the same well as Freud's oceanic self, as does the republican universalism that overwhelms difference or anchors it within a civic teleology. Although these discourses allow room for particularism, they do so only to the extent that such differences are assimilable into a single model of the subject that conceals real difference in favor of a uniform possibility of transformation and fluid exchange. The chapters in this volume focus intensely on this problematic. Through their engagement with mimesis, alterity, trauma, sovereignty, violence, or combinations of all of these, they extract the often tortuous logic that operated in colonial dominions and nascent postcolonies to situate the other in a universalist framework, whether through models of assimilation and association, civilization and culture, or state and subject.

The codependence of psychoanalysis and "progressive" or liberal colonialism and nationalism is thus, we argue, a missing link between Enlightenment universalism, with all its exclusions and absorptions, and the de facto universality of postmodern globalization, with all its fractured sub-jectivities. The unconscious of liberal humanism is not only its implicit categories of the inhuman but also the ego-id negotiation of boundaries between the human and the inhuman.

By relocating psychoanalysis in the domain of colonization, we seek to give new historical depth and political nuance to psychoanalytic elements of postcolonial theory. Our project is therefore as much one of retrieving as uncovering. Too often, the psychoanalytic has functioned as an unex-amined critical force, a sort of *deus ex machina* of postcolonial theory. In contrast, by inserting the globalized psychoanalytic subject in an explicitly postcolonial frame, we want to recover a specific political potential in psychoanalytic interpretations of trauma and sovereignty.

Ethnohistory, Colonialism, and the Cosmopolitan Psychoanalytic Subject

The research in these chapters is organized around two goals: bringing the history of psychoanalysis into colonial focus and employing this colo-nialized psychoanalysis for purposes of postcolonial critique. Chapters in the first part of the volume, therefore, address how empire, globalization, and the idea of psychological "otherness" have become imbricated in the continuing development of psychoanalytic discourse. Biographers have repeatedly emphasized the ways in which Freud was a product of his time; indeed, psychoanalysis is impossible to imagine outside the context of Western bourgeois modernity. Yet, scholars have paid significantly less attention to the implicit colonial assumptions of early psychoanalysis. From Freud's famous description of female sexuality as a "dark continent" to his conceptualization of "primitive" societies and the origins of civiliza-tion in "Totem and Taboo," much of psychoanalytic discourse is inextri-cable from the ideologies that undergirded European expansion.[1] At the time some members of the "native" elite in the empires were appropriat-ing an ego, many Europeans were beginning to suspect the destabilizing colonial tropics were lodged deep within their own mentality.[2]

In effect, the notions of the unconscious as a forbidden zone of irra-tional desire and passionate violence relied on imperial imaginings that continued to structure colonial space in starkly opposing terms. The di-chotomy between the cool exterior of the autonomous bourgeois ego and the inflamed turmoil of the colonized unconscious reflected the tensions of a "self-conscious" European modernity that defined itself against the unchanging "primitivism" of non-Western civilizations.[3] Although a range of social sciences in the early twentieth century embraced the idea of a universal unconscious that drew on assumptions about the "primitive" as a referent—often unconnected to any psychoanalytic dynamic—the colonized subject holds a special meditative place for explicitly psychoanalytic thinkers from Freud onward. Their writings reveal the powerful influence of ideas about the primitive gleaned from both research undertaken in tropical possessions and the florid reveries of colonial literatures. In the work of authors as diverse as W. H. R. Rivers, whose studies of sexuality and dream-life in the Solomon Islands informed his psychoanalytic practice in Britain, and Jacques Lacan, who drew on Claude Lévi-Strauss's reconfiguration of structural linguistics to elaborate his concept of the symbolic realm, the categorization of human societies under colonialism and the formation of the modern psychoanalytic subject are inseparable.[4]

Our work on the colonialization of psychoanalysis asks the following questions, in diverse global contexts: What did the self-consciously cosmopolitan psychoanalyst need from the "native"? How and in what ways has the "primitive" subject—illustrated in guises ranging from the child creator/fantasist in Sigmund Freud's family romance through Wulf Sachs's Black Hamlet and Octave Mannoni's Caliban to George Devereux's Plains Indian—been essential to the development of ideas about the universality of the unconscious? How was colonial desire implicated in psychoanalytic discourse and its infrastructural integration? In what ways are psychoanalytic self and liberal governmentality mutually constitutive?

In the "melancholic" modernity outlined by Ranjana Khanna in her concluding remarks, the difference between colonized cultures and bourgeois Euro-American societies threatened to blur some of the clearest lines of demarcation between psychoanalysis and other medical and social sciences informed by the idea of the unconscious. The "discontents" of the colonized individual were considered from a blind side of civilization: the Western fixation on racial hierarchy and an attending difficulty in fully conceptualizing the individual psyche outside of certain Western frames. An inability to imagine the psychic sovereignty of the colonized individual, and to apply the transferential and countertransferential structures of psychoanalysis fully across perceptions of racial and cultural difference, arguably nudged the dynamic basis of psychoanalytic dialogue a step closer to prescriptive and descriptive uses of the idea of the unconscious in related fields of medical and social sciences. Colonialism, like patriarchal treatments of femininity and nonhetero-sexual/gender orientations, presented a primordial challenge to notions of the global translatability of curative analytical work based on the social life of the unconscious.

As the chapters in this volume indicate, the implications of these entanglements operated in the clinical setting but also extended far beyond it and have persisted into the present. Where the Bengali analyst Girindrasekhar Bose grappled with the adaptation of Freudian concepts to the psychic needs and expectations of a Hindu clientele, the metaphorical and discursive links between the turbulent, primordial unconscious and the colonial "heart of darkness" have influenced transcultural interactions well into the era of globalization.

Writers and philosophers who embraced psychoanalytic methods for grappling with the problem of modern subjectivity—for example, Michel Leiris and Georges Bataille—borrowed significantly from ethnographic literature to articulate the fragmentation of the self as a manifestation of "primitive mentality" in the modern world.[5] In an era of rampant globalization, such ideas about psychological difference between postindustrial society and the Global South have proven intractable, rendering the multiple discourses of colonial psychoanalysis relevant to the interpretation of contemporary global processes. From the inclusion of dozens of "culture-bound syndromes" in the American Psychiatric Association's *Diagnostic and Statistical Manual of Mental Disorders-IV* to the operation of "ethno-psychoanalytic" clinics in hubs of south-to-north migration such as Paris and London, contemporary therapeutics has reembraced both the essentialism and the progressivism that evolved under colonialism.[6]

In the opening chapter of this volume, John D. Cash broaches the use of a "psychoanalytic turn" to account for the often tragic history of hegemony in cultural relations and notes that an oversocialized view of humanity has often resulted from the application of psychoanalysis to intersections of the social and the political. At the same time, the notion of a decentered subject is built into psychoanalysis in texts such as Freud's case study of the Rat Man, and as Cash states, postcolonial studies have been especially drawn to disruptions of "any idea of human subjects as cultural dupes or dopes." The cosmopolitan psychoanalytic subject, Cash in effect argues, is equally at home—and *unheimlich*, or not at home—as a paradigm in colonial or postcolonial settings. In his reading of the oriental traces in Freud's analysis of the Rat Man, Cash explores psychoanalysis as a mediator of discrimination and dehumanization, on the one hand, and, on the other hand, as a vector of resistance to dehumanizing ideologies and their symbolic and structural violence. The military tale of torture practiced "in the East" through the use of rats—to quote Cash, "the almost domestic, dirty animal; the uncanny, homely animal" that is emblematic of human subjectivity for Freud—produces the problem of sovereignty through the use of the rats to invade the corporeal spaces of the human. For Cash, the Rat Man's fantasies about this torture in the East encode not just a parable of the sovereignty of the subject but of the friend-enemy distinction and of dehumanization and the politics of inclusion in Abrahamic thought—in particular, the importance of such logics for extrahistorical structures of self.[7] Cash challenges us to consider the psychoanalytic relationship between civilizing processes and postcolonialism not as sequential or counterdiscourses but as mutually imbricated in the history of the case of the Rat Man.

The colonialization of psychoanalysis reveals these double tensions around psychological sovereignty and the governance of "excluded" or marginalized populations in a number of world contexts. Contributor Alice Bullard questions what French psychiatrist and analyst Henri Aubin desired from Africans, and Joy Damousi wonders what Géza Róheim required of Aboriginal Australians. What did these anthropologically minded analysts need these people to do? And what could they not allow them to do? What were they denying? At the same time Rivers looked for primitive "survivals" among the Todas, he appears to have disavowed the colonial predicament. So sensitive to the trauma of soldiers in the First World War, the colonial psychologist resisted Freud's more general engagement with the violence of the social tie and his insistence on the dissection of authority. As a later explorer of the tensions between psychoanalysis and anthropology, or the universal and the particular, Róheim similarly distinguished the psychological significance of past collective trauma from the social conditions of his recent informants, the victims of contemporary colonial violence. Yet, Róheim, unlike Freud, could not entirely prevent individual Aborigines from intruding on his musings about the primitive, and as a result, their modal subjectivity in the field kept becoming uncontrollably more complex and modern. Róheim claimed that his goal was to "find the latent wish-fulfillment formula in each specific type of social organization," yet he sedulously resisted any such interrogation of colonialism.[8]

Damousi's chapter forces us to consider what psychoanalytic questions and desires have since taken the place of Róheim's in studies of Aboriginal

Australians. According to Jennifer Rutherford, white intruders encountered Aboriginality as an unsymbolized remainder, something beyond signification, and a rupture with the law of the old world against which they needed to defend themselves aggressively.[9] For Ken Gelder and Jane M. Jacobs, the Aboriginal sacred continued to haunt settler nationalism, producing a sense of the uncanny, so "modernity is in a state of (dis)possession, never lost to itself but never properly secure either."[10] In Elizabeth Povinelli's analysis, Aboriginal Australians figured as fetishized diversity within the national imaginary, being made to desire adjustment to others in a liberal, multicultural state.[11] Thus, the discourse of "land rights" permitted alterity to be recuperated as multicultural citizenship. Though traveling multiple routes, these analysts are still trying to find some meaning in Aboriginality for debates over civilization, liberalism, or nationalism.[12] As Damousi notes, Róheim's work on the "savage" unconscious calls again into question the construction of the primitive and the universality of the psychoanalytic self.

The influence of empire on the making of the modern psychoanalytic subject is amplified through the use of psychoanalysis in the framing of colonial subjectivity and nationalist citizenship. Colonial psychoanalysis gave expression to a shift from notions of the "savage mind" to the idea that the subjectivity of elite "natives" was sufficiently complex and conflicted to render them capable of being psychoanalyzed and implicitly eligible for generic citizenship. The governing of the unconscious became a prerequisite for participation in nations and their history.

One of the critical problems of colonial administration in the late nineteenth and early twentieth centuries was the comprehension of the colonial "other"—that is, the fixing of native populations and their sociocultural complexity in the objectifying language of modern science. A broad range of medical, biological, and social-scientific disciplines converged in British, French, Dutch, and American imperial projects to produce specifically colonial forms of knowledge, including tropical medicine, disease ecology, and cultural and social anthropology.[13] Later, psychoanalytic concepts provided an essential logic for the interpretation of this information. In the 1920s and 1930s, both ethnographers who studied sexuality and childrearing and colonial administrators who struggled against growing nationalist movements came to lean on psychoanalytic language and ideas to describe unfamiliar human environments in understandable —and highly normative—terms.[14]

Psychoanalytic knowledge assisted in establishing a baseline for the native's personality, a critical dictum for the framing of colonial educational, judicial, and administrative policies in specific locales. As with an American therapeutic discourse about the modal personality of the "Negro" in the mid-twentieth century, such knowledge also fostered the development of deep social divisions even as it asserted its emancipatory potential.[15] As Hans Pols suggests in his chapter on the response to nationalism in the Dutch East Indies, psychological criteria helped to distinguish colonized elites from their social milieu and aided in the selection of "adaptable" subjects as local agents of colonial rule. Yet, these same colonized elites also frequently contested the knowledge on which their social positions were based. Colonial subjects who became fluent in the idiom of psychoanalysis transformed Freudian discourse as they adopted it, reversing standard interpretations of the Oedipal triangle, for example, with powerful implications for both the patriarchal structure of many colonial societies and the paternalism of colonial rule. A potential tool of domination that sought to inscribe the native personality indelibly, psychoanalysis could also provide a conceptual framework for negotiating self-government.

In some colonies, especially after 1920, the "talking therapy" of psychoanalysis might on occasion have been used to salvage elite neurotics, whether colonizers or colonized, and rehabilitate them as suitably modern subjects. Although French psychiatrists in the Maghreb occasionally dabbled in analytic methods, India was perhaps the most "psychologized" of colonies.[16] Medical doctors, two of them British, established the Indian Psychoanalytical Association in 1922. Among its leading figures were Girindrasekhar Bose, a Bengali physician, and Owen Berkeley-Hill, a socially defiant member of the Indian Medical Service and later the director of Ranchi Mental Hospital in Bihar.[17] Ashis Nandy has observed that because psychoanalysis came to India along with colonialism, "the new psychological man had to be by definition, a colonial subject." It was "as if psychology had to be, by definition again, the latest in a series of techniques of retooling Indians into a prescribed version of the nineteenth-century European."[18] According to Sudhir Kakar, colonial psychoanalysis produced "images of people who talk the European language with a quaint engagingness but whose inner life is bland and certainly far less complex than that of the writers' middle-class English, French or American friends."[19] Non-Western subjects of psychotherapy thus became, in a

sense, second-class citizens in psychological modernity, poorly understood and crudely enculturated.

In the global map outlined by our contributors, psychoanalytic theory
and practice arguably contribute to the liberal state's strategies of deferral.
In the social evolutionist schema, native elites remain abandoned in nationalism's waiting room.[20] Although the mentality and consciousness of
the colonized elite were less likely to be disparaged as altogether different,
they were increasingly represented psychoanalytically as profane copies
of more authentically complex and conflicted white mental processes.[21]
Many European analysts implied that native elites were stalled on the road
to psychological modernity, requiring continued supervision and discipline. And yet, these same elites could find in psychoanalysis a resource
for demonstrating their current fitness for self-government of body, mentality, and polity. Many were able to translate their eligibility for psychoanalysis into a structure of self that implied their satisfaction of the criteria
for citizenship. No longer cast as undifferentiated id, these elites strate-
gically appropriated an ego, thus mobilizing an imagined national public
that was similarly psychologically modern.

Christiane Hartnack's chapter on the acclimatization of psychoanalysis to colonial Calcutta and Mariano Ben Plotkin's chapter on the implantation of psychoanalysis in early twentieth-century Brazil showcase
what Hartnack terms "colonization of the mind" alongside related but
contrasting phenomena such as the "dialectics of defeat," coined by Govind Purushottam Deshpande, in which a retrieval and reinvention of traditional cultures might counterbalance colonial negations of cultural
value.[22] Bengali psychologist Girindrasekhar Bose, Hartnack notes, was
one of the first to adapt psychoanalytical concepts to Indian identity politics. Psychoanalysis among the local *bhadralok* elite foreshadowed Frantz
Fanon's later adaptation of colonial-era psychoanalysis to the construction
of anticolonial subjective and cultural sovereignty in French-occupied
North Africa. Hartnack's detailed description of the emergence of a psychoanalytic training and professional apparatus in Calcutta highlights the
cross-identarian uses of medical/cultural epistemologies of self under
globalization. In early twentieth-century Calcutta, psychoanalysis took on
peculiarly cosmopolitan dimensions in that it was practiced, Hartnack
concludes, "in those realms where British and Indian cultures merged,
competed, or clashed."

Plotkin's chapter ponders how some systems of thought, such as psychoanalysis, are capable of recasting the *Weltanschauung* of a century, even when displaced from their geographical and cultural origins. He demonstrates that psychoanalysis, not just as a therapeutic technique but as an artifact of cultural consumption, shifted in the twentieth century away from its German-language source origins to Anglophone sources and then to French and noncontinental Spanish-language cultural primacy. The uses of psychoanalysis broadened to what Plotkin describes as "an aesthetic and ideological tool." The reception of psychoanalysis in Brazil was tempered by concerns about race relations and national identity with the Brazilian elites' *habitus*. According to Plotkin, the concepts of repression and resistance—both notably central to the practices of colonization and decolonization—were key to a genealogy that Freud and his followers had relocated as a strategy for legitimation of psychoanalysis in medical and intellectual circles. In Brazil, such psychoanalytic concepts became important in the construction of national identity in the social imagination, not only within scientific circles, but also within the avant-garde *modernista* movement. Psychoanalytic ideas were integrated in relation to tensions around new European immigration and local histories of slavery, abolition, and Aboriginality.

Psychoanalysis and Anti- or Postcolonial Critique:
Trauma, Subjectivity, Sovereignty

Psychoanalytic delimitations of colonized subjects and the corresponding shallow psychological enculturation of "natives" in globalized structures of liberal statehood feed directly into the problem of postcolonial engagement with trauma and sovereignty in imperial modernity. Despite the numerous critiques of the notion of trauma as maladapted to national or ethnic or other collective experience, discussing large-scale phenomena of trouble and suffering *without* having recourse to discourses of psychic wounding is difficult, even though such discourses may be implicated in infringements of sovereignty.[23] Of course, Fanon felt free to use psychoanalysis in critique of colonial racism, even though he was aware that it was hardly an innocent or unencumbered critical resource.

Working through the paradoxes inherent in the project of postcolonial psychoanalysis is one of this volume's central goals. Just as the unconscious knows no contradiction, to paraphrase Freud, colonial practitioners saw no incompatibility in framing the so-called magical or irrational thought of "the native" in the omnipotent language of rational analysis.

They offered a sort of mirror image to artists, philosophers, and ethnographers who romanticized the "primitive" in the interwar era. As Plotkin notes concerning the Argentine and Brazilian reception of psychoanalysis, medical circles may have embraced the concept of sublimation and the attendant possibility of the "educability" of the population, but intellectual circles used psychoanalysis for a new appreciation of "wild" and exotic Latin cultures. Seeing the carnage of the Great War as the logical terminus of bourgeois civilization's itinerary, surrealists such as André Breton and his fellow travelers Bataille and Leiris saw redemptive potential in the social margins, including children not yet corrupted by education's moral straitjacket, "hysterical" women, madmen, and especially "the primitive," all of whom offered an antithesis to European modernity's social and intellectual strictures. The apparent irrationality of what Lucien Lévy-Bruhl famously termed the "primitive mentality" opened a pathway to aesthetic possibility ripe for cultivation and indulgence. Many analysts in the colonies and their metropolitan avatars agreed and even depended on the idea that any distinction between "civilized" and "primitive" mentalities could never be hard and fast. Yet, as a consequence, they also insisted that the "colonial unconscious" was subject to the same methods of dissection and analysis as the Western bourgeois psyche.

Psychoanalysis thus served as a critical organizing tool for those who considered "primitivism" to constitute the heart of the modern ego. If a central project of psychoanalysis was to demonstrate the universality of its central tenets, then finding vestigial traces of such "primitive" characteristics as the incest taboo, filial ambivalence, fetishism, and the tension between the indulgence and repression of the drives in modern Westerners provided an explanatory logic for the evolution of the "family of man." The irruption of savagery among the civilized was less pathology than it was atavism—no stranger than the vestigial hips of some snakes or the appendix in the human.

Psychoanalysis, as practiced and elaborated in colonial settings and, particularly, as adopted and adapted in the emergent postcolony, became reconfigured as a powerful critique of colonialism. The French analyst Mannoni, himself analyzed by Lacan in the late 1940s, took from psychoanalysis a theoretical tool kit for modeling the psychical development of Malagasy, based on his experiences as a colonial schoolteacher and as a witness to the bloody repression of the Madagascar uprising in 1947. Although bearing a surface similarity to other works on the modal personalities of ethnic "others," Mannoni's conceptualization of the Malagasy's "dependency complex" differed in that it posited a pathological personality structure that originated specifically in colonial political oppression. And while the psychiatrist Fanon was more a fellow traveler than an analyst, he, too, found inspiration in Lacanian models of the psyche when grappling with personality development among colonized peoples. It was his own experience as an Antillean medical student in France that served as the basis for the essays in his formative book *Black Skins, White Masks* and that eventually informed his model of colonial psychopathology in the Algerian conflict. He was among the first to point not only to the pathogenic nature of colonial domination but also the intense psychological compromises and conflicts of the "nationalist bourgeoisie" in the postcolonial state.

Fanon was working in a tradition that had already admitted, and attempted to codify, colonial alterity and mental conflict, but he took this psychic economy and rendered it political.[24] "Does psychoanalysis win out over Marxism?" Albert Memmi asked. "Does it all depend on the individual or on society?"[25] Fanon did not doubt that it all depended on psychogenesis within a specifically colonial social structure. "For the black man," he wrote, "historical and economic realities come into the [psychoanalytic] picture," which meant that "a black man's alienation is not an individual question."[26] A new generation of oppositional colonial psychiatrists would thus practice a politically informed socioanalysis as much as psychoanalysis. Relocated and socialized, psychoanalytic theory could inform an emergent postcolonial critique, one in which the recognition of instabilities of identity might be used to question essentialist fantasies rather than to recuperate them. Even so, much of the postcolonial theory that the work of Fanon has inspired fails to recognize how implicated psychoanalysis could be in colonial mentalities—how its relations with the colonial/postcolonial state might be as tender as they were tense.

More recently, some postcolonial theorists have elaborated extensively on Fanon's "socio-diagnostic psychiatry."[27] They recast the colonial setting as a place of fantasy and paranoia, of desire jostling against fear and loathing, thereby revealing the unsettling ambivalence and heterogeneity of encounters with alterity. Some would substitute this unsustainable projection and disavowal of difference for Fanon's simple Manichean dichotomy as the recurrent psychopathology of colonialism. Such play of identification and denial, of narcissism and paranoia, leads not to fixed and stable colonial categories but to the ramification of hybridity and ambivalence.[28] This insight has directed attention to how the latent articulation of the colonized might disrupt and disturb the ostensive identities of white male colonizers. For example, Ashis Nandy described Rudyard Kipling's "pathetic self-hatred and ego construction which went with colonialism," and Homi K. Bhabha observed more generally that "the colonizer is himself caught in the ambivalence of paranoic identification." Indeed, Bhabha went on to argue that by avoiding the earlier emphases on personal responsibility and on the recovery of masterful identity, it may be possible "to redeem the pathos of cultural confusion into a strategy of political subversion."[29] Yet, other postcolonial critics warn of the dangers of reducing "social and political problems to psychological ones, and of the substitution of poststructuralist linguistic manipulation for historical and social explanation."[30]

In this section on psychoanalysis and postcolonial critique, contributors range broadly, from chapters directly addressing psychiatry and psychoanalysis in the postcolonial era, to critiques of biopolitical knowledge in literary representations, to studies of trauma in colonial conquest, and in memory.

Hans Pols's chapter on Pieter Mattheus van Wulfften Palthe and the Indonesian struggle for independence investigates the problem of subjective sovereignty through psychoanalytic interpretations of anticolonial violence. Van Wulfften Palthe's writings on the so-called culture-bound syndromes, notably *amok*, served as a basis for his later historicization of Indonesian anticolonialism as "irrational" and "hypnotic" rather than as a product of the desire for self-determination and cultural sovereignty. A "family romance gone awry," Indonesian nationalist struggles were also seen by psychoanalytic observers as a historical literalization of "Totem and Taboo."[31] For van Wulfften Palthe, a Javanese failure to sublimate emotion led to the spilling over of accumulated aggression in struggles for autonomy. Anticolonialism, ostensibly characterized by a "dream-state" of wish fulfillment, played out similarly to Aboriginality in conceptualizations of civilization. John Colin Carothers's association of supernatural beliefs with the Mau Mau rebellion in Kenya provides another example of a psychiatric interpretation of colonialism that failed to consider, as Pols notes, the "narcissistic investment" of colonizers in "colonial subjects and possessions."[32]

Deborah Jenson takes on the challenge of placing Haiti in what Jacques

Derrida called "geopsychoanalytic space." She traces a creolization or interculturation of the unconscious, from eighteenth-century medical theories of *hypnose* (later called trypanosomiasis) as nostalgia or shock by electric manta rays, to the reception of animal magnetism or mesmerism in Saint-Domingue, to prepsychoanalytic European discourses of the unconscious and their positioning of the paradigm's applicability to the field of colonialism. The psychoanalytic concept of trauma both invites and resists application to social history and especially to history of imperial conquest, revolutionary decolonization, and neocolonial repetitions of colonial abuses. In Ruth Leys's problematization of the character of trauma as mimetic trauma or "traumatic mimesis," the victim unconsciously and almost hypnotically identifies with the aggressor and is open to imitation and therefore to repetition, in different subject positionings, of traumatic experience.[33] This interpretation of trauma threatens many historical interpretations of trauma in which "sovereign" victims are invaded by purely external traumatic structures and agents. Jenson argues that the paradigm of traumatic mimesis is, however, particularly apt for analysis of the Haitian Revolution (1791–1804) in which France and Haiti, Napoleon Bonaparte and Toussaint Louverture, and colonial trauma and postcolonial trauma operate as doubles, where the sovereignty of victim and aggressor is blurred by mimetic relationships and resistances. The psychoanalytic self here may be a "universal," but it is continually breached and structured by the colonized or colonizing other.

Richard C. Keller argues that although many social scientists and humanists have exhaustively explored the production of biopolitical knowledge and its implications, fewer have examined medicine as an explicit source of suffering and disenfranchisement. His chapter studies these phenomena by examining the complicity of medicine in the structural violence of the colonial situation, where the medical and psychiatric clinic often operated as a literal theater for colonial conflict and for the marginalization of indigenous subjects. For twentieth-century Algerian author Kateb Yacine, Keller maintains, psychiatry operated as a biopolitical machine for the regulation of a colonial order in which citizenship was a privilege of the European settler. Kateb's poetry, drama, and novels provide crucial sources for exploring literature as a site of resistance to a psychiatric paradigm that cast the Algerian as a noncitizen and for articulating legal consciousness in a context of colonial oppression. Keller's chapter probes the possibilities of applying methodologies borrowed from the social history of medicine and medical anthropology to literary works, with the goal of shedding light on the relationship between health, citizenship, and consciousness. By reading Kateb's work alongside critical documents in the history of colonial medicine, he points to the multiple axes of oppression that shape suffering, disenfranchise populations, and preclude "healing." Drawing on recent anthropological work on suffering and structural violence, Keller ultimately argues that Kateb's uses of medical language to reinscribe social experience are highly relevant in a world in which legal citizenship and the right to health remain closely entwined.

Whereas many of the previously discussed chapters in this volume point to the violence of colonial occupation and struggles for decolonization, anthropologist Didier Fassin stresses the ongoing traumas of the postcolonial in French republican discourses of development and immigration. Fassin takes on the paradoxes of republican universalism by tracing the development of "ethnopsychiatry" as a technology for negotiating the tensions of the welfare state in the context of postcolonial immigration. A product of the colonial period, ethnopsychiatry represented a confounded array of anthropological and psychological musings about the biocultural making of the colonized subject. The work of the psychoanalytically oriented Dakar School under Henri Collomb in the 1960s represented a culmination of such work, signaling without irony the possible merging of a universal personality structure and the regionally specific influences of particular forms of socialization. But the reuptake of ethnopsychiatry as practiced in France in the 1980s provided a stage for recognizing cultural determinism in a society that preached universalism. Ethnopsychiatric services emerged at a particular moment in French history: the 1980s witnessed both a transformation of national discussions about immigration from an official politics of inclusion to an unofficial one of illegitimacy and a remaking of the welfare state, with rights to health as a central pillar. As a consequence, ethnopsychiatry has become a venue for the inscription of cultural particularism in a society that refuses its recognition. Ethnopsychiatric research centers have become sites of official recourse for immigrants and their descendents who run afoul of French law or civic practice, as state physicians, social workers, and jurists have called on them to "treat" cases of "witchcraft" and *maraboutage* but also to reconcile social disputes, heal delinquency, and negotiate "cultural" practices such as forced marriage and excision. The problem, however, is that the emphasis on "culture" in such circumstances has both reinforced the second-class status of immigrant populations by marking them as particular exceptions to the rule of republican universalism and simultaneously elided the recognition of a deleterious and discriminatory political economy that perpetuated economic inequalities in postcolonial France.

Ranjana Khanna provides the closing remarks for this volume. Subjectivity—whether it refers to conscious beings, a consciousness of one's condition, a state of subjection, or grammatical attempts at sovereignty— needs to proceed from a questioning of what constitutes the human in current configurations of internationalist discourse. That is, one needs to understand how subjectivity is inscribed, partly in relation to the state and partly in conceptions of the international. In a world of intense pressures, psychoanalysis, with its investments in the sovereign subject as a vital location of the human and of history, yields to new problems of distinguishing between the social life of the subject in cosmopolitanism and globalization. In her chapter, Khanna proposes that "the international demands of psychoanalysis a new version of itself, as it did of Marxism some time earlier" and that modernist internationalism is generally characterized by loss. She contends that international psychoanalysis is optimally framed by Freud's failure to theorize melancholia adequately, particularly in relation to refugees, stateless people, and even the loss of a given ideal of the nation in decolonization. As Khanna concludes, this unresolved nature of melancholia both "impoverishes the unconscious dominion of psychoanalysis" and prevents its banal reification of cultural difference, leaving international psychoanalysis positioned in a liminal relation to hope, demand, and the perpetual.

Beyond the Psychoanalytic Fetish

In an influential series of articles, William Pietz observed that the problem of the fetish appeared at the point of exchange between different societies —that it arose between cultures in contact.[34] Psychoanalysis is similarly situated, though its intimate yet worldly ethnohistory has often been repressed. We need to face squarely the continuing past of psychoanalysis, whether as an alibi for colonial power or as positioned in dialectical relation to colonialism. The comforting notion that analysis is somehow separable from its conditions of possibility is hardly sustainable. As a corrective, we hope that the following chapters will illuminate the intercultural spaces where psychoanalysis developed and in which it continues to operate deconstructively, producing ambivalence or worse—adroitly performing its double act as colonial legacy and postcolonial critique.

In this sense, psychoanalysis cannot structure or inform any one theory arching over colonialism but rather functions as the disruptive or antinomial element within heterogeneous power relations—as corrosion, not architecture. That is, as a partial perspective on a pluralistic field, it works to disturb identity and homogeneity, to interrogate sovereignty, and to bring disavowal and denial to the surface. Psychoanalysis is thus intimately and disconcertingly part of the colonial imaginary and of our postcolonial histories and anthropologies, not tacked onto them as a theory or facile "psychologizing." Like the language we use, psychoanalysis is a flexible technology that is as useful in pulling apart as in building up, so long as it is used knowingly.

Notes

1. Freud, "Totem and Taboo."
2. Anderson, "Trespass Speaks"; Anderson, *Cultivation of Whiteness*.
3. Clifford, *Predicament of Culture*; Said, *Joseph Conrad*; Said, *Culture and Imperialism*; Rabinow, *French Modern*; and Torgovnick, *Gone Primitive*.
4. Rivers, *Conflict and Dream*.
5. Leiris, *L'Afrique fantôme*; Bataille, "L'Amérique disparue"; Bataille, *La part maudite*; and Dean, *Self and Its Pleasures*.
6. Benslama, *La psychanalyse à l'épreuve de l'Islam*; Devereaux, *Essais d'ethnopsychiatrie générale*; Elfakir, *Oedipe et personnalité au Maghreb*; Fassin, "L'ethnopsychiatrie et ses réseaux"; Fassin, "Les politiques de l'ethnopsychiatrie"; Gaines, *Ethnopsychiatry*; Good, "Culture and DSM-IV"; Kirmayer and Minas, "Future of Cultural Psychiatry"; Kleinman, *Patients and Healers in the Context of Culture*; Kleinman, "Anthropology and Psychiatry"; Latour, *Petite réflexion sur le culte moderne des dieux faitiches*; Nathan, *La folie des autres*; Roudinesco and Plon, *Dictionnaire de la psychanalyse*; and Said, *Freud and the Non-European*.
7. Schmitt, *Concept of the Political*; Derrida, *Politics of Friendship*.
8. Róheim, "Psychoanalysis of Primitive Cultural Types," 21.
9. Rutherford, *Gauche Intruder*.
10. Gelder and Jacobs, "Postcolonial Uncanny," 40.
11. Povinelli, "State of Shame."
12. Rose, *Not Being Able to Sleep*.
13. Anderson, *Cultivation of Whiteness*; Arnold, *Colonizing the Body*; Clifford, *Predicament of Culture*; Cohn, *Colonialism and Its Forms of Knowledge*; Kuklick, *Savage Within*; Prakash, *Another Reason*; Stoler, *Race and the Education of Desire*; Torgovnick, *Gone Primitive*; and Vaughan, *Curing Their Ills*.

14. Anderson, "Trespass Speaks"; Keller, *Colonial Madness*; and McCulloch, *Colonial Psychiatry and "the African Mind."*

15. Black, "Race and Unreason"; Jackson, *Social Scientists for Social Justice*; and Scott, *Contempt and Pity.*

16. Donnadieu, "Psychose de civilisation"; Keller, "Madness and Colonization"; and Keller, *Colonial Madness.*

17. See Berkeley-Hill, "Anal-Erotic Factor"; Berkeley-Hill, "'Color Question.'"

18. Nandy, *Savage Freud*, 139; Hartnack, "Vishnu on Freud's Desk."

19. Kakar, *Culture and Psyche*, 15. See also Khanna, *Dark Continents*; Vergès, "Chains of Madness, Chains of Colonialism."

20. Chakrabarty, "Postcoloniality and the Artifice of History"; Chatterjee, *Nation and Its Fragments.*

21. Bhabha, *Location of Culture*; Anderson, "Trespass Speaks."

22. Deshpande, "Dialectics of Defeat."

23. Fischer, *Modernity Disavowed.*

24. Gates and Appiah, *"Race," Writing, and Difference*; Vergès, "Chains of Madness, Chains of Colonialism."

25. Memmi, *Colonizer and the Colonized*, xiii.

26. Fanon, *Dying Colonialism*, 161, 13.

27. Bhabha, "Remembering Fanon"; Fanon, *Black Skin, White Masks.*

28. Bhabha, "Remembering Fanon."

29. Nandy, *Intimate Enemy*, 209; Bhabha, "Interrogating Identity," in *The Location of Culture*, 61.

30. Dirlik, *Postcolonial Aura.*

31. Gouda, *Dutch Culture Overseas.*

32. Carothers, *Psychology of Mau Mau.*

33. Leys, *Trauma.*

34. Pietz, "Problem of the Fetish," pts. 1 and 2.

PART I | Ethnohistory, Colonialism, and the Cosmopolitan Psychoanalytic Subject

Sovereignty in Crisis

Many many decades later, in the aftermath of that marvel of modern technology called the Second World War and perhaps that modern encounter of
cultures called Vietnam, it has become obvious that the drive for mastery
over men is not merely a by-product of a faulty political economy but also of a
world view which believes in the absolute superiority of the human over the
nonhuman and the subhuman, the masculine over the feminine, the adult
over the child, the historical over the ahistorical, and the modern or progressive over the traditional or the savage.
—Ashis Nandy, *The Intimate Enemy*

Within the human sciences, there is a long tradition of turning to psychoanalysis in order to develop more satisfactory
accounts of what Judith Butler has termed "the psychic life of
power."[1] Too often, however, such a turn has been employed merely
to supplement explanations of social order and social reproduction.
Hence, the internalization of social codes, the formation of a common or modal personality structure, or the interpellation of willing
or conforming subjects have been typical ways of drawing together
the social and the subjective. As Dennis Wrong has suggested, all
too frequently, the unhappy product of such an integration of psychoanalysis into social and political theory has been what he terms
an "oversocialized conception of man."[2]

The main tendency of this use of psychoanalysis has been to
produce an account of a subject centered in his or her internalized
and stabilized relation to power and authority. This is an odd outcome, as the very attraction of psychoanalysis lies in its resistance to

such commonplace notions of a centered subjectivity. Rather, as Butler, among others, highlights, psychoanalysis provides an intricate account of the decentered subject; a subject always in process, yet always somewhat organized for the moment; a subject always located within language, culture, and social institutions, yet always with the potential for reorganization.[3] It is this latter account of decentered subjectivity that holds the most interest for the human sciences, and particularly for postcolonial studies, if only because it breaks with any idea of a smooth continuity stretching from the cultural to the subjective and disrupts any idea of human subjects as cultural dupes or dopes. Instead, it leaves open issues of agency and resistance and can address such psychic and cultural formations as Frantz Fanon's Manichean delirium, Ashis Nandy's secret selves, and Homi Bhabha's fetish as stereotype.[4]

Given these characteristics, it is not surprising that this latter psychoanalytic account of human subjectivity as decentered, yet somewhat organized and passionately attached to power and authority, has held a strong attraction for postcolonial theory. With its focus on processes of identification, repression, and splitting and projection, psychoanalysis presents a rich account of the formations and deformations of subjectivity under conditions of intimacy, authority, and the play of power and violence. Sigmund Freud's *Civilization and Its Discontents*, for instance, develops an account of human subjectivities as so many compromise formations that struggle to repress, incorporate, sublimate, and integrate the inevitable tensions and conflicts between the drives, on the one hand, and specific cultural demands and ideals, on the other.

From this perspective, the cultural and psychological effects of colonialism are particular iterations and intensifications of these very civilizing processes. While rejecting the arrogance of any Western claim to universalism, as contained in even those masters of suspicion, Karl Marx and Sigmund Freud, Ashis Nandy nicely captures the attractions of psychoanalysis in such a colonized setting when he writes that "living in two worlds is never easy, and the new middle class in Bengal had lived for decades with deculturation, the break-down of older social ties, and disruption of traditional morality."[5] This theme of "living in two worlds" and the psychological and cultural effects such a split existence entails is a common theme within postcolonial studies, one that psychoanalysis is well suited to address. Nandy summarizes this affinity as follows: "Psychoanalysis with its complex, holistic approach to the human personality—

with its invocation of the person as a thinking, feeling, driven individual—at least allowed one to re-interpret its interpretations and to adapt them to the complexities of Indian society."[6]

Frantz Fanon's journey from the colony to the metropole is also a story about living in two worlds that invites psychoanalytic interpretation, whether in Fanon's own terms or in those of Homi Bhabha or, indeed, many others.[7] Fanon's encounter with the terrified child, presumably in Lyon, is exactly the prototypical moment that splits his world, the condensation of a series of nonrecognitions, indignities, and exceptions that plagued his existence in metropolitan France and revealed to him the inner workings of Western culture. Chapter 5 of *Black Skin, White Masks*, titled "The Fact of Blackness," begins with two epithets: " 'Dirty nigger!' Or simply, 'Look, a Negro.' " These epithets derive from a series of scenes displaced around a central condensation moment, the encounter with the child:

> "Look, a Negro!" It was an external stimulus that flicked over me as I passed by. I made a tight smile.
>
> "Look, a Negro!" It was true. It amused me.
>
> "Look, a Negro!" The circle was drawing a bit tighter. I made no secret of my amusement.
>
> "Mama, see the Negro! I'm frightened!" Frightened! Frightened! Now they were beginning to be afraid of me. I made up my mind to laugh myself to tears, but laughter had become impossible.[8]

Other scenes clustering around this condensation point include the condescension of his "neighbor in the university," the hostility and contempt of "one of those good Frenchmen on a train," the precarious position of the "Negro physician" for whom any mistake "would be the end of him and all those who came after him," and the fear and anxiety of the parents and others accompanying or nearby the frightened child.[9] In a composite scene, these moments are collapsed: " 'Look at the nigger! . . . Mama, a Negro . . . Hell, he's getting mad . . . Take no notice, sir, he does not know that you are as civilized as we.' "[10] This is the characteristic experience of all those who venture from the colony to metropolitan France, "that feeling which pervades each new generation of students arriving in Paris."[11] As Fanon puts it in a footnote, "Quite literally I can say without any risk of error that the Antillean who goes to France in order to convince himself that he is white will find his real face there."[12] The discovery is traumatic:

"What else could it be for me but an amputation, an excision, a haemorrhage that spattered my whole body with black blood?"[13] Hence, he insists, "I am overdetermined from without . . . I am *fixed*."[14]

"The Antillean who goes to France" is a refrain that echoes throughout *Black Skin, White Masks*. It stages the trauma of being "overdetermined from without" as a repetition of traumatic moments that are compelling because they originate and reiterate beyond the subject as an everyday feature of street-life France, yet return to the subject as a narcissistic wound that punctures the imaginary "I" that he, or she, had taken themselves to be; the white mask shrouding the black skin. This is the psychopathology of living in two worlds, a veritable repetition compulsion from without that haunts the subject. In chapter 6, "The Negro and Psychopathology," the theme of trauma, as a series of such traumatic scenes, is explored through reference to some of Freud's early work with Josef Breuer.[15] Fanon subsequently announces that "since the racial drama is played out in the open, the black man has no time to make it unconscious. The white man, on the other hand, succeeds in doing so to a certain extent, because a new element appears: guilt. The Negro's inferiority or superiority complex or his feeling of equality is *conscious*."[16] Here, we see an example of what Nandy has termed a "re-interpret(ing) of (psychoanalytic) interpretations" that "adapt(s) them to the complexities" of, in this case, the Antillean who goes to France.[17] Fanon's split between a white unconscious and a black "conscious" is informed by psychoanalytic conceptualizations, even as it radically adjusts them.[18] Underlying this dubious splitting, however, is a deeper reliance on the psychoanalytic account of trauma and repetition compulsion and on those central features of the dream-work, condensation, and displacement. If mimicry as contradiction and reversal floats across the surface of Fanon's reinterpretation, its deep structure is shaped by its reliance on psychoanalysis, even as it shifts, in a profound move, to overdetermination from without. Indeed, here we find an uncanny resemblance to Lacan's discussion of the purloined letter in *The Ego in Freud's Theory and in the Techniques of Psychoanalysis*, for the Antillean who goes to France finds himself, or herself, subjected to a signifier—indeed, a discourse—that has moved. As Lacan recognized,

> Every human drama, every theatrical drama in particular, is founded on the existence of established bonds, ties, pacts. Human beings already have commitments which tie them together, commitments which have

determined their places, names, their essences. Then along comes another discourse, other commitments, other speech. It is quite certain that there'll be some places where they'll have to come to blows. All treaties aren't signed simultaneously. Some are contradictory. If you go to war it is so as to know which treaty will be binding.[19]

Such interpretive strengths of psychoanalysis do not contradict the fact that psychoanalysis was also a technique deployed in the "normalizing" and "governmentalizing" of the colonized elite. In "The Savage Freud: The First Non-Western Psychoanalyst and the Politics of Secret Selves in Colonial India," Nandy draws our attention to such contrary potentialities in Freud's own work. He argues that Girindrasekhar Bose, as the first non-Western psychoanalyst, was well positioned to appreciate "the other Freud," who had "opened up immense possibilities, some of them invisible to those close to Freud culturally."[20] Most important, argues Nandy, "was the scope to construct a Freud who could be used as a radical critic of the savage world and, at the same time, a subverter of the imperial structures of thought that had turned the South into a dumping ground for dead and moribund categories of the Victorian era."[21]

As Nandy's references to the "savage world" and "imperial structures of thought" highlight, the psychoanalytic conceptualization of human subjectivity and of the vicissitudes of becoming a human subject, and the psychic and cultural traces left by this becoming, carry significant implications for any analysis of the ideologies of distinction, discrimination, and dehumanization that have routinely organized and haunted colonialism. Likewise, they also carry significant implications for any social and/or ethical movement, or political project, of resistance that anticipates the displacement of dehumanizing and exclusivist ideologies and the eradication of the structural, symbolic, and embodied violences that they license and support. In what follows, I explore such implications by drawing on the work of Sigmund Freud, Melanie Klein, Jacques Lacan, and Julia Kristeva to explore aspects of the psychoanalytic account of human subjectivity and its implications for such psychic and cultural phenomena as those listed previously—namely, Manichean delirium, secret selves, and the fetish as stereotype. To do so, I look closely at one of the foundational moments of psychoanalytic theory and at an instance of what we might regard as its principal source; one of Freud's case studies: the case of the Rat Man. I locate this discussion within a consideration of Ashis

Nandy's detailed analysis of the "intimate enemies" created by colonization and with reference to Jacques Derrida's reflections on "the beast and the sovereign."

The Intimate Friend/Enemy

In his analysis of the British colonization of India, *The Intimate Enemy*, and in his reflections titled "Towards a Third World Utopia," as elsewhere, Ashis Nandy is alert to the ways in which colonization successfully institutes its power and authority when it "colonizes minds in addition to bodies and it releases forces within the colonized societies to alter their cultural priorities once for all."[22] In this formulation, Nandy first of all captures the role that a violently transformed culture plays in establishing new codes of propriety through which what counts as the proper form of identity is regulated. With the British colonization of India, this alteration of cultural priorities manifested, principally, in the displacement of the established set of relations between categories of sexed identity. The net effect of this displacement was to produce a hard distinction in which a hypermasculinity contested with a docile "femininity in masculinity," this latter "the final negation of a man's political identity."[23] Hence, both colonizer and colonized were locked into a battle for the hypermasculinist position, one in which the dice, as well as the guns, were heavily loaded against the colonized.[24] Nandy emphasizes, however, that the perverse consequences of this battle impinged on both parties, in both body and mind, producing "psychologically deformed oppressors and their psychologically deformed victims (both seeking secondary psychological gains) [who] find a meaningful lifestyle and mutually potentiating cross-motivations."[25] An enforced cultural alteration, then, stabilized itself through an instituted pattern of distorted and distorting communication that promoted strict, stratificatory boundaries between self and other. These dichotomies that began to populate the colonial culture successfully displaced more permeable differences and distinctions between identities, whether they were based on sex or on age, another of Nandy's principal themes. The imposed imperial sovereignty repressed those "non-dualist traditions" embedded in the "religions, myths and folkways" of "many defeated cultures." Bounded and impermeable distinctions between self and other displaced more dynamic and permeable differentiations and were used to assert civilizational superiority and inferiority. As Nandy puts it, the defeated cultures try to protect the faith—increasingly lost to the modern world—that the borderlines of evil can never be clearly defined, that there is always a continuity between the aggressor and his victim, and that liberation from oppressive structures outside has at the same time to mean freedom from an oppressive part of one's own self. This can be read as a near compromise with the powerful and the victorious; it can be read as cultural resistance to the "normal," the "rational" and the "sane."[26]

In this analysis, the colonized as intimate enemy is culturally obligated to mobilize the friend-enemy distinction and prompted to compete, unequally, to occupy the same hypermasculinist discursive position. Yet, this same friend-enemy formation is haunted by the ambivalence of intimacy.

Nandy's work is replete with such insights and perspectives based in psychoanalytic theory, and these can be schematized around a model of colonized and colonizing subjects and their discontents. Hence, Nandy discusses the ambivalence of compromise and resistance, or collaboration and defiance. He notices identifications with the aggressor. He describes how the cruelties, inequities, and the suffering imposed by imperialism or authoritarianism "distort the cultures and minds" of both colonizer and colonized.[27] For Nandy, then, there are only victims: either immediately recognizable ones or those "camouflaged" ones, who, "at an advanced stage of psychosocial decay," continue to regard themselves as victors.[28] Finally, he identifies a "cultural pathology" in the West's "devastatingly sterile concept of autonomy and individualism which has increasingly atomised the Western individual."[29] Psychoanalysis is, at once, both a further iteration, as a normalizing—indeed, colonizing—discourse, and a radical deconstruction of this devastating cultural pathology. Significant to my later argument, Nandy links this distorting cultural demand for disconnected and sovereign-like hyperautonomy to the anthropocentric worldview of the post-Enlightenment West, the features and consequences of which are so aptly summarized in the epigraph to this chapter. Therein, Nandy itemizes a series of stark dichotomies, beginning with that between the human and the nonhuman; dichotomies that stereotype, stigmatize, and split in the interests of cultural hegemony, narcissism, mastery, and self-sovereignty.

The Beast and the Sovereign

In several of his last publications, and perhaps most centrally in his 2001–2002 seminar, "The Beast and the Sovereign," Jacques Derrida noticed and explored the trace of the animal—the wolf, the fox, the lion, the whale (as leviathan), and so forth—in conceptualizations of sovereignty.[30] The sovereign's exceptional position beyond any need to answer or to respond, allied with a potential for both domination and excess, carry the mark of a deeply embedded distinction within Western thought, and more broadly within Abrahamic thought, Derrida argues. This is the recurrent tendency within the Western heritage (and others) to insist on the application of a dichotomy—of an inviolable boundary between the human and the animal: one that treats all animals as equivalent insofar as they supposedly react rather than respond and have an inability to learn from history and its instituted imaginaries—to learn from its contingent, but consolidated, stocks of know-how. As a consequence, animals are thought to lack free will and are to be understood as hardwired, innately programmed organic machines—the absolute other of the human.

Another place we see this drawing of a stark boundary between the human and the animal is within the friend-enemy distinction; in certain ideologies of race, nation, class, ethnicity, and gender that rely on a dehumanization of the other as a way of removing that other from entitlement to hospitality or inclusion.[31] Such ideologies typically mark and validate the exclusion of the other (human) by casting that other as animal-like or thing-like, as another type of life entirely, or as something that lacks life. This raises the question as to why this split or dichotomy, with its entailments, is so entrenched, so resilient, and so difficult to displace. That is the question that led me to speculate that a review of some salient aspects of Freud's Rat Man case might prove valuable in thinking into these issues of sovereignty, politics, and ideologies of exclusion raised, in different registers, by both Nandy and Derrida.[32] For, in the case of the Rat Man, we are offered a study of a self-sovereignty in crisis, organized around the signifier of the rat: the almost domestic, dirty animal; the uncanny, homely animal that is itself emblematic of the Freudian account of human subjectivity. It is this account of human subjectivity and its implications for a postcolonizing politics of inclusion that I am principally concerned with, and I take up this theme in a manner that throws into question sovereignty's presumed indivisibility and asks at what cost such a narcissistic presumption can be maintained.

The Rat Man

The case of the Rat Man has one of its beginnings when a young man— Ernst Lanzer, as we come to learn much later (Freud names him Paul Lorenz)—goes on military maneuvers as part of his military service requirement. While there, an old army sergeant tells him of a terrible torture practiced "in the East": "The criminal was tied up . . . a pot was turned upside down on his buttocks . . . some rats were put into it . . . and they . . . *bored their way in.*"[33] As soon as he hears this tale, young Ernst has the terrible but, for him, quite delicious thought that this torture should be performed on Gisela, the love of his life, and on his father, who has been dead for some time. Immediately after he has these thoughts, he feels dreadfully guilty, and yet he remains fearful that something terrible will happen to Gisela and to his father. So, he invents a complicated ritual about catching trains, posting letters, and getting people to hand money to each other. But this is no real answer to the dilemma of his desire, as the ritual is so internally contradictory that it preserves, unresolved, his dual passion to both harm and protect Gisela and his father. Soon after this experience, the young man goes to visit Freud, who, we are not surprised to learn, readily agrees to treat him.

The most striking aspect of this precipitating scene is the reference to "in the East." With that one phrase, the cruel captain invokes a whole fantasy structure about oriental despotism and the careless cruelty of the sovereign—he who dominates and whose every wish is a command. It is of passing historical interest, I think, that such an instance of orientalism, splitting, and the friend-enemy distinction should play such a prominent role in the case that Freud presented to the very first meeting of the International Psychoanalytic Congress in Salzburg in 1908. Consider the phrasing Freud uses to describe young Ernst's face as he recounts the story of the cruel captain and the torture practiced in the East: "At all the more important moments while he was telling his story his face took on a very strange composite expression. I could only interpret it as one of horror at pleasure of his own of which he himself was unaware."[34]

Here, we have Freud's major observation: there is a subterranean, unconscious process that is in deadly conflict with this young man's attempts to govern himself. It generates pleasure but also fear and anxiety—fear for himself and for those whom he loves. It is exactly a Hobbesian fear—but this young man finds it impossible to sign up for the compact that would offer protection against the fear. He is, like all of us (only, in all likelihood, more so) a divided self—a decentered subject for whom the social contract is a sacrificial contract that he resents even as he assents.

As a very young boy (between the ages of three and four), Ernst had done something naughty—perhaps it was sexual; perhaps he bit someone. His father beat him as a punishment, and in response, the little boy flew into a rage and hurled abuse at his father. Having no "bad language" to use, he resorted to the names of common objects. So, he screamed at his father, "You lamp! You towel! You plate! and so on."[35] Although, on first impression, this seems a rather cute story, we should not fail to notice that here we have a moment of terror, violence, and fury. The resort to naming the father as a series of inanimate objects is itself a dehumanizing move. This is reinforced by the indication that from this time forward, Ernst was a coward; a coward not exactly out of fear but rather "out of fear of the violence of his own rage."[36] In this, we see a further instance of the fragility of his self-sovereignty and the intensity of his occluded "secret self."

If the young Ernst was almost lost for words of abuse, one of the major aspects of the case is the way in which a whole series of words comes to signify the Rat Man's unresolved ambivalence—what Freud terms a "regular rat currency."[37] Apart from scenes of biting, of worms in his anus (like the rats of the story from the East), of rats at his father's grave, of rats being killed, and so on, there are all those little rat signifiers that, like so many rats' tails, hang off a series of words that accumulate in the analysis. So, we have *spielratte* (referencing his father, the gambler, in colloquial German); we have *hofrat* (the new honorific attached to Fraulien Lina, the girl who was his nurse and object of desire when he was a child, with whom he took "a great many liberties," and who later married a judge, thereby transforming herself into Hofrat Lina); and we have the worries about the cost of the analysis and the condensation of *ratten* and *raten*, which supposedly include Freud putting his daughter on the stairs—the girl, in Ernst's dream, whose beautiful eyes turn to dung.[38] In a massive condensation, the signifier rat inserts itself throughout all aspects of the case. It is as if the words he did not have when he was a violent but impotent child have taken form but remained unconscious around the image and significance of the rat. In the process of attempting to become a civil subject via mechanisms of identification, mirroring, repression, splitting, and projection, the young boy who becomes the young man Freud meets has established a boundary between the human and the animal that he subsequently uses—very unsuccessfully—in order to present himself as a loving son, a suitable husband, and a competent worker. But isn't this a characteristic of becoming a civil subject: a deeply sedimented, culturally—and indeed, civilizationally—ordained way? In particular, isn't this an intensified, overdetermined feature of the post-Enlightenment European imaginary? Aren't these processes of abjection that support the drawing of the categorical boundary between human and animal, friend and enemy, along with the dehumanizing of the other as a means of distancing, disenfranchising, and attacking that other? Isn't this exactly what is at stake when we posit ourselves as sovereign subjects?

In the case of the Rat Man (like all of us, according to this psychoanalytic understanding), this is played out in the place of the other scene, which is beyond any intentional speech and which contains a knowledge that he does not know he has: the scene of the unconscious. Even though this other scene is beyond any intentional speech, it slowly unfolds and displays itself as the Rat Man speaks. It inheres within his speech and slowly declares itself in its very insistence and repetition. Of course, the Rat Man attempts to intentionally reveal himself to Freud, but he actually says more than he intends. He intends to tell Freud about how he is a loving son, a loyal fiancée, and an ambitious law student who somehow finds himself assaulted by thoughts and feelings that are quite alien to him and that he has to work very hard to subdue and keep at bay. But in the very process of telling this story about himself, he gives himself away, as it were. There is something in his speech that insists and persists, which repeats and eventually is heard, first by Freud and then by the Rat Man himself. This is the "regular rat currency," as Freud puts it: that accumulation of rat signifiers that keep recurring in his speech.

So, let me raise this question: According to this psychoanalytic understanding, how do we become a sovereign subject—a proper subject who has subjected himself, or herself, to the sovereign and who has signed up ("fessed up," as it were) to the social contract? What are the psychosocial and psychopolitical implications—indeed, effects—of subjecting ourselves to the law in order to be recognized as a sovereign subject? And in particular, how does this relate to the deeply embedded cultural habit of drawing and policing such a strict boundary between the human and the animal, the friend and the enemy?

In a famous comment, after considering the assault on human narcissism contained within the discoveries of Nicolaus Copernicus and Charles Darwin, Freud reflected on what he regarded as the third and most profound blow to human narcissism—the blow contained within psychoanalysis itself:

> But these two discoveries—that the life of our sexual instincts cannot be wholly tamed, and that mental processes are in themselves unconscious and only reach the ego and come under its control through incomplete and untrustworthy perceptions—these two discoveries amount to a statement that *the ego is not master in its own house*. Together they represent the third blow to man's self love, what I may call the *psychological* one. No wonder then that the ego does not look favourably upon psychoanalysis and obstinately refuses to believe in it.[39]

In the context of this discussion, it is worth noting how Freud understands the relationship between narcissism and our relation to nature. Just a few lines before the preceding quotation, Freud writes,

> In the course of the development of civilization man acquired a dominating position over his fellow-creatures in the animal kingdom. Not content with this supremacy, however, he began to place a gulf between his nature and theirs. He denied the possession of reason to them, and to himself he attributed an immortal soul, and made claims to a divine descent which permitted him to break the bond of community between him and the animal kingdom. Curiously enough, this piece of arrogance is still foreign to children, just as it is to primitive and primeval man. It is the result of a later, more pretentious stage of development.[40]

Freud tells us, then, that the ego is not master in its own house. Moreover, he tells us that humanity, in the history of civilization, comes to break the bond of community with the animal and to place a gulf, an absolute dichotomy, between human nature and animal nature. It is this gulf in which the Rat Man gets trapped and to which we all remain susceptible.

But what becomes of the presumed-to-be-sovereign subject? Is that presumed autonomy as stable as it imagines itself to be? What becomes of civilization's discontents? The formation of the subject takes place in a world of self and others—a world of bodies and parts of bodies and of sensations, memories, and phantasies. It proceeds through processes of abjection, incorporation, identification, internalization, mirroring, repression, and the entry into culture and language. To achieve a capacity to speak and act in the world, we come to exercise sovereignty over ourselves —but this is always subject to disruption by the unconscious. Psychic organization always leaves traces that persist. Our apparent sovereignty, then, is achieved at a cost: the repudiation of aspects of self and others; of bodies and parts of bodies; of sensations, memories, and phantasies; and of desires that cannot be incorporated into the organization of the "I/me" that I take myself to be. This positing of an "I/me" emerges from the capacity to locate or situate the "I" that I take myself to be within a symbolic order as a speaking and acting subject who has some capacity to decide, to choose, and to respond. What we have seen is that this positing of an "I/me" that can act, choose, and respond involves the splitting of the subject. Part of what is split off—part of what becomes unfamiliar or uncanny—is those aspects of myself and my relation to others that have been repudiated and repressed in order to establish an ego or "I." These repressed, split-off aspects remain as part of my unconscious, but they resist recognition by the "I" that I take myself to be. However, they have been preserved as part of my psychic organization—a repressed part—and they insist on some form of representation. Typically, they are recognized as other than me: as strangers or enemies—or as the uncanny. As Freud writes, in regard to the idea of the uncanny double, "There are also all the unfulfilled but possible futures to which we still like to cling in phantasy, all the strivings of the ego which adverse external circumstances have crushed, and all our suppressed acts of volition which nourish in us the illusion of free will. But . . . nothing in this more superficial material could account for the urge towards defence which has caused the ego to project that material outward as something foreign to itself."[41]

Freud then traces this splitting and projecting back to an origin: "When all is said and done, the quality of uncanniness can only come from the fact of the 'double' being a creation dating back to a very early mental stage, long since surmounted—a stage, incidentally, at which it wore a more friendly aspect. The 'double' has become a thing of terror, just as, after the collapse of their religion, the gods turned into demons."[42] If this doubling and splitting persists—as it tends to do—then the only recognition I can give to these repudiated, repressed parts of myself is to see them as the disliked, hated, or despised aspects of others whom I regard as unlike me: strangers, foreigners, or those whom I can successfully construe as different. In this way, what we broadly regard as the dehumanizing, stereotyping, and scapegoating of others proceeds. It is, however, haunted by an uncanny recognition of the other as a desired or detested "object" of and for the subject—a repository for secret desires and not-so-secret aggressivities; an intimate friend-enemy. So, Freud concludes that "this uncanny is in reality nothing new or alien, but something which is familiar and old-established in the mind and which has become alienated from it only through the process of repression."[43]

It is this thought that Julia Kristeva draws on when she proposes that we are strangers to ourselves.[44] She goes on to suggest that to remain as such in the contemporary postcolonial world of interdependency, globalization, and mass migration is to remain in a psychic state that supports aggressive nationalism, dehumanizing racism, and ethnic particularism as defenses against the anxiety generated by the presence of the imagined-as-other within our familiar territory. In the contemporary globalizing world, in what Ulrich Beck has termed the "global risk society," the presence and persistence of othering mechanisms—serving as psychic and cultural defenses against the anxieties generated by change—is itself a major hazard, a source of conflict, and war and destruction. Yet, these othering mechanisms play such a central role in the formation of the "I" that I take myself to be—and in the organization of our psychic structures—that it is very difficult to see how they might be displaced. Moreover, these same othering mechanisms—as I am terming them—have a deeply sedimented place within the Western (and, perhaps, Abrahamic) traditions. They are, at once, both subjective and culturally instituted. As such, they constitute one predominant way of dealing with the manifold insecurities of social existence. As we have seen, this splitting or othering process is evident in the recurring dichotomies between the human and the animal and in the friend-enemy distinction. Supported by this deeply embedded cultural imaginary, the split and decentered subject leans on and exploits such sharp distinctions, and the culturally available splitting mechanisms, in order to appear, to itself and others, as sovereign. In the case of the Rat Man, his very failure to manage this trick of self-cultivation reveals its inner logic. But there is another aspect to this. Where does sovereignty lie in the case of the enraged boy who curses his father in epithets that suggest he doesn't have the (im)proper words to say? Surely, it lies, if anywhere, in that fantasy that turns him into a coward—the fantasy that if let loose, his fury would annihilate his father. It is this sovereign fantasy, like a scene from the seraglio, that, through a culturally and psychically demanded reversal, plunges him into a life of fearfulness for those whom he loves. It binds him to these loved (and hated) others as internal objects with which he has identified, which he has defied, and with which he has also collaborated—"under the garb of obsequiousness," as Nandy puts it, regarding the colonized subject.[45]

Enough has been said to highlight that the location of sovereignty is undecidable—because it is, despite its own fantasy of itself, decentered. Sovereignty is, at once, within and without the law and thoroughly dominated by the friend-enemy distinction, due to its very need to construe itself as entirely autonomous, self-identical, and centered. Is the Rat Man sovereign when he subjects himself to the law of the father or when he asserts his aggressivity and violence in defiance of the father? Or should we pay attention to that other composite scene, so resonant of Hamlet, in which the Rat Man, having studied assiduously, as if to please his dead father, in the hour after midnight opens the door to his apartment and inspects his genitals in the mirror, as if to flaunt his sexuality against the will of the father? In retelling this scene, Freud writes,

> This crazy conduct becomes intelligible if we suppose that he was acting as though he expected a visit from his father at the hour when ghosts are abroad. He had on the whole been idle at his work during his father's lifetime, and this had often been a cause of annoyance to his father. And now that he was returning as a ghost, he was to be delighted at finding his son hard at work. But it was impossible that his father should be delighted at the other part of his behaviour; in this therefore he must be defying him. Thus, in a single unintelligible act he gave expression to the two sides of his relation with his father.[46]

Such instances illustrate the very ambivalence that lies at the heart of the sovereign subject, an ambivalence that is symptomatic exactly because of the cultural demand that it be repressed. When located within the field of social and political relations, this demand to ward off, or defend against, a self-recognition as decentered subject, as a stranger to oneself, readily turns into the friend-enemy distinction and its destructive sequelae. This leads us to imagine, as its displacement and replacement, the possibility—indeed, the urgency—of a beyond of sovereignty; perhaps what Derrida has termed a "democracy to come," what Nandy terms a "recovery of self," and what Kristeva discusses as a new cosmopolitan ethic in a world of nations without nationalism.[47]

Conclusion

In this chapter, I have revisited Freud's Rat Man case in order to draw out some aspects and implications of the psychoanalytic understanding of human subjectivity and its reliance on and resistance to culture, and I have been rather eclectic in the way I have gone about that. In particular, I have drawn out how a common mixture of abjection, narcissism, and defense against anxiety gives rise to recurrent splitting, evident in both the human-animal dichotomy and in its more overtly political parallel, the friend-enemy distinction, and thereafter, in a series of culturally telling distinctions such as those Nandy identifies as the "alter(ed)" categories of sexed identity in colonized India. If processes of abjection, narcissism, and defense are, at once, both fundamental to our becoming human subjects and the source of such recurrent splitting in our relation to self and others, and if these same psychic processes are embedded within cultures and institutions, then both presumptions about sovereignty and sovereignty's own presumptions about itself contain a set of major hazards.[48] These hazards are multiplied in a context of globalization and can be found, prototypically, in such instances as George W. Bush's post–September 11, 2001 observation that "every nation, in every region now has a decision to make. Either you are with us, or you are with the terrorists."[49] Such psychic mechanisms of splitting and projection are deeply embedded within ideologies, cultures, and institutions. They are part and parcel of a certain, rather hegemonic, common sense and compete to declare themselves and their effects as the proper reality principle. Given their pervasive presence within discourses of nation, class, gender, race, and ethnicity, they are difficult to escape. But there are, within the psychoanalytic tradition, attempts to conceptualize the psychic supports for what Derrida has termed the "democracy to come" and what Kristeva has characterized as a cosmopolitan ethic.[50] In its account of the depressive position, Kleinian theory offers a characterization of a mode of thinking, feeling, and relating that incorporates or contains ambivalence—without resort to splitting—and that generates constructions of self and other that are multifaceted and reparative.[51] These psychic processes may also take on an institutional and cultural location and operate as the support for an alternate reality principle, one that promotes reconciliation with both the stranger within and the imagined-as-other. Political and ideological projects that attempt to institute such a competing, inclusivist imaginary as the proper reality principle will inevitably meet with resistance and, quite often, with violence. The somewhat hegemonic ideologies that rely on processes of splitting and projection will attempt to recolonize the ideological field and establish or reestablish themselves as the sole and proper reality principle. This highlights that the emergence and consolidation of any cosmopolitan or inclusivist ethic involves more than a transformation at the level of the subject—a political recognition that is oddly occluded in Kristeva's argument about accepting the stranger within, yet nicely captured in Nandy's emphasis on the significance of the reordering of cultural codes for the potential recovery of both self and society. Such a recovery of self and society involves a battle within discourses and institutions about the establishment of reconciling modes of being and relating to self and others and to processes of power, authority, and violence.[52] In this respect, sovereignty is transformed through an acceptance of its internal division, an acceptance that contains rather than splits ambivalence. This involves a qualitative change that installs an ethic of care and concern, of reparation and reconciliation that is forever undoing the violence of a paranoid-schizoid mentality and culture.

The psychoanalytic perspective resolutely confronts the residues of our becoming human subjects and of our entry into culture. Such residues of abjection, narcissism, and splitting and projection cannot be extinguished, either from subjectivity or from cultures and institutions. But they may be incorporated and contained. Such a qualitative change can ameliorate and displace the violence of sovereignty, but the conflict itself cannot be finally eliminated. Herein, we glimpse a strength of Derrida's understanding that "democracy to come" remains a potentiality. Most significantly, the psychoanalytic perspective returns us to the routines of politics and policy with, perhaps, a keener sense of what is at stake. Any democracy to come does not and will not come of its own. I would suggest that it will only emerge, recur, or appear as a movement, or a series of such, that slowly comes to know its own name(s)—and as a movement, or series, whose very (recurrent) coming into being gives rise to countermovements determined to annihilate it. This is humanity's shared version of the Rat Man's dilemma, especially in a globalized postcolonial world.

Let me conclude with three further scenes. In April 1908, in Salzburg,

Freud presented the case of the Rat Man to the first international congress of psychoanalysis. His biographer, Ernest Jones, characterized this presentation as "both an intellectual and an artistic *feast*": "Delivered without any notes . . . it began at eight and at eleven he offered to bring it to a close. We had all been so *enthralled*, however, at his *fascinating* exposition that we *begged him* to go on, and he did so for another hour. I had never before been so *oblivious* of the passage of time."[53] The italicized words highlight the extent to which this was a sovereign moment for Freud—as he established both his own preeminence and the new institution of psychoanalysis as an international movement. It resonates interestingly with the occasion on which Freud took young Ernst into his family home for a meal, acting as the sovereign by breaking all the rules of professional conduct and professional distance that he had come to require of his followers.

On October 30 and November 6, 1907, Freud had presented an earlier account of the Rat Man case to the Vienna Psychoanalytic Society, under the title "Beginning of a Case History." This presentation was recorded in the minutes of the Vienna Psychoanalytic Society, minutes taken by Otto Rank in his role of salaried secretary of the society. In all, minutes were kept for the period from 1906 until 1915, when Rank began military service in the First World War. Thereafter, Freud himself retained possession of these foundational minutes until he fled Vienna in 1938. Upon leaving Vienna, Freud entrusted Paul Federn, the acting president of the Vienna Psychoanalytic Society, with the minutes, and Federn took them with him when he, in turn, fled Vienna. None were published until after Federn's death, with one exception. That exception is the combined protocol of the two meetings of October 30 and November 6, 1907, when Freud first discussed the Rat Man case with his colleagues. Interestingly, in the context of this discussion, this protocol was first published in a "somewhat modified form," along with Federn's annotations, "in the East"—more precisely, in the journal of the Indian Psychoanalytical Society, *Samiksa*, itself first published in the latter years of Girindrasekhar Bose's presidency of the society.[54]

The final scene is in the trenches of Europe during the First World War, where the Rat Man's story has returned to a place of military maneuvers. Only now, they are more deadly, and young Ernst, like so many others, is killed, leaving Gisela, whom he has married, to grieve and mourn. Having settled with his own ghosts through his analysis—at least having settled sufficiently to choose, to respond, to work, and to love—he encounters even more deadly ghosts at large "in the West."

Notes

1. Butler, *Psychic Life of Power*.
2. Wrong, "Oversocialized Conception of Man in Modern Sociology," in *Sceptical Sociology*. See a similar discussion of this point in Gay, "From Couch to Culture," in *Freud for Historians*.
3. This argument is developed in Cash, "Conclusion."
4. These references are to Fanon, *Black Skin, White Masks*; Nandy, *Savage Freud*; and Bhabha, "Other Question" in *Location of Culture*.
5. Nandy, *Savage Freud*, 113.
6. Ibid., 114.
7. Fanon, *Black Skin, White Masks*; Bhabha, "Interrogating Identity," in *Location of Culture*.
8. Fanon, *Black Skin, White Masks*, 112–13.
9. Ibid., 113 (the university neighbor), 121 (the good Frenchman), 117 (the black physician), and 112 (the parents and others nearby the frightened child).
10. Ibid., 113.
11. Ibid., 153.
12. Ibid.
13. Ibid., 112.
14. Ibid., 116.
15. The source of this quotation from Freud is not cited by Fanon. It comes from Freud's first lecture at Clark University in the United States in 1910. Freud refers to Breuer's discovery of the "talking cure" before commenting, within the quote selected by Fanon, that "in contrast, however, to what was expected, it was not always a single event that was the cause of the symptom; most often, on the contrary, it arose out of multiple traumas, frequently analogous and repeated." *Black Skin, White Masks*, 144. Notice that this characterization, in chapter 6, of trauma arising from a series of analogous traumatic scenes coincides exactly with Fanon's rendition of his own trauma in the preceding chapter, "The Fact of Blackness."
16. Fanon, *Black Skin, White Masks*, 150.
17. Nandy, *Savage Freud*, 114.
18. My argument here accords with Bhabha when he comments on this dubious splitting between a white unconscious but a black "conscious": "We cannot agree with Fanon that 'since the racial drama is played out in the open the black man has no time to make it unconscious,' but that is a provocative thought. In occupying two places at once—or three, in Fanon's case—the depersonalized, dislocated colonial subject can become an incalculable object, quite literally, difficult to place." "Remembering Fanon," 121.
19. Lacan, *Ego in Freud's Theory and in the Techniques of Psychoanalysis*, 197. Lacan's discussion draws implicitly on Freud, "Group Psychology," and anticipates,

so to speak, Louis Althusser's account of interpellation without jettisoning (class) antagonism and conflict. Of course, this highlights the limiting and entirely unnecessary character of the dichotomy Fanon draws between conscious and unconscious and overdetermination from "the inside" as against "from without."

20. Nandy, *Savage Freud*, 136.

21. Ibid.

22. Nandy, *Intimate Enemy*, xi.

23. Ibid., 8.

24. In Nandy's account, Mohandas Gandhi's transformative capacity was based in his refusal to conform to and compete in terms of such a restricted cultural code. *Intimate Enemy*, pt. 1, sc. 6; pt. 2, 100–107.

25. Nandy, "Towards a Third World Utopia," in *Bonfire of Creeds*, 446.

26. Ibid., 451.

27. Ibid., 445.

28. Nandy, *Intimate Enemy*, xvi.

29. Nandy, "Towards a Third World Utopia," in *Bonfire of Creeds*, 465.

30. I was fortunate to be able to attend Jacques Derrida's seminar, "The Beast and the Sovereign," presented at the University of California–Irvine in April and May, 2002. A keynote lecture from that seminar series presented at Irvine is now in print. See Derrida, "Transcendental 'Stupidity.'" The immediately preceding French iteration of this seminar series, presented from December 2001 to March 2002, has been published in English as *The Beast and the Sovereign*.

31. For the classic statement of the friend-enemy distinction, see Schmitt, *Concept of the Political*.

32. My discussion of Freud's Rat Man case was first presented in 2002 to the "small seminar" convened by Jacques Derrida as an accompaniment to his public seminar at the University of California–Irvine on "the beast and the sovereign."

33. Freud, "Case of Obsessional Neurosis," 47.

34. Ibid., 47–48.

35. Ibid., 86.

36. Ibid.

37. Ibid., 94.

38. Ibid.

39. Freud, "A Difficulty in the Path of Psycho-Analysis," 143.

40. Ibid., 140.

41. Freud, "'Uncanny,'" 236.

42. Ibid.

43. Ibid., 241.

44. Kristeva, *Strangers to Ourselves*.

45. Nandy, "Towards a Third World Utopia," in *Bonfire of Creeds*, 459.

46. Freud, "Notes Upon a Case of Obsessional Neurosis," 84–85.

47. Kristeva, *Nations without Nationalism*.

48. A classic group psychoanalytic study with this emphasis is Menzies-Lyth's study of institutional cultures as defenses against anxiety. See Menzies-Lyth, "Functioning

of Social Systems as a Defence against Anxiety," first published in 1959, in *Containing Anxiety*.

49. President G. W. Bush, "Address to a Joint Session of Congress and the American People," September 20, 2001, Washington, DC. Available online at: http://georgewbush-whitehouse.archives.gov/.

50. See, for instance, Derrida, "On Forgiveness," in *On Cosmopolitanism*, esp. 55–58; Derrida, *Rogues*.

51. See Klein, *Envy and Gratitude*; Kristeva, *Melanie Klein*; and Burack, *Healing Identities*.

52. For a more detailed discussion of such processes, see Cash, "Troubled Times."

53. Jones, as quoted in Gay, *Life for Our Time*, 244 (my emphasis).

54. See Nunberg and Federn, *Minutes of the Vienna Psychoanalytic Society*, introduction and chapter 28.

Denial, La Crypte, and Magic
Contributions to the Global Unconscious from
Late Colonial French West African Psychiatry

In her book *Imperial Leather*, Anne McClintock discusses a European imperial identity created via the negation of difference, a psychological predisposition she links to theories of phallocentric fetishism.[1] The circulation of fetish from the medieval Iberian worries over religious rectitude into fifteenth-century Africa and then back to Europe via the mercantilist trade routes marks the long-standing globalization of ideas as well as economies. Consciousness and diseases of the mind emerged as objects of scientific study within this globalizing, imperialist network. The Portuguese, in the fifteenth century, transferred *feitico* to the sacred and magic objects they encountered in African trading voyages. The French scientist Alfred Binet was the first, in the 1880s, to deploy the term "fetish" in a psychiatric discussion of sexual deviance. Carrying psychiatric discussion of fetishes back into the colonies was the work, in the early twentieth century, of Dr. Henri Aubin. The circulation of fetishes marks the long process of the globalization of the unconscious.[2]

Aubin's interest in psychoanalysis fed a long preoccupation with the processes of denial, magic, mana, and what he called *la crypte*. Each of these terms was a means of expressing affective projections and the transformations of consciousness and human relationships that arose in the wake of such projections. The psychoanalytic outlook through which Aubin could express insights into such processes was itself a critical addendum to the empirical tradition of scientific study of the mind and mental illness. Reaching back into the decidedly unscientific realm, where magic and denial could shape the human world and change realities, Aubin tapped into a way of thinking and perceiving from which he—as a medical doctor trained in Western scientific thinking—would normally be excluded. Scientific objectivity defined itself against the occult; scientific rationality stood in opposition to superstition and the belief in magic. Recuperating an understanding of magic via psychoanalysis was a way for Aubin to broaden the reach of Western psychiatry. His techniques allowed him to open the rational, scientific mind to processes scientists had fought hard to overcome and repress. However, his rediscovery of magic and denial via African psyches was necessarily limited by his commitment to psychoanalysis. No matter how seriously Aubin discussed la crypte, magic, and denial, he reserved for himself and others like him a sphere of scientific inquiry colored by rationality and objective empiricism. The universal "crypte" that in his thinking underwrote all human consciousness was, in his own thought processes, heavily circumscribed. The universal psyche he explored in this manner was curiously denuded of the power of terror experienced by those more truly open to—and therefore less protected from—affective projections.

Aubin's psychiatric theories appropriated knowledge of magic, denial, and la crypte from his African patients and assimilated this into a universal theory of the psyche. His work represents a considerable advance beyond the biological racism of the Algiers School, to which he had some professional ties, and lays the groundwork for the emergence of transcultural psychiatry in the postcolonial era. Focusing on the emergence of the globalized unconscious allows us to recognize that the bridge Aubin built between colonial and postcolonial psychiatry was also (perhaps necessarily) a bridge that assimilated difference. This chapter also takes stock of an intimately related dynamic: the problematic relationship of the French psychiatrist to colonial subjects and the consequent development of a science built upon a doctor-patient relationship fraught with fear, tension, and denial. Finally, a similar force has been at work in the history of psychiatry that routinely overlooks the role of colonial psychiatry in creating metropolitan practices. Denial in multiple instances and locations emerges again and again to shape and direct the psychiatrists' and the historians' interests. Denial, to complete the circle of references, became a central focus of Aubin's research and theorizing.

The Psychiatric Scene: Recuperating the Colonial
into Postcolonial and Metropolitan Psychiatry

Elisabeth Roudinesco's magisterial *Jacques Lacan* somehow fails to mention prominent psychiatrists from the colonies who made contributions.[3] The omission of Marie-Cécile and Edmund Ortigues is most suprising, given the strong relationship they had with Jacques Lacan and the impact of their *Oedipe Africain*, which was developed in relation to debates that circled around Lacan.[4] This forgetting of contributions from the colonies leads to a misshapen history of psychiatry; it leads to a history that mirrors the troubled relations between the colonizer and the colonized rather than reflecting on, or resolving, this relationship. By focusing on Aubin's contributions to psychiatry, this chapter investigates the fraught relations between colonial and postcolonial psychiatry, between psychiatry and ethnography, and between the French psychiatrist (in this instance, Aubin) and his African patients.

Aubin is largely a forgotten figure in the history of French psychiatry. If his name is recognized at all in current circles of psychiatrists and historians of psychiatry, it is probably because of his entries in Antoine Porot's *Manuel alphabétique de psychiatrie*, and most especially because of his entry on "primitivism," which employs the much-criticized ideas of Lucien Lévy-Bruhl on primitive mentality.[5] Just as some historians would prefer to forget the widespread influence of Lévy-Bruhl's theory of primitivism, there is perhaps a predisposition to forget the psychiatrist who wrote about primitivism—Henri Aubin. To be sure, at distinct moments and junctures, Aubin's writings cry out for objections and resistance, if not outright dismissal. And yet, lest we risk engaging in our own denial of multiplicitous pasts, to properly construe the history of psychiatry in the postcolonial era, Aubin must be taken into account. We should note that Aubin did hedge and qualify the terms "primitive" and "primitive mentality." Perhaps it is the quality of straining at the limits of his race, class, and epoch that granted his writings a dimension that we are at pains to uncover and recuperate.

Aubin was a curious, hybrid figure. His work took shape within the era of late imperialism and after the initial breakthroughs in developing psychoanalysis. He straddled the seemingly oppositional psychiatries of the colonial Algiers School and the postcolonial transcultural psychiatry of the Fann group.[6] He collaborated with Antoine Porot (the leader of the Algiers School) but overcame the biological racism of that school and pursued research inspirational for the celebrated Fann group at the University of Dakar in the early postcolonial era. Working in the fresh terrain developed by the giants Pierre Janet, Sigmund Freud, and others, Aubin sought to make his mark by bringing specific case studies of African mental illness into theoretical play. Like Freud in "Totem and Taboo," he thought the African studies would illuminate European psychic processes, but unlike Freud, Aubin actually worked with Africans suffering various psychic crises.

Fascinated by occult practices, Aubin created an oeuvre centered on denial, la crypte, and magic as universal biopsychological forces. La crypte expressed Aubin's conviction that a biopsychological dimension underlay all human psyches. Hidden, difficult to access, archaic, and mysterious, la crypte contained the sacred and the corpse, mana and the magical. It buried, contained, and preserved the strongest common dimensions to human psyches.[7] The influence of Carl Jung's "collective unconscious" on Aubin is clear; however, Aubin sensed it was possible to go beyond Jung's insights on myths and archetypes as expressions of the collective unconscious; he aimed to unlock fundamental driving processes of the human spirit.

Although Aubin worked explicitly with psychoanalytic concepts, he did not psychoanalyze African patients.[8] He sought, rather, to bring cultural analysis into the psychiatric arena. In that project, he relied on a broad array of cultural anthropologists but most notably on the *L'Année sociologique* scholars (Emile Durkheim, Marcel Mauss, and Henri Hubert), along with their collaborator, Lévy-Bruhl. Aubin followed Freud's conviction that "primitives" revealed universal human psychological processes; he termed this universal psychic dimension "bio-psychology." He followed Carl Jung in seeking to understand a collective unconscious, yet unlike Jung, he attempted to access primal energy flows (magic and mana) rather than cultural archetypes and myths. Working closely with African patients, Aubin drew on cultural analysis to formulate psychiatric and psychoanalytic concepts. Identifying magic, mana, taboo, and sympathy (or "participation") as bedrock elements in human psyches, Aubin then sought to work with these in the European context. Denial, conversion, and projection drew his sustained attention.

Aubin, as was usual among French colonial psychiatrists, made his career in the military. He specialized in neurology at the medical university in Bordeaux, from which he graduated in 1927. He supplemented this degree with further studies in colonial medicine and naval hygiene at Marseille. In 1933, he earned his specialist degree in psychiatry and legal medicine from the University of Paris. Aubin's colonial career began in Pondicherry, where he was the chief medical officer at the colonial hospital in 1929. From 1933 to 1935, he worked in a psychiatric service in Fez, Morocco. He then moved to the Michel-Lévy Hospital in Marseilles, where he worked with interned *tirailleurs Sénégalais*. He personally treated 120 of these hospitalized African soldiers and supplemented that knowledge with 160 cases he found in the hospital archives.[9] Subsequently, he worked in Algeria, where he served from 1939 as the chief of the psychiatric service in Oran.

Doctors Gaëtan Gatian de Clérambault, Frank Cazanove, and Emmanuel Régis were the doctors to whom Aubin felt personally indebted as a young psychiatrist. Dr. Angelo Hesnard, who served the dual role of bringing Freudian analysis into French psychiatric practices and of carrying it with him on his tours of duty in the colonies, must be recognized as well. Hesnard's seminal book of 1914, cowritten with Dr. Emmanuel Régis, presented Freudian analysis to the French public with a critical air. However, Hesnard—who, in 1914, was just embarking on his career—continued on to become a major advocate of psychoanalysis in France. Hesnard's influence in the colonial world, where he served as a medical doctor, extended to providing training analysis for certain psychiatrists or psychologists (Henri Collomb, the founding director of the Fann Hospital in Dakar, was one of his analysands).[10] Hesnard directed the *Revue Française de psychanalyse*, which enjoyed the explicit blessings of Sigmund Freud, from its founding in 1927. Freud, Marie Bonaparte, Hesnard, and René Laforgue figure prominently among the early contributors. The *Revue* featured explicit cross-cultural and comparative dimensions, with early contributions on the Hindu castration complex, hunting trophies and the atavistic pleasure of killing, and Chinese dreams. The famous pioneer of ethnopsychiatry, Géza Róheim, presented to the Société psychanalytique in 1928 on racial psychology and the origins of capitalism.[11]

Aubin's success as a colonial psychiatrist entailed a substantial history of publications spanning more than forty years, from 1927 to 1971, and amounting to some 250 total. While his career took him across the French empire, his writings ranged widely, from neurology to ethnography, from organic diseases to theories of magic, denial, and repression. His broad range of interests included a psychiatric study of the poet Arthur Rimbaud and of the fifteenth-century explorer Vasco da Gama. In the pages of *L'Evolution psychiatrique*, Aubin reviewed the works of many of the most prominent theorists and psychiatrists of his day, including Michel Foucault's *Histoire de la folie*; Marie-Cécile and Edmund Ortigues' *L'Oedipe Africain*; Maud Mannoni's oeuvre; Paul Parin, Fritz Morgenthaler, and Goldy Parin-Matthey's *Whites Think Too Much*; and Angelo Hesnard's theories of phenomenology and psychotherapy.[12]

In 1938, Aubin reported on psychiatric services in the colonies at the Congrès des aliénistes et neurologistes de France et des pays de langue française based in Algiers. This report parallels and updates the comparatively well-known 1911 report by Henri Reboul and Emmanuel Régis.[13] In this work, Aubin noted the role of divine and occult forces in popular accounts of mental illness, while maintaining an emphasis on biological etiology in psychopathologies. Malaria, amoebic infections, sleeping sickness, leprosy, pneumonia: each such infection was cited by Aubin as causal of specific cases of psychopathology. Psychiatrists, he argued, played a vital role in discovering organic infections via psychiatric diagnosis. Unfortunately, he contended, "It is still common to view psychosis as a mysterious effect of destructive Occult Forces against which no real defense is possible." Evil spirits or heavenly curses, he remarked, are as present in the minds of the civilized as among those they seek to civilize.[14]

Even as Aubin produced psychoanalytic studies, they remained underrecognized. The most prominent contemporary evaluation of French West African psychiatry, written by Madeleine Ly in 1948 as a medical thesis, despaired over the underdeveloped psychiatry of West Africa and specifically lamented the absence of a psychoanalytic tradition in the colonies.[15] Ly's evaluation of the state of West African psychiatry—seemingly oblivious to Aubin's work—focused on Dr. Cazanove's "Memento de psychiatrie coloniale africaine," published in 1927.[16] Ly argued that because Cazanove was a student of Régis (who was intimate with and yet critical of psychoanalysis), Cazanove repressed material that cried out for psychoanalytic understanding. Her argument depended heavily on Cazanove's repeated references to demonology, which she regarded as material especially suited to psychoanalytic treatment.[17] Ly, however, undervalues the dual reliance of Cazanove on psychiatry and ethnology, an interdisciplinary move essential to the development of transcultural psychiatry. Indeed, even his 1927 article was dedicated to his "maîtres"—Dr. Régis, the cele-brated psychiatrist, and Maurice Delafosse, the ethnographer and colonial administrator.[18] While Cazanove stopped short of engaging psychoanaly-sis, his unusual advocacy of studying beliefs in magic, possession, and African rituals opened a path for Henri Aubin.

Cazanove's achievements in integrating ethnographic knowledge into medicine appear more clearly when contrasted with the resilient resis-tance among doctors to such knowledge. Ethnography interested and served government officials more frequently than doctors. For example, Charles Monteil's 1931 study of divination in Afrique occidentale fran-çaise (AOF; French West Africa) sought to represent the role of magic in African thinking, but Monteil sought to apply this to governmental strate-gies rather than to the practice of medicine.[19] The posthumous publica-tion of Dr. Émile Mauchamp's *La sorcellerie au Maroc* documented vari-ous magical medical practices, but it aimed to expose superstition and ignorance rather than to build a bridge between medical practices. In 1907, Mauchamp was murdered by a mob in Marrekesh, reportedly after a German spy spread rumors that Mauchamp's medical skills included the ability to administer poison that took two or three years to be fatal.[20] The French then took this murder as a pretext for expanding colonial rule. As Mauchamp's father opined, it was time for France to clean up the moral miasma that caused Moroccans to rot and become ferocious.[21]

The impasse between French colonial doctors and West African healing —whether composed of ignorance, disdain, or perhaps unwitting fear— was upheld in part by the allegiance of medical men to science. Science was the source of medical authority in France, with major battles to wrest authority over mental illness from religious authorities fought in the nine-teenth century.[22] Identifying himself as a man of science willing to wage war on metropolitan as well as colonial superstitions, Aubin nevertheless dem-onstrated a marked interest in and sympathy for various forms of magic, divination, possession trances, and other mystical beliefs. He perceived the importance of magic and the occult or divine in European as well as African societies. He maintained that all colonial psychiatrists should study ethnol-ogy and insisted as well that metropolitan psychiatrists should be prepared to treat peoples from the colonies.[23]

Aubin explicitly rejected the racial stereotyping too frequently prac-ticed by his colleagues. Hence, while he collaborated with Antoine Porot on various projects, he cannot be identified with Porot's contention that

colonial psychiatrists confront "constitutional insufficiencies, a primitivism caused by mental indigence, ignorance, credulity and suggestibility."[24]
Indeed, as we shall see, Aubin emphasized the merits of specific psychic
characteristics among Africans. A similar contrast is found between Hesnard and Aubin. Hesnard looked at the *tiralleurs Sénégalais* in order
to identify an "ethnic factor" in their illness. He was especially impressed
by the "extraordinary impulsivity of transplanted Senegalese, who, although normally pliant under military discipline and candidly devoted,
even childishly attached to their officer or doctor, when faced with the
slightest infection or anxious reaction to being up-rooted, are capable of
sudden and brutal homicide of Whites who are caring for them."[25] While
Hesnard suggested a racial causality in these psychotic rages, Aubin suggested instead that each case merited individual investigation, which likely
would reveal a great diversity of causes for the psychotic breakdowns.[26]

By 1952, Aubin published *L'Homme et la magie*, a synthesis of his
analytic theories.[27] His subsequent research continued to span a broad
array of topics, only a small percentage of which focused exclusively on
Africans. Rather, one of the facts that makes Aubin's work compelling is
his insistent effort to incorporate his ethnographic knowledge and theories into works that addressed European psychiatric issues. Rather than
cutting off the colonial world as an isolated case study, Aubin sought to
integrate insights and truths he learned via practicing psychiatry with
Africans into his work with other populations. His specific interest in
African dances, African art, and magical practices resonate in his broader
treatises on eternal magic, healing through art, and other works.[28] However, the assimilation of African practices and beliefs into his general
psychoanalytic theories also constitutes the denial of difference through
which the global unconscious was built. An accounting of what was lost in
this assimilative move includes the power of the fetish, of the occult, and
of fear itself.

The Fetish and Colonial Denial

Andràs Zempléni, the Fann Hospital researcher renowned for his systematic study of the psychotherapeutic value of Lebou possession rituals,
remarked that the defining feature of a fetish-object is that it possesses
intentionality.[29] The uses of the terms "fetish" and "fetisher" in colonial-era
documents were much looser. In general, fetish and fetisher referred to
objects involved in animist or Islamic religious, ritual, or ceremonial uses

and those who engaged in such activities, respectively.[30] Fetishes and fetishers variously provoked disdain or curiosity among colonial doctors. What they did not provoke was either a measured appreciation of their positive attributes or an acknowledgement of their spiritual power. Fetishers, also sometimes called sorcerers or witch doctors, in French colonial West Africa included traditional healers from ancestor-worshipping cults and Islamic marabouts. Both groups—animist healers and marabouts— threatened French colonial authority and were subject to various campaigns to limit their influence. Marabouts distributing protective amulets (what a European of the time would call a fetish and what locally was called a *gris-gris*) during an epidemic, for example, were subject to arrest for the unlawful practice of medicine and the transgression of quarantine boundaries.[31] The colonial authorities feared the combined spiritual-medical power of the marabouts, especially those belonging to the Mourides, because these men offered an alternative to allegiance to the French.[32] Even these colonial officials acknowledged that the marabouts emanated an "occult power" capable of attracting allegiance from diverse ethnic groups— capable even of attracting the allegiance of the mixed-race Catholics. Their converts willingly donated large sums of money, which was used in part to build mosques, themselves an incarnation of the marabouts' power and a rallying point for their followers. "There is a danger in this occult power that I must point out," reported one local official. "This is a peril for our administration."[33]

French medical doctors and African assistants trained in colonial hospitals served, wittingly or not, the colonial regime's goal of displacing the spiritual authority of healers and marabouts.[34] One French perspective on the treatments given by African healers in Afrique équatoriale française (AEF; French Equatorial Africa) was represented by M. le Médecin-Major Huot's report from Loango, in which he emphasized the need to protect the mentally ill "from the power of a revolting barbarity which is imposed on them by the fetishers."[35] Colonial laws prohibited healers, marabouts, and witch doctors from openly pursuing their healing arts. Arrest, imprisonment, fines, and even execution could befall the unlucky practitioner apprehended by French authorities. Sorcery was proscribed, as was magic and "charlatanism" (which included some instances of traditional healing), with infractions carrying a punishment of fifteen days to six months imprisonment. Even in situations where all parties consented, colonial law prohibited divination through the administration of poison.

"Calumnious denunciation" (which included accusations of witchcraft) was also illegal.[36]

These laws were unevenly enforced and thus did not entirely constrain customary practices. Moreover, customary law was allowed precedence in situations that did not shock the French "sense of humanity."[37] In other words, sometimes, superstition or magical practices were tolerated because they appeared inoffensive or relatively harmless. However, the repressive colonial laws were applied to customs that threatened lives, such as divination by poison, accusations of witchcraft, and cannibalism. The repressive laws were enforced, for example, through the series of trials in the Casamance (in southern Senegal) in the 1920s for *necroanthropophagy*, which arose out of allegations of widespread murder and feasting on the dead.[38] In these trials, 161 Diolans from the Casamance were arrested for belonging to a secret society centered on cannibalism. At least six were sentenced to death, while others received sentences of imprisonment of ten to twenty years.[39] The colonial authorities presented the Diola trials as an effort to stamp out barbarous practices and to extend the reach of French standards of civility.[40] These trials demonstrate the willingness of colonial authorities to entertain a terrifying otherness as an aspect of West African culture. The "difference" represented by the alleged cannibalistic cult elicited the full repressive powers of the colonial regime; in the imperial logic, recognized difference needed to be expunged. The trials illustrate the distinction between difference entertained as a harmless amusement and difference figured as powerful and threatening.[41]

The global unconscious relies on a disarming of such threats. Witches who travel in the night to murder and then eat their victims, as in these trials, are extirpated from society, not integrated into it. The difference signaled by necroanthropophagy was a perceived threat. Acknowledging this difference entailed combating it. The ethnographic understanding of witchcraft, which usually emphasized that witches ate only souls, not flesh, gained adherents by the mid-twentieth century. This view removed the criminal dimension to witch cannibalism. Killing a soul, after all, does not constitute homicide. The ethnographic outlook simultaneously disarmed the metaphysical evil of eating souls via a resolutely secular outlook that deprived soul-eating of its metaphysical resonance. The rising power of the ethnographic perspective is exemplified by Marcel Griaule, an administrator-ethnographer who opposed the 1950 legislative agenda that sought to strengthen the prohibitions on witchcraft. Griaule adopted a secular and pragmatic outlook, successfully arguing that in an area with one doctor for every 45,000 inhabitants, healers were needed.[42]

The psychological approach to witchcraft and cannibalism relied on integrating ethnography into psychological theories and therapies. This attained full flower among the Fann Hospital practitioners of the 1960s and 1970s, who refused to recognize any real threat from witchcraft or magic. While professing to respect the beliefs and traditions of the Wolof, Serer, and Lebou, the psychologists and psychiatrists at Fann Hospital never entered into the religious realities that sustained witchcraft practices and accusations. Neither did they truly believe in the other forms of "spirit crisis," whether spirit possession or magical enchantment. Taking refuge in psychological and psychoanalytic interpretations of these beliefs, the Fann practitioners could claim to respect the West African spirit crises and healing traditions while never actually feeling threatened by them. This difference is a type of difference that can be approached, studied at leisure, and then assimilated in some guise into the universal.

Aubin was a precursor to the Fann practitioners. Working from the 1920s to the 1950s, he integrated ethnographic studies of magic and witchcraft into his psychiatric practice. He, like the Fann practitioners, took the fetishers seriously and yet psychologized (and so disarmed) their essentially religious realities. What is gained and what is lost in psychologizing spiritual beliefs is illustrated by contrasting Aubin's theories to missionary perspectives on these phenomena. The reflections of Père Boilat and Raoul Allier, both religiously minded rather than psychologists, are strikingly similar to Aubin and yet diverge sharply on issues related to the ultimate nature of good and evil, morality and truth. This comparison demonstrates how Aubin both recognized and discounted differences and thereby achieved a universal theory of the unconscious.

Denial in the Colonized and in the Colonizers

Aubin found uncovered in his West African patients aspects of the psyche that in his European patients were covered with elaborate disguises. One of the most compelling processes he recovered from his work with African patients was *reniement*, or denial.[43] When Aubin's theory of denial is contextualized in terms of the colonial ethnography of Père Boilat and Raoul Allier, and also in terms of Frantz Fanon's comments on the topic,

the differences that are obscured emerge more clearly, as do certain imperialist imperatives. Globalizing denial relied, as demonstrated here, on
its own peculiarly compulsive denials.

Reniement became one of Aubin's fundamental themes, one to which
he returned time and again and which eventually served him as a major
explanatory device for African as well as European psyches. Denial developed as a point of focus for Aubin as he reflected on the psychiatric
aliments of black African soldiers who had served in the French army in
the First World War.[44] Inside French psychiatric hospitals, black African
spirit crises appeared to doctors other than Aubin as unfathomable psychotic rage; the cause usually postulated was some type of biological inferiority or weakness. Aubin, however, understood the psychotic rages
and subsequent denial of them as intimately linked to the fear of demons.
This link was later confirmed by Fann Hospital clinicians who worked
with Wolof, Serer, and Lebou peoples suffering what they understood
within their own culture as spirit crises. The black African beliefs about
spirit crises, as well as black African therapeutic practices related to them,
were not studied by French doctors in a systematic manner prior to the
founding of the Fann Psychiatric Hospital at the University of Dakar in the
postcolonial era.[45] In trying to understand the causes of black African fear
and denial, Aubin is breaking new ground, and yet even in the identification of his patients as "Senegalese," he entertains a false sense of unifor-
mity by overlooking the multiple geographic locales and ethnicities represented among the *tiralleurs Sénégalais*.

Aubin's work at the Michel-Lévy Hospital involved him intimately with
black Africans suffering spiritual/psychological collapse in the wake of
military service. He built his published theories from the 120 black Africans whom he treated, combined with information he gleaned from dos-
siers on 160 more patients. Using this material, Aubin created a portrait of
black African psychotic regression and developed a theory of the curative
dimensions to the black African habitual denial of psychotic episodes.[46]
"The furious paroxysms of the Senegalese soldiers," reflected Aubin, "are
the cause of unfortunately frequent dramas . . . These are delirious, blind
explosions which quickly reach their height; the patient, beside himself,
gesticulates and mutters, or, turned in on himself, sorrowful, mute, . . . he
seems animated by an implacable hatred of everyone . . . insensible to all
exhortations, he ferociously strikes everyone who tries to approach and

destroys everything within reach."[47] Once the paroxysm takes hold, according to Aubin, it spends itself quickly, especially if the individual has been isolated.[48]

Aubin was struck by the prominence of denial and the ease and frequency with which it was used by these soldiers. He elaborated on his theory several times throughout the ensuing decades. In a 1939 study, Aubin emphasized how the Senegalese deny their mental illness. Even when confronted with physical evidence of psychotic fits, they would nevertheless repeatedly deny that any such fits had taken place. Aubin reflected the common reaction among the doctors to this denial, commenting, "We are stupefied *to see them tranquilly and categorically deny all their previous claims.*"[49] He singled out for discussion one case in which a man in full delirium started to describe the Lilliputian devils which were tormenting him, but terrorized, he refused to recount what they said to him, saying "that would make him die."[50] Aubin accorded a certain respect to this man's terror, explaining that in Senegal, someone who has seen the devil must not speak of it for a period of three months, lest they risk the pain of further haunting and suffering.[51] Such evidence demonstrated to Aubin that denial functioned as a form of mental hygiene by preventing suffering. Aubin theorized that the reniement of the "primitives" was a tool of mental hygiene that they discovered via instinct.[52] Reniement, he contended, liquidizes individual episodes that otherwise take up an inordinate amount of psychic energy and are liable to create automatic activities in the mind, almost completely dissociated from reflective activity, which creates a nervous exhaustion that is itself generative of neurosis. Following the insights of Pierre Janet, Aubin claimed, "These patients would be immediately cured if they forgot the event."[53]

This case, for Aubin, exemplified the sentiment that animated systematic denial. Aubin chose the word "sentiment" deliberately, intending to invoke the Durkheimian theory of collective representations.[54] For Aubin, denial served as a central, collective sentiment; it was a motivating affective force in mental processes. Affect, Durkheim had theorized, occupied a visceral substratum to thinking, opinions, and even to conscious will or desires. Collective sentiments, such as denial, expressed pervasive, culturally specific underpinnings to cognition and other more conscious mental processes. Aubin deployed the Durkheimian theory to express the power and pervasiveness of denial among black Africans. He then extended his argument, pointing out that denial was highly apparent among mentally ill Europeans as well as Africans and that even among the healthy, Europeans as well as Africans, denial was a normal feature of the mind.

Aubin recognized the psychotherapeutic value of other diverse African practices, claiming that "primitives" have other means in addition to reniement to liquidate the disturbing event. He remarked, in particular, on magic ceremonies, diverse forms of exorcism, the removal of an evil presence by a sorcerer or a relative, sacrifices, pilgrimages, and so forth.[55] In this brief allusion to African means of "liquidating" disturbing events, Aubin marked the route for future transcultural and ethnopsychiatric studies. The inauguration of this new transcultural science was demarcated in 1957 in a World Health Organization–sponsored symposium. At that event, Roger Bastide argued explicitly for the psychotherapeutic value of the Brazilian ritual of *candomblé*; in so doing, he broke explicitly with prior medical opinion.[56] Bastide also defended African cults as part of healthy social and mental life, arguing that better medical understanding necessitated familiarity with ethnographic knowledge and local practices of African immigrant populations.[57]

In 1950, *L'Evolution psychiatrique* hosted a discussion of Aubin's general theory of denial, a discussion that ranged broadly over various psychological mechanisms of defense.[58] By this time, Aubin had formulated a general theory of the "systematic denial of transgression," which he found to be very active among both "primitives" as well as Europeans. The purest form of this psychic defense, he claimed, was among unassimilated Africans: "Among primitives denial achieves the level of 'willed forgetting' which for Janet figured as an ideal means liquidating affective traumas."[59] As previously, Aubin asserted here that the half assimilated lost this facility for denial and were given to endless pondering of perceived grievances and paranoid reactions. For Aubin, the Freudian discussion of pathological repression generative of neuroses was merely a failed form of denial. Through the denial of inopportune pregnancies, of illness, or of setbacks or defeats in one's career, Europeans routinely deployed the device Aubin found revealed so clearly among Africans.

Aubin's focus on denial as a universal in the global unconscious encourages us to look more closely at how denial figured, unconsciously, into his own theorizing. Twin pillars of obfuscation support his theorizing, as is demonstrated by comparing his work to the religiously informed ethnographic observations of the priest Boilat and the protestant missionary Allier and then by broadening that comparison to include the psychiatrist and anti-imperialist critic Frantz Fanon. Allier's global unconscious had one foot in the modern (as it denied the power of the supernatural and the terror it inspires) and another firmly rooted in imperialism (as it denied the power of imperialist power and the terror it inspires). These denials sustained Aubin's ability to assimilate the differences he acknowledged into a universal unconscious.

Father Boilat was deeply loyal to France and deeply Catholic in his outlook. Religious and imperialistic, Boilat took his metaphysics seriously and campaigned heartily for the expansion of the rule of Christian civilization.[60] The battle against demonic forces, in Boilat's worldview, entailed a battle against metaphysical evil. Boilat's father was a French military officer; his mother came from the mixed-race, partially assimilated Signare community in Saint-Louis. Orphaned at a young age, Boilat was raised by priests; he studied in France and Italy and eventually returned to Senegal to serve in the priesthood. Boilat's transcultural roots granted him access to various ethnic groups in western Senegal, an access that was strengthened by his spiritual convictions. He fully credited the forces of God and demons in the world and did not dismiss such beliefs as mere superstition, as a secular-minded Frenchman would have. On the contrary, Boilat describes and ruminates at length on the spiritual realities he observed, including marabout diviners, spirit possessions, soul-eating witches, hypnotism, and the manufacture and uses of *gris-gris*. In the mid-nineteenth century, Father Boilat took a special interest in Wolof marabouts, seeking to understand the extent of their "diabolical" powers. As Boilat understood the Wolof use of the term, "marabout" referred to an Islamic priest, which included any man of good moral standing who observed the religious laws. The "grands marabouts" avoided the use of protective amulets, or *gris-gris*, and generally offered aid to their people by simple laying on of hands and prayer.[61] Marabouts who were advanced in age assumed the status of god-like figures so that touching their hair was thought to bring long life. Village marabouts, in charge of educating the children, usually also made and sold *gris-gris*. Boilat took a dim view of these village marabouts, describing them as liars and deceivers who were taken for true prophets by the credulous villagers.[62] Village marabouts could sometimes sell *gris-gris* for enormous prices, as they were believed to make their wearers invulnerable to any misfortune: "With them, no bullet can penetrate you; any sword, knife, spear, or arrow, would break if you touched them."[63] To the martial powers of *gris-gris*, Boilat added yet more powers, describing how they "could be designed to protect against witches, or against the nocturnal noises that signaled the presence of the devil, or to cure any disease, or to kill one's enemies; what do I know? For all the needs of humanity, to protect and serve in all the different situations of life."[64]

Boilat was convinced that most marabouts-diviners were imposters, but some of his experiences led him to believe in the power of some to foresee truths "only accessible through the intervention of higher spirits."[65] In Gorée, Boilat witnessed the performance of one particularly adept marabout, a Mandingue from the Gambia who worked by tracing cabalistic signs in the sand. Eager to know the source of his prodigious insights, Boilat asked to know whom the marabout invoked. In an answer confounding to a Catholic priest, the marabout answered that "he only addressed himself to the devil."[66] To his own testimony of marabouts' fortune-telling powers, he adds that of several other missionaries.

The diabolic powers worked wonders in Boilat's Senegal. He portrayed a world populated by demons and only gradually enlightened by Jesus:

> We know that before the coming of Our Lord, and even during his mortal life, the demon was adored across the entire world under different names, that he had his oracles and temples, that he performed the most surprising wonders, and that he could even possess people and speak different languages through their mouths. We know that Our Lord and the apostles, working in His name, as well as many of the saints, exorcised demons from the bodies of infidels and even from Christians. To the extent that faith spreads throughout the universe, the power of the demons diminishes, and their feats become more rare; but in regions not yet enlightened by Christian truths, in countries where infernal spirits are worshipped and invoked, they [i.e., the infernal spirits] appear to me to still possess much power and to perform wonders that exceed the reach of human intelligence.[67]

Boilat began his career as a missionary convinced that marabouts always worked through lying and swindling the people. However, after six years of preaching against Senegalese superstitions, Boilat was persuaded to admit that the maraboutic practices were indeed diabolic and hence truly powerful. Denying the power of the marabouts, Boilat finally understood, denied the truths "that people had seen with their own eyes, touched with their own hands, and heard with their own ears."[68] Denying this power, he finally accepted, would only harden the believers into fanaticism. Convinced of the power and truths possessed by the Senegalese peoples, Boilat undertook a type of ethnographic study, searching out possessions, healers, and the like, seeking to discover the "infernal truth" of these cultures.

On May 19, 1848, Boilat witnessed a possession firsthand. As he describes the event, he and his companions had gone to bed for the night and just fallen asleep when "infernal cries that made our hair stand on end and made us shiver despite ourselves" awoke them.[69] M. Vidal, the *préfet apostolique*, stricken with uncontrollable trembling, instructed Boilat to find out what was going on. Father Boilat went with another priest, Father Carmarans, to investigate the source of the cries in a neighboring house. There, they found a young woman, about twenty-two years old, lying on a straw mattress, a pillow under her head. A crowd of people filled the house. The young woman's head was like a pendulum racing at an incalculable pace. As Boilat recalled, "In a tone that one could feel in an inexpressible way, she chanted all sorts of prophesies. All the Blacks were beside themselves, deeply inhibited, and could not aid her. What ails her? I asked. They responded, 'a spirit has seized her body; you who are educated, you might be able to find a way to drive it out.'" Responding to this challenge, Father Boilat began by asking the woman's name, and he was told it was Sophie. But when he addressed the woman directly, "Sophie, Sophie, in the name of Jesus-Christ answer me, Sophie," the response came, "I am not Sophie, I am not a girl to have such a name, I am Samba-Diob, the great demon worshiped by the Serers in the village XX in Baoul. I am a spirit, I go where I like on the wings of the winds."[70] Then, Samba-Diob, or Sophie, continued to chant. Suddenly, she began a different song in a language unknown to Father Boilat. Father Carmarans, who was there with Boilat, claimed in an astonished voice that it was a shepherd's song from his home in the Aveyron. Overcome with emotion, Father Carmarans asked Boilat to stay with the young woman while he went to the chapel to pray for her. Boilat stayed watchfully by her side but sent someone to his room to fetch his Virgin Mary medal. When Carmarans returned and the medal arrived, Boilat proceeded to perform an exorcism. Only with great difficulty could he get the Virgin's medal to stay on the woman's contorting body. Six men helped to hold her steady while Father Boilat placed the medal on her head, only to have it thrown to the other end of the room by her violent jerkings. They found it, brought it back, and fixed it again in the same place. This time, the convulsions stopped immediately. "We could not help admiring the power of Mary," reflected Father Boilat.[71]

Then, Samba-Diob began chanting that he would leave soon if the medal was removed and flour was put on Sophie's feet. Father Carmarans cautioned that this was a ruse of the demon and that he should not be given anything at all. Boilat wrote, "The Negresses were already arriving with their flour, but we prevented them from throwing it. The evil spirit, forced by the name of Mary to depart, sounded a song of leave in a voice loud enough to be heard down the whole street, and continued, gradually in softer tones, as though he were further and further away. The Wolof words to the song were, 'I am a spirit, I came here on the wings of the winds, I fly where I like, and in the blink of an eye I disappear, I return to my realm where the homages of divinity are given me.'"[72] After this song, Sophie lay on the bed as if she were dead, then fell into a deep sleep. The next morning, Sophie was exhausted, looking as though she had not slept in a long time. Boilat recalled, "She was very surprised to find a Virgin's medal attached to her hair, and she threw it off, saying that already in Dakar someone had given her one, and that her mother had made her get rid of it. She had no memory of what had happened the previous night."[73]

Completely overlooking any implications of Sophie's oblivion regarding her fit—that is, overlooking precisely what Aubin found so essential and universal—Boilat focused instead on how to understand the events. "Was this a possession, an obsession, or a simple epilepsy?" asked Boilat. He consciously refused to resolve this puzzle, writing, "It is not for me to decide."[74] Rather, his primary desire seemed to be to reveal the different possible understandings of the experience of Sophie—or Samba-Diob. Later, he recounted what he portrayed as a less ambiguous case of a young Wolof girl, about twelve years old, who was subject to such seizures, during which she made frequent prophesies in many different languages. In this instance, Boilat did not credit the European view of such possessions as medical crises but relied instead on a belief in speaking in tongues. The "demonic" origin of these possessions was not doubted by Boilat, who pointedly remarked that the most prominent languages of prophesy were either Serer or Nones; that is, languages "spoken by people who are fetishists." This girl's spirits, however, also seemed related to the Islamic world, since while prophesizing, she demonstrated superb knowledge of the Qur'an and of Arabic, although she was in fact illiterate.[75]

Boilat describes how for many years, as he had traveled around Senegal, he had heard of demon possessions. The crises were viewed very differently by Europeans and Africans; as he wrote, "The Negroes remove the possessed person to a quiet house, while the Europeans comment simply that it was an epileptic attack." Epilepsy? Possession by a "subtle spirit"? Such a possession, he reports, "was like a wind which seizes the body, shakes it violently, and makes them able to foretell the future."[76] Boilat's Catholic faith led him to consider these events as demon possessions, but his knowledge of local cultures and languages forced him to consider the discrepancy between a "demon possession" and the more apt translation "to be seized by a spirit." However, even as Boilat's Catholicism provided him a certain degree of access into the spiritual view of the Senegalese, it also limited this access. In the Catholic point of view, demons are unequivocally bad or evil. Spirits in the animist worldview, on the other hand, can be good or bad, playful or mischievous, troublesome, helpful, or perhaps even neutral. Boilat's hesitancy in his translation—between "demon possession" and "to be seized by a spirit"—reveals his own tensions between his Senegalese ancestry and his allegiance as a Catholic priest to a metaphysical world clearly divided between the good (including God, Jesus, Mary, and other recognized saints) and evil (including Satan and other demons). The partially Islamicized peoples of Senegal, meanwhile, lived in a world in which spirits did not align so neatly into good and evil.

The earliest French medical observations of such possessions—including those of Huot, Cazanove, and Aubin—date from the first half of the twentieth century and rely on secular, scientific reasoning. Dr. Huot, writing in 1912, remarked that understanding such mental crises as spirit possession was "nothing other than the doctrine of demonic possession, as old as the world."[77] Jean-Martin Charcot, working in Paris in the mid-nineteenth century, famously seized hysteric fits and possession crises from the authority of the Catholic Church and brought them within the empire of psychiatric medicine.[78] Aubin regarded his own work as falling in the same tradition, combating superstition both in France and in colonies.

Spiritual beliefs, however, carry forces that can pervade cultural systems. The protestant missionary Raoul Allier explored in great depth the implications of living under the rule of demonic forces. This preoccupation led Allier to recognize that the chief characteristic of such lives is the omnipresence of terror.

Allier was a historian of religion, of conversion, and of psychology.[79] His point of view occupies a cusp position, straddling an objective, secular outlook and an outlook rooted in Christian religiosity. As such, Allier took the prospect of magic, sorcery, and witchcraft rather more seriously than did Aubin. While both men saw in such practices evidence of universal human inclinations toward magical thinking, Allier felt compelled to address the reign of terror provoked among people who lived in fear of witches. Both Allier and Aubin recognized that the conviction one had been bewitched could provoke a deep terror and ensuing death. Allier looked closely at such beliefs, arguing that the search for magical causes disrupted or prevented reasoning based in empirical causality and that it encouraged people to accept things as real when they were not real at all. This indifference to factual reality, for Allier, was at the heart of a predisposition to lying: "This indifference toward the truth that seems to characterize the non-civilized, . . . should we be surprised that it takes on its gravest feature in an inveterate predisposition for lying?"[80]

Allier provided long documentation of such carelessness with the truth, culled from the records of the missionary Hermann Dieterlen, who commented repeatedly on the seemingly instinctual impulse to lie. Allier recounts instances of lying that seem to be self-protective (i.e., refusing to admit a pregnancy or a venereal infection) but also uses as an example a woman's denial that she had heard the noise of a certain waterfall. In local lore, it was reputed that those who heard this waterfall would certainly die. The woman's lie, and lying in general, acknowledged Allier, "became a sort of paradoxical defense. Used without the slightest regard for the truth."[81] In Allier's view, this psychic defense mechanism, much celebrated by Aubin, led to mental impairment, stunted intelligence, and moral decrepitude. "In the atmosphere of magic," commented Allier, "the natural candor of the mind diminishes and disappears." The belief in magic and witchcraft discouraged the development of the intellect. Allier reasoned that "a creature who finds it fatiguing to habitually use reason easily becomes the plaything of his passions."[82]

In the life-world of those for whom witchcraft is real, life is full of the unknown, of uncertainties, of mutual suspicions, and hence of fear. The desire for magical powers—powers to protect oneself and one's family against witchcraft and also the power to gain riches, a desirable mate, or healthy children—can push people to commit crimes.[83] Among the wealth of examples Allier offered, the most extreme was the search for powerful medicine fabricated from human body parts seized from living victims.[84] In Allier's analysis, the penchant for dishonest and unclear thinking combined with rule of fear and avarice were the root causes of such vicious behavior.

If Allier saw lying as an understandable yet ultimately corrupting defense mechanism, Aubin focused on the positive dimensions to prevarication. Aubin's emphasis on the positive role of denial distinguished his psychiatric outlook from some of his peers, who were more likely to invoke sweeping negative generalizations of the *tirailleurs*. The widely held belief that natives were inveterate liars and not to be trusted was, from Aubin's point of view, based in a fundamental misunderstanding. Aubin was intrigued by Raoul Allier's 1927 book, *Le non-civilisé et nous*, which discussed lying by "primitives," but he commented with disappointment that Allier viewed "systematic negation" only as a negative feature leading to moral dissolution rather than perceive its potentially positive impact on mental health.[85]

At least one other psychiatric opinion on the role of lying among the colonized should be considered here, and it is that of Frantz Fanon. In 1955, Fanon delivered a paper at the francophone psychiatric Congrès titled "Conduites d'aveu en Afrique du Nord" (The Algerian and Avowal in Medico-Legal Practice).[86] He argued that Algerians are not prone to confession in colonial courts precisely because of their resistance to the colonial order. "The colonized does not let on," wrote Fanon. "He does not confess himself in the presence of the colonizer."[87] Fanon's view of the resistance to colonization was sharpened as the Algerian Revolution continued. In *A Dying Colonialism* (published originally in 1959), Fanon wrote unstintingly of the alienation of Algerians from every aspect of the colonial order: "The colonial situation is precisely such that it drives the colonized to appraise all the colonizer's contributions in a pejorative and absolute way. The colonized perceives the doctor, the engineer, the schoolteacher, the policeman, the rural constable, through the haze of an almost organic confusion."[88]

Fanon's emphasis on the anger of the colonized returns a political dimension to Aubin's concept of *reniement*. Indeed, as Ly mentions in her 1948 thesis, the French public were introduced to colonial anger in 1921 by René Maran's widely read novel, *Batoula, veritable roman nègre*.[89] Like Fanon, Maran was an assimilated (or *évolué*) colonial; he served as a colonial official in French Equatorial Africa. In *Batoula*, the hostility of the colonized for the colonizer enters into every aspect of their relationship: "Behind the grimacing smile of welcome is rancor, and covered by apparent good will is the hope for a liberating massacre—'We will kill them all, one day, long from now.' "[90]

The furious outbursts of psychotic and homicidal rage described by Hesnard, for example, take on new meaning when set side by side with Fanon and Maran. Aubin and other psychiatrists did not entirely overlook this anger, yet neither did they assign colonial politics primary significance.[91] Aubin, like many psychiatrists, asserted that it was *"precisely the relatively* évolué *individuals* who have the most accentuated paranoid tendencies; this evolution, it is true, has *ordinarily been defective* and too rapid; it provoked the premature abandonment of certain ancestral beliefs and institutions (which are capable of reigning in the dangerous drives of each ethnic group), before a new civilization could be assimilated."[92] Aubin at least acknowledged a political grievance that often animated the heart of such rancor: "The cult of justice, so strong among them and exalted by the predication of egalitarianism, is often stymied by the discovery of actual inequalities between Whites and himself; from this a latent sentiment of *distrust, injustice and hostility* grows—all of it encouraged by the *vanity of the natives*."[93] Distrust, hostility, and a sense of injustice, according to Aubin's reasoning, arise among the colonized because of their resentment of racial inequality. Aubin seemed to naturalize this racial inequality so that the "native's injured vanity" that provokes their resentment, and in turn causes paranoid psychosis, appears ridiculous and unjustified. Nowhere in Aubin's medical psychiatry was there a serious appraisal of the impact of unjust legal regimes.

Aubin's leap to racialized rationalizations of colonial anger betrays his own anxiety experienced as denial seizes his consciousness. As we have seen, Aubin normally rejected racialized explanations in favor of careful case studies. This exception proves the strength of the compulsion to deny colonial injustice and reveals the anxiety that such denial will prove inadequate. At length, however, he shook himself free from the compulsive denial of the political. Without retracting his compulsive racializing, he recalled himself and his readers to his commitment to specific case studies and resolved to cut short his discussion of the paranoid psychoses of the half assimiliated: "We will not pursue this psychogenetic reasoning any further, since it can only be approximate given the considerable psychological differences between the diverse primitive ethnic groups."[94]

Aubin's ability to assimilate black African denial into a global uncon-scious—his ability to equate African with European denial—relied on twin pillars of obfuscation. He denied the power of the occult that pervaded his patients' lives, and he denied the power of French imperialism that simi-larly pervaded their lives. As a man of scientific medicine, Aubin was proud of his opposition to "superstition." As a product of the colonial era, he was apparently blind to his own denial of the relevance of political oppression. In both instances, his thinking offers backhanded proof of his claim that denial itself is a universal mechanism, prominent among Euro-peans just as among Africans. Boilat and Allier, who took their meta-physics more seriously than did Aubin, cannot assimilate all humans into a universal without first extirpating evil and its pervasive effects. Fanon, the anti-imperialist psychiatrist, chooses sides with the colonized, defend-ing difference against imperialism. Aubin's balancing act—defending the secular, the scientific, and the universal unconscious—incorporates what appears to be difference as a dimension of the universal.

Magic and Mana

Secure in his denial of the terrorizing power of the occult, Aubin con-tinued his studies, focusing increasingly on magic. In 1952, he published his major work *L'Homme et la magie*, which centered on excavating the contents of la crypte.[95] Professor Henri Baruk, the chief doctor at the Maison Nationale of Charenton, aptly cast Aubin's *L'Homme et la magie* as a seminal interdisciplinary investigation in ethnography and psychiatry. Baruk described how Aubin had used his long years of service in India and North Africa as an opportunity for studying the characters of his patients. In these groups, Baruk contended, one could observe "the fundamental sentiments of human nature, which are less masked, less compressed, less repressed."[96] The magical mentality, according to Aubin, is part of the depth psychology of all humans. Civilization, he explained, caused the ongoing and cumulative repression of the magical mentality so that it is more and more contained under the sediments of logic and rationality. Nonetheless, Aubin contended, human intelligence remains governed by very powerful sentiments and affects and remains, in its foundations, ridden by magic.[97] Notably, the magical governing forces on which Aubin dwelt were seemingly bereft of the power to do real harm to him. Aubin gained access to la crypte precisely because the world of the occult held little power over him. This freedom—discussed previously as established via denial or alternately understood as a reason's liberation from super-stition—demonstrates the circumscription of Aubin's own point of view. He can perceive the power of magic but is protected from its realm.

At its heart, *L'Homme et la magie* is a history of human moral sensi-bilities—tracing the historical emergence of causality, rationality, individ-ualized identity, and responsibility—and as such, it creates a type of uni-versal history. The driving force of this history was the gradual distinction between self and the surrounding world, entailing the separation of mind and emotion from all the diverse elements of the environment, including other people, animals, plants, and objects. Through this history, Aubin placed magical thinking at the foundation of a long series of human trans-formations that included the emergence of concepts of justice, respon-sibility, rights, culpability, emphasis on individual responsibility rather than group redemption, and punishment for the one proven guilty rather than for the group arbitrarily or magically held at fault.[98] Aubin believed that the "non-civilized thinks endlessly about the occult forces that sur-round him," but he believed as well that the civilized repressed such magic only to have it reemerge in countless dimensions of their lives.[99]

La crypte, magic, and mana, in Aubin's estimation, all expressed the same force. In psychoanalytic terms, he rendered this as projection, sym-pathy, and contagion (the ability of emotional energy to transfer from one vessel to another). Aubin understood magic as the diffuse and omnipres-ent work of mana in linking the visible and invisible worlds. He described mana, following Robert Henry Codrington's *Melanesians*, as "the most exalted of powers; the true efficacy of things that re-inforces mechanical action without obliterating it. It is mana that makes the net hold, that makes the house solid, that makes the canoe seaworthy. In the field, it is fertility, in medicine it is the force for health or mortality."[100] Mana, in other words, is the intentionality of the fetish-object; it is the power of something to act with will. Aubin assimilated affective projection to taboo and mana, explaining them as communicable, powerful charges, and sup-plemented these with the concept of "participation," which "implies magi-cal connections between the individual and his or her setting, between things that for us are heterogeneous, between things, that to our eyes, have no relation to each other."[101] In his most lucid formulation, he ex-plained, "We [moderns] localize sentiments in the self and in ourselves, whereas the primitive localizes his sentiments outside of himself in the world he experiences." Aubin demonstrated affective projection by explaining that while a modern individual might claim he feels terror when confronted with a king or a priest, a primitive would say that the priest or king is taboo (possesses mana). A modern person would say, "I am afraid of dead bodies," whereas a primitive would say, "Cadavers are taboo" (or possess mana).[102]

If the Durkheimians wished to see mana as a collective force of the social group—a force perceived by individuals that gives rise to intense collective representations—Aubin did not disagree, yet he was driven to investigate the more individualized experiences of mana, most particularly, of course, the highly idiosyncratic experiences of the mentally ill. His examples include one troubled young woman who believed she could fly and who broke her legs jumping out a window.[103] In another example of individualized magical thinking, Aubin presented the case of a young man, with an Arab father and a European mother who had converted to Islam, who developed phobic delusions after he had suffered a head injury.[104] He developed a conviction that he could feel the finger of God on his head and that he was destined to become a saint. Then, he became obsessed with a delusion that people were trying to prevent his saintliness by tricking him into eating pork. This phobic delusion eventually led him to murder his sister. Aubin discussed this case in psychoanalytic terms of the contagion of a repugnant impurity, the sense of revulsion at being forced to participate in this impurity, and then the attempt to free himself via transgressing an interdiction (i.e., murdering his sister), which itself brought automatic retaliation. Notably, he made no reference to racial etiologies or the special challenges of assimilating to European civilization.[105]

Aubin's conclusion to *L'Homme et la magie* enumerated twenty or more clinical, therapeutic, political, and sociological uses of the knowledge of the magic and la crypte. From the point of view of psychiatry for the colonized, he pointed out that the ability to heal is culturally and geographically specific. This is an insight that the Fann group developed in its careful collaboration with traditional healers in Senegal in the 1960s. He also remarked that individuals transplanted from the colonies are likely to suffer excess of spleen because of the absence of participation between the individual, the group, and the country. Frantz Fanon's celebrated article "North African Syndrome" covered similar terrain in 1952, two years after Aubin's *L'Homme et la magie* was published.[106] Aubin emphasized again that pejorative opinions of natives should be revised, especially with respect to the positive role of lying in maintaining mental equilibrium. The concepts of taboo and mana, according to Aubin, explained the phobia toward hospitals and careers as nurses and also the apparent ingratitude of some patients for the treatment they received. Indeed, the experiences of Africans trained in mental health professions demonstrate that approaching the spirit world without magical protection can incur costly sacrifices. The history of the directors at Fann Hospital— one prematurely dead, the next incapacitated for many years, reportedly because of a spirit possession—demonstrate the power of taboo and the courage required to confront such taboos directly.[107]

Focused as he was on the individual, Aubin neglected to consider magical thinking widely shared among Europeans. This is a blind spot in his thinking, which is nonetheless heavily characterized by the division of populations into broad categories of moderns and primitives. For him, primitives exhibited magic; moderns hid it. Black Africans played the role in Aubin's theories of illuminating the crypte that was common to all humanity. For him, black Africans symbolized the primitive, which in turn symbolized magic. This chain of symbols contrasts to those documented and critiqued by Fanon in *Black Skin, White Masks*. Published in the same year as Aubin's *L'Homme et la magie*, Fanon's book theorized that European thinking was characterized by "Negrophobia."[108] Following a psychoanalytic and Durkheimian analysis closely similar to Aubin's and expressly attributed to Aubin's colleague Angelo Hesnard, Fanon pointed out that phobias arise out of prelogical thinking in which symbols come to stand for powerful affective projections. Negrophobia, as Fanon theorized, embodied the Europeans' fear and anxiety that well from within and then was projected upon Blacks so that they carried the negative affective charge. Fanon was unstinting in his confrontation with negative racializing: "In the remotest depth of the European unconscious an inordinately black hollow has been made in which the most immoral impulses, the most shameful desires lie dormant. And as every man climbs up toward whiteness and light, the European has tried to repudiate this uncivilized self, which has attempted to defend itself. When European civilization came into contact with the black world, with those savage peoples, everyone agreed: Those Negroes were the principle of evil."[109] Aubin's project was to focus the primal associations away from rigid pejoratives to the infinitely malleable dimensions of mana, magic, or fetish. Fanon's concept,

Negrophobia, recalls the threatening force of the occult; Aubin's magic entails power than can threaten weak individuals (i.e., the mentally ill) but did not inherently threaten those in the modern world.

Aubin's discovery of denial and magic (la crypte) in African colonial subjects and his integration of these into a universal psychoanalytic theory relied heavily on disempowering magic, rendering the crypte relatively harmless and thereby finding it tolerable. Religiously minded men such as Boilat and Allier had comparatively little tolerance for occult forces, sensing in them a metaphysical danger. Fanon similarly viewed the repressed as deeply threatening, as containing the principle of evil. Aubin's ability to assimilate the crypte into a universal psyche relied heavily on this denial of power and danger. His access to the forces of magic and participation was limited; the African patients he treated had a much greater access to this domain and more fearful reactions to its forces. This chapter has sought to recuperate these theories of Aubin, placing them back into a Eurocentric history of psychiatry that has denied their significance. Perhaps of greater significance than his universal psychoanalytic theory, Aubin opened a window into African consciousness and culture. While of limited scope, hedged with denial of the occult power to terrorize, and with denial of imperial injustices, nonetheless, this window opens to a broader, more powerful, and less easily appropriated terrain of West African spiritual health and spirit crises.

Notes

1. McClintock, *Imperial Leather*, 189–92. On the emergence of "fetish" in French psychiatry, see Nye, *Masculinity and Male Codes of Honor in Modern France*, 110–13.
2. The debate on whether psychoanalysis can be universal has traditionally focused on the Oedipus complex. See Li, "Marshall Sahlins and the Apotheosis of Culture," 201–88; Malinowski, *Sex and Repression*; Manfredi, "Ìgbo Initiation"; Obeyesekere, *Work of Culture*; and also Bullard, "L'Oedipe Africain," esp. 183–92. For an exceptionally insightful treatment on the historicity of mental illness and the unconscious, see Storper-Perez, *La folie colonisé*.
3. Roudinesco, *Jacques Lacan*.
4. See Bullard, "L'Oedipe Africain," 192–94.
5. Lévy-Bruhl, *Les Fonctions mentales dans les sociétés inférieures*; Lévy-Bruhl, *Primitive Mentality*. Relatively recently, Shore, in *Culture in Mind*, appropriated Lévy-Bruhl's theory of "participation" to drive innovations in cognitive philosophy. The most incisive and appreciative criticism remains Pritchard, "Levy-Bruhl's Theory of Primitive Mentality."

6. For a brief history of the Fann group, see Bullard, "Imperial Networks and Post-colonial Independence." *Psychopathologie africaine*, established in 1965 and still in press, published most of the pioneering Fann Hospital studies.

7. Aubin, *L'Homme et la magie*, 21.

8. Some might contend that Wulf Sachs was the first to publish a psychoanalysis of an African. See his *Black Hamlet*, with a new introduction by Saul Dubow and Jacqueline Rose. However, Ortigues and Ortigues, in *Oedipe Africain*, argue convincingly that true psychoanalysis must be driven by the questions and demands of the analysand, and by that standard, their own work takes precedence over that of Sachs. For an extensive discussion, see Bullard, "L'Oedipe Africain."

9. Aubin, "Introduction à l'étude de la psychiatrie chez les Noirs," 213.

10. This revises Ohayon, *L'Impossible rencontre*, in which she overlooks Hesnard bringing psychoanalysis into colonial situations (67–70).

11. Róheim, "La psychologie raciale et les origines du capitalisme chez les primitifs."

12. Aubin, "A Propos de l'ouvrage de Maud Mannoni"; Aubin, "Deux ouvrages de psychiatrie transculturelle"; Aubin, "Foucault et sa conception idéologique de l'histoire de la folie"; and Aubin, "Conceptions phénoménologiques et psychothérapie instituionnelle d'après l'oeuvre de Hesnard."

13. Reboul and Régis, "L'Assistance des aliénés aux colonies."

14. Aubin, "L'Assistance psychiatrique indigène aux colonies," 150.

15. Ly, *Introduction à une psychoanalyse africaine*, 79.

16. Cazanove, "Memento de psychiatrie." See also Cazanove, "Les conceptions magico-religieuses."

17. Ly, *Introduction à une psychoanalyse africaine*, 80, 91.

18. For a description of Delafosse's contribution to French colonial policies, see Conklin, *Mission to Civilize*, 177–78.

19. Monteil, "La Divination chez les noirs de l'Afrique occidentale française," 134–36.

20. Bois, "Étude documentaire sur l'auteur," 23.

21. Mauchamp, "Lettre de M. P. Mauchamp à J. Bois," 3.

22. Charcot and Richer's *Démoniaques dans l'art* redescribed what artists throughout the ages had portrayed as spiritual ecstasy as in fact nothing other than hysteria or neurasthenia. See Goldstein, *Console and Classify*, 326, 363–67.

23. Aubin, "L'Assistance psychiatrique indigène aux colonies," 196–97.

24. Porot, "Discussion du rapport d'assistance psychiatrique," 178.

25. Hesnard, "Discussion du rapport d'assistance psychiatrique," 183.

26. Aubin, "L'Assistance psychiatrique indigène aux colonies," pt. 2, 196.

27. As a counterpoint, in the following year (1953), Aubin published a French translation of John Colin Carothers's World Health Organization–sponsored project, *African Mind*.

28. See, for example, Aubin, "Pensée magique et psychiatrie"; Aubin, "Médecine magique et arts sculpturaux de l'Afrique"; Aubin, *La guérison par l'art*; and Aubin, "La magie eternelle."

29. Zempléni, "From Symptom to Sacrifice," 137n67.

30. On some of the implications of the choice of these terms, see Mann, "Fetishizing Religion."

31. De la Rocca, Chef du Bureau Politique, Tivaouane, Cercle de Cayor, Rapport Politique Annuel, 18 February 1925, Sous Serie 6M 323, Bobine 178, Senegal National Archives.

32. Robinson, *Paths of Accommodation*, provides a compelling account of French negotiations with Muslim marabouts to govern large segments of West Africa. Although he is interested in the "cultural capital" of the marabout, Robinson does not address their medical activities. See also Babou, "Amadu Bamba and the Founding of the Muridiyya."

33. Rapport Politique, 1926, Sous-série 6M 323, Bobine 178, Senegal National Archives.

34. On the French-trained African doctors and the deliberate use of medicine to extend French civilization, see Huémavo-Griamud, *Médecins Africains en AOF*.

35. Huot, as quoted in Reboul and Régis, "L'assistance des aliénés aux colonies," 98–99.

36. See Afrique occidentale française, *La justice indigêne en Afrique occidentale française*, 31, 38–39.

37. Pautrat, *La justice locale*, 92.

38. Rapport Politique Générale Annuel, Territoire de la Casamance, 1926, 42 pages, dated 17 February 1927, signed L'Administration Supérieur (signature illegible), Senegal National Archives, 2 G26–66, p. 4; Baum, "Crimes of the Dream World." More generally on witchcraft and soul cannibalism, see Simmons, *Eyes of the Night*; Ames, "Belief in 'Witches' among the Rural Wolof of the Gambia."

39. Territoire de la Casamance, Rapport Politique Générale Annuel, Territoire de la Casamance, 1926, 42 pages, dated, 17 February 1927, signed, L'Administration Supérieur (signature illegible), Senegal National Archives, 2 G26–66, p. 6.

40. Ibid.

41. Robert Baum's careful history of these trials argues that they served aspiring local elites in their efforts to solidify their status vis-à-vis the French administration by ridding themselves of their rivals.

42. Griaule, *Conseiller de l'Union Française*, 91.

43. Of course, few now would agree that denial is an appropriate route toward mental health. It might be considered more appropriate in honor-based cultures (i.e., see Nye, *Masculinity and Male Codes of Honor in Modern France*). See also Hacking, *Rewriting the Soul*, in which he entertains Pierre Janet's therapeutic encouragement of forgetting as a dimension of his adherence to honor (195–97) and then argues against this induced false consciousness (260–65).

44. The black African soldiers were drawn mainly from French West Africa and also from French Equatorial Africa and yet were collectively called *tirailleurs Sénégalais*. For a good social history of the *tirailleurs*, see Echenberg, *Colonial Conscripts*.

45. Bullard, "Imperial Networks and Postcolonial Independence."

46. This study of psychotic regression can be contextualized in later medical litera-

ture that depicted a relative ease of regression and quick recovery among black Africans, as contrasted to Europeans, who are more resistant to psychosis but in whom psychosis proves more intractable. Marie-Cécile and Edmond Ortigues theorized that early infantile object substitutions and fixations could account for these differences. See their *Oedipe Africain*, 105–6; Bullard, "L'Oedipe Africain," 180–83, 190–91.

47. Aubin, "Introduction à l'étude de la psychiatrie chez les Noirs," pt. 1, 13.

48. Ibid., 18.

49. Ibid., 3.

50. Ibid., 12.

51. I qualify my reference to Aubin's respect for this fear because his respect does not extend to a belief in the demonic forces that threatened the Senegalese. Here, Aubin allows a difference between himself and the West Africans to remain unbridged. However, in passing over this difference in silence—that is, by not reflecting on the difference between really feeling fear of demons and merely recognizing that someone else feels threatened by demons (that Aubin does not seem to believe even exist)—Aubin is able to assimilate the version of West African denial into European denial more easily. Taking the demons seriously would necessitate that Aubin leave the confines of psychology to grapple with metaphysics. Raoul Allier (discussed later in this chapter) engaged in such attempts and arrived at a much stronger respect for difference and yet also with a strongly hierarchical conviction of European moral superiority.

52. Aubin, "Introduction à l'étude de la psychiatrie chez les Noirs," pt. 1, 28.

53. Ibid. His reference is to Pierre Janet's encouragement (i.e., via hypnosis) of forgetting as a means of curing patients suffering dissociation consequent to trauma. See Hacking's discussion in *Rewriting the Soul*, 195–97.

54. Aubin, "Introduction à l'étude de la psychiatrie chez les Noirs," pt. 1, 12.

55. Ibid., 28.

56. Bastide, "Psychiatrie, Ethnographie et Sociologie," 227.

57. Ibid.

58. Aubin, "Refus, Reniement, Repression." See also Aubin, "Conduites de refus et psychothérapie."

59. Aubin, "Refus, Reniement, Repression," 31.

60. Boilat, *Esquisses Sénégalaises*, 301–3, 315–16.

61. Ibid., 301.

62. Ibid., 302.

63. Ibid.

64. Ibid., 303.

65. Ibid., 454.

66. Ibid., 455.

67. Ibid., 447–48.

68. Ibid., 449.

69. Ibid., 449–50.

70. Ibid., 450–51. Boilat remarks that he could not remember the name of the village.

71. Ibid., 452.

72. Ibid.

73. Ibid., 453.

74. Ibid.

75. Ibid., 453–54.

76. Ibid., 449.

77. Huot, as quoted in Reboul and Régis, "L'Assistance des aliénés aux colonies," 101.

78. Goldstein, *Console and Classify*, 361–77.

79. Of his long list of publications, the most relevant here is Allier, *La psychologie de la conversion chez les peuples non-civilisés*.

80. Ibid, 87.

81. Ibid., 90–91.

82. Ibid., 91.

83. Ibid., 113–15.

84. Ibid., 116–17.

85. Aubin, "Introduction à l'étude de la psychiatrie chez les Noirs," pt. 2, 213. See Allier, *Le non-civilisé et nous*. In contrast, decades later, in his 1968 review of *Whites Think Too Much*, Aubin found support for his outlook in Parin, Morgenthaler, and Parin-Matthey's emphasis on "negation." See Aubin, "Deux ouvrages de psychiatrie transculturelle," 185.

86. Haakon Chevalier provided the Anglophone title in his translation of Fanon's *A Dying Colonialism*; Fanon's original title is "Conduites d'aveu en Afrique du Nord."

87. Fanon's comment on his 1955 paper in *A Dying Colonialism*, 127n2.

88. Ibid., 121.

89. Maran, *Batoula*.

90. Maran's *Batoula*, as cited in Ly, *Introduction à une psychoanalyse africaine*, 121.

91. For instance, compare to André Ombrédane on the Asalampusa as discussed in Bullard, "Critical Impact of Frantz Fanon and Henri Collomb."

92. Aubin, "Introduction à l'étude de la psychiatrie chez les Noirs," pt. 1, 25–26.

93. Ibid.

94. Ibid.

95. Aubin, *L'Homme et la magie*. Aubin dedicated this comprehensive study to Dr. Henri Ey, Professor Henri Baruk, Dr. Angelo Hesnard, Daniel Lagache, Antoine Porot, and Léon Pales. These men represent a cross-section of the most prominent psychiatric and ethnographic practitioners of that era. Hesnard and Porot, we have encountered previously; Ey was the chief editor of *L'Evolution psychiatrique*, Lagache was a leading French psychoanalyst, and Pales was the associate director of the Musée de l'Homme.

96. Compare this outlook to Freud's in "Totem and Taboo," in which a direct comparison between "primitives" and the mentally ill is made. The assumption of a universal human psyche is common between Baruk, Freud, and Aubin, with an

added belief that "more civilized" peoples possess psyches that are more highly elaborated or developed via various processes.

97. Baruk, in the preface to Aubin, *L'Homme et la magie*, 10.

98. While recognizing the criticism of comparing adult primitives with civilized children, Aubin cites Bastide's *Sociologie et psychanalyse* in defense of the comparison, arguing that infantile traits are consolidated in adult primitives. Aubin clarified his comparison, stating, "The alienated will never turn back into a primitive, no more than the primitive could be considered a madman." He dissociated himself from any claim that there was an absolute or strong distinction between "civilized" and "primitive" peoples or that "primitive mentality" was somehow "prelogical." Aubin, *L'Homme et la magie*, 16, 19, 30; Bastide, *Sociologie et psychanalyse*, 185.

99. Aubin, *L'Homme et la magie*, 19.

100. Ibid., 21–22. Aubin is relying on Codrington, *The Melanesians*. Freud also relied on Codrington's *The Melanesians* in "Totem and Taboo." Aubin relies heavily as well on Hubert and Mauss, *Esquisse d'une théorie générale de la magie*.

101. Aubin, *L'Homme et la magie*, 23.

102. Ibid., 31; hence, the fascinating power of the HBO television series, *Six Feet Under*, in which all the characters are infused with the taboo powers of death.

103. Ibid., 23.

104. Ibid., 27.

105. Notably absent from his analysis was any causal reference to race or the racial constitution demanded by European civilization (in contrast, for example, to Donnadieu, "Psychose de civilisation," 30–37). Aubin retained here the fundamental role of biological etiology, as he notes that the episode began after a traumatic blow to the head.

106. Fanon, "Le Syndrome nord-africain," 237–51. This article is reprinted in pt. 1, chap. 1 of Fanon, *Toward the African Revolution*.

107. See my further discussion in Bullard, "Imperial Networks and Postcolonial Independence," 210–11.

108. Fanon, *Black Skin, White Masks*, 154; originally published as *Peau noire, masques blanques*. Fanon relied on Angelo Hesnard's definition of phobia.

109. Fanon, *Black Skin, White Masks*, 190.

Géza Róheim and the Australian Aborigine
Psychoanalytic Anthropology during the Interwar Years

Since Freud wrote his famous book, *Totem and Taboo*, we who follow in his footsteps have been trying to build up a new science.
—Géza Róheim, "Psychoanalysis of Primitive Cultural Types"

In 1952, writing toward the end of his life, the psychoanalytic anthropologist Géza Róheim reflected on the very existence of the academic field to which he had devoted his professional energies. "Is there such a thing as a psychoanalytic anthropology?" he asked. "From a practical point of view psychoanalysis and anthropology are two different professions. A psychoanalyst sits in his office and receives patients who want to be cured. An anthropologist goes to some tribe in the desert or jungle and tries to understand those people—who certainly do not want to be cured, indeed, they could teach us a lesson in happiness." Despite these and other marked differences Róheim identified between the two disciplines, he was hoping to "build up a new science. We sometimes call it psychoanalytic anthropology but we all believe that it will be the only anthropology of the future."[1] Róheim's optimism, however, was not shared by others, and his vision to bring forth a new discipline did not eventuate, as neither psychoanalysts nor anthropologists embraced his methodology with much conviction. While his work did not spawn "new methods, new results, new problems"[2] as he had hoped, Róheim's attempted integration between anthropology and psychoanalysis is worthy of examination for his efforts to psychoanalyze the indigenous self, for a number of reasons.

This chapter attempts to explore the paradox at the heart Róheim's work. From the outset, Róheim assumes that the Australian Aborigines are a "primitive race" and that a study of them can capture a snapshot of an undeveloped human subjectivity before the onset of "civilization." At one level, then, Róheim's gaze is unquestionably colonial in the way it positions his subjects as "uncivilized" as compared to the white, Western self. But he also takes his analysis in directions that complicate indigenous subjectivity and challenge any characterization of it as simplistic. Although he attempts to normalize and modernize the "savage"—that is, to make the savage Western and familiar—Róheim takes his discussion beyond that of clichéd paradigms of the "simple savage." In doing so, the question that underlines his work is one that is at the heart of psychoanalysis: How universal is the psychoanalytic self? Is the unconscious universal, or is it bound by cultural determinants? For Róheim, the answer is paradoxically yes to both questions. In sustaining both these positions, Róheim at once offers psychoanalytic theory as a potentially liberating set of ideas that, by arguing for the complexity of the indigenous self, challenges contemporary ideas of primitivism. But in doing so within a colonialist Western paradigm, he cannot escape its equally oppressive interpretations.

Róheim was born in Budapest in 1891. He was a trained anthropologist who, in 1919, occupied the first chair of anthropology at the University of Budapest, a position he held until 1938. He became a convert to psychoanalysis while in Germany, training in geography and anthropology at the universities of Berlin and Leipzig.[3] In 1915, he combined both his intellectual passions by establishing the discipline of "psychoanalytic anthropology."[4]

Róheim pursued his psychoanalytic interests through his involvement with the Hungarian Psychoanalytic Society, a multidisciplinary, eclectic group that reached its zenith immediately after the First World War. He was involved in the society during its heyday—when Sandor Ferenczi was its inspiring and flamboyant leader, followed by Michael Balint. During the 1920s, Róheim studied with Ferenczi and Melanie Klein. One of the distinctive features of the Hungarian Psychoanalytic Society was its emphasis on the interpersonal impact of the mother-infant relationship, where one "cannot speak of an independent self in the infant" in the "first months of life." The society made an important contribution to discussions about the mutual relationship between analysand and analyst.[5] One of Róheim's major contributions to psychoanalytic ideas was the identification of the phenomenon of "collective trauma" during the course of his studies in Australia. He argued that the impact of these traumas could be deciphered in the myths and rituals of a given culture.[6]

Róheim's beliefs were defined by a number of understandings. First, in what has been termed his "folklore studies," Róheim believed that cultural artifacts could be "interpreted in terms of the psychology of the individual." He ignored the possibility that the various customs and beliefs he studied would have "economic, religious or sociological meanings."[7] Myths, for him, were a reflection of the "inner psychic experiences of the individual," but these were "unknown to the individual himself"—a myth was treated "very much like the manifest content of a dream." Second was his belief in the "psychic unity of mankind"—that modern Europeans "did not differ in the slightest from the rudest primitives." He believed in a "static human psyche."[8] Finally, he believed that myth and ritual "have a contemporary significance."[9]

Róheim was primarily an academic anthropologist who applied psychoanalytic interpretations to the observations made by others who undertook fieldwork. In 1921, he was awarded the Freud Prize for a paper on "Australian totemism." Although his interest in Australian Aborigines had been longstanding, it was not until 1929 that he undertook his first extensive field trip to Australia, arriving in Adelaide in February and staying for ten months.

The Róheims were welcomed to Adelaide by Dr. Herbert Basedow, anthropologist, state parliamentarian, and formerly first chief protector of Aborigines in the Northern Territory, who was able to arrange meetings for them with South Australian Aboriginal communities. The Róheims then spent four months at the Lutheran mission at Hermannsburg, where Géza Róheim made contact "with the desert tribes known to science only by name or not at all" (Pichentara, Pindupi, Yumu, Nambutji, etc.). In November, he returned to Adelaide, where he wrote up his results and prepared for his onward journey to New Guinea, Africa, and the United States.[10]

Anthropology and Psychoanalysis

Róheim, of course, was not alone in attempting to combine psychoanalysis with anthropology. Many of Róheim's views reflected those of analysts who saw virtue in drawing together the insights of these disciplines. In an address to the Royal Anthropological Institute in 1924 on psychoanalysis and anthropology, Sigmund Freud's biographer, Ernest Jones, began by telling his audience that he was all too aware of the pitfalls of a scholar in one discipline instructing those in another. It "behoves [the speaker] to do so in a duly tentative and modest spirit," he cautioned. This was especially the case, he believed, in relation to psychoanalysis, where one could "count only on incredulity and opposition from those not familiar with the subject."[11]

Jones argued that a belief in "occult forces" by savages was a projection of their unconscious. He observed that "the extent to which savages seem to be preoccupied with thoughts about wizardry, witchcraft, and evil spirits of all kinds inevitably makes a psychoanalyst suspect that their unconscious minds must contain specially intense wishes of a hostile nature, which have been extensively projected into the outer world."

Taking incest as his example, Jones pointed to the role of the Oedipus complex in such societies and "the endless initiation rites, the numerous myths and cosmogonies where the content is either openly or symbolically incestuous, and the vast problem of totemism itself" to suggest how this connection between the two disciplines may "throw a flood of light on some of the most obscure problems in anthropology." On the more contentious issue of the relationship between savage and civilized peoples, Jones argued that the "supposed . . . lack of concentration, reason, powers of discrimination and logic" among "primitive peoples" is not due to a lack of these qualities but rather to a "different orientation of emotional interest from our own." What was this "different orientation"? Jones located it in the unconscious: "It is possible that the conscious thinking of savages is more directly and extensively influenced by unconscious factors than is that of civilised peoples, just as is so with the child." In making this suggestion, he wished "to guard [himself] against the charge of underestimating the complexity of the relationship in question." Lest he be accused of comparing savages to children, he argued that in psychoanalysis, there is "more of the infant in the adult than is commonly recognised, and also more of the adult in the child." This resulted, he believed, "in a greater respect for the mind of the child and a less respect for the mind of the adult."[12]

Although Jones's address was the first time a psychoanalyst had spoken to a group of anthropologists, Freud had famously made these and other connections between psychoanalysis and anthropology in 1913 in his ambitious and controversial work "Totem and Taboo." In identifying the unconscious, projection, incest, and totemism as the key concepts to a psychoanalytic reading of primitive peoples, Jones was drawing heavily on Freud's speculations.

In four articles, Freud draws on a study of primitive peoples in order to gain some psychological insight into the condition of neurotics in his society as well as the psychodynamics of contemporary culture. Drawing examples from Australia, Melanesia, Polynesia, the Solomon Islands, and Africa, Freud discusses incest and the Oedipal phase in the first chapter. He makes the observation that "savage peoples" believe that incestuous wishes, which become unconscious, are regarded as "immediate perils" that need to be repressed. Freud includes material on his neurotic patients in the discussion, arguing that neurotics either failed to free themselves from the psychosexual conditions of childhood or they have returned to them. In both cases, the contribution of psychoanalysis is that it identifies the role of the infantile in cultural and individual behavior.[13]

Although Freud considered the cultures he discussed not to have reached the level of his own "civilization," he believed a study of their rituals, customs, and taboos could offer insight into contemporary neurosis. In this regard, he resisted any dismissal of them as society had similarly dismissed the psychology of children:

> I am under no illusion that in putting forward these attempted ex-
> planations I am laying myself open to the charge of endowing modern
> savages with a subtlety in their mental activities which exceeds all
> probability. It seems to me quite possible, however, that the same may
> be true of our attitude towards the psychology of these races that
> have remained at the animistic level as is true of our attitude to-
> wards the mental life of children, which we adults no longer under-
> stand and whose fullness and delicacy of feeling we have in conse-
> quence so greatly underestimated.[14]

Freud sought to find underlying links between psychoanalysis, social anthropology, philology, and folklore, but his observations were, in the end, only academic—he himself never went out into the field. It was up to his followers to absorb his interpretations and apply them. One of Freud's most committed and devoted disciples was Géza Róheim, who traveled to Australia to seek confirmation of some of his theories. Róheim was keen to prove Freud right; his was an intellectual and theoretical pursuit rather than a political fascination. His writings and observations are framed by the way in which he perceives himself as a worthy successor to Freud through his own efforts to connect anthropology and psychoanalysis.

Psychoanalysis as a Colonialist Discourse

Although Jones was cautious about how he framed the psychology of the savage, there can be no denying that, as many scholars have pointed out, psychoanalysis has been a colonizing discourse. In *Dark Continents: Psychoanalysis and Colonialism*, Ranjana Khanna characterizes psychoanalysis as a "colonial discipline." It "disciplines" a "way of being," an "idea of being that was dependent on colonial political and ontological relations, and through its disciplinary practices, formalized and perpetuated an idea of uncivilized, primitive, concealed, and timeless colonized peoples." It shaped a "form of civilized being" in late nineteenth-century and early twentieth-century Europe, a national-colonial self that was "brought into existence, or perhaps more accurately, into unconcealment."[15] In the context of anthropology, this takes various forms. Psychoanalysis aims to give people a personal history; it gives the analysand a rationalization of what "cannot be accounted for in the guise of the unconscious." On the other hand, an anthropology that is "built upon a racist evolutionary philosophy posits the contemporary 'primitive' as a version of the early stages of human society, and the primitive can therefore have no history." These peoples have no past, memory, or history.[16] The question of whether there is cultural *difference* in regard to conditions like madness has also aroused debate. For instance, Jonathan Sadowsky has shown that during the nineteenth century, European missionaries did not understand madness as relative but as "something they could recognise." He argues that madness is not universal or relative to different cultures, but it is both, and different historical circumstances can stress one or the other. During the nineteenth century, the stress was on difference.[17] Ashis Nandy's study of psychoanalysis in the Indian context has shown that it was also used to demystify aspects of Indian cultural life, and as a tool that could be used against the West.[18] Furthermore, psychoanalysis has also been seen as "criticizing the native culture and . . . as a legitimating ideology for colonial domination."[19]

Stephen Frosh has mapped out the various criticisms against psychoanalysis in racial terms. "Rooted in a colonizing society," he argues, psychoanalysis has "spoken 'for' others without genuinely allowing itself to *encounter* otherness."[20] In the context of the British Empire, as Roland

Littlewood and Maurice Lipsedge observe, some of the stereotypes associated with the emotional states of blacks in the British Empire compared them with children; they were believed to be simpleminded and, like the Afro-American, were seen as "cunning and infantile but faithful and superstitious and insensitive to pain."[21] The black man "did not even possess an individual mind but shared a communal mind, attuned to the elementary collective consciousness of his tribe."[22] The "civilized man" assimilated and worked through his conflicts, while the "primitive split them off and dissociated himself from them."[23]

Psychoanalysis and psychiatry in the earlier part of the last century worked within a model that assumed the ascendancy of white civilization, progress, and the Enlightenment. It is true, as Littlewood and Lipsedge argue in their work on psychoanalysis and race, that indigenous populations within the British Empire were often considered "more physical than psychological."[24] It was often assumed, for instance, that the apparent lack of depression and insanity revealed that "Africans and Asians were incapable of examining their feelings, had difficulty expressing their emotions and were less likely to have a distinct personality." Their apparent tendency not to become insane was interpreted as living in a "state of primitive simplicity," with no cares and concerns in the world.[25] After all, Freud himself had suggested that neuroses arose from the demands of the pressures of Western civilization and modern life. The insane were often compared to primitive peoples. The British physician Henry Maudsley had argued decades before that the mentally insane shared with primitive men a regression into a rudimentary state.

During the interwar years, anthropological ideas were built on these views but were also moving in different directions in Australia. Social anthropologists in the 1920s predicted the end of Aboriginal culture and racial decline. Others believed they could be saved from extinction—a view expressed by humanitarian and pro-Aboriginal groups. Those such as Daisy Bates were steadfast in their conviction that the most humanitarian act would be to ensure their decline was as painless as possible. Both at a physical and psychological level, the evolutionary framework informed scientific interpretations of the fate of the Aborigine. The anthropologist Stanley D. Porteus, in his book *The Psychology of a Primitive People*, argued that it was "universally considered" that Aborigines belonged "in the most primitive stages of culture" and believed that they were less developed than Europeans.[26] Modernity—with its assumptions of the rational, scientific, and linear self—positioned the indigenous population as savage, irrational, and unscientific.

By the 1930s, anthropologists were using notions of the psyche to explore the so-called dream-life of Aborigines. According to Adolphus Peter Elkin, an Anglican clergyman and leading anthropologist, a dream "to the Aborigines is not a passing fantasy, but a real objective experience in which time and space are no longer obstacles, and in which valuable information and help is gained by the dreamer." Aborigines, Elkin observed, showed a "faith in the manifestations of the dream-life."[27] Unlike his contemporaries, who believed that the Aborigines were a dying race, Elkin staunchly believed in offering assistance and creating further understanding and support for Aboriginal communities.[28]

Subsequently, Aboriginal religion expert Tony Swain has argued that Elkin popularized the term "dreamtime" and that anthropologists and others adopted it uncritically. Like Róheim, Elkin applied Western views of dreaming and what he referred to as the dreamtime. The key to reading these was through symbolism, especially through the "dream-totem," where "to see another person's dream-totem while asleep is to learn something about him." He felt that symbolism held the key. "The phenomena of dream-totemism," Elkin argued, "show the important part played by symbolism in the life of the Aborigines, more especially in the dream-life." For Elkin, the dreamtime was related directly to dreaming, for these examples "show the depth of the Aborigines' faith in the manifestations of the dream-life." Thus, Elkin believed, it was important to consider the "traditionally and socially conditioned patterns and purpose of dreams and visions."[29] This highlights cultural differences in relation to self-scrutiny, which was seen by anthropologists to be noticeably absent from indigenous cultures.

In the colonialist environment that continued during the interwar years, human rights and citizenship were denied to the indigenous population. Across Australia, citizenship rights of the indigenous population during the interwar years were determined by the states of Australia. John Chesterman and Brian Galligan argue that at this time, the states became more authoritarian in how they dealt with Aborigines, "reaching a low point in the 1930s."[30] This was indeed a period when the definition of "Aboriginality" underwent intense scrutiny as various eugenicist categories emerged for the first time in legislation, such as "native blood," "half blood," and "crossbreed." Government regulations dictated wages and working and living conditions, as well as movement and marriage; they created a situation where Australian Aborigines were living under conditions that were oppressive and exploitative and that denied them the most basic human rights. Ideologically, the contemporary view that prevailed was that Aborigines were a primitive race—one that was removed from evolutionary developments and could not survive in a modern, "civilized" world.[31] Anthropologists, scientists, and medical practitioners promoted the purity of a white race, and eugenicist ideas promoted the concept of "breeding out" the Aboriginal race through what was termed the "half-caste."[32] The forcible removal of Aboriginal children from their communities was premised on racially driven understandings of Aboriginality based on purity and whiteness that were bound by Western rationality.[33] Several organizations and groups of both whites and Aboriginal leaders formed in order to assist Aboriginal communities and promote their interests and welfare. During the interwar years, these included the Australian Aboriginal Progressive Association in New South Wales; in Victoria, the Australian Aborigines' League; and in Western Australia, the Native Union. The Communist Party of Australia and women's organizations such as the Australian Federation of Women Voters, as well as Christian progressives, through groups such as the United Aborigines Mission, challenged assumptions about the conditions in which Aboriginal communities lived in a "civilized" country.[34]

The view of the "simple Aborigine" destined to extinction, however, remained a dominant discourse. In 1934, when addressing the Sydney Bushwalkers Club, Charles Price Conigrave, who had lived for many years in northern Australia, reported that the "average native . . . possessed the mentality of a child." Therefore, any policy should be based on "an understanding and appreciation of his limitations, and not upon the desire to give him a position of equality among white people, who had had the advantage of eras of evolution and education."[35] Medical assumptions were deduced from the apparent "simple life" of the Aborigines.[36] A belief in Aboriginal culture as a museum relic worthy of preservation also prevailed at this time. To preserve Aboriginal culture amounted to "a wish to preserve this strange link with our yesteryears."[37] The discipline of anthropology in Australia at this time reflected the discipline as it was taught and understood worldwide. It was, as Julie Marcus has observed, a discipline "filled with hope," as it offered insights and reflections into other cultures as a means of reflecting on the civilization of the West. During the 1930s, she adds, anthropology presented challenges to the order of European societies, while at the same time, it provided deeply conservative views on the supremacy of the West.[38] The development of anthropology as an academic subject received a major boost with the appointment of Professor Alfred Radcliffe-Brown in 1927 to the University of Sydney. Although his studies were later criticized, he did develop new ways of thinking about Aboriginal welfare and culture. The view that Aborigines were "dying out" also provided a heightened sense of the need for immediate action to study those who had survived.[39]

These were the views that held sway at the time, and they reflected modern notions of the "rational," the scientific, and the linear progress of civilization. Psychoanalysis was bound similarly by notions of the rational, as well as individualism. As Alan Roland argues in his work on cultural pluralism, classical psychoanalysis "always emphasised a resolution of unconscious conflicts so that rationality can once more prevail."[40] In the Australian context, psychoanalytic ideas were not widespread, and they were largely restricted to medical use. During the 1920s and 1930s, a growing body of Freud's work was being published in English, and many of his theories gained further exposure and began to inform academic disciplines and intellectual forums. Religion, feminism, sexuality, psychology, and anthropology were but a few of the areas influenced, and what intellectuals had in common was the way in which they applied Freud's ideas liberally and eclectically to their individual disciplines. In his later life, Freud became increasingly preoccupied with this kind of eclecticism and what he saw as the watering down of his methodology by those from outside the field of psychoanalysis. While this trend was obviously a problem worldwide, nowhere was it as marked as in Australia, where the lack of a psychoanalytic training institute and low numbers of trained analysts meant that there was no real yardstick of orthodoxy. The ideas behind psychoanalysis, unattached as they were to any real practical application, remained just that—ideas: theories that could be appropriated at will by Australian intellectuals and incorporated into their own philosophies and practices.[41]

To what extent did Róheim's psychoanalytic gaze reflect these prevailing colonialist views about Aborigines?

Róheim's Technique

The key element in Róheim's decision to travel to Australia was his belief that Australians "represented the most primitive existent race."[42] Paul

Robinson argues that the theory that most likely inspired him to pursue observations of Australian Aborigines was found in Freud's *Civilization and Its Discontents*. If it was the case, as Freud argued, that civilization was based on repression, then it followed that the most primitive culture "should also be the most permissive, and its members the healthiest, psychologically, of living men."[43]

Róheim wrote a number of studies of the Australian Aborigines during the interwar years, including several lengthy articles and two major works: *Australian Totemism: A Psycho-Analytic Study in Anthropology* (1925) and *The Riddle of the Sphinx* (1934). In *Australian Totemism*, Róheim made the myths and rituals of Aboriginal culture and society the focus of his study. Although he did detour occasionally, Róheim applied Freud's original assumptions in "Totem and Taboo" mechanistically. He aimed to explore the unconscious meaning of ritual and was especially concerned to read myths through the Oedipus complex.

Animals in particular represented unconscious symbols for Róheim. Of one "complex" he identified, he argued that "the projection into the environment of those unconscious concepts and feelings [has occurred] where animal species symbolically represent father-mother complexes."[44] Through a close reading of myths, he concludes that these "myths afford us some insight into the unconscious mechanism of Arunta ritual and tradition."[45] The Oedipus complex figured prominently in Róheim's interpretations:

> We remind the reader that the kangaroo as father and the emu as mother have very definite symbolic meanings in the proto-totemic complex of the Australian tribes. Thus the means by which a man procreates his own child appears in the light of a breaking through the cardinal taboos; he symbolically kills his own totem, that is, he either kills his kangaroo-father or has intercourse with his emu-mother. Thus all children owe . . . their birth to an unconscious (symbolic) realisation of the Oedipus complex—from their own point of view in a fight with their own father and intercourse with their own mother, whilst from their father's point of view it is a revival of his own infantile Oedipus complex.[46]

An evolutionary perspective emerges in his writings. "The poverty and the extreme primitiveness of the material culture of the Central Australian natives," he writes, "is perhaps best emphasised by the fact that they have not yet completely attained the stage of evolution in worldly goods that clearly marks off Man from the Animal Kingdom . . . The Australian native has conserved the rudiments of a pre-human stage of development." [47]

Róheim argued that a striking characteristic of the culture of the Australian Aborigine was its masculinity: men were aggressive, women were excluded from ceremonial functions, and female representation in myths, dreams, and children's games were portrayed as masculine. He traced collective trauma to this experience of the masculinization of the culture, thus shifting the emphasis from the "history of the race to the history of the individual."[48] As a disciple of Freud, Róheim understood "trauma" as childhood trauma rather than that of the trauma of the destruction of the race.

Through the course of his work with Aborigines, Róheim adopted two novel approaches to his investigations: that of observing child's play[49]—he found that using Melanie Klein's methods of play analysis indispensable for observing Aboriginal children's behavior[50]—and of psychoanalyzing individuals through dream analysis. In both of these, he draws on the *unconscious* as a global, or generic, category. In doing so, I would argue that he reveals the savage self as more layered and complex than the representation of the "dying savage" that is so common among the work of his colleagues. In Róheim, we see the paradox where psychoanalysis is an enabling discourse that complicates the unconscious, yet pathologizes and marginalizes the savage as primitive within a white, Western discourse.

The analysis of children is a telling example of this in his work. In *Children of the Desert*, Róheim analyzed children largely through the Oedipus complex. He observed children of the Aranda, Loritja, Pitchentara, and Jumu tribes, writing that "although of course they are not free from anxiety in the clinical sense, they certainly enjoy greater freedom of body and soul than an average white boy." Róheim clearly finds them intriguing —the Western marvel of the "primitive other": "The desert . . . is the nursery of these children. Their eyes are trained to see lizards, to detect the places where they can dig for witchetties, and they eat what they can get. Play and school is one and the same thing, for as they grow their aims will grow with them, till when they have reached to age of ten or twelve they can deal with the kangaroo himself."[51] The case study of one child, Depitainja, is a lengthy one, so I will draw on a few elements of it to provide an example of Róheim's application of the Oedipus complex and the way in which he attempted to read the boy's behavior through Freud's theory. For Róheim, there is a recognition of the specificity of the culture of the Australian Aborigine, implying a more complex subjectivity, but he is also attempting to draw out generic conclusions about the Oedipus complex. In his analysis, there is also an inverted aspect of the Oedipus complex:

> While the snake represents him in his aggressive male attitude, there is always a certain amount of indecision regarding the sex of the nanny-goat. First he calls it a little girl and makes it kiss the mother (monkey). The kiss is repeated on the vagina and we know that he himself is always trying to do this to the girls. Now he makes a group consisting of snake (father), monkey (mother) and nanny-goat (himself). The nanny-goat is now treated as a male. It has intercourse with the mother while the snake does the same to the nanny-goat per anum. Here we have the Oedipus attitude in both aspects; the boy who loves the mother, but is also beloved by the father, and is therefore both a boy and a girl.[52]

Róheim believed that Depitatinja's mental makeup and sexual habits were both similar to and different from that of "what we might expect if he were a European child of the same age." The latent motive, he argued, "is always and everywhere the Oedipus complex." He also noticed that "the degree of openness" with which the boys discussed "the sexual significance of their games" differed from their white counterparts.[53]

In *Australian Totemism*, Róheim drew evidence from Australian mythology, ritual, and social structure in support of the primal crime hypothesis.[54] He also found proof of "homo-erotic" ties, which gave "cohesion to the brother clan, and thus to society as a whole." In other observations, he wrote that the origins of stone culture can be traced to "the primal crime." He noted how "the psychic origins of stone culture were to be found in the particular manner in which the father of the horde was murdered by his sons."[55] In other analyses, he observed the ways in which economic revolutions were reduced to their psychological motivations.[56] He also believed that the totem represented the mother and that the animal consumed at the totem meal "was only secondarily a representative of the father."[57] This points to the issue of sexuality and his view of it as it was played out in cultural activity and individual psychology: there was "a massive confusion of masculine and feminine elements."[58]

These details reflect the paradox that Róheim's interest in his subject was framed with the colonialist paradigm of "accessing" the primitive and unfolding the mystery of the primitive other. He stated explicitly that he aimed to get "a glimpse into the prehistoric period of humanity" and to understand it "through a correct psychological interpretation of the data afforded by the study of cultural areas."[59] Róheim did discuss, however, the *unconscious* as a cross-cultural, generic concept, and he applied a universal understanding of it. I would argue that in Róheim's analysis, the Australian Aborigine possessed a complex subjectivity, despite his insistence on its primitive nature. In this way, he represented the primitive unconscious as having a dynamic agency. The unconscious knew no racial hierarchies in his work. According to Montague David Eder, who wrote the introduction to *Australian Totemism*, "The hypothesis must be framed that the unconscious of a person of lowly culture is in quality the same as that of persons of the higher culture, and that the unconscious, strictly unconscious, motives which influence both alike are those discovered in the laboratory of the psycho-analyst."[60]

The issue of whether the self is culturally universal is one that has preoccupied anthropologists and psychoanalyst cultural theorists. Roland notes the way in which some anthropologists search for universals—and believe that while cultures vary enormously, everyone fundamentally shares the same psychology. "Psychological universalism" does not allow for differences in self perception or in the relationship between the inner and outer selves. A relativist approach, on the other hand, involves a recognition of the way in which each culture has its "own internal consistency and validity related to the indigenous culture and its social patterns." The problem that arises here is that "there are no common categories or standards for comparison or criticism across cultures."[61] Róheim's analysis combines this tension; he applies universal categories of psychoanalysis and works within the assumption that there is a universal framework, but he is also acutely aware of cultural differences. For instance, with regard to free association, in the "case of a primitive man you cannot make him associate freely, you must wait till he does it involuntarily."[62] At once, he wrestles with the notion of a universalist unconscious with an evolutionary one. It is beyond question that Róheim applies a European model of analyzing the self. His approach, I would argue, is one that takes as normative the principle of Western individualism. And yet, despite privileging this paradigm, in applying Freud, he paradoxically provides a level of interrogation and analysis that renders indigenous subjectivity more complex than any other theorist writing at the time.

Róheim adopts a technique whereby he analyzes rituals as a reflection of a generic unconscious. In doing so, he provides a methodology that offers a complicated—if contestable—reading of indigenous rituals. Of one such ritual, he concludes by observing that "the totemic magic is the result of a compromise formation between the libido (as personified by the old men) and repression (represented by the resisting women). It seems also to indicate that the repression is directed primarily against the incestuous manifestation of the libido." He believed that by pointing out "certain seemingly unimportant but ever-recurring details in the complicated and elaborate structure of a variable ritual and find[ing] out the meaning of these details, we shall be probably very near to the unconscious meaning of the ritual itself."[63] What does he read into the ceremonies and rituals? As he writes, "In certain traditions we find magical and totemic ceremonies as a substitute for coitus. Intercourse is attempted by the hero but was declined by the women, whereupon the hero straightway proceeds to perform magical ceremonies. An old man named IIIipa came to a camp of Yelka . . . women and tried to cohabit with one of them. She resisted him; he struck her on the neck with his tomahawk and killed her (killing = coitus)."[64] There is no doubt that however much the unconscious of Aborigines is deemed "equal" to that of Westerners, the primitive status was undeniable for Róheim when considering material possessions:

> The poverty and extreme primitiveness of the material culture of the Central Australian natives is perhaps best emphasised by the fact that they have not yet completely attained the stage of evolution in worldly goods that clearly marks off Man from the Animal kingdom . . . The Australian native has conserved the rudiments of a pre-human stage of development; his culture is autoplastic . . . in a certain degree he uses materials derived from his own body for practical, ornamental and ceremonial purposes. Strings used for various purposes are made of human hair.[65]

These were also related to a psychoanalytic reading: "But it is very natural that this poverty of external resources should go hand in hand with a corresponding autoerotic fixation of the libido which is demonstrated by the still greater ceremonial use of portions of their own body, or objects unconsciously equated with such portions."[66] Although Róheim interprets this material deprivation as evolutionary, his aim was to approximate clinical analysis in the field by transference, free association, and dream analysis. "You must be good friends with the natives or to put the same thing in the technical language of psychoanalysis you must get a *transference*," he writes.[67] In discussing the various dreams, Róheim constructed himself very much as a scientific clinician: "Just as the analyst in clinical analysis will be able through analyzing the transference to construe the original infantile libido situation the analyst in the field will be in possession of a reliable clue that helps him to understand the original libido situation and the character of people."[68] Through such an analysis, Róheim was attempting to "normalize" and make "knowable" the "Australian savages" through the white, Western discourse of psychoanalysis. He was attempting to "understand" the savage by translating his or her behavior through the prism of Western rationality. Analyzing transference through these categories presented another challenge: "Transference of course is the basis of all anthropological work although the non-psychoanalytical anthropologist . . . knows nothing about its infantile origins . . . I do not mean to say that the psychoanalyst will or should work according to a merely conscious scheme. He too must find the right attitude instinctively i.e.—through what has been called the dialogue of the unconscious . . . The anthropologist . . . on the other hand works with an unanalyzed transference and especially what is worse still with an unanalyzed counter-transference." The ambivalence of Róheim's views between universalism and cultural specificity are articulated as follows: "The anthropologist although theoretically [believes] in the unity of mankind and therefore expect[s] to find that the black or brown man has striving, yearning and fears like his own is still the child of a different race and civilization."

The strategy of free association was also different for the savage. In his discussion of analyzing the savage, Róheim identified the differences and similarities in the technique of doing so. As an analyst, the culture is similar to the analysand, as they "both speak the same *language* not only technically using the same words, but also psychically, using the same social values." In the field,

> the use of the principle of free association [is] to get a complete picture of the culture he is studying and get much information which he could

never have got by direct questions. However, we know very well how a patient will use or abuse the principle of free association and press it into the service of resistance . . . The informants will give you endless amounts of songs, myths, garden magic so that you should have no time to make enquiries regarding dreams, sexual life or black magic. You must then decide for yourself whether the information you are getting is worth having or whether you can risk losing a few details, perhaps even losing your time for some days, in order to get information of the kind they may be withholding.[69]

He distinguished his approach from the "lifeless" study of anthropologists Baldwin Spencer and Carl Strehlow. Unlike their behaviorist approach, he aimed to do the following after a ceremony: "I must get all the explanations that may be connected with that ceremony. And not only an explanation of details but also chance associations connected with the ceremony and last but not least with the dreams connected with that ceremony."[70] He was aware of the ways in which psychoanalysis, as a practice, and anthropology both differed from and resembled each other. In combining the two techniques, Róheim attempted to create a "new anthropology." He distinguishes between the "savage informant" and the "patient" who comes to an analyst. The interaction and dynamics vary considerably between the primitive and the Westerner who utilizes psychoanalysis: "Do not forget that your savage informant is not a patient. He does not come to you with a conflict that he desires you help him with and he is certainly not willing to pay for the privilege of relating his dreams." The power relationships are defined in very different terms between the indigenous and the white patient:

In order to get into touch with him at all you must invert the usual analytic proceeding and offer him something instead of making him see the value of your work by paying for it. To all natives a white man is a superior person who disposes of many desirable things in the shape of tea, flour, tinned meat, sago, tobacco or rice, and a white man who wouldn't give him anything would be a wicked being indeed.[71]

He identified cultural difference in that the response from the primitive race was not that of the white man: "Talking, especially about himself, means work for a primitive man and he would not do it day after day without any recompense. Not only that primitive man [is] not patient, but the amount of psychical strain he can bear is far smaller than a civilised man is prepared to cope with."[72] Inevitably, Róheim came up against cultural differences in what was to be spoken and not spoken of. He very quickly learned that speaking about dead parents was taboo in the culture he aimed to study, but he immediately drew similarities:

> Now I knew that there was a taboo against mentioning the name of the dead, but I did not know that it was taboo to talk about them. When after this first manifestation of collective resistance I began to enquire into this matter I was told that it is not exactly taboo but people don't like it. Finally, I got some information that threw light upon the subject: if a man talks freely about his dead father he will lay himself open to the suspicion that he has killed him by evil magic, in other words, wished his death. Well, I thought, they were not very far from my own point of view after all.[73]

Róheim characterized all anthropological work as transference—"the basis of all anthropological work, although the non-psychoanalytical anthropologist does not call it transference and knows nothing about its infantile origins." But this was often an unexplored aspect of the work of the anthropologist, who "works with an unanalysed transference and especially, what is worse still, with an unanalysed counter-transference."[74] Róheim believed that anthropologists were prone to idealizing the native—what he believed was itself a form of transference.

It was commonly believed at the time that because of their "simple" existence, Aborigines did not have depth of feeling or complex adult emotions. For this reason, they were deemed to be unlikely to suffer from "insanity." The impact of colonization was identified as the cause of insanity, with the introduction of Western diseases playing a major role. In his analysis, Róheim attempted to provide the Aboriginal rituals and myths with more than a stereotype or a simple view of Aboriginal behavior. Whatever the judgment of the applicability of Western ideas about repressions and Oedipus, in his analysis, he attempted to explore what he believed was the *complexity* of Aboriginal subjectivity, beyond the stereotype of a primitive savage.

Some have labeled Róheim a romantic; others have characterized him as a Freudian radical who pursued Freudian interpretations with "relentlessness." Paul Robinson includes him in his study of radicals because "he took it upon himself to denounce the repressiveness of modern civilization."[75]

By treating the unconscious as generic, Róheim was indeed contradicting some of his own statements that the Australian Aborigine was primitive. The paradox was that while he was initially drawn to the primitive state of the Aborigines, in his detailed analysis of their myths, rituals, and ceremonies, he aimed to complicate the understanding of the "simplicity of the savage."

Although Róheim indulged in "a ruthless psychological reductionism,"[76] failing to identify the political reasons for the displacement and dispossession of the Aboriginal people, not to mention the eugenics and scientific theories that were emerging at the time, he did attempt, on the other hand, to problematize an indigenous subjectivity as complex, intricate, and multilayered. In arguing that the self was universal, Róheim was positioning the unconscious of the indigenous self as a subject worthy of analysis and interrogation and not an inquiry to be dismissed as simple-minded or childlike. This signifies an important contribution at the time to challenging colonialist assumptions. For this reason, I would agree with Paul Robinson when he describes Róheim as "an unduly neglected individual" in the history of psychoanalysis.[77]

Notes

1. Róheim, "Psychoanalytical Techniques and Field Anthropology," folder 4, box 2, MS 46, p. 55, Róheim Papers, University of California, San Diego.
2. Róheim, "Psychoanalysis of Primitive Cultural Types," 22.
3. Robinson, *Freudian Left*, 80–81.
4. Meszaros, "Tragic Success of European Psychoanalysis," 207; Robinson, *Freudian Left*, 81.
5. Vikár, "Budapest School of Psychoanalysis," 73–74.
6. Ibid., 66.
7. Robinson, *Freudian Left*, 83.
8. Ibid., 88.
9. Ibid.
10. Róheim, introduction to "Psychoanalysis of Primitive Cultural Types," 3.
11. Jones, "Psycho-Analysis and Anthropology," 114.
12. Ibid., 125–29.
13. Freud, "Totem and Taboo," 69–70.
14. Ibid., 157–58.
15. Khanna, *Dark Continents*, 6.
16. Ibid., 73.

17. Sadowsky, *Imperial Bedlam*, 21.

18. Nandy, *Savage Freud*, 83.

19. Ibid., 140.

20. Frosh, *For and Against Psychoanalysis*, 214.

21. Littlewood and Lipsedge, *Aliens and Alienists*, 66.

22. Ibid.

23. Ibid., 67.

24. Ibid., 302.

25. Ibid., 61.

26. Porteus, as quoted in McGregor, *Imagined Destinies*, 107.

27. Elkin, "Notes on the Psychic Life of the Australian Aborigines," 51–52.

28. Markus, *Governing Savages*, 150.

29. Elkin, "Notes on the Psychic Life of the Australian Aborigines," 51–56.

30. Chesterman and Galligan, *Citizens without Rights*, 121.

31. Markus, *Governing Savages*, 37–38.

32. See Anderson, *Cultivation of Whiteness*; McGregor, *Imagined Destinies*.

33. Haebich, *Broken Circles*.

34. McGregor, *Imagined Destinies*, 115–22.

35. *Sydney Morning Herald*, August 20, 1934, 5.

36. Nye, "Blood Pressure in the Australian Aboriginal," 1000.

37. "The Aborigine's Future," *Argus* (Melbourne), April 28, 1934, 24.

38. Marcus, *Indomitable Miss Pink*, 57.

39. Ibid., 58.

40. Roland, *Cultural Pluralism and Psychoanalysis*, 7.

41. See Damousi, *Freud in the Antipodes*, 79–106.

42. Robinson, *Freudian Left*, 100.

43. Ibid., 101.

44. Róheim, *Australian Totemism*, 57.

45. Ibid., 100.

46. Ibid., 151.

47. Ibid., 221.

48. Robinson, *Freudian Left*, 103, 105–6.

49. See Róheim, "Psychoanalysis of Primitive Cultural Types," 2–198.

50. Robinson, *Freudian Left*, 102.

51. Róheim, "Psychoanalysis of Primitive Cultural Types," 23.

52. Ibid., 26.

53. Ibid., 32.

54. Robinson, *Freudian Left*, 92.

55. Ibid., 94.

56. Ibid.

57. Ibid., 95.

58. Ibid., 96, 97.

59. Róheim, *Australian Totemism*, 16.

60. Eder, introduction to *Australian Totemism*, 11.

61. Roland, *Cultural Pluralism and Psychoanalysis*, 15.

62. Róheim, "Psychoanalysis of Primitive Cultural Types," 18.

63. Róheim, *Australian Totemism*, 217.

64. Ibid.

65. Ibid., 221.

66. Ibid., 222.

67. Ibid., 64–65.

68. Róheim, "Psychoanalytical Techniques and Field Anthropology," 81.

69. Ibid., 117–19.

70. Ibid., 124.

71. Róheim, "Psychoanalysis of Primitive Cultural Types," 15.

72. Ibid., 16.

73. Ibid.

74. Ibid.

75. Robinson, *Freudian Left*, 75.

76. Ibid., 121.

77. Ibid., 79.

Colonial Dominions and the Psychoanalytic Couch
*Synergies of Freudian Theory with Bengali Hindu Thought
and Practices in British India*

In colonial literature, "the colonized" tended to be conceptualized as a single entity. The vast differences between respective regional histories, differences relating to gender and social strata, the colonizing impact of the European powers, and the time frames of colonization were often overlooked or ignored. Underlying concepts of such literature were dichotomies that split along a colonial divide—for example, a monolithic "West" or "Europe" versus an undifferentiated "colonized world."

Because the actions of colonized subjects threatened their interests, the respective colonial powers invested in empirical research. Some of these works were basic investigations, such as a census of the population in a colonial territory. Others were of immediate relevance, like a study on how to train East African peasants to become efficient plantation workers. Although stereotypic attributions and judgments prevailed in the resultant studies, they nevertheless shed light on the agency of and differences among the colonized.

More recently, a growing number of postcolonial studies by Asian, African, and Latin American intellectuals differentiate along parameters such as time frame and the kind of colonial domination, region, gender, and social strata. Moreover, recent research points out that the precolonial past itself needs further differentiation. As the Indian historian Gyan Prakash writes,

The continual and residual power of pre-colonial (in their diversity) and colonial pasts in Indian history has . . . always been confronted with a wide range of cultural influences. One could thus also speak of already hybrid history after the impact of Moghul rule in most parts of India. What we have is thus a culturally rich patchwork of influences . . . at those moments, repressed knowledges and subjects returned, not as timeless traditional entities, but as figures of subalternity to reclaim some ground.[1]

In sum, current scholarship in the field has replaced the simple binary formulation of colonizer and colonized with multifaceted perspectives and the concept of a multitude of colonial dominions.

Vertical as well as horizontal differentiations complicate the study of colonial dominions. Because precolonized societies had an existing social structure in place upon which further hierarchies were imposed as a result of colonization, multiple layers of power could be found within a single colonial setting. Such social differentiations provide a clearer picture of the realities of life among the colonized. When taking a closer look at lower-class British soldiers in British India, for example, one finds that a social hierarchy existed among the colonizers as well.

Psychiatric case studies from the European Mental Hospital in Ranchi, India, show that many of the poorer British subjects were not in a position to actively cope with the challenges of life in a colony. Others coped somehow but suffered tremendously because they were directly and constantly confronted with a social and natural environment that differed considerably from the one they were accustomed to in England. Unlike the upper strata of the colonial officials who hardly ever interacted with Indians other than their servants, they could not withdraw from daily chores into a world that was seemingly British—for example, retreat into their clubs and hill stations, go big-game hunting, or even take trips home.[2]

The dissolution of the oversimplifying binary of colonizer and colonized in favor of more horizontal and vertical differentiation does not, however, refute the fact that colonialism had caused lasting imprints on the former colonies. Similarly dramatic, yet less visible than depleted forests, strip mines, and colonial buildings, were colonizations of the mind. These effects were strongest within the privileged sector of the urban population because these were the people who had the closest contact with the colonizers. Yet, the repercussions extended beyond this social stratum. As Srimati Svarna Kumari Devi Ghosal, a pioneer in the early Indian women's movement and a prolific Bengali writer, has shown, issues of identity and colonial dominion were also of concern to Bengali women in colonial India. In her novel *An Unfinished Song*, she wrote, "This is the story of life among the Reformed Party of Bengal, the members of which have to some extent adopted Western customs. It shows the change that touch with Europe has brought upon the people of India, but in their inner nature the Hindus are still quite different from Western races. The ideals and traits of character that it has taken thousands of years to form are not affected by mere external change."[3]

Because British colonial rule did not completely destroy the multi-faceted and rich cultural traditions that existed in India, cultural resistance could gain in strength by drawing on precolonial modes of thinking and behavior. Glorifications of real—or sometimes imagined—intellectual as well as material achievements of the past served an important psychological function in the first part of the twentieth century. This helped to restore self-esteem and national pride that was shattered as a result of colonialism. Govind Purushottam Deshpande concluded his article "Dialectics of Defeat" by stating that "colonialism resulted in the suppression of the Indian people. At the same time, and because of it, it led to the retrieval of cultural, classical traditions and languages."[4] Activities that aimed at restoring—or inventing—a cultural identity generally strove to find positive aspects to those facets of Indian culture that were deprecated by British colonial administrators.

A classic example of such dynamics within colonial dominions is Mohandas Gandhi's attempt to imbue the broad-based anticolonial resistance with Hindu morals.[5] Furthermore, whereas *Satyagraha*, *Ahimsa*, and *Swadeshi* belonged to the realm of politics, the renowned Bengali writer, poet, and artist Rabindranath Tagore creatively blended European, Persian, East Asian, and Bengali Hindu traditions in his literature, drama, music, and work in the visual arts; and the often-cited physicist and plant physiologist Jagadish Chandra Bose "Indianized" colonial imports in science. His research at the "Bose Temple of Science," as his laboratory at Calcutta University was commonly called, sought "the ultimate unity which permeates in the universal order and cuts across the animal, plant and inanimate lives." In that they were "considered proof of the superiority of Indian holistic thinking over imported European ideas," his findings were used for nationalistic purposes.[6] Moreover, the militant Bengali politician Subhas Chandra Bose praised J. C. Bose's research as having "generated a passion for a new awakening in the history of this country."[7] As will be seen, similar synergy between European and Indian knowledge can be found in the creative fusion of elements of psychoanalysis with Bengali Hindu ways of thinking and healing.

The Colonial Couch

For almost a hundred years, the leading address for the treatment of the psychological and psychiatric problems of British-educated urban Bengalis has been 14 Parsibagan Lane in Calcutta. The first therapist who tried to ease the suffering of those who came to this location was Girindrasekhar Bose (1887–1953).[8] In Calcutta, he studied chemistry and science at Presidency College before continuing his studies at the medical college of Calcutta University, where he obtained his MD degree in 1909. In the introduction to his dissertation, Bose mentioned that he had been "keen on practising hypnosis to therapeutic ends" while still a student, before he came across psychoanalysis in 1909.[9] When graduate-level courses in psychology were introduced at Calcutta University in 1913, Bose registered immediately. In 1917, he obtained a master's degree in experimental psychology; in 1921, he was awarded the first doctorate in psychology ever earned at an Indian university. From 1917 onward, he was a part-time lecturer in abnormal psychology at Calcutta University. One of his decisions there was to make courses in psychoanalysis compulsory for all students of psychology.

Bose belonged to a well-to-do family of the writer's caste. As was customary in his circles, he regularly opened the doors of the family's mansion at 14 Parsibagan Lane to Bengali writers and intellectuals, who read and discussed their latest works in progress. This Utkendra Samiti (Eccentric Club) provided a window to the West as well as an important network for people sharing a passion for Bengali Hindu identity politics. It was also a source of inspiration for the development of Bose's psychoanalytical concepts, for it was in these meetings that imported psychoanalytical ideas were related to prevailing concepts and conditions in Bengali Hindu culture. Once the Indian Psychoanalytical Society was founded in 1922, the members convened at 14 Parsibagan Lane, which has been the institutional address for the Calcutta branch of the Indian Psychoanalytical Society ever since.

The Indian Psychoanalytical Institute was formally opened in 1932. Its candidates had to attend lectures at the Department of Psychology at Calcutta University, read prescribed literature from the society's library, and complete a minimum of two hundred sessions of personal analysis. The training program required that they undertake analysis of at least two cases of one hundred sessions each under the guidance of either Bose or Owen Berkeley-Hill, a British psychiatrist who was an old friend of Ernest Jones and superintendent of the European Mental Hospital in Ranchi. On May 1, 1933, with the help of his brother Rajsekhar, Bose established a psychiatric outpatient clinic at the Carmichael (now R. G. Kar) Medical College and Hospital at Belgachia in north Calcutta.[10]

At its founding, the Indian Psychoanalytical Society included fifteen members. Among them were seven medical doctors, two of whom were European—Berkeley-Hill and R. C. McWatters—and in the Indian Medical Service and thus part of the British colonial administration. Another seven were psychologists, five from the Department of Psychology at Calcutta University and one each from Patna and Dacca. The society continued to attract new associates, mostly writers and other members of the Bengali intelligentsia who did not intend to practice psychoanalysis like members from the medical professions. By 1934, the Indian Psychoanalytical Society listed fifteen members and twenty associates, and by 1945, there were sixteen members and fifty-four associates.[11] Even though not all members were as active as Bose, and certainly none as prolific a writer, nonetheless, over the years, a substantial body of articles was published by the other members of the Indian Psychoanalytical Society. Most articles appeared in the *Indian Journal of Psychology* and a few in the *International Journal of Psychoanalysis*. In 1947, the Indian Psychoanalytical Society started its own journal titled *Samiksa*.

In contrast to Freud's plush couch in Vienna, the essential piece of equipment in Bose's consulting room was a simple striped foldable deck chair. It is symbolic, if not ironic, that in choosing a colonial piece of furniture, Bose "went West." By covering his heavy couch with an oriental rug, Freud, on the other hand, "went East." The "colonial couch" reflected the social and cultural background of Bose's patients: the well-to-do British-educated sectors of Bengali society who were attracted to something imported. The reception of psychoanalysis had the advantage that it was self-motivated and not imposed, and that it originated in continental Europe, not in Britain. As journal articles and even radio broadcasts in Calcutta in the 1920s and 1930s reveal, psychoanalysis was considered modern, even avant-garde.

In general, Bose's patients belonged to the British-educated urban elite whose professional life was interwoven with the interests of the colonial rulers. They were similar to Berkeley-Hill's patients, even though these were mostly lower-class British subjects or Anglo-Indians, in that they were among those groups most exposed to a dually British and Indian world. Psychoanalysis was practiced neither in the zenana—the enclosed women's section of traditional Bengali households—nor in British officers' clubs but in those realms where British and Indian cultures merged, co-existed, competed, or clashed.

The challenge for Bose was to adapt theoretical concepts and therapeutic procedures that were developed by Freud according to the needs and expectations of a socially and culturally very different group in Vienna to the requirements of his particular patients in Calcutta. Although Bose spoke Bengali with his patients and retained many aspects of his Hindu cultural traditions, essential elements of his therapeutic work were European imports. Aspects of Freudian theory and practice that traveled well, for example, were the technique of free association, the concept of the unconscious, and the use of dreams in psychoanalysis. By creatively integrating selectively imported European and specific Bengali Hindu concepts into his therapeutic work, Bose overcame the colonial dichotomies of British versus Bengali, modern versus traditional, and public versus private.

Guru Girindraskhar and His Bengali Hindu Pillars of Identity

According to accounts by his contemporaries, Bose was a charismatic figure, to the extent that some people referred to him as "Guru."[12] He never gave up wearing traditional Bengali clothes and following Bengali Hindu customs. To gain a better understanding of Indian psychological knowledge, he sought the help of a Pandit who guided him in his studies and exercises.

In a speech given to the Indian Philosophical Congress in 1930, Bose presented his article titled "The Psychological Outlook of Hindu Philosophy" and communicated his knowledge of classical Hindu scripts. As an example of one of the psychological questions raised roughly before the seventh century BCE in the Upanishads, Bose quoted the following:

"Which are the sense organs that go to sleep and which are the ones that keep awake? How do dreams arise? Which is the agent in the body that feels pleasure? What is the source of the vital energy of the body?"[13]

In his 1938 speech to mark the twenty-fifth anniversary of the Department of Psychology at Calcutta University, Bose proposed that more work be done in the field of Indian psychology and added that the Board of Higher Studies in Psychology at the University of Calcutta had recently proposed including the study of yoga in its syllabus.[14] Bose also praised Mallinaga Batsayana, the author of the Kama Sutra, for his knowledge of sexual matters. Following a summary of his main observations, he wrote that "although Batsayana wrote his great work about 2,000 years ago, his views are worthy of serious attention even from the most advanced modern sexologist."[15]

In addition to his guided reading of classical Hindu scripts, which had a considerable impact on his thinking, writing, and practical work, Bose was also interested in learning more about folk wisdom and customs and included some of his personal observations in his publications. In an article on dreams, he described a popular shrine devoted to Siva where, due to continued fasting, praying, and not sleeping, the suffering person falls into a state of physical and mental exhaustion. The resulting hallucinatory dreams were considered to provide solutions to the seeker's problems.[16]

Moreover, Bose integrated an essential element of popular cultural traditions into his psychoanalytic theory. As Deborah Bhattacharyya points out, according to popular Bengali beliefs, wishes play an essential role in the sourcing of psychic disturbances.[17] By giving the concept of wishes a central place in his publications and by innovatively including wishes in his therapeutic work, Bose set yet another "pillar of identity" into his theoretical and practical oeuvre.

THE IMPORTANCE OF WISHES

Bose's most comprehensive theoretical publication, "A New Theory of Mental Life," contains a systematic description of his views on wishes. He considered psychological energies in the form of wishes, not biologically founded instincts or drives, to be essential to human life. Bose defined a wish as a "peculiar psychic process—conscious or unconscious—preceding or accompanying the intention of the organism in its effort to change."[18] A major point of difference in relation to Freudian theory was that in Bose's view, resolution of psychic disorders could come about not by sublimation but by the recognition and gratification of repressed wishes. Thus, wishes should be fulfilled, as they would otherwise disrupt an individual's psychic well-being.

According to Bose, wishes have an inherent polarity; that is, each wish contains the logical tendency to strive for a realization of its opposite. Or as Bose phrased it, "Every wish that arises in consciousness is accompanied by its opposite which remains in the unconscious. Thus, an active wish is accompanied by an unconscious, passive wish. The wish to strike somebody is accompanied by the unconscious wish to be struck."[19] Because both wishes cannot be satisfied simultaneously, one of them will be repressed while the other becomes manifest. This situation can switch, with the manifest aspect becoming the repressed and the repressed, manifest.

THE SEE-SAW METHOD

Besides vacillating, two opposing wishes can block each other in the flow of energies—for example, when they are in conflict with each other. In Bose's model, psychoneurosis is the result of a conflict between repressing and repressed forces; thus, the essential task of the psychoanalyst is to liberate these repressed elements.

To uncover repressed wishes, Bose used what he termed the "see-saw method."[20] In his therapeutic interventions, he might ask a patient to reverse the subject-object relationship in a daydream or fantasy by changing perspective and identifying with another of the elements (person, animal, item) found in the narrative or dream sequence. Thus, the action itself would be kept functionally the same, only subject and object would be reversed. Another approach employed by Bose was to ask patients to try to imagine the feelings of the object. Bose strongly emphasized that the mere unearthing of one repressed wish is not enough but that the active application of this see-saw technique as a kind of forced association tool was essential in resolving internal conflicts.

THE PRINCIPLE OF UNITY

For Bose, the guiding principle underlying all wishes is a striving for unity.[21] He considered all wishes to be efforts toward a unification of subject and object and rejected Freud's notion of a "pleasure principle." In Bose's view, pleasure arises when the efforts toward a unification of subject and object are successful. Pain results when a unification of subject and object fails.

This notion of unity is not only well rooted in Bengali Hindu traditions, but it was also in vogue among the *bhadralok*. As Gyan Prakash points out, "Jagadish Chandra Bose, addressing a literary conference, argued for the unity of knowledge. Stating that while the West was known to compartmentalize knowledge, the Eastern aim has been the opposite, namely that in the multiplicity of phenomena, we never miss their underlying unity."[22]

Another interesting remark by Bose that reveals his identification with cyclic Hindu traditions, on the one hand, and contemporary professional models, on the other, is that in his professional role, he considered himself akin to an engineer who fixes interrupted circuits.[23] This is a very different image than the one expressed by Freud, who said that he identified himself with an archaeologist who digs into a patient's personal past and uncovers hidden layers. Whereas Bose chose references to cycles, Freud used a metaphor that was entirely linear.

Bose Speaks Up against European Dominance

The strong anticolonial urges in the first part of the twentieth century strengthened a sense of belonging to the majority and nurtured feelings of cultural identity, especially among the Bengali elite, the *bhadralok*.[24] Through the political involvement of his brother Rajsekhar, a famous writer, as well as through other relatives and friends, Girindrasekhar Bose stayed in close contact with Bengali members of the Indian independence movement. Some members of the Indian Psychoanalytical Society are also reported to have been close to Mahatma Gandhi.[25] Therefore, it should not be surprising that beyond reaffirming Bengali Hindu traditions by integrating these into his psychoanalytical theories, several of Bose's writings expressed an explicitly anticolonial stance.

Keeping in mind this context, it is revealing that in 1923, at the height of revolutionary political activities in British India, Bose's definition of mental disease specifically exempted martyrs and patriots: "If we assert that whatever is against the preservation of [the] individual is a diseased condition, we are confronted with the same type of difficulty. The sense of morality and duty often leads us to self-destructive actions, e.g. the feeling of the patriot or martyr."[26] In a 1931 speech, he also again made explicit references to political and social conditions by saying, "The distinction [between normal and abnormal mental states] is more or less an arbitrary one necessitated by the demands of society."[27]

In regard to Freud's theory of the dissolution of the Oedipus complex, Bose wrote in 1929, "I do not agree with Freud when he says that the Oedipus wishes ultimately to succumb to the authority of the super-ego. Quite the reverse is the case. The super-ego must be conquered and the ability to castrate the father and make him into a woman is an essential requisite for the adjustment of the Oedipus wish. The Oedipus [conflict] is resolved not by the threat of castration, but by the ability to castrate."[28] Bose cautioned against accepting all psychoanalytic findings as "truths." In his article "The Reliability of Psychoanalytic Findings," he questioned psychoanalytic generalizations and criticized psychoanalysts who "do not hesitate to dogmatize on their findings and regard them as 'settled facts' even when the analysis has been of a very cursory nature."[29] This is most likely in response to the writings of British members of the Indian Psychoanalytical Society—among them Berkeley-Hill, who used psychoanalysis to justify colonial measures.

Like his colleagues, Bose was not allowed to teach in Bengali at Calcutta University. It was only in 1938 that Tagore (a Nobel Prize winner) could present an honorary lecture in his mother tongue; before then, all instruction and writing for publication had to be in English.[30] So, too, Bose's dissertation and all the articles that he had published in Indian academic journals and international journals were in English. But Bose was very proud that his work also appeared in various Bengali publications, and he wrote that his British colleagues should learn Bengali if they were interested in these texts.[31]

Although Freud was obviously not a British subject, there is nevertheless an air of distancing, if not anti-European sentiment, to be discovered in Bose's attitudes toward Freud. In 1922, Bose sent Freud an imaginative portrait drawn by a famous Bengali caricaturist and family friend. This penciled sketch wherein Freud resembles a stereotypical British colonial officer amused Freud; he wrote to Lou Andreas-Salomé, "Naturally, he makes me look the complete Englishman."[32] Less subtle was Bose's remark in his book *Everyday Psychoanalysis* in which he criticized Freud for running the International Association for Psychoanalysis "like a church."[33] While this association and the gift indirectly conveyed his view of Freud, Bose's distancing from Freud can also be detected in his writing.

Freud's Shattered Conquistadorial Dreams

Freud had dreamed of a "psychoanalytic international." He assumed that his theory and therapeutic methods would be universally valid and applicable; that is, they would not change due to time, location, or the personal experiences and diverse backgrounds of his followers. Because the schisms in the psychoanalytic movement were manifold, he invested considerable energy in fending off critics and guarding his theories against revision. Bose's remark that Freud handled institutional matters in an authoritative clerical manner hit a nerve. Though Jewish by birth, Freud was nevertheless socialized in a Catholic milieu.[34] Moreover, he grew up at a time when European colonialism was in full bloom. It is therefore not surprising that in letters to his friend Wilhelm Fliess in the late nineteenth century, Freud confessed to identifying with conquistadors and colonizers.[35] Much later, in a letter to Bose on December 13, 1931, he went on to mention "the proud conquests it [psychoanalysis] has made in foreign countries."[36]

In contrast to his later adversary Carl Gustav Jung, Freud's attitudes toward various elements of Indian culture remained highly aloof, if not disparaging.[37] None of his "dirty old gods," the hundreds of antique statues he had collected, derived from South Asia. Freud's conversations and letter exchanges with Bruno Goetz (a student of philosophy and Sanskrit at Vienna University), Romain Rolland, Rabindranath Tagore, and the Bengali linguist Suniti Kumar Chatterji confirm his lack of interest in, if not outright denigration of, Indian culture.[38]

Considering Bose's strong anticolonial and to some extent also anti-European attitudes and Freud's views on Indian cultures, it is all the more surprising that the Bose-Freud correspondence spans the years from 1921 to 1937.[39] Herein, Bose confronts Freud with his view that not all elements of psychoanalysis are transculturally universal. It can be read as documentation of a struggle between Freud's sweeping assumptions of universal applicability and Bose's focus on particularities and his claim of differentiation in regard to psychoanalytic findings.

On January 31, 1929, Bose sent thirteen of his psychoanalytical articles to Freud. In his reply, Freud basically defended his own theories against this challenge but tried to balance his criticism: "I have read all of your papers . . . You directed my attention to the Oedipus wish especially and you were right in doing so . . . I confess I am by no means convinced of the validity of my own assumptions. We have not yet seen through this intricate Oedipus matter. We need more observations."[40]

On January 1, 1933, after receiving Bose's most comprehensive work entitled "A New Theory of Mental Life," Freud wrote him a long letter that reveals Freud's regrets about his earlier lack of interest in Bose's psychoanalytical work: "The first letter of this new year goes out to you. I did study the essay you were so kind to send me and am deeply impressed by it . . . I see that we did neglect the fact of the existence of opposite wishes . . . These phenomena have to be worked into our system to make us see what modifications or corrections are necessary and how far we can acquiesce to your ideas."[41] Freud did not anticipate that the Indian members of the Indian Psychoanalytical Society would turn out to be so disloyal to him. Yet he noticed that the "Freudian Orient," namely the wholesale reception of psychoanalysis in India, was not what he had hoped for. Despite his public stance, Freud intuitively sensed the importance of cultural differences. On the occasion of his seventy-fifth birthday, the Indian Psychoanalytical Society sent him an ivory statue of Vishnu along with a Sanskrit poem. Not only did his letter of thanks not reveal any interest in the symbolism of the gifts, but he dubbed the statue his "trophy of conquest." When the statuette later developed cracks, he made the following entry in his diary: "Can the god, being used to Calcutta, not stand the climate in Vienna?"[42] Thus, Freud, in the privacy of his diary, expressed a premonition that psychoanalysis would not travel easily.

Bose's Interfaces versus Fanon's Black Skin–White Mask Dichotomy

Because not many non-European psychiatrists worked under colonial conditions, and even fewer of them were prolific writers who expressed their criticism of a simple importing of mainstream psychological and psychiatric theories into non-European settings, it is interesting to compare the life and work of Bose with that of Frantz Fanon (1925–1961).[43] As will be seen, despite their similarities, these two representatives of anti-colonial and critical psychiatry had little in common. In fact, their differences support the earlier claim of the importance of differentiations in colonial contexts.

As an African-Caribbean, Fanon remained an outsider, first in France and then in Algeria, where he was confronted with racism, prejudices against non-Muslims, and prevailing sentiments against intellectuals who had come to Algeria as French citizens and members of the colonizing mission. Even after he had changed sides and joined the Algerian National Liberation Front (FLN), Fanon continued to experience the racism and alienation he described so powerfully in his first book, *Black Skin, White Masks*.[44] Because Fanon died at the early age of thirty-six, and also because of the political choices he made—for example, joining the FLN and working for the Organization of African Unity (OAU)—his practical psychiatric experience was limited. As a result, his psychiatric analyses and psychotherapeutic contributions also focus on the political context. They do not specify sociological, gender-specific, or religious factors in the aetiology and treatment of psychological and psychiatric disorders. He was first of all an anticolonial political thinker, writer, and activist who attempted to change the political conditions to overcome the assumed causes of his patients' sufferings. Because of this, his writings were translated into several languages and set off waves of political debate and action until long after his death.

Bose, on the other hand, belonged ethnically to the majority population of India; within his native Bengali Hindu culture, he was highly privileged in terms of his status, financial situation, education, and social networks and stayed deeply rooted in his native culture. He hardly ever left Calcutta, not even for a visit elsewhere, and he never moved away from his family home. His pronounced anticolonial attitudes were conformist within the circles to which he belonged. Unlike his brother and other relatives and friends, he did not actively engage in the anticolonial independence movement. Instead, Bose spent over forty years of his life trying to ease the suffering of members of the *bhadralok*. As a result, in his psychological and psychoanalytical writings, he charted new territory.

Bose's creative efforts to integrate elements from European and Bengali Hindu psychological and psychoanalytical thought and practice were unprecedented in the field of academic psychology and psychiatry in colonial times and thus were groundbreaking. Instead of the binary concept of black skin–white mask that Fanon adhered to, Bose opted for interfaces (in the very sense of the word). His work was not limited by dichotomies but rather strove to establish connections. In that respect, his views and practical experience have remained relevant. The contemporary postcolonial globalized world, with its increased transfers and circulations of people, goods, and ideas, is not only a world of multiple dislocations and separations but also one of new arrivals and amalgamations. Yet, as in Bose's time and place, these ever-shifting relationships, with their concomitant effects on power structures and social hierarchies, have repercussions in the dominions of the individual and collective unconscious.

.

Notes

1. Prakash, *After Colonialism*, 81.

2. Hartnack, *Psychoanalysis in Colonial India*, 23–25.

3. Ghosal, preface to *Unfinished Song*.

4. Deshpande, "Dialectics of Defeat," 2176.

5. Bondurant, *Conquest of Violence*.

6. Nandy, *Alternative Sciences*, 54.

7. Bose, *Indian Pilgrim*, 82.

8. Mitra, "Prof. Girindrasekhar Bose"; "Dr. Girindrasekhar Bose (Obituary)"; Edwards, "In Memoriam"; and Nandy, "Savage Freud."

9. Bose, "The Concept of Repression," 5.

10. Sinha, "Short Life Sketch of Girindrasekhar Bose," 68.

11. For details, see the Indian Psychoanalytical Society's annual reports for the years 1923, 1926, 1928, 1929, 1930, 1933, and 1935.

12. Sinha, "Development of Psychoanalysis in India," 431.

13. Bose, "Psychological Outlook of Hindu Philosophy"; Bose, "Is Perception an Illusion?" 150.

14. Bose, "Progress of Psychology in India during the Past Twenty-Five Years," 345.

15. Bose, "Duration of Coitus," 252.

16. Bose, "Dream," 82–84; Bose, "Yoga Sutras."

17. Bhattacharyya, *Pagalami*.

18. Bose, "New Theory of Mental Life," 154.

19. Bose, "Opposite Fantasies in the Release of Repression," 32–33.

20. Ibid., 34–35.

21. Bose, "New Theory of Mental Life," 154.

22. Prakash, "Science Between the Lines," 78.

23. Bose, "Analysis of Wish," 10.

24. For a discussion of the term *bhadralok*, see Chatterjee, *Nation and Its Fragments*, 35.

25. Gandhi, "Interview to Indian Psycho-Analytical Society," 109–10.

26. Bose, "Reliability of Psychoanalytic Findings," 115.

27. Bose, "Psychology and Psychiatry," 144.

28. Bose, "Genesis and Adjustment of the Oedipus Wish," 236–37.

29. Bose, "Reliability of Psychoanalytic Findings," 113.

30. Bose, "Asutosh Mukherjee," 310; Majumdar, *History of Modern Bengal*, 491.

31. Bose is reported to have said, "If my works are of any worth, . . . they will be translated by the foreigners in their own languages. No Englishman will write his works in Bengali for the benefit of the Bengalees!" As cited in Chandak Sengoopta, "Girindrasekhar Bose: Explorer of the Psyche," *Statesman* (Calcutta), January 11, 1987.

32. Freud to Lou Andreas-Salomé, 13 March 1922, in *Sigmund Freud and Lou Andreas-Salomé Letters*, ed. Ernst Pfeiffer, 114.

33. Bose, *Everyday Psychoanalysis*, 254.

34. Schorske, *Fin-de-Siecle Vienna*; Beller, *Vienna and the Jews*.

35. Freud, *Complete Letters of Sigmund Freud to Wilhelm Fliess*, 398ff.

36. Freud to Girindrasekhar Bose, 13 December 1931, as cited in Sinha, "Development of Psychoanalysis in India," 431. Though metaphors like conquests were of a military nature, they had entered medical and biological terminology in the late nineteenth century. They were thus part of Freud's professional environment; cf. Otis, *Membranes*.

37. Coward, *Jung and Eastern Thought*.

38. In a letter to Rolland written on January 19, 1930, Freud commented on Rolland's enchantment with Indian culture: "I shall now try with your guidance to penetrate into the Indian jungle from which until now an uncertain blending of Hellenic love of proportion, Jewish sobriety, and philistine timidity have kept me away." As cited in Fisher, "Sigmund Freud and Romain Rolland," 38–39.

39. Because Bose made copies of his letters to Freud and carefully preserved Freud's letters to him, it is possible to reconstruct aspects of their correspondence. In 1956, at the request of Anna Freud, Bose's widow, Indrumati Bose, gave the letters to the Sigmund Freud Archives. Thereafter, parts of the correspondence were published by the Indian Psychoanalytical Society in the *Journal of the American Psychoanalytical Association* and the *International Journal of Psychoanalysis*. Ramana, "On the Early History and Development of Psychoanalysis in India," 113–34; Sinha, "Development of Psychoanalysis in India," 428.

40. Freud to Bose, 9 March 1929, as cited in Sinha, "Development of Psychoanalysis in India," 430, and in Ramana, "On the Early History and Development of Psychoanalysis in India," 125.

41. Freud to Bose, 1 January 1933, as cited in Sinha, "Development of Psychoanalysis in India," 431, and in Ramana, "On the Early History and Development of Psychoanalysis in India," 125.

42. Freud, *Diary of Sigmund Freud*, 115.

43. For literature on Fanon, see Bulhan, *Frantz Fanon*; McCulloch, *Black Soul, White Artifact*.

44. Fanon, *Black Skin, White Masks*; Fanon, *Studies in a Dying Colonialism*; Fanon, *Toward the African Revolution*; and Fanon, *Wretched of the Earth*.

Psychoanalysis, Race Relations, and National Identity
The Reception of Psychoanalysis in Brazil, 1910 to 1940

Psychoanalysis has been one of the two systems of thought to define the "long twentieth century," the other one being Marxism. The term "psychoanalysis" does not only refer to a psychological theory or a particular psychotherapeutic technique but, in the words of poet W. H. Auden, to a "whole climate of opinion."[1] For sympathizers and detractors alike, Sigmund Freud's creation has become a necessary referent for defining such issues as sexuality, personality, the self, the unconscious, and many other key words, which became key words precisely as a result of their association to psychoanalysis. As John Forrester points out, "There is something irreversible about what Freud has done to twentieth-century culture."[2] Why certain systems of thought (such as the two just mentioned) that were not particularly easy to understand and were emerging at the fringes of the intellectual life of their time became powerful transnational ideological systems that, to some extent, determined the *Weltanschauung* of a whole century—even in cultural spaces that are very different and located very far away from those where they originated—while other systems of thought fell into oblivion is a question that cannot be easily answered. Certainly, the analysis of the multiple processes of reception in different cultures, processes that are neither passive nor lineal, can provide a good starting point for understanding the success of a given system of thought (psychoanalysis in this case) because, after all, its history cannot be separated from the history of its successive interpretations, readings, and appropriations.[3]

Since the 1930s, there has been a displacement of the centers of production and, more importantly, consumption of psychoanalysis: first from continental Europe to the Anglo-Saxon world and, more recently, from the North to the South; that is to say, from Europe and the United States to South America, or, in other words, from the center to the periphery. Today, countries such as Argentina and Brazil not only have more psychoanalysts and patients in proportion to their population than probably any other country in the world, but psychoanalysis also occupies a central place in the urban culture of both countries.[4] Although the massive dissemination of psychoanalytic thought in Brazil is a relatively recent phenomenon, no more than forty years old, the reception of psychoanalysis in that country, however, is a long-term phenomenon. As early as 1899, there was at least one professor lecturing on Freud and his concept of hysteria at the prestigious medical school in the state of Bahia. In the 1930s, psychoanalytic ideas were incorporated into the public educational policies both at the federal and at the state level.

The reception of psychoanalysis (or of any other system of thought) in a given cultural space is shaped by the particular vision that each society develops of itself. Norbert Elias has defined the "national habitus" as the particular way in which "the fortunes of a nation over the centuries become sedimented into the habitus of its individual members," or, in other words, how the process of state formation is connected to changes in the vision of the world and the construction of subjectivity of individuals.[5] Elias's concept of habitus articulates the macro- and microlevels of analysis. It can be argued that the particular form in which a system of thought is received, appropriated, and redefined in a particular society is closely connected to the national habitus developed in that society. Elisabeth Roudinesco has shown, for instance, that the implantation of psychoanalysis in France was modeled by a certain preexisting and typically "French" notion of the unconscious that emerged from the historical social and political conditions that form the French habitus (although Roudinesco does not use this notion).[6] Brazil, a country that achieved its independence from Portugal in 1822, that did not develop an autonomous medical tradition, and that did not even have an integrated system of higher education until the 1930s, is, of course, not comparable to France. However, in Brazil, too, a habitus that gradually formed during the colonial times shaped the early reception of psychoanalysis. In particular, psychoanalysis was "read" through the filter of the Brazilian elites' preoccupations with race, race relations, and national identity—preoccupations that constituted a central dimension of the Brazilian habitus.

This chapter focuses on the early reception of psychoanalysis in Brazil. The reception (I prefer to use "reception" as opposed to "implantation," which suggests a static phenomenon) of a system of ideas in a particular culture is a complex and multidimensional process that takes place in different cultural levels and at different speeds. Here, I will concentrate on three interrelated areas of reception that show the articulation between the reaction to psychoanalysis and deeper elements of Brazilian national culture. After a short discussion of Brazil's history and formation of a national habitus, I focus on the reception of psychoanalysis by medical circles, the impact of psychoanalysis in the artistic avant-garde "modernista" movement, and the influence of psychoanalysis in Brazilian social sciences. Of course, there was overlap among these different areas of reception. Some doctors, for instance, were very close to avant-garde artists and shared spaces of socialization with them. Other doctors, most notably Artur Ramos, also became distinguished anthropologists and social scientists. However, as Jorge Luis Borges has suggested, even if things happen simultaneously in reality, language can only convey them in successive images; therefore, while the processes I discuss here took place more or less at the same time and were informed by each other, I can only deal with them one by one. The time frame of the discussion starts in the 1910s (when psychoanalysis began to be discussed in medical circles of São Paulo, Rio de Janeiro, Salvador de Bahia, and elsewhere) and ends in the 1940s, before it became institutionalized through the creation of psychoanalytic associations recognized by the International Psychoanalytic Association (IPA). The creation of such associations promoted the standardization of the practice and study of psychoanalysis. Although this standardization has not totally eliminated the national, and even regional, components in the diffusion of psychoanalysis, here I analyze the period when the absence of an orthodoxy allowed for different readings and appropriations of a discipline in a moment when no one could claim the monopoly of legitimacy in its practice and definition.

Brazil: Slavery, Race, Monarchy, and the Formation of a National Habitus

Since the late seventeenth century, Brazilian economy depended on black slaves imported from Africa to work on sugar plantations located in the northeastern part of the colony. Until the mid-nineteenth century, Brazil received more black slaves than any other country in the Western Hemisphere, including the United States. In the eighteenth century, the discovery of precious metals and stones in the south, and later the diffusion of coffee plantations in the areas of Rio de Janeiro and São Paulo, displaced the economic center from the north to the south. Coffee plantations, however, continued to be labored mostly by slaves. In 1822, Brazil achieved its independence from Portugal in a unique manner. It was Dom Pedro (the son of João VI, the king of Portugal who had established himself in Brazil in 1808 after Napoleon's invasion of Portugal) who declared independence after his father was summoned back to Portugal by the Portuguese Cortes, thus becoming Pedro I, Emperor of Brazil. Brazil would be the only country in Latin America to gain its independence without a war and also the only one to keep a monarchy for over sixty years after proclaiming it. Until the end of the nineteenth century, members of the Brazilian social elite still held titles of nobility.[7] In 1831, the increasingly authoritarian Pedro I was forced to abdicate in favor of his five-year-old son, also named Pedro, who, unlike his father, was born in Brazil. Until the child was granted majority in 1841 (at the age of fifteen) and crowned as Pedro II, the country was ruled by a council of regency. During the first half of the century, the monarchy secured for Brazil a level of political stability that was unknown in the emergent republics of the fragmented former Spanish colonies. Although during the nineteenth century, the Brazilian social and intellectual elites held, at least formally, a liberal credo, they did not believe that republican practices could be compatible with the presence of a large population of black slaves.[8] However, beginning in the 1870s, a growing republican movement emerged in the urban centers of the country. Progressive Brazilian intellectuals started seeing both the monarchy and slavery as anachronisms that impeded the development of the country. Monarchy outlived the abolition of slavery in 1888 by only one year: in 1889, Emperor Pedro II was overthrown by a military revolution that established a republic more in tune with the rest of the continent. This oligarchic republic (known as the Old Republic), which was controlled by regional elites of planters, lasted until 1930 when a revolution led by Getulio Vargas, from Rio Grande do Sul, introduced a new era of a centralized state. In 1937, Vargas established the authoritarian *Estado Novo*, vaguely inspired by fascism and the Catholic authoritarian government of Oliveira Salazar in Portugal. Vargas ruled the country from 1930 through

1945, when he was overthrown by a military coup, and again from 1950 to 1954, when, facing the prospect of another coup, he committed suicide.

Since the nineteenth century, modernization has been, to Brazilian intellectual elites, synonymous with "whitening" the country. Brazilian intellectuals looked at Argentina's massive European immigration as a successful model to follow. However, although a large number of foreign immigrants went to Brazil beginning in the late nineteenth century, the country was never as successful as its neighbor in attracting the coveted white European immigrants. Thus, in Brazil, the formulation of national identity was closely related to the possibilities and limitations of integrating the different ethnic groups that composed its society, particularly Aborigines and blacks. However, while the former (less visible in the cities) were idealized by a generation of nineteenth-century romantic poets and writers,[9] the latter were despised as an inferior group. In any case, the presence of a sizable black and mixed population was perceived by members of the Brazilian elite as a hindrance to the country's progress and as a problem that had to be urgently addressed.[10] Brazil became an icon of exoticism in Latin America.

The construction of a national identity and of a national habitus in Brazil was closely connected to the existence of a large mixed population. High levels of coupling and reproduction among members of diverse racial groups had existed in Brazil since colonial times, thus giving rise to a large population of people of color and to the myth of Brazilian racial democracy.[11] Brazil developed as a multiracial society in which possibilities of social mobility were closely tied to "whiteness," although whiteness could be achieved by wealth and social prestige. It was possible for Brazilian mulattoes and even for blacks to rise to the top of society.[12] During the nineteenth and the beginning of the twentieth centuries, however, doctrines of "scientific" racism originating in the ideas of Count Arthur de Gobineau, Louis Agassiz, and a particular reading of social Darwinism were combined with the idea that a gradual whitening of the population was possible through European immigration and through competition for survival, because the "superior" white race would prevail. Thus, most educated Brazilians considered blacks and mulattoes as degrading elements in society.

The first decades of the twentieth century were a period of great disruption in the country. Former slaves, emancipated in 1888, were left without education or any kind of social safety net. Many of them migrated to the cities, producing an urban underclass of people of color that fed nascent Brazilian industrialization. As a result, Brazil, a traditionally rural country, went through a process of rapid urbanization. The population of the city of São Paulo almost doubled between 1893 and 1900. European immigrants who poured into the country after abolition also greatly contributed to urban growth. This accelerated process of urbanization put a strain on public services, which were still in a primitive stage of development. Housing conditions and public health deteriorated.

The Brazilian state was active in promoting measures of social hygiene and public health. But unlike its Argentine counterpart, the Brazilian government did not involve itself, at least until the 1930s, in an active program of public education. In the 1920s, seventy-five percent of the Brazilian population was still illiterate. Similarly, while in the former Spanish colonies, universities had been established in early colonial times (sixteenth and seventeenth centuries), the first full-fledged Brazilian universities were only established in the late 1920s and 1930s. Earlier, children of the Brazilian elite obtained their higher education in independent professional schools or in more prestigious European universities. In this general context, psychoanalysis arrived in Brazil.

Medical Reception of Psychoanalysis

The reception of psychoanalysis in Brazilian medical circles started early in the twentieth century, precisely when the effects of the crisis provoked by the abolition of slavery and the end of the monarchy were becoming apparent. It is noteworthy that unlike the situation in other Latin American countries (most notably in Argentina) where doctors who showed an early interest in psychoanalysis were generally the younger members of the profession, who occupied a relatively marginal position in the medical field, in Brazil, some of the most prestigious psychiatrists (particularly in the state and city of Rio de Janeiro) felt attracted to Freud's theories. As early as 1899, as was mentioned previously, Dr. Juliano Moreira, a reputed professor at the School of Medicine of Bahia, and who is today considered the founding father of modern Brazilian psychiatry, began discussing Freud's writings in his classes. Although he did not publish specifically on psychoanalysis, his interest in Freud and psychoanalysis had a strong influence on some of his students. When Moreira was appointed director of the Hospital Nacional de Alienados (Brazil's national mental hospital; Moreira occupied this position between 1903 and 1930), he established a psychoanalytic ward.[13] Already in the 1910s, medical students began writing the first dissertations on psychoanalysis. At the same time, other prestigious doctors in São Paulo, such as Franco da Rocha, also became interested in psychoanalysis.[14] This interest in psychoanalysis was not restricted to medical circles. Articles discussing psychoanalysis appeared routinely in major Paulista newspapers. Both Moreira and da Rocha became members of the short-lived Brazilian Psychoanalytic Association created in São Paulo in 1927 by Dr. Durval Marcondes, a student of da Rocha.

Brazilian doctors had a particular reading of Freud's ideas—a reading that was influenced by broader preexisting social concerns. Within the positivistic-somatic paradigm that was then in fashion in Brazil and elsewhere in Latin America, degeneracy theory was a major current in Brazilian psychiatry and social thought until at least the 1930s.[15] This theory, formulated in the nineteenth century by French doctor Bénédict Augustin Morel and later modified by Valentin Magnan, was based on the idea that mental and physical diseases were inherited from generation to generation, each time in a more destructive dose. In Brazil, degeneracy was linked to race: the seeds of degeneration were thought to be found in the black and mulatto populations. According to Bahiano doctor Raymundo Nina Rodrigues—one of the most prestigious doctors of his time who inaugurated anthropological studies of the black and mulatto populations and who was paradoxically a mulatto himself—the practice of African religions and rituals were evidence of the "extreme neuropathic or hysterical" and "profoundly superstitious personality of the Negro." Others thought that spiritism practiced by blacks and mulattoes "could induce madness in any participant individual, with or without a predisposition."[16] Through their religious rituals and also (particularly) through their exaggerated sexuality that led to perverse practices, blacks and mixed populations introduced the germ of degeneracy into Brazilian society.

The reception of psychoanalysis in Brazil was linked to local elites' perception of the "exotic" and "wild" elements of their own society. In Brazil, psychiatrists, eugenicists, and mental hygienists linked social and political problems to the biological constitution of the Brazilian man. According to prevalent views, the presence of degenerated aspects of "inferior races"—that is to say, native Brazilians and particularly blacks—contributed in turning Brazilians into an indolent and undisciplined population.[17] Within this mental framework, sexuality was perceived as a particularly dangerous dimension of degeneracy. The alleged uncontrolled sexuality of blacks provided further evidence of the "primitive" nature of the Brazilian population.

Psychoanalysis allowed doctors and intellectuals who were unhappy with the prevalent racist view to introduce nuances into the racialist thought. As Jane Russo points out, while racial theories condemned the country to failure and backwardness, psychoanalysis provided a possible way out. If uncontrolled sexuality had been seen as evidence of primitivism, psychoanalysis provided new tools to approach the problem. First, the idea of sublimation, crucial to the medical reception of psychoanalysis in Brazil, inserted into a neo-Lamarckian matrix prevalent among Brazilian doctors introduced the possibility of "educability." Thus, the excessive sensuality of primitive races need not be an impossibility for progress. Second, the very concept of "sexual excess" and primitivism came to be seen under a different light because in itself, sexuality was neither good nor bad, as psychoanalysis had shown. Sexuality, under the new perspective, was responsible both for the worst and the best of what humanity could do. At the same time, it was recognized that everyone had a primitive dimension to his or her personality. Interestingly, in Brazil the attitude toward sexuality seems to have been more open than in other Latin American countries. As Jane Russo points out, sexuality was discussed in "popular courses on sexology, special celebrations such as the Day of Sex, radio broadcasts about sex, and sex education campaigns." Some thinkers found in sexuality the origins of Brazilian identity.[18] This relative openness toward sexuality paved the way for a reception of psychoanalysis as the "science of sexuality." According to the Brazilian doctors' point of view, all Brazilians, independently of their race, had a "primitive ego," which, identified with the Freudian id, needed to be disciplined, civilized, and transformed. It should not be surprising, therefore, that early reception of psychoanalysis in Brazil was closely linked to education and to a Haeckelian, and at the same time neo-Lamarckian, reading of Freud's ideas.[19] Both the notion that ontogenesis reproduced phylogenesis and the Lamarckian emphasis on evolution through the inheritance of acquired characters that could be induced from the outside left room for optimism because they implied that Brazilian primitivism could be civilized through education and other state-sponsored measures. Arthur Ramos, a disciple of Nina Rodrigues who was active in the fields of medicine, education, and anthropology, as well as a student of black culture in Brazil, and whose doctoral dissertation on "Primitive and Madness," defended in 1925, was informed by psychoanalysis, created—following Carl Gustav Jung but also Lucien Lévy-Bruhl's work on "primitive mentality"—the concept of "folkloric unconscious" that would explain the persistence of primitive mental elements in the contemporary human. This folkloric unconscious became visible under certain conditions, such as dreams, mental disorders, artistic creation, and others. Ramos refuted the theses concerning the racial inferiority of the black population. Instead, he proposed an ethnopsychoanalytic diagnosis of the Brazilian people, imprisoned, he believed, in a "mental atavism" originating in the influence of Afro-Brazilian culture evident in some fetishist rituals. The condition of the Brazilian black population was, according to Ramos, "the consequence of magic, pre-logical thought, which is independent from the anthropological-racial question, because it can emerge, under different conditions and in any other ethnic group . . . This idea of 'primitivism,' of 'archaic' is purely psychological and has nothing to do with the issue of racial inferiority."[20]

Other prestigious doctors, most notably Júlio Pires Porto-Carrero (born in Pernambuco but active in Rio de Janeiro since the late 1920s; author of five volumes on psychoanalysis; translator of Freud's work into Portuguese; member of the Brazilian League of Mental Hygiene, whose psychoanalytic clinic he directed for years; and secretary of the Rio de Janeiro branch of the short-lived Sociedade Brasileira de Psicanálise, created in 1927), interpreted psychoanalysis as a tool for the regeneration of the population, particularly through state-sponsored sexual education and also through eugenic measures, including a liberal policy toward abortion.[21] A proponent of a strong state managed by an elite group of capable technicians (he distrusted democracy), for Porto-Carrero, the school should not be seen as the continuation of the home but rather as the opposite: the home should be the continuation of the school. Because Brazilian homes, affected by weaknesses related to the vestiges of primitivism carried by local families, could not secure social discipline and civilization, it was up to the state to carry out this task through the sublimation of children's sexual impulses by imparting sexual education inspired by psychoanalytic theory in public schools. As he pointed out in 1927, "Given the influence of sexuality in the formation and operation of the infantile psyche, it is not fair that education ignore the sexual side of life and repel sexual manifestations and knowledge simply as immoral. It is urgent to introduce sexual education."[22] For Porto-Carrero, however, sexual education consisted mostly of sublimation through control and discipline of children's sexuality. He proposed an education without excessive rigor or tenderness (both could originate deviations in children's sexuality) and suggested that the use of such devices as pacifiers and bottles should be limited and carefully monitored. According to Porto-Carrero, psychoanalysis provided a scientific foundation to what pedagogists such as Maria Montessori had been doing empirically. He claimed that the price of ignoring psychoanalysis in education would be an increase in crime and perversion.[23] This is why he insisted on educating parents and teachers in psychoanalysis. Pedagogy and psychoanalysis, he repeated, would preclude penology, for once society was rebuilt on the foundations laid by psychoanalysis, crime would cease to exist.

Porto-Carrero, who treated patients by using his own version of the psychoanalytic method and considered himself a self-taught psychoanalyst,[24] thought that Brazil's problems were associated with three interrelated kinds of taboos, originating first in the traditional patriarchal family, second in an exclusive idea of fatherland, and third in the presence of superstitious forms of religion. Although he considered that religion could constitute the basis for morality—he criticized Freud's *The Future of an Illusion* as a utopia—Porto-Carrero warned against the fetishistic manifestations of religion so common in Brazil. The three races that converged in Brazil, particularly the two "savage" ones (natives and blacks), contributed to the development and diffusion of these taboos. A good moral education, he insisted, should start by an opportune sexual education that would dissolve the taboos.[25]

Porto-Carrero also combined psychoanalysis and criminology. While earlier criminologists like Nina Rodrigues associated criminality with race, arguing that blacks and mulattoes could not be considered fully responsible for their acts and therefore could not be held legally competent to stand trial in a civilized court of law, Porto-Carrero displaced the question of criminal responsibility from race to the realm of the unconscious.[26] For him, no criminal could be held responsible for his or her acts because criminal actions were the consequence of problems located in the unconscious. Moreover, the criminal was, according to Porto-Carrero, a social emergent: "The criminal embodies the guilt and sadistic anxieties of the whole society."[27] Porto-Carrero proposed a general reform of the penal code that would eliminate punishment for criminals. According to him, punishment was an act of revenge inflicted by society that originated in a feeling of collective guilt rooted in the Oedipus complex. In Porto-Carrero's view,

> Punishment, sentence . . . is deeply egoistic, animal . . . Those misfits, criminal or not, will be studied and observed by technicians in medicine, psychology and pedagogy. The sick ones will be given the appropriate treatment as it is done in mental hospitals. The rest, after an appropriate isolation which will not take place in a prison, will be reeducated through the use of pedagogic methods and through psychoanalysis, the only currently existing means to dive into the unconscious of individuals and to reconstruct the super-ego, that is to say, to reconstruct his ability to adapt.[28]

Porto-Carrero was not alone in associating psychoanalysis with education. Several Brazilian doctors and intellectuals who approached psychoanalysis in the 1920s and 1930s were active in their states' educational systems. Dr. Ulisses Pernambucano, who developed an interest in psychoanalysis and entered in analysis with Porto-Carrero, was director of the Escola Normal de Pernambuco. Furthermore, Dr. Durval Marcondes, from São Paulo, created in 1938 the mental hygiene section of the Paulista public school system and headed it until 1974.[29] There, he entered into contact with other educators, most notably Virginia Bicudo, who would later become a member of the first generation of IPA-affiliated Paulista analysts. Arthur Ramos was director from 1934 to 1939 of the Secção de Ortofrenia e Higiene Mental of the Institute of Educational Research, set up as part of a broader program of educational research promoted by the Getulio Vargas government after 1930—one of the first measures taken by Vargas was the creation of a new Ministry of Education and Health—and led by fellow Bahian Anísio Teixeira in Rio de Janeiro.[30] Ramos promoted interdisciplinary research on the family environment of children with behavioral or learning problems. Similarly, Deodato Moraes, author of *A psicanálise na educacão* (1927), was appointed school inspector of the Federal District and was member of the board of directors of the Brazilian Educational Association. According to Luiz Fernando Dias Duarte, during the 1930s—at least until the establishment of the authoritarian Estado Novo in 1937—there coexisted in Brazil different political projects that concerned themselves with issues of civilization and of national identity: right-wing Catholics, liberals, philo-fascist authoritarians, and pro-

Soviets. All these projects included defenders of an education based on some type of psychological knowledge.[31]

Most doctors interested in psychoanalysis were also members of the Liga Brasileira de Higiene Mental, founded in Rio de Janeiro in 1923. Like in other countries, in Brazil, the mental hygiene movement—originally created in the United States—was very receptive to psychoanalysis.

The authoritarian government of Getulio Vargas was peculiar because it attracted intellectuals regardless of their ideological colors. Patterns of collaboration between intellectuals, most of whom belonged to elite families (and to the poor branch of aristocratic families, as Sergio Miceli has shown),[32] and the state had existed in Brazil since the times of the monarchy. Vargas's program of state-led social and cultural modernization was compatible with the role that many Brazilian intellectuals had constructed for themselves, providing guidance to an incapable and uneducated people. The Vargas regime offered them the possibility of an association to a strong state willing to work with intellectuals on a broad program of social, political, and cultural reforms. Thus, it was relatively easy for Brazilian doctors and educators already interested in psychoanalysis to introduce it into the official educational agencies and hospitals when the opportunity emerged. Moreover, psychoanalysis was appropriated and reinterpreted by Brazilian intellectuals and doctors who made it fit into their ideas of social reform. Psychoanalytically oriented doctors, together with avant-garde artists and social scientists, found a place in Vargas's modernizing programs. Psychoanalytic thought, or at least some versions of it, fit into Vargas's modernizing programs, as well as into his plans of creating a "healthy and patriotic" youth.

Unlike in Argentina, the institutionalization of psychoanalysis in Brazil through the creation of IPA-endorsed associations was not seen as a rupture with previous patterns of reception, as it was elsewhere. When Durval Marcondes created his short-lived association in São Paulo in 1927 (which obtained provisional recognition from the IPA), most doctors who had been interested in psychoanalysis joined it. Franco da Rocha was elected president, while Juliano Moreira became president of the Rio de Janeiro branch and Porto-Carrero became its secretary, among others. The Paulista association published a single-issue journal, but for reasons that are not clear, it disappeared a few years later.[33] After the demise of his society, Marcondes continued corresponding with Abraham Arden Brill and other prominent members of the international psychoanalytic establishment, letting them know that Brazil would happily receive European analysts who were escaping from Nazism. Finally, Dr. Adelaide Koch arrived in Brazil in 1936 after escaping from Nazi Germany. Once established in her new country, she began to provide formal training to would-be analysts (including Marcondes himself) at—of all places—the Marcondes consulting room.[34] Meanwhile, Marcondes campaigned to obtain official support for an IPA-affiliated Brazilian psychoanalytic association. Later, Marcondes and Koch would lecture together with Virginia Bicudo on psychoanalysis at the recently created Escola Livre de Sociologia e Política of São Paulo, a prestigious institution of research and teaching of the social sciences created by members of the Paulista industrial elite in the 1930s.

Psychoanalysis and Avant-Garde Art

Medical circles did not constitute the only space for the diffusion of psychoanalysis in Brazil; psychoanalysis also proved to be attractive to other sectors of the intellectuality of that country. Since the 1920s, there was a general growing perception that psychoanalysis was not only an innovation in psychology and psychiatry but also an essential component of cultural modernity. After all, as Roudinesco has shown, French literati and intellectuals, for instance, were much more receptive to Freud's ideas than were French doctors.[35]

The post–First World War crisis of ideologies had an impact on Latin America in general and on Brazil in particular. During the 1920s, radical groups from the right and from the left (and sometimes mixed) appeared in the country. Between 1921 and 1922, right-wing Catholics organized themselves around the Centro Dom Vital that published the influential magazine *O Ordem*; at the same time, the Brazilian Communist Party was created, and the first *Tenentista* rebellion (organized by antiliberal, vaguely antibourgeois midranking officers) took place. Furthermore, in the period after the First World War, Latin American intellectuals began questioning previous certainties. The barbarism that was unchained in Europe repositioned the whole discussion around European civilization and the supposedly primitive nature of Latin American societies. Particularly in Brazil, this kind of discussion had important consequences because Brazil was the only country of the continent to actually send troops to fight in Europe. The primitive and savage aspects of Brazilian culture began to be seen under a new light. This revisiting of these old themes had a deep impact on the arts and, more generally, on the Brazilian intellectual field.

In February 1922, during the celebration of the centenary of Brazilian independence, the Modern Art Week took place in São Paulo. The eight days of public exhibits followed by three days of festivals (lectures, readings, and concerts) were calculated to scandalize the bourgeois public of the city.[36] The Modern Art Week was the crystallization of a movement that had started taking shape in the previous decade around, among others, writers such as Mario de Andrade and Oswald de Andrade (no relation to the former); poets such as Menotti del Picchio; musicians such as Heitor Vila-Lobos; and painters such as Lithuanian-born Lasar Segall, Anita Malfatti, and Tarsila do Amaral, the future wife of Oswald de Andrade. Modernism in Brazil was the equivalent to avant-gardism elsewhere and permeated into all forms of art and also into social thought. Modernists were deeply concerned about the formulation of a truly Brazilian cultural identity. Although influenced by Dada, fauvism, and futurism, Brazilian modernism did not mimic any of those movements. The several modernista manifestos emphasized the idea that Europe had profited from Brazil for a long time, and now it was high time for Brazilian culture to "cannibalize" Europe, meaning to take whatever was useful from Europe and to creatively digest it to create something new (and to excrete whatever could not be put to use). As critic Antonio Cândido points out, modernism was at the same time a well-defined artistic movement beginning in 1922, a less clearly defined aesthetic worldview that promoted the end of current and accepted forms of arts, and a historical period. Modernism had its most dynamic moment in the 1920s.[37] During this period, the movement diversified and took different forms in different regions of the country.[38] Gradually, it became a very heterogeneous movement, with a right wing that emphasized order and nationalism and a left wing that stressed irrationalism and aesthetic and social revolution. In general, modernism was associated, above all, with freedom from the artistic academic paradigms that were hegemonic between the 1890s and the 1920s.

Modernists—particularly the most radical ones—made heavy use of psychoanalytic concepts and ideas but did so from a point of view that was very different from the one held by psychiatrists. While for the latter, as it has been discussed, psychoanalysis was a tool used for understanding and taming the wild components of Brazilian culture or, in the best of cases, a possible way out from biologic determinism, for the artists, psychoanalysis provided a tool for the construction of an aesthetic and an ideological movement that exalted precisely those exotic and wild elements of Brazilian culture.[39] The native, the "mestizo," and the black were now reinterpreted as the creative forces of Brazilian culture and society. The *Pau-Brasil* (Brazilwood) movement of 1924 (the same year in which André Breton published the Surrealist Manifesto) led by Oswald de Andrade, Tarsila do Amaral, and Paulo Prado emphasized primitivism and the discovery of the self.[40] During his trips to Paris, Oswald de Andrade discovered that the primitive cultures that excited European avant-garde artists were part of everyday life in tropical Brazil: "barbarian and ours," or, as Oswald de Andrade would put it four years later in his "Manifesto Antropófago," "Tupy or not tupy, that is the question."[41]

In the "Manifesto Antropófago," Oswald de Andrade mentioned Freud three times: he was characterized as the man who solved the enigma of women, who identified the evils that "antropofagia" came to end, and who understood the oppressive nature of the social reality. Moreover, the idea of the taboo turned into a totem through antropofagia pervades the whole manifesto, which was dated the 374th year of the "deglutition of the Bishop Sardinha" (a Catholic bishop killed and eaten by the Caeté Indians in 1556). Thus, the modernists exalted as the most creative component of Brazilian culture what the psychiatrists sought to tame. According to Mario de Andrade, the unconscious was the driving force of all artistic creation.[42] Or, as historian and modernista author Sergio Buarque de Holanda pointed out, "Today, more than ever, all poetic art must be, principally, a declaration of the rights of dreams . . . We have to seek paradise in unexplored regions. Only night stays clear."[43] Thus, as Cristiana Facchinetti claims, psychoanalysis attracted the interest of modernists and their friends in two opposite ways: as an instrument to criticize civilization as shaped by the European mold and as a device to valorize peripheral cultures and their primitive components. Modernists appropriated psychoanalytic concepts (and also ideas from Karl Marx and Friedrich Nietzsche) as tools for the subjective and social revolution they promoted.[44] According to Oswald de Andrade, Marx and Freud could show the path toward authenticity and toward destruction of the patriarchal order.[45] Freud's name and his ideas made conspicuous appearances in many of the avant-garde journals published by modernists. In the modernists' appropriation, however, Freud's ideas were also subjected to antropofagia. Modernists took what they could use of psychoanalysis, combined it with other theoretical frameworks, most notably Théodule-Armand Ribot's psychology, and reinterpreted it to make it fit into their aesthetic and political agenda. Unlike surrealists, the modernists approached psychoanalysis from a nontheoretical perspective; for them, psychoanalysis was an aesthetic and ideological tool. Moreover, in contrast to their French counterparts, modernists were not interested in issues related to mental health. While the surrealists exalted the hysteric woman to the role of a muse, modernists sought inspiration in the primitive components of Brazilian culture.

Given the convergence of interests between psychiatrists and artists, it is not surprising, therefore, that when Dr. Durval Marcondes established his Brazilian Psychoanalytic Society in 1927, more than a few of the artists who had participated in the Modern Art Week joined in immediately.[46] In fact, Marcondes himself had a connection with the modernista movement; he even wrote some poetry that was published in the avant-garde journal *Klaxon*.

Psychiatrists and avant-garde artists both became interested in psychoanalysis. Although the appropriation that these two groups made of the Freudian system was different, in both cases, it was based on the same set of problems that had constituted a major preoccupation for Brazilian social and intellectual elites since at least the nineteenth century and that defined an important aspect of the national habitus: how to deal with the primitive but constitutive dimension of Brazilian culture and society. This primitivism was associated with the issue of race relations. Nonetheless, while doctors tried to use psychoanalysis as a tool to domesticate this aspect of Brazil, artists, on the other hand, attempted to use psychoanalysis to exalt it.

Psychoanalysis and the Social Sciences

Social sciences constituted another space for the reception of psychoanalysis in Brazil. Unlike their older Spanish American counterparts, Brazilian universities, created in the 1930s with the purpose of educating a modern intellectual and state elite, were from the beginning of their existence inserted into a dense transnational intellectual and institutional network: they were already born modern. French, Italian, and American professors (some of whom were members of "cultural missions," as in the case of the Europeans sent by the governments of their own countries) soon populated the faculties of Rio de Janeiro and particularly of

São Paulo. Foreign sociologists, anthropologists, and historians such as the Frenchmen Claude Levi-Strauss, Roger Bastide, and Fernand Braudel, together with American Donald Pierson and many others, stayed in Brazil doing research and teaching for more or less extended periods of time. In the case of the French professors, they became part of the system of promotion for young French scholars who, after spending some time in Brazil, would earn prestigious positions in France. Therefore, modern social sciences together with transnational research agendas and mechanisms of validation and funding were introduced and institutionalized earlier in Brazil than in most other Latin American countries, where the modernization of social knowledge would only be concluded by the late 1950s. Moreover, in Brazil, the social sciences were at the center of university projects aimed at creating a new breed of national and local intellectual and technical elites.

By the time foreign intellectuals arrived in Brazil, psychoanalysis already had been incorporated into the theoretical toolbox of social analysts in Europe and the United States. Brazil, with its large primitive population, whose unconscious was supposedly located more on the surface than that of urban civilized European people, was seen by foreign scholars as particularly apt for a psychoanalytic approach.[47] For Brazilian (or Brazilian-based) social scientists, the reception of psychoanalysis was also associated with the exotic components of Brazilian culture. Thus, beginning in the early 1930s, the Escola Livre de Sociologia e Política included courses on psychoanalysis taught by Durval Marcondes and Virginia Bicudo (both future founding members of the IPA-affiliated Paulista Psychoanalytic Association). At the University of São Paulo, on the other hand, formal courses on psychoanalysis would be introduced only in 1954 as part of the training for clinical psychologists.

Arthur Ramos,who occupied the chair in anthropology and ethnology at the newly created Universidade do Brasil, analyzed Brazilian black culture and found there the origin of primitive elements that permeated into all sectors of Brazilian society. Ramos began the first volume in 1934 of his monumental three-volume work *O negro brasieleiro*, devoted to the study of Afro-Brazilian religion, by wondering what influences operated on the psyche of the African people after the forced contact with other races and other environments.[48] From the very beginning, Ramos made clear that primitive collective representations were present in all culturally backward social formations, regardless of race: "Those concepts of 'primitivism' and 'archaic' are purely psychological and have nothing to do with racial inferiority."[49] This displacement of primitivism from the realm of race to the realm of psychology and culture (and the fact that primitive religious elements permeated even into the upper ladders of Brazilian society) left a door open for social and cultural improvement. However, before eliminating these vestiges of primitivism, it was necessary to understand scientifically those forms of atavistic thought. Psychoanalysis (and Levy-Bruhl's theories on primitive mentality) provided the tool for such knowledge and understanding. Ramos analyzed myths and rituals of African origin from a psychoanalytic point of view.[50]

Another social scientist (not linked to medicine) was French sociologist Roger Bastide, who had an enormous influence on the first generation of Brazilian social scientists. Bastide had developed an interest in themes related to psychoanalysis before going to Brazil. He had written extensively on the mystical life of primitive people, and their manifestation in poetry and the arts. "The primitive," said Bastide in 1931, "is a slave of his emotions."[51] In 1933, he wrote an article titled "Matériaux pour une sociologie du rêve" in which he tried to launch a sociology of dreams.[52] Once in Brazil, Bastide became immediately fascinated by the relationships between different races and cultures, relationships where he found the key to the originality of Brazilian culture. However, in contrast to Mario de Andrade—with whom Bastide established a fruitful dialogue—according to Bastide, the mixture of races should be understood as a juxtaposition of different cultural elements and not as a "digestive synthesis." Bastide shared with modernists an interest (or, perhaps, an obsession) for defining the authenticity of Brazilian cultural production. In 1941, Bastide wrote his influential article "Psicanálise do cafuné" in which he analyzed from a psychoanalytic-sociological point of view a particular ritual of African origin that was very popular in the Brazilian patriarchal family during the empire: the caresses administered by female slaves to their mistresses' heads with the apparent purpose of killing lice.[53] As Bastide points out, the main purpose of the article was methodological: to conciliate psychoanalysis and sociology through a particular example. Bastide begins his argument by discussing the libidinal dimension of the *cafuné*: it generated pleasure of a sexual kind; in other words, it was a substitute for masturbation. Bastide concludes that *cafuné* was associated with the sexually subordinate place of women in plantation patriarchal families and with the separation between sex and marriage for which this kind of social formation allowed. Marriages were arranged, but while men had free rein to satisfy their sexual desires with the black female slaves, women, on the other hand, were forced to observe a strict sexual morality. *Cafuné*, then, was in Bastide's eyes a substitute for women's sexual satisfaction, "and thus it had a useful function, because it protected morality."[54] A few years later, Bastide wrote in French his *Sociologie et psychanalyse* based on his lectures at the University of São Paulo.[55] As Bastide remembered in the preface to the second edition, "psychoanalysis was [then] in fashion" in São Paulo.

Sociologie et psychanalyse is a methodological work in which the author shows that although there was an incompatibility between classical (e.g., Durkheimian) sociology and traditional psychoanalysis, there was nonetheless a fertile ground for interdisciplinary work between renovated social sciences and new versions of psychoanalysis. The last chapter of the volume is a comparative analysis of the encounter of two societies: blacks and whites in Brazil and in the United States. Based on his own ethnographic research in the former country and on similar works carried out in the latter, Bastide tries to explain the relations between the two ethnic groups in the United States, and particularly certain phenomena such as the apparent existence of a sexual taboo between black men and white women, as the result of a displaced Oedipus complex. In the era of slavery, the white mistress to some extent had occupied a maternal position for the blacks. The taboo of the white woman is "identical to the taboo of incest," concludes Bastide. Although slavery had been abolished long ago, the taboo remained.[56] The other side of the Oedipus complex—the feeling of hate toward the father—is also present in the relations between black and white males. However, and here is where Bastide parts company with "traditional Freudians," these sexual elements must be understood in a broader social context and manifest themselves differently according to gender and social class.

In a country like Brazil, on the other hand, where racial lines were not so well defined, as Bastide points out, things developed differently. Whereas blacks in the United States (particularly those belonging to the upper social strata) tried to incorporate themselves as best they could into the white society by internalizing white values, in Brazil, Bastide found the survival of a large number of African cultural elements, particularly those of religious or folkloric nature. Following the work of Arthur Ramos, Bastide wondered whether the survival of myths and rituals of African origins among Brazilian blacks was due to the fact that they continued to fulfill (although in a distorted and modified form) the same kind of unconscious needs that they had fulfilled in Africa or whether it was simply the result of the "conservative power of traditions" existing among religious groups. Unlike the previous generation of doctors and writers who associated certain African rituals with mental diseases, Bastide maintained that "it is necessary to note that the characterization of mystical trance as hysterical collides with the fact that hysteria is a white disorder, extremely rare or even inexistent among blacks . . . The cult of *candomblé*, far from being the root of pathology is, on the contrary, a form of social control of the unconscious. Therefore, it is a factor of psychophysical equilibrium."[57] The trance, therefore, should be explained both by psychological and sociological factors. According to Bastide, the *candomblé* is a particular form of Jacob Levi Moreno's psychodrama. In sum, for Bastide, the African rituals that survived in Brazil were a synthesis between collective representations imposed by an ancestral religion and unconscious tendencies that were controlled by tradition. What for earlier Brazilian psychiatrists had been a form of pathology was for Bastide, in the words of Dias Duarte, "a balm and compensation for the excesses of civilization."[58]

Conclusion

Until the creation of IPA-affiliated psychoanalytic associations in the late 1940s, psychoanalysis was considered in Brazil to be more of an instrument of social analysis than a therapeutic technique. The interest that Brazilian doctors, social scientists, avant-garde artists, and the general public developed in psychoanalysis was closely connected to a series of social concerns that had formed the national habitus since the late colonial times—particularly, the problem of how to deal with the "wild" and "primitive" dimension of Brazilian culture. This problem was indistinguishable from the broader problem of race relations. According to the prevalent view of the Brazilian intellectual elites, in order to enter into modernity, Brazil had to come to terms with its heterogeneous population. The topic of race relations (or rather racialized sexual relations) was also at the center of the formulation of a Brazilian national identity.

The perception of the role of blacks and mulattoes in Brazilian culture changed over time. Until the 1930s, it was broadly accepted that blacks and mulattoes were the carriers of the seeds of degeneracy. Even Paulo

Prado, who was very close to the modernista movement, in his celebrated work *Retrato do Brasil* (1928) considered "Brazilian sadness" to be the result of the exaggerated sexuality of the inferior races.[59] However, particularly in the 1930s, some thinkers contributed to the reformulation of this idea. In 1933, Pernambucano sociologist Gilberto Freyre published his influential work *Casa-grande e senzala*. There, Freyre claimed that the origins of Brazilian national identity had to be traced to the space defined by the sugar plantations in the northeastern part of the country during colonial times. In particular, Freyre emphasized the importance of illegitimate sexual relations between the white male planter and the black female slave. These relations not only gave origin to the large Brazilian mixed population but also had important cultural consequences, defining the relatively mild (particularly when compared to the United States) contacts between races. Thus, in spite of his contrasting approach, sex was also at the center of Freyre's analysis, which cited the works of Oskar Pfister.

Psychoanalysis circulated in Brazil as the scientific knowledge that could provide explanations for sexuality and also displace the discussion about Brazilian exoticism and primitivism from the realm of race to the realm of the unconscious. Doctors, educators, social scientists, and avant-garde artists found in psychoanalysis an adequate instrument for their social and cultural projects. These encounters with psychoanalysis, however, had different points of departure that only the plasticity of a doctrine like Freud's could render compatible. In spite of those differences in the approaches to psychoanalysis, all those groups interested in it shared basic social preoccupations that were at the center of the formulation of a Brazilian national identity and that were a crucial component of a national habitus.

Needless to say, the notion of psychoanalysis put forward by Brazilian doctors, artists, and social scientists had little resemblance to the idea of psychoanalysis established by orthodox analysts and would seem even more different to the Lacanian orthodoxy established decades later. Nevertheless, those different interpretations of the Freudian theory are as much a part of the history of psychoanalysis as those promoted by one orthodoxy or the other. Moreover, when psychoanalysis becomes institutionalized in a given society, it does not happen in a vacuum but in a cultural humus already fertilized by earlier forms of reception. Brazilian analysts were aware of this, and unlike their Argentine counterparts, they constructed a genealogy for their discipline that included the precursors as well as the pioneers and accepted the nontherapeutic dimension of psychoanalysis.[60]

Notes

1. "If often he was wrong and, at times, absurd to us he is no more a person / now but a whole climate of opinion / under whom we conduct our different lives: / Like weather he can only hinder or help." W. H. Auden, "In Memoriam Sigmund Freud," as cited by Forrester, *Dispatches from the Freud Wars*, 184.

2. Forrester, *Dispatches from the Freud Wars*, 2.

3. In recent years, there has been an impressive production of scholarship on the diffusion of psychoanalysis in different countries. What follows is only a small sample of it. For the diffusion of psychoanalysis in France, see Roudinesco, *La bataille de cent ans*, and Turkle, *Psychoanalytic Politics*; for Russia, see Miller, *Freud and the Bolsheviks*, and Etkind, *Eros of the Impossible*; for the United States, see Hale, *Freud and the Americans*, and Hale, *Rise and Crisis of Psychoanalysis in United States*; for Argentina, see Plotkin, *Freud in the Pampas*; and for Australia, see Damousi, *Freud in the Antipodes*.

4. Some authors make the distinction between Freudism and psychoanalysis, defining the former as the loose collection of discourses and practices inspired in Freud's ideas and the latter as a more formalized therapeutic practice. See Vezzetti, *Aventuras de Freud en el país de los Argentinos*. I believe that this distinction is unnecessary. I prefer to use a broad definition of psychoanalysis that includes all practices and discourses that seek legitimacy in a (real or imagined) Freudian origin. See also Plotkin, introduction to *Freud in the Pampas*.

5. Elias derives his conception of "habitus" from psychoanalysis: "[Freud] attempted to show the connection between the outcome of the conflict-ridden channeling of drives in a person's development and his or her resulting habitus." *The Germans*, 19. Analogous connections could be established for societies. I prefer the (historical) concept of "national habitus" to the (ahistorical and essentialist) idea of "national character."

6. Roudinesco, *La bataille de cent ans*.

7. Lilia Moritz Schwarcz notes that during the Brazilian monarchy, a system of titles imported from Europe that included dukes, counts, viscounts, barons, and the like was mixed with indigenous names. Thus, there was the Viscount of Pirajá, the Viscountess of Tibají, the Baron of Bujurú, and so forth. See Schwarcz, *As barbas do imperador*.

8. On the paradoxical place of liberalism in nineteenth-century Brazilian elites' thought, see Schwarz, "Las ideas fuera de lugar."

9. Natives became a romanticized symbol of nationality even for the monarchy. The regalia of Pedro II were full of elements associated with the native population.

10. For a discussion of the evolution of ideas on race in Brazil, see Skidmore, *Black into White*.

11. See da Costa, "The Myth of Brazilian Racial Democracy."

12. Many of the most prestigious Brazilian intellectuals active in the late nineteenth and early twentieth centuries were black or mulatto, including Machado de Assis, the most important Brazilian writer and founder of the Brazilian Academy of Letters; Raymundo Nina Rodrigues, a prestigious (and racist) psychiatrist and anthropologist who worked in Bahia; Juliano Moreira, considered the founding father of Brazilian modern psychiatry; and many others. It is interesting that in most cases, their color was forgotten. A Brazilian colleague told me that after working for many years with Moreira's work and reading all his (numerous) biographies, she learned that her subject was black only when she came across a picture of him in an archive. None of Moreira's biographers mentioned this; his blackness had been "repressed."

13. Russo, "A Psicanálise no Brasil-Institucionalizacão e Difusão entre o Público Leigo." Moreira was an enthusiastic follower of Emil Kraepelin, whose theories he read with a neo-Lamarckian tone. See Venancio and Carvalhal, "Juliano Moreira."

14. See da Rocha, "Do delírio em geral," later reproduced in da Rocha, "A psicologia de Freud." In 1920, da Rocha also published a book titled *O Pansexualismo na doutrina de Freud*. The idea that psychoanalysis was a pansexual doctrine had French origins. In the second edition of the work (in 1930), "pansexualismo" was dropped from the title, which became *A doutrina de Freud*.

15. Skidmore, *Black into White*; Borge, "Puffy, Ugly, Slothful and Inert."

16. Moreira-Almeida, de Almeida, and Neto, "History of 'Spiritist Madness' in Brazil," 11.

17. Nunes, "Da Medicina Social à Psicanálise," 69.

18. Russo, "A Difusão da Psicanálise no Brasil na Primeira Metade do Século XX."

19. Neo-Lamarckism and Haeckelianism were in fact constitutive elements of Freud's thought. See Sulloway, *Freud, Biologist of the Mind*.

20. Ramos, *O negro brasileiro*, as cited in Schreiner, "Uma aventura para amanhã," 157. Ramos was also the author of *Estudos de Psychanalyse*.

21. Porto-Carrero believed that abortion should be permitted, after a technical commission reviewed each case, for six reasons: (1) therapeutic; (2) prophylactic; (3) eugenic; (4) moral; (5) aesthetic (in the case of women for whom the aesthetic of their body constitutes the basis of their contribution to society, like dancers such as Isadora Duncan); and (6) professional (women who make crucial contributions to society and whose pregnancies and motherhoods would impair them in fulfilling their professional roles, such as scientists). He also promoted birth control. See Porto-Carrero, *Psicanálise de uma civilizacão*, 164ff. See also Russo, "Júlio Porto-Carrero."

22. Porto-Carrero, "O carácter do escolar, segundo a psychanalyse," as cited in de Oliveira, "Os primeiros tempos."

23. In 1928, Porto-Carrero and Pedro Deodato de Moraes taught a course on psychoanalysis applied to education at the Brazilian Association of Education. In that opportunity, they listed the names of the Brazilian doctors who were interested in psychoanalysis. All of them occupied very prominent positions in the profession.

24. In a footnote to the 1929 edition of a paper on psychoanalysis delivered in 1925 to

the Sociedade Brasileira de Neurologia, Porto-Carrero points out that "in spite of the exposition of methods done here four years ago, the author uses today only the methods of Freud and the 'active' method of Ferenczi." Porto-Carrero, "Aspectos clinicos da psychanalyse," 124. In the paper, Porto-Carrero mixed psychoanalysis with other kinds of therapies. I want to express my appreciation to Professor Jane Russo for giving me access to this and other works by Porto-Carrero.

25. Porto-Carrero, "Bases da educacão moral do brasileiro."

26. Mokrejs, *A Psicanálise no Brasil*, chap. 4.

27. Porto-Carrero, "Conceito psychanalytico da pena," 185.

28. Porto-Carrero, *Criminologia e psicanálise*, 63, as cited in Russo, "Júlio Porto-Carrero," 135.

29. In 1926, Durval Marcondes presented a thesis titled "O simbolismo estético na literatura" (the aesthetic symbolism in literature) to compete for a chair in literature in the state secondary school system.

30. See Artur Ramos, *Educacão e Psychanalyse*, a kind of textbook on psychoanalysis for educators.

31. Dias Duarte, "Em busca do castelo interior."

32. On Brazilian intellectuals, see Miceli, *Intelectuais e classe dirigente no Brasil*; Pécaut, *Entre le peuple et la nation*.

33. It is noteworthy that in 1967, the newly created *Revista Brasileira de Psicanálise* declared itself to be the continuation of the journal of 1928.

34. See Russo, "A Difusão da Psicanálise no Brasil na Primeira Metade do Século XX"; de Almeida Prado Galvão, "Notas para a história da psicanálise em São Paulo"; and Sagawa, "A psicanálise pioneira es os pioneiros da psicanálise em São Paulo."

35. Roudinesco, *La bataille de cent ans*.

36. Morse, "Multiverse of Latin American Identity," 18.

37. Cândido, "A Recolucão de 1930 e a Cultura."

38. Cândido and Castello, *Presenca da literatura brasileira*, 9.

39. Porto-Carrero, for instance, criticized modernists precisely for their glorification of what is primitive and infantile. See Porto-Carrero, *Psicanálise de uma civilizacão*, 37.

40. However, Paulo Prado—a member of one of São Paulo's most prominent families—would write in 1928 a widely read work of interpretation titled *Retrato do Brasil*. Mario de Andrade criticized the work because, according to him, it was a "pre-Freudian" piece.

41. Oswald de Andrade, "Manifesto Antropófago," 142–47; in English in the original. Tupy Guaraní was one of the native groups found by the Portuguese when they arrived in Brazil in the sixteenth century.

42. Sometimes, Mário de Andrade seems to confuse the Freudian unconscious with an idea of subconscious—that is to say, something that is below consciousness. See, for instance, his "Prefacio Interesantissimo" in *Paulicéia Desvairada*. In the first paragraph, he writes, "[I] write without thinking all what my unconscious yells at me." Later, in the same piece, however, he writes, "I believe that lyrism is born in the subconscious," 22. See also his "A escrava que não e Isaura": "What really exists is the

subconscious sending telegrams and more telegrams to the intelligence—to use Ribot's comparison," 43. Mario de Andrade's library included a large amount of psychoanalytic literature.

43. Sergio Buarque Holanda, *Estética*, 3n, as cited in Facchinetti, *Deglutindo Freud*, 162.

44. Facchinetti, *Deglutindo Freud.*

45. Oswald de Andrade, *Estética e política.*

46. See Perestrello, "Primeiros econtros com a psicanálise"; Sagawa, "A psicanálise pioneira es os pioneiros da psicanálise em São Paulo."

47. Similarly, in 1929, Hungarian anthropologist-psychoanalyst Géza Róheim took an extensive trip to Australia to carry out a psychoanalytic-anthropological study of native groups. See Damousi, *Freud in the Antipodes*, 93–96. See also Damousi's contribution to this volume (chapter 3).

48. Ramos, *O negro brasileiro*, 17.

49. Ibid., 32.

50. Ibid., 236. Ramos established an association between the levels of development of religions and the stages of libidinal development according to the psychoanalytic point of view. Thus, in native Brazilian myths predominated by pre-Oedipal fantasies and in African myths of Nagô origin, Ramos discovered more elaborate conflicts of Oedipal origin (241).

51. Bastide, "Materiaux pour une sociologie du rêve," 625.

52. Bastide, "Matériaux pour une sociologie du rêve." An excellent analysis of Bastide's intellectual trajectory can be found in Peixoto, *Diálogos Brasileiros.*

53. Originally published in 1941, "Psicanálise do cafuné" was reproduced in Bastide, *Sociologia do folclore brasileiro.*

54. Ibid., 320.

55. Bastide, *Sociologie et psychanalyse.*

56. Ibid., 242.

57. Ibid., 251.

58. Dias Duarte, "Em busca do castelo interior."

59. Oswald de Andrade, a friend of Prado, wrote a critical review of *Retrato do Brasil* in which he wonders how "a man *à la page* like my good friend, could write a pre-Freudian book on Brazil." "Retoques ao retrato do Brasil." Although in Mario de Andrade's library there was a copy of Freud's "Three Essays on the Theory of Sexuality," given to him and dedicated by Paulo Prado, we know that in 1925 (when he was already working on *Retrato do Brasil*), Prado wrote to his friend Blaise Cendrars to ask for bibliographic advice on the topics of melancholy and sadness. Prado mentions that he knew of books written by Alfred Binet and Alexandre Dumas; no mention of Freud appears in the letter.

60. See, for instance, *Revista Brasileira de Psicanálise.*

PART II | Trauma, Subjectivity, Sovereignty: Psychoanalysis and Postcolonial Critique

The Totem Vanishes, the Hordes Revolt
*A Psychoanalytic Interpretation of the
Indonesian Struggle for Independence*

The Indonesian struggle for independence from the Netherlands, which lasted from August 1945 to December 1949, was unusually violent; widespread atrocities and callous aggression against civilians were committed by both sides. It commenced with Indonesia's declaration of independence by Sukarno and Mohammad Hatta on August 17, 1945, two days after Japan had capitulated, and ended with the transfer of sovereignty from the Netherlands to Indonesia on December 27, 1949. In the meantime, fierce battles with British forces, which occupied parts of Indonesia in 1945 and 1946, and the Dutch armed forces, which organized two military interventions, took place. Because of the pressure from the United States and the United Nations, the Dutch position became increasingly untenable. After Indonesia gained independence, its relationship with the Netherlands remained tense and was fraught with mutual mistrust. The conflict over West Papua (Irian) during the late 1950s and early 1960s constituted the nadir of this relationship.

Accounts of the *bersiap* period (as the Dutch call it) and the Indonesian revolution (as the Indonesians call it) are inherently contestable.[1] In this chapter, I will analyze the psychoanalytic interpretation of the Indonesian struggle for independence by the psychiatrist Pieter Mattheus van Wulfften Palthe, who had been associated with the medical faculty in Batavia before the Japanese occupation. He was able to observe the events after the Indonesian declaration of independence firsthand. His interpretations were in-

fluenced by Sigmund Freud's "Totem and Taboo," which relates how revolting hordes kill an all-powerful father, only to resurrect him in the form
of a totem to which they vow unconditional allegiance.[2] According to van
Wulfften Palthe, in the Dutch East Indies, the all-dominant father figure
had vanished *twice*, not because of the murderous acts of revolting hordes
but as a consequence of unrelated events. In 1942, the Dutch capitulated to
the Japanese imperial forces after a few months of mostly symbolic resistance; in 1945, the Japanese surrendered after American advances on
Japan and the dropping of the atomic bomb. In both cases, van Wulfften
Palthe argued, the vanishing of the totem was unrelated to the struggles of
the Indonesians. Indonesians were therefore left without an object to
which they could project their ambivalent feelings of aggression they had
felt toward the Japanese, which they then transferred to the Dutch. In van
Wulfften Palthe's description, the struggle for independence was a surreal
affair in which the Dutch became the inadvertent object of Indonesian aggression. In an act of displacement on an international scale, the Dutch became the object of the wrath the Indonesians had felt toward the Japanese.

Van Wulfften Palthe's analysis of the Indonesian struggle for independence reflects his attempt to come to terms with its abhorrent violence,
the origins of the Indonesian desire for independence and hatred of the
Dutch, and, ultimately, the loss of the Indies as a colony.[3] It is a psychoanalyst's attempt to understand the excessive violence that occurred in a
place most Dutch remembered as a tropical paradise inhabited by the
meekest and most gentle people on earth. Relying on general ideas of the
primitive mentality of the indigenous population, crowd psychology, and
psychoanalysis, van Wulfften Palthe located the ultimate reasons for the
Indonesian struggle for independence in factors entirely extraneous to the
Dutch and the way they had governed their colonial empire. In this chapter, I will provide a general background of the Indonesian revolution and
psychiatric writings on the nature of the Indonesian mind, including van
Wulfften Palthe's writings on amok and primitive mentality. I will then
proceed to his interpretation of the Indonesian struggle for independence
and the nature of banditry of Java, which were an essential part of this
analysis.

The Struggle for Independence

On March 8, 1942, about two months after the first invasion on the outer
islands and a mere eight days after the Japanese invaded Java, the Dutch

army surrendered control over the Indonesian archipelago. The Dutch had proven powerless against the overwhelming military might of the Japanese army, which made a great impression on the Indonesian population. Some nationalist leaders welcomed the change of power and cooperated with the Japanese as a way of furthering their nationalist agenda. After the first year of the Japanese occupation, most Indonesians felt that the repression under the Japanese was worse than what they had experienced previously. On December 7, 1942, Queen Wilhelmina of the Netherlands promised in a radio broadcast that the Netherlands would enter negotiations to reform the relationship with its colonies after hostilities had ended. Sukarno and Hatta proclaimed the independence of the Indonesian republic on August 17, 1945, two days after the Japanese capitulated.[4] The British, who controlled the southern part of the Pacific Theatre of Operations, requested the Japanese troops to maintain peace and order until British reinforcement could arrive. On Java, this led to a paradoxical situation. The Japanese did not want to fight the nationalist forces they had previously supported. They decided on a voluntary internment in the countryside, virtually leaving the cities. They halfheartedly disarmed the indigenous military forces they had trained during the occupation and hardly offered resistance when these forces attempted to gain control over weapon depots. It took more than a month before a small number of British troops arrived, and when they came, they did not bring sufficient reinforcements.

The first few weeks after the Japanese capitulation were remarkably peaceful but also somewhat unreal. Many Dutch individuals who had survived the Japanese internment camps attempted to find their relatives. They were only vaguely aware that the political situation in the colonies had changed dramatically and that a return to prewar life was unlikely. The Indonesian members of the Japanese police forces and militias started to arm themselves by looting Japanese army depots. These forces consisted of young men (called *pemuda*, literally "youth"). Late in September, they staged demonstrations and started to attack civilian targets (mostly Dutch citizens), often armed only with knives and bamboo spears. At the same time, former Indonesian soldiers of the Dutch colonial army (KNIL) staged attacks as well. Hostilities increased when the British landed (beginning on September 8, in modest numbers), although the British did not want to interfere with what they considered an internal conflict. When the Dutch landed, beginning in October, violence escalated. This later led to what the Dutch have called the "police actions" (because they dealt with internal affairs within the national borders) but that are more appropriately named military incursions or a colonial war.

For most colonial officials and Dutch politicians, the Indonesian aspirations for independence came as a surprise; they had been acquainted with a compliant and mostly docile population that seemed to appreciate their presence. As a matter of fact, the Dutch had expected to be welcomed by the Indonesians as liberators from Japanese repression. By exiling most leaders of the various nationalist movements in the 1920s and the 1930s, they had successfully silenced the opposition to colonial rule. When they were met with violent opposition, they had great difficulty coming to terms with it. Van Wulfften Palthe's writings are one of the attempts to explain the hostility of the Indonesians and what could be done to ameliorate the situation. In his analysis, he relied on a long tradition of psychiatric writing on the nature of the "primitive" Indonesian mind.

Colonial Life as a Family Romance

Frances Gouda has pointed out that colonial life and the relationships between colonizers and colonized have often been depicted in terms of family life, where natural, amicable, and benevolent relationships between parents and children, teachers and pupils, and masters and servants obtained; similarly, colonial strife has often been portrayed as a disturbance in family relationships or as a family romance gone awry.[5] In Dutch popular writings, Indonesians were portrayed in an ambivalent manner, at times as children who were emotional, dependent, pleasing, and eager to acquire the superior cultural heritage of their parents and at other times as fractious, subordinate, stubborn, unreliable, and unwisely resisting benevolent paternal authority. This portrayal was reinforced by theories of racial and social evolution, which placed the different ethnic groups inhabiting the globe in a graded series, their place depending on the level of evolution attained. The Australian Aboriginal represented the most primitive stage of evolution, while the advanced civilizations of the West (Dutch, English, or American) were portrayed as the pinnacle of the process of social evolution.[6] From this perspective, Indonesian ethnic groups were the adolescents of humankind: their intellectual faculties had developed quickly, but they were, as yet, untrained and undisciplined, subject to mood swings, and overly eager to attain a status of autonomy and independence for which they were not yet sufficiently mature. Using these images of family life, the highly artificial and repressive nature of colonial society could be described as natural and even necessary. It also provided reasons for not taking the Indonesian struggle for independence too seriously.

The views on the primitive nature of the indigenous population of the Indonesian archipelago had existed for a long time and relied on stereotypes common in colonial life, which also informed scientific and medical writings. These views became much more prevalent during the 1920s, when the increasingly vocal and vibrant nationalist movements started to express their desire for meaningful political participation and ultimate independence. At the same time, Indonesians were ever more depicted as lazy, emotional, fractious, and fickle. When the leaders of several nationalist movements were imprisoned and exiled, the participation of Indonesians in the *Volksraad* (Popular Council, the colonial parliament, founded in 1918) became meaningless. Instead of initiating or continuing a dialogue with these leaders, a few politicians came to advocate a psychological colonial policy in which scientists would study the nature of the native psyche as a guide for colonial policy.[7] The Western-trained Indonesian intellectuals who participated in the nationalist movements were portrayed as alienated, uprooted, disgruntled, and out for their own profit; they were utterly unable to represent the Indonesian people. At the same time, politicians and social commentators considered the real needs of the Indonesians to be so opaque that only systematic scientific study could reveal them.

In the colonial Dutch East Indies, there was, on the one hand, an outspoken disdain for the lazy, emotional, childish, and uneducated native who could not possibly benefit from Western education; on the other hand, there was also an exaltation of Javanese Eastern spirituality and high culture, which had existed for thousands of years and had been handed down from generation to generation. Dutch theosophists praised the *wayang kulit* shadow-puppet theatre, which carried spiritual messages the West needed to respect and hear.[8] They associated the wayang with the spiritualism of India, bypassing Islamic culture that had become dominant in the Dutch East Indies more recently. In the portrayal of the Javanese as spiritual, an essential difference between Western and Eastern culture is assumed, although Eastern culture is conceived as superior. Because the spiritual superiority of Javanese culture was located in a distant past, it led to a veneration of an imagined past culture rather than to dialogue about present-day political concerns. It led to attempts to unearth and discover true and essential Javanese culture as it was before Western interference commenced—and attempts to restore Javanese culture to this state. Therefore, it can be considered an attempt to orientalize or particularize the Javanese.

Amok and the Nature of the Native Mind

Pieter Mattheus van Wulfften Palthe (1891–1976) has always been known as a highly energetic individual with numerous interests.[9] During his medical studies at the universities of Leiden and Utrecht, he became second lieutenant (reserve) of the Fourth Regiment of the Hussars, a regiment of the Dutch army. He also was a jockey. From an early age, he was fascinated by airplanes and flying; he obtained his pilot's license in 1913. During the First World War, he was a lieutenant-flyer at the military airfield near Soesterberg, where he became director of medical services in 1918. His 1927 dissertation on the sensory and psychic functions during flight was the first book on aviation medicine published in the Netherlands.[10] In 1927, van Wulfften Palthe arrived in the Dutch East Indies to take up a position as instructor in neurology and psychiatry at the STOVIA, Batavia's medical school, which became the Faculty of Medicine two years later.[11] During his long stay in the Indies, he wrote many articles on somatic treatments and neurology.[12] He maintained a busy private practice and had a longstanding interest in psychoanalysis, which is apparent in the few articles he wrote on what later were called the culture-bound syndromes (amok, lata, and koro) and medico-legal issues, which combined psychoanalysis, crowd psychology, anthropology, and earlier psychiatric theories on the nature of the primitive psyche. During the war, he was interned in Batavia's Kramat and Tjideng camps, where he provided medical services and looked after displaced psychiatric patients.[13] In 1946, he became president of the emergency university in Batavia.[14] In 1948, he returned to the Netherlands and became the director of the first aeronautic laboratory at the Soesterberg military airfield four years later.

Van Wulfften Palthe has been recognized as one of the most authoritative writers on amok, which is currently understood as a culture-bound syndrome in which a male individual, often in a situation of extreme embarrassment, attacks and kills people indiscriminately in a state of frenzy. Several Dutch colonial psychiatrists proposed theories on the nature of amok. Van Wulfften Palthe's predecessor at the STOVIA, Feico Herman Glastra van Loon classified it as an acute and emotional state of confusion instigated by a highly charged emotional experience involving great public embarrassment (*malu*).[15] A state of amok could more easily be induced during a fever (due to malaria or an infection) or in patients with tertiary syphilis. Van Loon, like his colleague Petrus Henrie Marie Travaglino, ascribed the prevalence of amok (and lata) to the emotional and infantile character of Indonesians, who they characterized as child-like, impulsive, emotional, lazy, and as having poorly developed second-ary processes (involving rationality, foresight, and planning).[16] According to both psychiatrists, Indonesians had a lower level of mental develop-ment, resembling that of Western children. Both van Loon and Travaglino equated primitivism and infantilism, leading to comparisons between both states (as well as to questions as to how the Indonesians could be raised or educated to attain a higher, Western level of civilization). The Eastern and the feminine were also equated, mutually reinforcing West-ern male stereotypes about non-Western individuals and women.[17]

Van Wulfften Palthe developed an explanation for amok with distinct psychoanalytic elements. According to him, societies—and thereby the personality types that are most prevalent—could be characterized by the relative importance of civilization versus culture.[18] Civilization repre-sented an emphasis on rituals, morality, and rules. Highly civilized societies were characterized by taboos, prohibitions, rituals, conformity, rigidity, and a distinct respect for social hierarchy. Soldiers were highly regarded, as were courage and sacrifice. There was a sense of superiority toward other ethnic groups. Government was autocratic and dictatorial; life was ori-ented toward the community. Highly cultured societies, on the contrary, were characterized by freedom of emotional expression, tolerance, non-chalance, patience, and self-deprecating humor. Soldiers were not appreci-ated at all; war was despised, while cosmopolitanism and pacifism were cherished. People tended to be realistic, materialistic, and afraid of illness and misadventure. Societies tended to be democratic and egalitarian, and social control was rather loose. Specific communities could be character-ized by their level of civilization in combination with their level of culture, which encouraged the formation of specific personality types, the expres-sion of certain kinds of mental disorders, and the repression of others.

Using this typological characterization, van Wulfften Palthe classified the Javanese as a highly civilized group with a very low level of cultural development. Because of this, there were very few avenues for the expres-sion of accumulated tension, frustration, and aggression. As he stated,

"We have come to know our Javanese as a people with a very high civilization in all classes and layers of the population . . . In this respect, they are more civilized and more controlled than we are. However, this condition also provides the possibility that mental tension can accumulate, even by normal emotionality."[19] He argued that individuals in the West had a great number of ways to abreact accumulated emotions at their disposal, among them drinking alcohol, dancing, shouting, driving cars, watching or participating in sports, and listening to music, which aided them in coping with delay of gratification, denial, and repression. These feelings could also be sublimated in artistic or religious activity. These methods were generally not available to the Javanese; consequently, aggressive energy and mental tension could "accumulate to such an extent that the control mechanisms are no longer sufficient and the dam suddenly and irresistibly breaks, allowing expression of *ur*-instincts and aggressive impulses in amok."[20] When placed in a state of public embarrassment, the accumulated frustrations could burst out in an explosive way. Amok was one of the very few patterns of behavior available to the Javanese that could serve as an outlet for pent-up aggression.

In his analysis of amok, van Wulfften Palthe attempted to shed light on the nature of a specific mental disorder prevalent in Southeast Asia, the nature of the normal indigenous psyche, and the nature of Indonesian society as a whole: amok was a condition inherent to Indonesian culture and could be explained by a "disharmony between a high level of civilization . . . and a small amount of living culture."[21] Because of the close association between personality structure, mental illness, and society, all three had to be taken into account. In this respect, van Wulfften Palthe followed the legacy of Emil Kraepelin, who had visited Java in 1904 to conduct research in comparative psychiatry, and a number of Dutch psychiatrists who had followed his ideas.[22] According to Kraepelin, an analysis of the relative prevalence of mental illness and the different symptoms in which mental illness is expressed would illuminate the ethnic, cultural, or climactic components in the development of mental illness. In addition, it could shed light on the nature and character of different ethnic groups, thereby contributing to a *Völkerpsychologie*, a project of his one-time teacher Wilhelm Wundt.[23] His ideas also closely paralleled those of the culture and personality school in the United States.[24] Van Wulfften Palthe used his psychoanalytic insights on the nature of amok and Javanese culture to analyze specific social phenomena in the Dutch East Indies and used these insights when social developments in the Indies took unexpected turns.

A Psychoanalytic Interpretation of the Indonesian Revolution

Van Wulfften Palthe's analysis of the Indonesian struggle for independence started with Japan's capitulation on August 15, 1945, and Indonesia's declaration of independence two days later. Independence could hardly be considered an accomplishment; after all, the Japanese had not surrendered because of Indonesian resistance or as the result of prolonged fighting. Instead, the Japanese capitulation was announced and the republic established, but nothing further happened. According to van Wulfften Palthe, this led to a rather uncanny situation: "The iron hold of Japanese discipline, which held the whole population in its grip, suddenly disappeared without anything taking its place."[25] Some older Indonesians expected the Dutch to return to reestablish law and order and bring peace and prosperity to their colonies once again. They were disappointed because the Dutch did not return for another four or five months. The nationalists expected a violent struggle for independence, but after Sukarno's declaration, they had achieved what they wanted without any effort. There was no resistance to overcome, although the Indonesian state did not receive any recognition from abroad, either. For the nationalists and the restless former members of the militias organized by the Japanese, this led to an almost unbearable situation: "In the first two months [after the proclamation of independence], the pent-up craving for action found no object to express itself towards, it was like kicking against a loose curtain."[26] The totem had disappeared; the ambivalent feelings held toward it no longer had an outlet. The pent-up aggression against the Japanese was suddenly left without an object, and clear indications on how to proceed were lacking. Because there was no one to fight and no forces to resist, an artificial calm prevailed for the time being.

During the peaceful weeks after the Japanese capitulation, emotional tension was building under the surface. Van Wulfften Palthe commented, "The tension found no outlet, the people became apathetic and felt empty, ill at ease, and uncertain; they remained expectant without knowing exactly what they were waiting for; because of this anxious expectation they no longer worked regularly."[27] The totem, or the object of ambivalent Oedipal attachment, the former placeholder of which were the Japanese, had left, and nothing had taken its place. This meant that the feelings the Indonesians harbored toward this authoritarian father figure—among them love, admiration, hatred, resentment, and fear—no longer had an object. As a consequence, Indonesian emotions split into two components. A new mother complex was formed, and affections of love and attachment were transferred to the mother country (*ibu pertiwi*), the republic. The feelings of hatred and resentment previously harbored against the Japanese were transferred toward the Dutch, replacing the affectionate feelings they previously held. The Japanese propaganda, which invoked hatred against the Europeans, retroactively presented an ideal wish fulfillment; its emphasis on Eastern superiority aided this process.

The emotional needs of the Indonesians, who had suffered three years of brutal repression, remained unfulfilled by the lack of action after independence was declared. The nationalists made symbolic attempts to provide alternative outlets with slogans and red-and-white flags and by organizing marches to celebrate the establishment of the republic. This, according to van Wulfften Palthe, was not sufficient; therefore, "one could observe a regression to a more primitive level of development in the leaders and their followers, in the first instance to a kind of dream-state, a trance, a possession by images and wishes far removed from all reality and logic."[28] Here, the mechanisms that had held Javanese bands of bandits and millenarian religious movements together resurfaced. The nationalists and the newly armed members of the former Japanese police forces were guided by imaginary ideas aimed at wish fulfillment rather than by rational considerations. Because the British did not intervene, they became convinced that they were much stronger and that Lieutenant-General Sir Philip Christison (the British officer in charge of Indonesia) had actually recognized the republic. Van Wulfften Palthe commented that "this trance, this dream-state inhibited any efficient action."[29] People moved, in large vans, from one village to the other, displaying large banners, or began to travel aimlessly around the country, waving flags and expecting the establishment of an earthly paradise.[30]

The bands of bandits, which van Wulfften Palthe later asserted had been endemic in Indonesian life before the war, reappeared in great numbers. They had appeared immediately after the Dutch capitulation as well, but the Japanese had been able to suppress their activity. At this moment, there was no central army or police force that could control them. The nationalist forces attempted to make them serve the new republic, with only limited success. Superstition played an important role: some groups were convinced that independence had to be established before January 1, 1949; otherwise, great unrest would result.[31] In the ensuing unrest, the boundaries between gangs and religious movements started to fade. Ill-defined groups became increasingly violent and began to attack defenseless Dutch civilians. A state of collective amok ensued in Java: "In their totality they form a horde, unaffected by reason and living in a mystic-magical world of make-belief, in which the most primitive instincts of aggression and cruelty have free play."[32] Abduction, abuse, rape, arson, and destruction occurred on a regular basis.

The older supernatural beliefs, which, according to van Wulfften Palthe, had once been part and parcel of bands of bandits in Java, reappeared with a force not witnessed previously. Bands were convinced of their own invulnerability and were guided by an *ilmu* (an amulet, often a small piece of bamboo worn around the neck). Groups of young Indonesians, often only armed with bamboo spears, regularly attacked British soldiers. Van Wulfften Palthe observed that "attacks with sharpened bamboo sticks on Sherman tanks indicated their faith in their invulnerability; their loss of a sense of reality is indicated in the way they themselves describe how enemy bullets deviated from their course."[33] The activities of these gangs made Java a dangerous place for Europeans; it appeared that there was a general "regression to the times before the Dutch arrived, before the *Pax Neerlandica* had ended the mutual wars and when gangs still operated freely."[34] These hordes, manned by neurotic fanatics fueled by anger and resentment, made the whole country regress into a barbaric state of violence. In van Wulfften Palthe's analysis, the hatred of the Indonesians toward the Dutch only came into being after the Japanese capitulation and in essence was transferred from the Japanese to them. Only then did the attitudes of the Indonesians become pathological. This view also supported the necessity of a strong military presence to function as a superego for the Indonesian population because the superego of individual Indonesians had not yet sufficiently developed.

Van Wulfften Palthe's characterization of the Indonesian resistance against the Dutch is not entirely unusual; it resembles that of the British psychiatrist John Colin Carothers in his attempt to understand the motives for the Mau Mau rebellion in Kenya.[35] Instead of analyzing political repression in Kenya and the appropriation of the lands of the Kikuyu, Carothers elaborated on the childlike nature of the African mind, the role of superstition, and the belief in supernatural powers that buttressed the

Mau Mau rebellion. Carothers also pointed out the erosion of African culture by the presence of Europeans in the colony. As a consequence, the Kikuyu "had lost the supportive and constraining influences of their own culture."[36] In many ways, Mau Mau seemed to be an adolescent rebellion based on persistent beliefs in magic that had their basis in primitive culture, which was in the process of being modernized by the presence of the British. In Carothers's account, the appropriation of the land of the Kikuyu and the repressive colonial regime had little to do with it.

Based on his psychological analysis of the current state of affairs, van Wulfften Palthe offered some advice as to which military strategy to follow. He finished his first writings on the topic near the end of 1945 and made them available to the administration of the Dutch and English occupying forces in Indonesia, who chose to ignore them and prevent their further circulation.[37] According to van Wulfften Palthe, only the most repressive military approach could be expected to yield results. One could not expect that being reasonable or dropping pamphlets from airplanes would have positive results. Neither was there a point in negotiating with moderate Republicans (of whom Sutan Syahrir was an example).[38] Revealing his earlier association with the military and his acceptance of its values, van Wulfften Palthe advocated the "forceful, purposeful, and consequent application of force."[39] A gentle and careful approach would only be counterproductive and encourage more bloodshed. Because of the irrational nature of the gangs that were opposing the Dutch, only brutal force could be expected to have any effect: "Once in motion, the hordes rush against the machine guns and the evidence of a great number of casualties dislodges the mystic-magical belief in its invulnerability as little as the failure of an African witchdoctor damages his reputation."[40] When law and order had been reestablished, the Indonesians would be much more open to negotiation.

In addition to the violent suppression of the insurrection, van Wulfften Palthe argued that a number of preventive activities should be undertaken as well. First of all, the freedom of assembly should be suspended immediately, which would prevent the formation of hordes.[41] Schools would have to be closed and festivities cancelled; *pasars* (markets) could only be held under military supervision, and train and tram services could only be available for the transportation of goods. The movement of groups in the countryside had to be monitored with air reconnaissance, after which they could be dispersed. Because of the emotionality and lack of individuation of the Indonesians, religious groups and gangs held sway over the population without encountering much resistance. The only way to prevent these groups from forming was to keep people apart from each other. Using brutal force and preventing groups from forming remained as the only options for the Dutch to reassert their authority and reclaim their position in colonial society.

The Role of Indonesian Intellectuals

In his analysis of the political situation in the Dutch East Indies after the Japanese capitulation, van Wulfften Palthe carefully distinguished between the masses and the intellectual elite. He described the behavior of the masses, or the hordes, as irrational, archaic, and not amenable to rational arguments. He acknowledged that the small elite of intellectuals who had received their Western education in Dutch schools and mostly served in positions of the colonial government had reasonable arguments for independence.[42] However, he asserted that in the chaotic state of affairs after the capitulation of the Japanese, even Indonesian intellectuals had regressed to a state in which narcissistic desire and wish fulfillment were more important than reason and negotiation. Unfortunately, many intellectuals had harbored anger and resentment against the Dutch for a long time, which interfered with their ability to handle the situation in the best way for both parties.

Van Wulfften Palthe acknowledged that the educated Indonesians had had the most intensive interaction with the Dutch before the war. They had been educated in Dutch schools and occupied the lower ranks in the colonial administration. In many ways, these intellectuals had embraced Western values. Unfortunately, according to van Wulfften Palthe, their prolonged interaction with the Dutch had been damaging to their self-esteem. Although they officially had equal rights to the Dutch and almost all positions had been open to them, their daily interactions with the Dutch had often been stilted and at times humiliating. This was, in the first place, due to the behavior of some Dutch individuals who, because of inferiority feelings, had expressed arrogance and feelings of racial superiority toward all Indonesians, irrespective of their education and accomplishments. Even more damaging, in van Wulfften Palthe's opinion, had been the attitudes of progressive Dutch individuals who admired Javanese culture and had attempted to support the Indonesians in all possible ways. He was most critical of this group, who were "active during the last few decades before the war, who found everything beautiful and praiseworthy about the Javanese and who were critical of the rough and derelict nature of Dutch colonial officials; they were more Indonesian than the Indonesians."[43] Van Wulfften Palthe was probably commenting on the activities of progressive Dutch intellectuals who were greatly interested in ancient Javanese and Balinese culture and had been supportive of the nationalist movement. These comments could also reveal a deep disappointment with some of his former students; after all, many students had joined the struggle for independence.[44]

According to van Wulfften Palthe, Dutch individuals representing the ethical policy and members of progressive groups (such as *De Stuw* and the Java Institute), rather than the reactionary politicians of the 1920s and the 1930s, had earned the ire of the Indonesian nationalists. As he commented wryly, "There is no better way to make someone an enemy for life than to aid him continuously in his career, his development, and his aspirations."[45] Those Dutch who admired Javanese culture had often provided condescending support that was fueled by a feeling of superiority caused by an infantile identification with the helpless Javanese. In this case, too much help and too much encouragement had led to an unreasonable amount of guilt in Indonesians, as well as great amounts of pent-up anger. The resentment the Indonesians had built up went unnoticed by the Dutch: "In the symbiosis of the Dutch with the Indonesians of this group [the intellectuals], under the tranquil surface intense tensions built up, which most Dutch because of their complacency did not recognize and which the Indonesians knew to hide masterfully behind an appearance of peacefulness."[46] The education the Dutch had brought had only focused on intellectual development, which was not sufficient to fulfill the emotional needs of this emerging class of Indonesians.[47] During the military actions of the Dutch in Indonesia, the same groups of Dutch admirers of Javanese culture took the side of the Indonesians and criticized all efforts of the Dutch army and government.[48]

Banditry in Java

Because the United East Indies Company had sold off tracts of land around Batavia for the establishment of plantations, creating vast areas that were sparsely populated and that could not be policed effectively, bands of bandits became active around the city from the second part of the nineteenth century on.[49] Van Wulfften Palthe's views on banditry in Java were formulated after he had developed his views on the Indonesian struggle for independence in an attempt to further explain the origins of its extraordinary violence and appear to have been influenced by the prewar sensational coverage in the colonial press. Interestingly, they form his most influential contribution to the historiography of the Indonesian revolution and the role bandits and gangs played in it.

According to van Wulfften Palthe, bands of bandits had been operating in Java's countryside for a very long time; their leaders were feared and venerated. Van Wulfften Palthe had investigated gang members after their arrests to provide psychiatric testimony about their mental state to the courts. On the basis of his observations, he provided his own psychoanalytic views on the nature of these bands of bandits.[50] Their nature, according to him, was rooted in superstition, archaic thought, and animistic beliefs, as well as transference to the leader of the group. Because of the generally low level of development of the Javanese (whose thought processes allegedly were characterized by prelogical thinking, mystical beliefs, and superstition), the members of the group were tied to the leader in a way that resembled a hypnotic trance. Consequently, these gangs resembled primeval hordes in which any sense of individuality was lost and in which the leader had ultimate power. Van Wulfften Palthe's ideas were inspired by crowd psychology, which elaborated on the destructiveness of hordes, the power of charismatic leaders, and the process of deindividualization that occurred in crowds. Gustave Le Bon, whose *Psychologie des Foules* is mentioned by van Wulfften Palthe, was one of the best-known representatives of this genre.[51] Apart from the clinical examination of a few gang members, it appears that his judgment was also influenced by the highly sensationalized coverage of gangs in the newspapers of the Dutch East Indies.[52] Western literature, in particular the German author Karl May's *Winnitou* stories on the Wild West, and movies—Westerns had been very popular in the Dutch East Indies—provided highly romanticized images of gangs and criminals, which influenced public perceptions of bandits.

Physicians, anthropologists, and others had previously commented on the nature of superstition among the Javanese.[53] According to van Wulfften Palthe's analysis, the leader of the gang was responding to a calling, which was based on the time of his birth, his name, some physical feature, or some other omen. Because of this, the leader was thought to have been bestowed with magical powers and invulnerability. Members of the gang were chosen by divination; the gang was held together by an *ilmu* (a charm, amulet, or secret code), which it believed gave the gang extraordinary powers by making it invisible and invulnerable. Through divination and complex numerological calculations, the day, time, method, and victims of the next *rampok* (attack) was decided. According to van Wulfften Palthe, the psychological character of these gangs closely resembled that of religious mass movements that sprang up in the Indies every once in a while. These movements were also based on mystical insight or divination based on old scriptures and were organized in the expectation that paradise would be established on earth (Buddhist-Hindu beliefs) or that the Mahdi (Messiah) would return (Muslim beliefs). These spiritual movements were often guided by individuals who, through visions obtained while in trance, inspired the population. These popular movements were inspired by archaic beliefs and could cause the population to become extremely restless.

Before the Dutch had established the *Pax Neerlandica* on the Indonesian archipelago, indigenous groups, van Wulfften Palthe argued, had ample opportunity to engage in rampok in the form of warfare between tribes, head hunting, and other violent encounters.[54] Because of Dutch intervention, this was no longer possible, leaving gang membership as one of the only ways of releasing pent-up tension through coordinated group activity. Rampok became, in this perspective, the social equivalent of running amok. It was facilitated by the transference of Oedipal feelings to the group leader, which lowered the individuality and level of consciousness of every group member and tied the band (or the horde) together in a form of collective hypnosis.

Discussion

In the account of van Wulfften Palthe, the Indonesian struggle for independence could be explained in terms of crowd psychology and psychoanalysis, which also explained the mechanisms responsible for amok and banditry in Java. The highly emotional nature of the Javanese made them prone to the influence of charismatic leaders. The disharmony between their civilization and culture made it impossible for Indonesians to drain inner tension and frustration. Combined with a culture in which superstition, animism, divination, and mystical powers played a central role, this led to an explosive situation after the Japanese capitulation. Because there was no object for their anger and resentment, and because their freedom had been achieved without any struggle, the Indonesians transferred the hatred they had felt toward the Japanese to the Dutch. This led to the situation in which the brutal military intervention organized by the Dutch in 1946 had become inevitable. In van Wulfften Palthe's narrative, the Dutch appeared to be scapegoats rather than aggressors.

Van Wulfften Palthe firmly stood in the tradition of psychiatric commentary on colonial affairs by emphasizing the infantile character of the Indonesians.[55] He delegitimized the Indonesian resistance against the reassertion of Dutch rule in the colonies by explaining it as the outcome of neurotic processes and the irrational, erratic, and violent behavior of hordes. In his perspective, the hatred against the Dutch originated in the few weeks after the Japanese capitulation. In other words, they were not based on the exploitative nature of colonial society, which had existed for over three centuries. His ire was particularly directed against Indonesian intellectuals who, through their occupations and positions in the colonial government, had come to accept Western culture and who, in this respect, resembled the colonizers most closely. It appears that van Wulfften Palthe felt that a safe distance between the colonizers and the colonized would be one of the most effective ways of maintaining peace and order in the colonies. This view is ironic for a teacher at Batavia's medical faculty; the medical school had been one of the primary institutions in which Western knowledge and values had been transferred to Indonesians.

His explanations offered for the violence of the Indonesian revolution (and earlier violence as well) are culturalist in nature because they refer to essential and unchanging elements in Javanese and Indonesian culture. These explanations are attractive because they repress the cumulative effects of over three centuries of repressive Dutch colonial rule, military pacification actions, and how the Dutch, by enlisting indigenous elites to rule the population, had established an extremely exploitative regime.[56] Such explanations have been pervasive; as Robert Cribb argued, discussing the Indonesian violence in East Timor, "One of the few refreshing features of writing about the massacres in East Timor is that they have not been blamed on Indonesian culture . . . there has been no serious attempt to explain the Timor massacres in terms of the Bratayudha or running amok."[57] In recent years, scholars of Indonesian society have criticized culturalist explanations and have instead proposed analyses emphasizing specific historical circumstances that explain the development of specific forms of violence and the repression of others.[58]

The Dutch psychiatrist's psychoanalytic interpretation of the Indonesian revolution leaves many questions unanswered. Van Wulfften Palthe, for example, did not investigate the narcissistic investment of the Dutch in their colonial subjects and possessions; he only mentioned in passing that they had come to consider Indonesia as their second home and invested the land with feelings of love and affection. He also failed to investigate the frequent violence and cruelty committed by the Dutch in their attempt to maintain their former colonies, even after offering independence during the war and even though international opinion had turned against them. Most of all, he failed to investigate the blatant failure of the Dutch to observe the vibrant and increasingly vocal nationalist movement that clamored for independence decades before the Second World War. The Batavia medical school was known as a hotbed of nationalism; van Wulffthen Palthe must have had extensive interactions with a number of leaders of the Indonesian revolution (which could explain the ire toward them in his writings). It can be argued that, despite the Second World War, the Dutch had not yet relinquished their highly idealized image of *tempo dulu*—the golden period of the colonial era when white and brown had lived in a harmonious colonial family. Because of the trauma of the German and Japanese occupations, the Dutch contrasted an imagined past of colonial peace and harmony with the newly developed political situation in Indonesia. When their colonial dream was brutally disturbed by the struggle for independence, the Dutch encountered Indonesians in a way they had never imagined them to be.

Van Wulfften Palthe's views on bandits and crime are particularly interesting because they constitute one of the main elements of his psychoanalytic interpretation of the Indonesian struggle for independence. His psychoanalytic interpretation of banditry in Java was written when the Indonesian revolution was nearing its end and the transfer of sovereignty from the Netherlands to Indonesia was approaching. In addition, it was written *after* his first psychological analysis of the Indonesian revolution and appears to be an attempt to make sense of its violence by unearthing historical pedigrees. Only a small part of his brochure dealt with banditry before the war; the rest is devoted to the Indonesian struggle for independence. As a consequence, his analysis of bandits greatly overestimated their power and organizational abilities before the war. Bands of bandits did operate in the countryside before the war, but they were much more haphazardly organized and far more opportunistic than he makes them out to be. Because all Indonesian life was rife with superstition, it cannot be too surprising that we see some of that in gangs. Nevertheless, it cannot be argued that magic, a belief in invulnerability, and the use of *ilmus* set bandits apart from the rest of the Indonesian population.

In van Wulfften Palthe's account, the activities of bandits in Java were not related to poverty and economic necessity (or the desire for monetary gain), opportunism (the lack of police power in the areas surrounding Batavia), or a form of resistance against wealthy landowners or the intrusive colonial government. By placing this type of social movement within the realm of the pathological, the criminal, and the insane, he forcefully delegitimized them. In her extensive analysis of the gangs operating in and around Batavia, Margreet van Till concludes that they were far less organized than van Wulfften Palthe claimed and also much less violent (their goal was obtaining goods; they generally avoided killing people).[59] She also emphasizes that superstition did not play an overly important role (not more or less than in other areas at the time).[60] Van Till concludes that the highly sensationalized and paranoid images of criminals and bandits in the Dutch East Indies media were a significant factor in mythologizing them. Van Wulfften Palthe's account appears to have been influenced by these media reports.

Van Wulfften Palthe was the first author to connect the activities of bandits to the Indonesian revolution (although he merely wanted to elucidate the psychological mechanisms that were operative in both). His pamphlet on gangs, which appeared in a series of brochures reporting the lectures held before the (Dutch) Psychiatric-Legal Society, is rather obscure. It is therefore somewhat surprising that it has inspired Benedict Anderson and Robert Cribb in their writings on the Indonesian revolution. In *Gangsters and Revolutionaries*, in which Cribb analyzes the many connections between bandits and revolutionary activities, the connection between bandits and revolutionaries is central.[61] In Anderson's *Java in a Time of Revolution*, van Wulfften Palthe's ideas appear when he emphasizes the importance of bandits and their charismatic leaders, the *jagos*. Anderson states that "the hand-me-down Freudianism tends to mar his argument," but he copies van Wulfften Palthe's emphasis on the charisma of bandits.[62] Both Cribb and Anderson, following van Wulfften Palthe, emphasize the long historical roots of banditry in Java as well as the latter's characterization of the nature of bandits—in particular, their reliance on charms and divination. Van Wulfften Palthe also appears in Eric Hobsbawm's *Bandits*, in the chapter discussing the conditions under which bandits can become part of a revolutionary moment.[63] Interestingly, Hobsbawm uses van Wulfften Palthe's work to analyze how bandits can become revolutionaries, while van Wulfften Palthe's views on the violence of the Indonesian revolution had informed (and distorted) his views on bandits operating before the war, making them precursors for the Indonesian struggle for independence.

The emphasis on the role of the supernatural in van Wulfften Palthe's descriptions of both bandits and the groups fighting in the Indonesian revolution can be interpreted as revealing a deep anxiety, common in colonial empires, for a somewhat indeterminate, unremitting, and menacing "silent force"—a threatening, mysterious, and supernatural force that most often appeared at night and that threatened to undermine colonial society.[64] One familiar figure in Indies colonial literature is that of the rejected *nyai*, or Indonesian housekeeper. Many European men had housekeepers or concubines, who were expelled from the household after the men had accumulated sufficient wealth to marry European women (although at times, they continued to live in the household as servants). In colonial narratives, the jilted *nyai* took revenge by resorting to *guna guna* (black magic), which led either to the death of her former lover or to his blind obedience, as if cast under a spell.[65] In these narratives, sexuality, the primitive, magic, and lethal aggression were inextricably related.

In a similar vein, criminals, crime, and bandits formed highly charged topics that received ample attention in newspapers as well as in colonial novels, serials, and theatrical performances. In colonial life, bandits inspired both fascination and paranoia. Colonial narratives on crime centered on the *jago*, the fighting cock or the charismatic macho bandit who flaunted the colonial order through his cunningness, overpowering sexual appeal, and hypnotic hold on the members of his band. In the narratives on banditry and *jagos*, aggression, the primitive, magic, and sexuality were inextricably related as well. In van Wulfften Palthe's writings on the Indonesian revolution, it appears that the dark and hidden forces that were repressed in colonial life were about to overpower the last vestiges of civilization. The fear of being overwhelmed by the oppressed/repressed was a colonial nightmare; his writings can be seen as an exaggerated expression of the persistent colonial fear of being overpowered by the irrational forces of the colonial unconscious. The only way he felt the Dutch could react was by firmly asserting the control of the colonial ego and forcefully repressing the primitive forces that threatened civilization.

The measures he proposed (repress any congregation of more than three individuals, close all schools and means of public transportation, etc.) probably reflected his earlier military training and were so extreme that he implicitly admitted that the forces of the hordes could no longer be held in check.

Conclusion

In his writings, van Wulfften Palthe presents an account in which amok, crime, collective regression, and the release of primitive and murderous emotions toward the totem are woven together in a theoretical narrative with elements from psychoanalysis, Le Bon's crowd psychology, and psychiatric views on the nature of primitive mentality. By explaining the Indonesian uprising by referring to the nature of Javanese culture and the unbridled aggressive impulses of primitive hordes, he delegitimized the Indonesian demands for independence. By locating the reasons for their resistance in the period of the Japanese occupation, he craftily displaced the anger many Indonesians felt toward the Dutch colonial powers onto the Japanese and repressed the often brutal nature of the Dutch colonial administration. By reducing the subjectivity of Indonesians to a primitive level and by depicting them as primitive savages devoid of reason and led by brutal forces unleashed from unconscious realms, he denied the possibility of any form of meaningful dialogue with the newly established Indonesian government. He discredited the Indonesian intelligentsia by asserting that they had been reduced to irrational brutes as well. In many ways, van Wulfften Palthe regressed to earlier discourses on the nature of Indonesians and repressed the gains made by small groups of progressive Europeans who maintained a dialogue with the leaders of the Indonesian nationalist movement. His analysis appeared to be guided by the wish that the harmonious colonial family could be restored and constitute a firm defense of colonialism at a moment in which its disappearance was a near certainty.

Notes

1. "Bersiap!"—bahasa Indonesia for "Get ready!"—was the call to action heard in villages when Dutch soldiers arrived.
2. Freud, "Totem and Taboo." Van Wulfften Palthe was closely familiar with psychoanalysis and published in psychoanalytic journals. See, for example, van Wulfften Palthe, "Koro."

3. Van Wulfften Palthe's reactions to the Indonesian revolution appear in three publications: "Psychologische Beschouwing omtrent den Huidigen Toestand op Java," *Over het Bendewezen op Java*, and *Psychological Aspects of the Indonesian Problem*, which consists of the English translation of both Dutch articles with some additional commentary.

4. The Indonesian revolution or struggle for independence has been covered in many sources; among them are Anderson, *Java in a Time of Revolution*; Cribb, *Gangsters and Revolutionaries*; Bussemaker, *Bersiap! Opstand in het Paradijs*; Vickers, *History of Modern Indonesia*; and Cribb, *Modern Indonesia*.

5. These ideas have been developed in Gouda, *What's to Be Done with Gender and Post-Colonial Studies*, and Gouda, "Languages of Gender and Neurosis in the Indonesian Struggle for Independence." In the latter article, Gouda provides many illustrations of the pervasiveness of this metaphor in political discussions on the Indonesian struggle for independence. She also discusses van Wulfften Palthe's work extensively.

6. See, for example, Gouda, *Dutch Culture Overseas*, esp. chap. 4, "Native 'Other' as the Medieval, Childlike, and Animal 'Self' (or as Fundamentally Different)"; Breman, *Imperial Monkey Business*; and Alatas, *Myth of the Lazy Native*.

7. See Pols, "Nature of the Native Mind." For an early example of these ideas, see Kohlbrugge, "Psychologische Koloniale Politiek."

8. Sears, *Shadows of Empire*.

9. The biographical information on van Wulfften Palthe is derived from de Langen, "Bij het 25-jarig Hoogleraarschap in de Psychiatrie en Neurologie van Prof. Dr. P. M. van Wulfften Palthe," and from newspaper clippings, biographical information, and articles made available by the Dutch Institute of Military History, Dutch Ministry of Defence.

10. Van Wulfften Palthe, *Zintuigelijke en Psychische Functies Tijdens het Vliegen*.

11. STOVIA stands for School ter Opleiding van Indische Artsen (School for the Education of Indies Physicians). Medical teaching in Batavia commenced in 1851 with a two-year course for vaccinators and was expanded greatly in the early twentieth century. The Faculty of Medicine, which granted degrees equivalent to those granted by medical schools in the Netherlands, was opened in 1927, gradually replacing the STOVIA (which, beginning that year, did not accept any new students but allowed students who had started in previous years to transfer to the medical faculty or to complete their studies). For overviews of medical education in the Dutch East Indies, see Luyendijk-Elshout, *Dutch Medicine in the Malay Archipelago*; de Knecht-van Eekelen, "Tropische Geneeskunde in Nederland en Koloniale Geneeskunde in Nederland-Indië."

12. Most of these articles appeared in the *Geneeskundig Tijdschrift voor Nederlandsch-Indië* (Medical Journal of the Dutch Indies). His most important articles have been collected in van Wulfften Palthe, *Neurologie en Psychiatrie*.

13. The Tjideng camp was located just east of the Koningsplein, later Lapangan Merdeka, in the neighborhood of Tanah Abang (Central Jakarta). For Tjideng and brief references to van Wulfften Palthe's role as physician there, see Kemperman, *De*

Japanse Bezetting in Dagboeken.

14. For the emergency university see: van Wulfften Palthe and Kerstens, *Opening Nood-Universiteit.*

15. Van Loon, "Acute Verwardheidstoestanden in Nederlands-Indie"; van Loon, "Amok and Lattah." For a general overview of psychiatric theories on amok, see Kua, "Amok in Nineteenth-Century British Malaya History."

16. See Pols, "Psychological Knowledge in a Colonial Context."

17. For an analysis of the gendered images of the Dutch for the indigenous population, see Gouda, "Gender and 'Hyper-Masculinity' as Post-Colonial Modernity during Indonesia's Struggle for Independence."

18. Van Wulfften Palthe elaborated on this theory in several places. See, for example, van Wulfften Palthe, "Geestesstoornis en Gemeenschapsstructuur."

19. Ibid., 2066.

20. Ibid., 2067.

21. Van Wulfften Palthe, "Forensische Psychiatrie in Nederlandsch-Indië," 11.

22. For Kraepelin, see Bendick, *Emil Kraepelins Forschungsreise nach Java.* Statements about the nature of the indigenous psyche (the "inlandsche psyche") have been made by Kohlbrugge, van Loon, and Travaglino.

23. See Diriwachter, "Völkerpsychologie."

24. See, for example, Kluckhohn and Murray, *Personality in Nature, Society, and Culture.*

25. Van Wulfften Palthe, "Psychologische Beschouwing omtrent den Huidige Toestand op Java," 425.

26. Ibid.

27. Ibid.

28. Ibid.

29. Ibid., 426.

30. Van Wulfften Palthe, *Over het Bendewezen op Java*, 5.

31. Van Wulfften Palthe, *Psychological Aspects of the Indonesian Problem*, 30–31.

32. Van Wulfften Palthe, "Psychologische Beschouwing omtrent den Huidigen Toestand op Java," 426.

33. Van Wulfften Palthe, *Over het Bendewezen op Java*, 14.

34. Ibid., 15.

35. Carothers, *Psychology of Mau Mau.*

36. Ibid., 15.

37. Van Wulfften Palthe, "Psychological Aspects of the Indonesian Problem," 4119. Van Wulfften Palthe had printed a brochure containing his analysis that was discussed by a group of Dutch intellectuals in Jakarta as part of a group dealing with the future of Indonesia. For the Jakarta discussion group, which ran from 1946 to 1949, see the archive of J. W. Meyer Ranneft, Dutch National Archives, access number 2.21.121, file 486.

38. See Mrázek, *Sjahrir.* For the different approaches of older Indonesian intellectuals, who favored dialogue and diplomacy, and the *pemuda*, who favored armed struggle, see Anderson, *Java in a Time of Revolution.*

39. Van Wulfften Palthe, "Psychologische Beschouwing omtrent den Huidigen Toestand op Java," 427.

40. Ibid., 426.

41. Travaglino had argued the same in the 1920s. See Travaglino, "Politiek en Psychologie."

42. Van Wulfften Palthe, *Psychological Aspects of the Indonesian Problem*, 1.

43. Van Wulfften Palthe, *Over het Bendewezen op Java*, 9.

44. The occupants of the dormitory for the Faculty of Medicine, located at Prapatan 10, became one of the centers of armed resistance against the Dutch. See Engelen et al., *Lahirnya Satu Bangsa dan Negara*.

45. Van Wulfften Palthe, "Psychologische Beschouwing omtrent den Huidigen Toestand op Java," 430.

46. Van Wulfften Palthe, *Over het Bendewezen op Java*, 8.

47. Before the war, there had been sustained criticism of providing a Western-style education to the Indonesian elite. Critics decried the intellectual emphasis of this education, which they felt should be focused on building character instead. See, for example, Nieuwenhuis, *Opvoeding tot Autonomie*.

48. Van Wulfften Palthe, *Psychological Aspects of the Indonesian Problem*, 18–21.

49. The most thorough analysis of both the role of bandits and the way they were represented in the colonial press is van Till, *Batavia bij Nacht*. See also Bussemaker, *Bersiap! Opstand in het Paradijs*; Cribb, *Gangsters and Revolutionaries*; and Nordholt and van Till, "Colonial Criminals in Java."

50. Van Wulfften Palthe, *Over het Bendewezen op Java*, 7.

51. Although Le Bon is not cited explicitly, the title of his main work is. See Le Bon, *Psychologie des Foules*; Le Bon, *Crowd*. See also Nye, *Origins of Crowd Psychology*; van Ginneken, *Crowds, Psychology, and Politics*.

52. Van Till, *Batavia bij Nacht*.

53. Most prominently in Kohlbrugge, *Blikken in het Zieleleven van den Javaan en Zijner Overheerschers*.

54. Van Wulfften Palthe, *Over het Bendewezen op Java*, 7.

55. Pols, "Psychological Knowledge in a Colonial Context."

56. Cribb, "Misdaad, Geweld en Uitsluiting in Indonesië."

57. Cribb, "From Total People's Defence to Massacre," 234.

58. See, for example, Colombijn and Lindblad, "Introduction"; Nordholt, "Genealogy of Violence"; and Colombijn, "What Is So Indonesian about Violence?" These critics consider Benedict Anderson's article on the concept of power in Javanese culture as the most influential recent culturalist explanation of violence in Indonesian culture. See Anderson, "Idea of Power in Javanese Culture."

59. Van Till, *Batavia bij Nacht*.

60. See also the reaction by Meijer, "Over het Bendewezen op Java," which makes similar points.

61. Cribb, *Gangsters and Revolutionaries*. Cribb quotes Van Wulfften Palthe, both *Over het Bendewezen op Java* and *Psychological Aspects of the Indonesian Problem*.

62. Anderson, *Java in a Time of Revolution*, 156n. It should be noted that van

Wulfften Palthe does not employ the term *jago*, which was introduced in a reaction to his original brochure by Meijer, "Over het Bendewezen op Java."

63. Hobsbawm, *Bandits*. Quotes from van Wulfften Palthe's writings appear on p. 99 and p. 102; the description of Javanese bands on p. 52 is entirely derivative of van Wulfften Palthe: "Thus the traditional Javanese 'rampok' band is essentially a group formation of a magical-mystical nature, and its members are united, in addition to other bonds, by the *ilmoe* (elmu), a magical charm which may consist of a word, an amulet, an adage, but sometimes simply personal conviction, and which in turn is acquired by spiritual exercises, meditation and the like, by gift or purchase, or which comes to a man at birth, designating him for his vocation. It is this which makes robbers invisible and invulnerable, paralyses their victims or sends them to sleep, and allows them to fix, by divination, the place, day and hour of their exploits—but also forbids them to vary the plan once it has been divinely determined."

64. The reference to the "silent force" is derived from the famous novel *Hidden Force* by Couperus, which describes the downfall of a European administrator as he becomes entangled in a mysterious web of degeneration and primitive sexuality.

65. Wiener, "Dangerous Liaisons, and Other Tales from the Twilight Zone."

Placing Haiti in Geopsychoanalytic Space
Toward a Postcolonial Concept of Traumatic Mimesis

Of course Freud never speaks of imperialism.
—Gayatri Spivak, *A Critique of Postcolonial Reason*

The patient who develops a symptom on a particular day—whether owing to unrest in San Domingo [Saint-Domingue] or elsewhere—is always inclined to attribute it to his doctor's advice.
—Sigmund Freud, *Studies on Hysteria*

Creolization of the Unconscious

In the introduction to this volume, we ask, to what extent is the psychoanalytic subject, that figure of European high modernism, actually a colonial creature? The ostensible universality of the unconscious, lauded by the surrealists in the slogan "Surrealism is within the reach of the unconscious of the whole world,"[1] is perpetually moved out of reach by the fact that, as Dipesh Chakrabarty puts it, the universal can only exist "as a place holder, its place always usurped by a historical particular seeking to present itself as the universal."[2] Exploration of the globalization of the unconscious targets this transregional "placing" of historical and particular claims for the universality of the unconscious, with the obvious caveat that some "geopsychoanalytic" sites (to quote Jacques Derrida) provide easier access than others.

In "Geopsychoanalysis 'and the rest of the world,'" Derrida reflected that "In Algeria, the country I come from and that I left for the first time only at age nineteen, the psychiatric and embryonically psychoanalytic apparatus was in the main, before the war of independence, an emanation of the apparatus in the 'metropole' . . . African psychoanalysis was European, structured in the deepest way by the colonial state apparatus."[3] Although in this comment, Derrida signals the absence (and implies the repression) of a North African psychoanalytic particular, he indirectly highlights the translational conundrum of claims for the unconscious outside of certain specific forms of twentieth-century coloniality. Colonial discourses determine the legibility not only of psychoanalytic ventures outside of the European metropoles of their emergence but also of departures from them. This paradox is particularly manifest in the fertile research ground of psychoanalysis in India, where, as Christiane Hartnack has noted, Owen Berkeley-Hill and Claude Dangar Daly applied concepts from the work of Sigmund Freud, Ernest Jones, Karl Abraham, and Sándor Ferenczi to provide "scientific justification for British feelings of superiority to an alien people" and "took part in the psychoanalytic activities of Bengali intellectuals," functioning as "a link between them and the International Psychoanalytic Association."[4] Despite the ethnocentrism of the colonial psychoanalytic encounter with India—Freud would write in a thank-you note to Grindrasekhar Bose, "As long as I can enjoy life it will recall to my mind the progress of Psychoanalysis, the proud conquests it has made in foreign countries"[5]—it marks the spot of archives, practitioners and theorists, and texts and countertexts.

A similarly fecund discursive axis is found in the United States and in Argentina and Brazil, where large nineteenth-century *fin-de-siècle* to mid-twentieth-century European emigrations brought psychoanalytic discourses and institutional frameworks. Although the importation of psychoanalysis to Latin America is a complex story, as Mariano Ben Plotkin demonstrates, it became part of the infrastructure of everyday life.[6] This New World migrancy of European medical and cultural discourses and structures was overlaid upon a proto-European civic arena, issued from the print cultures of modernity that Benedict Anderson had attributed to "creole pioneers." Anderson, relying at least symbolically on the particular South American definition of "creole," or *criollo*, as those born in the Americas but of unmixed Iberian descent, identified the defining characteristic of the creole pioneers exemplified by Brazil, the United States, or the former colonies of Spain as their linguistic and genealogical commonality with their former metropoles: "Language was not an element that differentiated them from their respective imperial metropoles. All were shaped by people who shared a common language and common descent with those against whom they fought."[7]

Identifying geopsychoanalytic modalities and continuities in postcolonies with less twentieth-century commonality of European language(s) or descent with former metropoles is more challenging. The Caribbean—notably, where the category of the creole referred to those born in the Caribbean, whether of African or European descent—exemplifies the psychoanalytic outsider status denoted by the International Psychoanalytic Association (IPA) expression "the rest of the world," as quoted in Derrida's article title. In "the rest of the world," no matter how profound the psychic dialogue and dialectics emanating from colonial, indigenous, and diasporan encounters, specific textual traces of a psychoanalytic link remain elusive. Patterns of causality and influence between these parts of the world and psychoanalysis are largely unsounded. These geopsychoanalytic voids include not only Caribbean sites, in which the minority white colonial apparatus had become increasingly disaggregated after abolitions of slavery, such as Jamaica, but also Saint-Domingue, that hugely influential and profitable eighteenth-century colonial space where colonial rule was defeated by former slaves in the early nineteenth century, yielding the singular African diasporan autonomous and largely creolophone state called Haiti.

Although the recent vogue for the application of the concept of "creolization" to anything and everything certainly merits critiques such as Stephan Palmié's "Creolization and Its Discontents,"[8] I will contend here that the Haitian creolization of the unconscious is a legitimate and neglected field of inquiry. Edward Kamau Brathwaite famously defined creolization as "a cultural action—material, psychological, and spiritual—based upon the stimulus/response of individuals within the society to their environment and—as white/black, culturally discrete groups—to each other . . . one group dominant, the other legally and subordinately slaves."[9] For Brathwaite, an essential component of creolization was its mimetic quality, "its attendant imitations and conformities," not only in the form of the "white imitation" in which slaves served as "mimic-men" but also in its "two-way" status because "in white households the Negro influence was pervasive."[10] As Simon Beecroft summarizes, "Creolization is the name for the acknowledged and illicit processes of acculturation and interculturation during the colonial period."[11] Interculturation between the European and creolized scientific/cultural spheres, specifically as it concerns the evolution of the psychoanalytic notion of trauma, is the subject of this chapter. From early medical commentary on an African sleeping sickness, or "hypnosis" (*hypnose*), in Saint-Domingue, to the proposition by American physician Benjamin Rush that slavery in the West Indies produced melancholy and madness, to a decisive late-eighteenth-century creolized unfolding of mesmerism in the colony, to hypnotic modalities in French reactions to the Haitian Revolution and the upheavals of Napoleonic imperialism, to the origins of both psychoanalysis and trauma theory in hypnotic therapy, this chapter will attempt to place Saint-Domingue/Haiti on the geopsychoanalytic map that is being refined throughout this volume.

Although in a literal sense, any application of psychoanalytic models to history predating the late nineteenth century is anachronistic, no school of thought evolves in a vacuum, and psychoanalysis itself helps us to chart mimetic resistances and rivalries in the gestures through which any given school of thought decisively announces its originality and autonomy. History is fair game in the genesis of psychoanalytic constructs. Derrida cautions against privileging "a pure invention of psychoanalysis, that is, . . . a psychoanalysis that one might still dream would have innocently sprung forth already outfitted, helmeted, armed, in short, outside all history, after the epistemological cutting of the cord, as one used to say, indeed, after the unraveling of the navel of the dream."[12]

This nonhermetic model of a historically embedded psychoanalytic discourse and practice allows Anne Harrington, for example, to situate Freudian thought as one landmark in a larger transnational and chronologically expansive field of "the body that speaks": "This strange body stands at the center of a narrative about the dangers of repression and the healing power of confession that I call 'the body that speaks.' It is a narrative that is historically indebted, more than anything else, to the work of Sigmund Freud."[13] Earlier interventions in a culturally diverse history of dynamic psychotherapy unabashedly framed Freud at the forefront of the mind/body historical continuum. In the influential 1981 work *Discovery of the Unconscious*, Henri F. Ellenberger created a chronology moving from a non-Western, nonrationalist, or nonscientific "ancestry" to an implicit contemporary family of dynamic psychotherapy. This past/present organization rather than a contemporaneous cross-sectioning of diverse approaches to the unconscious suggests a teleology in which dynamic psychiatry and psychoanalysis triumph over centuries of "primitive" practices. In this structure, Ellenberger echoed Freud's own tendency to formulate cultural commentary on the hegemony of civilization primarily from the oblique distance of the archeological and anthropological past, as in his comment that Egypt's "imperialism was mirrored in religion as universalism and monotheism."[14] Such temporal abstraction from the global present on Freud's part, coinciding with a tendency to telescope between ancient and modern schemes of individual development,[15] facilitated a range of plausible readings of his subject positioning with regard to modern colonialism. Ranjana Khanna notes that Freud's writings "were never more than ambiguous on the topic of civilization. As Nandy has said, he could be read by the highly colonialist psychoanalyst Berkeley-Hill in India in a manner that would see him as a 'radical critic of the savage,' or by the first Indian analyst Grindrasekhar Bose as 'a subverter of the imperial structures of thought that had turned the south into a dumping ground for the dead and moribund categories of the Victorian era.'"[16]

Proto-Hypnosis in the Torrid Zone

Long before the formal advent of psychoanalysis, the "torrid zone" of the colonies, and especially Saint-Domingue as the richest and most prominent example of an eighteenth-century colony, was fertile ground for theorizing civilization's discontents as psychic disequilibrium. The Saint-Domingue colonist and ethnographer M. L. E. Moreau de Saint-Méry described a prevalent physical disorder uniting "all the extremes of the imagination, that magician of hot climates." The magician of imagination presided over a cultural scene in which "all passions were at play, in continual agitation."[17] Numerous international observers had warned that anyone going to Saint-Domingue should expect to fall prey to pathology, "because the climate change produces a universal revolution" in body and spirit.[18] Slaves were seen as particularly vulnerable to what in today's terms would be viewed as mental health symptoms. Racial inequality and enslavement caused medical observers to begin mapping the bodily expression of psychic pain.

The Saint-Domingue doctor Jean Damien Chevalier noted in 1752 that newly arrived slaves were extremely susceptible to "mal d'estomac" or stomach pain, which he attributed to their unhealthy food rations during the Middle Passage.[19] Jean-Baptiste Thibaut de Chanvalon in 1763, citing Chevalier on the phenomenon, argued instead that expatriation and grief made these African migrants vulnerable to a mal d'estomac characterized by overwhelming languor and hypnotic fatigue, leaving them incapable of movement or work, even when cruelly beaten. Thibaut hypothesized that the cause of this extreme lethargy was "the grief that seizes these free-born individuals, kidnapped from their homes, shackled in vessels like criminals," leading to a distinctive despair.[20] For Thibaut, where whites ardently pursued healing, "death was a matter of indifference to slaves," who had developed the "metempsychosis" that passing into death involved passing back into *Guinen* or Africa, framing ongoing life as, in effect, inevitable.

The Saint-Domingue physician Jean Bathélemy Dazille further developed the notion of a psychic pathology in 1776, noting that slaves were "subject to falling into a state of languor or melancholy that brings them to the point of utter discouragement."[21] Dazille simultaneously associated this melancholy of slavery with banal physical causes, notably parasitic infection. He also saw pathology in the very air breathed by the victims of the claustrophobic Middle Passage. For Dazille, the slaves, stacked body to body in putrid holds, breathed air that was endlessly recycled by the collectivity, ultimately losing its "elasticity" and other properties, leading to a fundamental impoverishment of slaves' health, even at the level of blood and its circulation.[22]

Benjamin Rush, the American physician, signer of the Constitution, and innovator in the treatment of mental illness, contributed to the consideration of slavery as a pathological state in his 1788 article "An Account of the Diseases Peculiar to the Negroes in the West-Indies, and Which Are Produced by Their Slavery" in *American Museum*. Rush described the mal d'estomac common to slaves in the French West Indies as "hipocondriasis."[23] By hypochondriasis, he meant not that the illness was imagined, as it was often fatal, but that it was somatoform rather than induced by poisoning, as colonists often believed: "It occurs soon after their importation, and often proves fatal, with a train of painful and distressing symptoms which are ignorantly ascribed to the effects of slow poison taken by themselves, or given to them by others. This disease, with all its terrible consequences, is occasioned wholly by grief, and therefore stands justly charged upon slavery."[24]

Rush also was interested in frenetic and trance-like affect among slaves as a sign of psychic trauma. He dismissed colonists' insistence that the singing and dancing of slaves was a sign of happiness, arguing instead that it was "an effect of mirth," a mirth framed as melancholic and stoic rather than lighthearted. To explain this concept, Rush described the story of a ship's crew, trapped on a burning vessel near helpless observers. The crew "for a while filled the air with their cries for help and mercy," but at a certain point "there was a cessation of these cries, and nothing was heard on board the vessel but a merry tune on a violin, to which the crew danced with uncommon spirit," until their immolation. This macabre anecdote illustrated for Rush the likelihood that the music and dances of slaves were "physical symptoms of melancholy or madness." He refused to contextualize them in the same category of leprosy or yaws because "they are both common in Africa," whereas he considered this melancholic, mad, or hypochondriac disposition to be a product of slavery in the French West Indies.[25] Rush's emphasis on somatoform and trance-like states framed the enslaved as a demographic situationally prone to altered consciousness with physical symptoms. Slavery was a traumatic state with concrete pathological sequelae. Likewise, in 1851, New Orleans physician Samuel Cartwright would reanimate the Greek association of the runaway slave with madness as "drapetomania, or the disease causing Negroes to run away," to be cured either by providing adequate living conditions or by whipping them "until they fell 'into that submissive state.'"[26] This diagnosis has since been conceptualized as "a disease called freedom."[27]

In 1861, an obscure marine surgeon named Dr. Nicolas, in an article in the *Gazette hebdomadaire de médecine et chirurgie*, would propose a neologism, *hypnose* or "hypnosis" (from the Greek *hypnos* or "sleep") to describe the illness that Chevalier and Dazille had described as "mal d'estomac," and which an increasing corps of colonial doctors now understood to be a sleeping sickness. From the moment of the publication of Dr. Nicolas's disproportionately influential article, the lexifer "hypnose" would then dominate discussion of sleeping sickness in the French domain through the first decade of the twentieth century, although the parasitic illness also concurrently began to appear by its current name, "African trypanosomiasis." Dr. Nicolas's casual renaming of this illness, which, as he noted, had been subject to confusion with severe anemia,[28] would engender a complex interweaving of the psychoanalytic and colonial medical traditions. By 1886, *L'Encéphale*, a "journal of nervous and mental maladies," would typically broach "the sleeping sickness of negroes" in the same breath with "maladies of nervous activity" and with "the symptoms and forms of hypnosis specifically studied in hysterics."[29]

Is the lexical cross-fertilization between a long-observed illness of newly arrived, traumatized slaves, and hypnosis in the early neurological and psychoanalytic tradition purely chance, or does it reveal a hidden but important colonial inspiration for the mechanisms of the unconscious?

Hypnosis, as Leon Chertok and Isabelle Stengers have noted, "constitutes not only, as Freud said, the best proof of the existence of the unconscious, but also the best means for transmitting the narcissistic wound the unconscious inflicts on us."[30] Chertok and Stengers outline the trajectory that led Freud "first to see in the mutative power of hypnosis the expression and the proof that the human psyche eludes ordinary causal categories, and then to abandon hypnosis as an instrument in order to invent the analytic setting, and finally to conclude that the setting did not have the power he had first supposed."[31] It is fascinating, however, that not only could one find statements such as, "Hypnosis is to be observed above all in negroes from the southern part of Africa,"[32] in scientific journals from the early 1860s onward, but that over time scientific writers retroactively inserted the notion of hypnosis into the eighteenth-century colonial medical tradition, as if in the assumption that Nicolas's neologism had been a part of the discussion of slaves' psychic maladies all along. Thus Gustave Reynaud, in his "Epidémiologie de la maladie du sommeil," would claim that in 1732 that the Saint-Domingue doctor Pouppé Desportes (or Pouppée-Desportes) had noted the presence of hypnosis, in the sense of trypanosomiasis, among African slaves in Saint-Domingue.[33] Reynaud posited that early modern observers in the Caribbean ascribed the origins of hypnose to several possible causes, including nostalgia, or slaves' languor in the face of the loss of their homeland; stings by electric rays or "torpedo fish"; and "spells by sorcerers administering poisons."[34] (The latter possible cause, it should be noted, coincides indirectly with the inducement of *zonbi* or zombie-like states in which poison and magic reduce the individual's affect and autonomy to the state of the "living dead.")

This category of pathology in newly arrived victims of the Middle Passage, with its associations with the depressive languor of nostalgia, electric shock by rays (which had been used in ancient times to treat headaches and other maladies), or magical and poisoning practices of taking control of another's spirit, strikingly parallels the "mutative power" of later psychoanalytic constructs of hypnosis and trauma. Hypnosis as sleeping sickness in Africa or in earlier captives emerging into New World slavery developed into a common focus of medical interest precisely at the time that hypnosis in the neuropsychiatric/psychoanalytic domains was gaining attention. Even in a purely medical and ethnographic context, hypnosis had a dual identity as both a sleeping sickness and a phenomenon of melancholy and nostalgia. As Maurice Buret summarized in *Questions diplomatiques et coloniales*, "In the past, the maritime physicians ascribed great importance to the depressive influence of nostalgia. Dr. Carles wrote, 'Hypnosis is a pathology of the *barracons* (warehouses of the slave trade) and of slavery.' 'It is not rare,' Dr. Guérin noted also, 'for the African, far from his wife, to become sad, lost, apathetic, and to contract this cruel illness.' "[35] Reynaud, in his reference to Pouppé Desportes, showed his intuition that hypnosis had a long Caribbean pedigree, even though, to my knowledge, Pouppé Desportes was one of the few medical ethnographers *not* to engage with the problem of slaves' trauma or of neuropathic lethargy among slaves.

The creolization of the unconscious between Europe and the Caribbean thus features, in an overdetermined and chronologically convoluted sense, the putatively psychosomatic epidemiological category that would become known as hypnosis, just before hypnosis became decisively psychoanalytic in its identity.[36] Another thread of this story is Saint-Domingue's prominent association with the mutative power of hypnotic states in both European and African cultural importations.

Mesmerizing Vodou

The complex colonial medical meaning of hypnosis had already been broadened by the creolization of a fundamental precedent to psychoanalysis: mesmerism. As Chertok and Stengers note, "At the end of the eighteenth century, what we now call hypnosis was named 'animal magnetism,' a term created by Franz Anton Mesmer."[37] Ellenberger, picking up an obscure anecdote concerning the establishment in Saint-Domingue of a branch of Mesmer's Société de l'Harmonie, or Harmonian Society, carried out detective work on "the birth, evolution, and vicissitudes of dynamic psychiatry between Mesmer and Charcot, that is, from 1775 to 1893." He began by citing, from the year 1775, "a clash between the physician Mesmer and the exorcist Gassner."[38] Mesmer's theories were dangerously associated in France, according to Karol Kimberlee Weaver, with the erosion of class boundaries between a religious public and a scientific elite.[39] Ellenberger's framing of the homophonies between Mesmer and Johann Joseph Gassner might suggest a categorization of mesmerism as a sideline of exorcism, but instead, he traces the processes through which, in the late nineteenth century, the theories of Mesmer and his followers were integrated "into the official corpus of neuropsychiatry by Charcot and his contemporaries."[40] Key to this trajectory was the importation of hypnotic magnetism to the colony of Saint-Domingue by the naval officer Antoine-Hyacinthe de Puységur.

As James Delbourgo and Nicholas Dew explain in *Science and Empire in the Atlantic World*, mesmerism "became popular among slaveholders, as well as the enslaved, each having their own *baquets* [tubs of magnetized water]." They note that in 1784, "Madame Millet, a respectable French woman settled in Saint-Domingue, recorded the effects of 'animal magnetism' on the inhabitants of the island in the following terms: 'A magnetizer has been in the colony for a while now, and, following Mesmer's enlightened ideas, he causes in us effects that one feels without understanding them. We faint, we suffocate, we enter into truly dangerous frenzies that cause onlookers to worry.'"[41] Ellenberger, in his account of mesmerism in Saint-Domingue, argues summarily that it created a "psychic epidemic" ultimately conterminous with the Haitian Revolution: "In Saint-Domingue, magnetism degenerated into a psychic epidemic among the Negro slaves, increasing their agitation, and the French domination ended in a blood bath. Later Mesmer boasted that the new republic—now called Haiti—owed its independence to him."[42]

Weaver provides the most historically nuanced account of mesmerism in Saint-Domingue, bypassing the established tendency to equate both magnetism and the Haitian Revolution itself with hysteria and noting instead the depth and cosmopolitan variety of healing practices among the enslaved as well as the avid consumption of "popular science" among the colony's privileged classes as preconditions for the rapt reception of mesmerism. Weaver argues that magnetist practices were soon adopted "by enslaved men and women interested in promoting and giving voice to an ideology of rebellion and freedom." By 1786, magnetism "had been forbidden to all those of African descent, free or not," as it had become associated with "jugglers," meaning black "practitioners of spiritual medicine," and with the vodou revolutionaries known as "Macandals," named after François Macandal, the maroon leader who had been executed in 1758 for a plot to overthrow white rule by poisonings.[43] Enslaved mesmerists were brought to trial for allegedly fomenting revolution in assemblies involving magnetism. Weaver concludes that magnetism resembled some vodou religious and healing techniques and was incorporated into the syncretist, mimetic, and cosmopolitan character of vodou. The use of magnetism by the enslaved to carry out healing risked becoming a healing of their enslavement itself through revolutionary decolonization.

The association between mesmerist hypnosis and hypnotic states in vodou is borne out by the contemporaneous adoption in ethnographic writings of a vocabulary of magnetism precisely to describe vodou. Moreau de Saint-Méry noted that a very striking dimension of vodou ceremonies was "the kind of magnetism that leads all those who are assembled to dance until they lose conscious thought."[44] The proof of the force of this hypnotic magnetism was that it affected "even whites spying" on the ceremonies, leaving them trembling and dancing in the assemblies they had come to denounce. Another indirect legacy of colonial mesmerism was the notion of "magnetic sleep," which indirectly linked the axis of sleeping sickness and nostalgia to the discourse of mesmerism.[45]

Channeling Civilization's Discontents in the Individual

Hypnosis and mortal nostalgia among newly arrived slaves, turbulent magnetism among slaves in the years leading up to the Haitian Revolution, and a somatoform Afro-diasporic grief generally are not placed on the same "speaking body" continuum as psychoanalysis because the familial, and inherently bourgeois, psychoanalytic subject is a figure of private Western subjectivity rather than of political collectivities. Chakrabarty contends that colonial, national, and economic life, versus individual psychic life, was only gradually conceptualized as systematically distinct over the course of the nineteenth century: "Accounts of 'strife and conflict in civil society' are gradually shifted to a 'site within the individual itself' until the individual becomes, by the end of the nineteenth century, the more familiar figure whose private self, now regarded as constituted through a history of psychological repression, can be pried open only by the techniques of psychoanalysis."[46]

Although prepsychoanalytic uses of the notion of the unconscious are plentiful, as Nicholas Rand has demonstrated,[47] Eduard von Hartmann's *Philosophy of the Unconscious* (1869), which tied psychic pathology to the problem of suffering in pessimist philosophy by Arthur Schopenhauer and others, was especially influential in articulating the parameters of the production of individuality. (Georges Palente later would summarize the association of pessimism and individualism with palindromic verve: "Does pessimism engender individualism? Does individualism engender pessimism?"[48]) Von Hartmann was dedicated to the principle of individualist unity but also eager to avoid the conflation of unities with individualism: "Every individual is a unity, but not all unities are individual." This distinction applied especially, for von Hartmann, to what he viewed as the deceptive rhetoric of physical or psychological continuity between metropole and colony: "Thirdly and lastly, the fact that a country lives off the products of its colonies, and that its colonies in their turn live off the products of the art of the *mère-patrie*, in an obvious reciprocity of action, does not mean, no matter how extensive the rapport may be, that the colonies and the *mère-patrie* should be regarded as a single individual."[49] The psychology of a colony and a metropole elude theorization for von Hartmann, regardless of their psychological and material imbrication.

Occasionally in the late nineteenth-century context, colonial expansion itself was explored in relation to the unconscious, primarily as a means of justifying rather than critically assessing European "transformism." The *Revue rose* noted, for example, that Jean Marie Antoine de Lanessan, in his 1886 work *L'Expansion coloniale de la France*, saw in settler colonialism "an unconscious movement of humanity, determined by evolution."[50] Ethnographic writings in some instances also pursued the parallelism between African diasporan spiritualist/healing practices and psychoanalytic diagnostic and curative constructs. One criminologist noted—in derisive terms—the parallelism between discourses of hypnosis and hysteria in Europe and occult practices in the colonies, not to suggest a continuum of psychic experience but rather a coincidence between colonial and early modern European magical thinking: "Blacks, continually attributed occult powers, end up believing that they possess them. In the colonies, people experience suggestive states analogous to hypnosis and hysteria, which bear similarity to the well-known phenomena of the sixteenth and first half of the seventeenth century in France."[51]

The next element of creolized interculturation of the unconscious that I will address in this chapter is the traumatic and hypnotic response— often a "mesmerized" response—of the colonial world to the radical power ruptures inherent to the successful decolonization of Haiti by its African diaspora.

Nineteenth-Century Postcoloniality and the Trauma of History

Unforeseen adversity is like the torpedo fish: it jolts you and then numbs you: the light that flashes before your eyes is nothing like the light of day. People, objects, facts, unfurl before you in a fantastic manner, moving as if in a dream . . . If this violent position of the soul is prolonged, it deranges the mind's equilibrium and becomes madness, . . . life becomes no more than a vision for the sufferer, a vision which he himself haunts like a ghost.

—Victor Hugo, *Bug-Jargal*

The role of Haiti in the creolization of the unconscious is best understood against the background of France's entry into the nineteenth century in a state of double postrevolutionary trauma. The reforms of the French Revolution had severely tested cultural identity, political solidarity, and economic viability within continental France. It had destabilized the forces of tradition and heritage that Edmund Burke would champion as fundamental rights in his conservative critique of the event.[52] By the time the young Corsican-born military hero Napoleon Bonaparte seized power in 1799, revolution was devolving into a discordant jumble of correctives and compensations. At the same time, another revolution was unfolding outside of the hexagonal boundaries of France—and this parallel revolution challenged the most radical principles of 1789 as insufficient and abortive.

In Saint-Domingue, through a concatenation of often contradictory rebellions and extensions of revolutionary claims, Toussaint Louverture and other important military leaders from the slave camp had seized emancipation and political power while retaining French colonial status. But Napoleon, who famously interpreted his own person as the locus of continuing revolutionary action and ideology after 1799, became determined to regain control of Saint-Domingue. By the end of 1803, the massive French expedition launched to quell revolution in Saint-Domingue, led by Napoleon's brother-in-law Charles-Emmanuel Leclerc, had failed. Recognizing defeat just before the proclamation of the independence of Saint-Domingue, renamed Haiti, on January 1, 1804, France sold Louisiana, in part to make up for the crippling cessation of colonial revenues.[53] In May 1804, Napoleon's founding of the French Empire signaled not only the will to suppress the significance of the defeat of French dominance in Haiti but also a refusal to articulate the traumatic legacies of a revolution that had on a certain level been too radical in metropolitan France and not radical enough in the colonial culture of slavery. Napoleon was central to the evolution of this incoherent postrevolutionary condition of France in the dual arenas of the Hexagon (continental France) and Haiti, through his triumph in the former and his loss in the latter.

Postcoloniality in the French-speaking world was thus coterminous

with a postrevolutionary modernity immediately reconfigured as imperialist modernity. The French/Haitian revolutionary double—a double
that internally represented a sort of revolutionary civil war fought not so
much over the content of Enlightenment emancipation ideology as over
its sources and audiences and beneficiaries, its sphere of applicability, and
its location of agency—yielded to the binary couple of an emerging postcolonial and imperialist French modernity.

The concept of early nineteenth-century postcoloniality parallels the
problem of anachronism in attempts to chart prepsychoanalytic developments of the unconscious in the Caribbean. The term "postcolonial" was
not used at the time, and postcolonial theory, as a dialectical movement
marked by poststructuralism, which undeniably first emerged as a philosophical and political discursive apparatus for new engagement with—or
from—the vast swathes of the world that were decolonized in the twentieth century, obviously did not yet exist. But the late twentieth-century
emergence of postcolonial theory should not, as Ania Loomba points out,
be conflated with the actual temporal parameters of the postcolonial:
"Formal decolonization has spanned three centuries, ranging from the
eighteenth and nineteenth centuries in the Americas, Australia, New Zea-
land and South Africa, to the 1970s in the case of Angola and Mozam-
bique."[54] There is, in fact, a two-way chronological valence to the risk
of anachronism because in the twenty-first century, postcolonial theory
without reference to the Haitian Revolution is vulnerable to charges of
anachronism in its turn. As Nick Nesbitt puts it, "Two of the processes
that came to distinguish the twentieth-century were invented in Haiti: decolonization and neo-colonialism."[55] For Frantz Fanon, the Haitian Revolution was such an exalted example of anticolonial agency that any political and psychological resolution of twentieth-century black alienation
would first require acknowledgment by the alienated that "I am not *only*
responsible for the revolt in Saint-Domingue."[56] The Haitian Revolution highlights a long continuum of discourses and actions generated
against colonialism by those subjugated within colonialism, independent
of the self-conscious discursive products of postcolonialism as a named
phenomenon.

The problem of Haiti's precocious postcoloniality intersects with the
problem of a prepsychoanalytic creolization of the unconscious, in that
French and Haitian accounts of this historical upheaval have a strongly
hypnotic quality and even refer, as in the excerpt at the beginning of this

section from Victor Hugo's novel on the Haitian Revolution, to the local continuum of mechanisms of neurological shock or pathology, such as the electric ray or torpedo fish. Romantic-era literature about the violent events in Saint-Domingue is singularly marked by interracial relationships organized around intense identifications, doublings, and rivalries. In *Bug-Jargal*, the young white protagonist filters all the violence of the slave insurrection through the problems of his simultaneous rivalry, attachment, and debts to a slave leader. The discordance of his pronounced ideological racism with these new power hierarchies and unexpected philosophical and human bonds is sufficiently raw and intense to create a dissociative split in subjectivity, exemplified by his inability to recognize his rival and the slave leader as one and the same man rather than two distinct individuals. The narrator muses that the "extraordinary events" and "catastrophes" of the time are like the shock of the ray. The "repose of the soul" is shattered by the contact with the fish, which "jolts you and then numbs you: the fearful light that flashes before your eyes is nothing like the light of day."[57] The power of shock and a kind of hypnotic paralysis of perception represent, for Hugo, the trauma of the Haitian Revolution.

As in Hugo's account of the young colonist's trauma, the traumatic sequelae of Haiti's decolonization make postcoloniality applicable to the vanquished colonial power as well as to the victorious decolonizing power, to France as well as Haiti. For the former colonial power, the overthrow of its rule "also specifies a transformed historical situation, and the cultural formations that have arisen in response to changed political circumstances."[58] Although Patricia Crone argues that "imperial trauma" is a paradoxical construct, in that the powerlessness experienced by the powerful can in no way be conflated with the powerlessness of the powerless, the sudden fall from power of French colonizers in the Haitian Revolution was an obvious blow to French imperial identity and projects.[59] In this sense, virtually all empires would end in the trauma of their disintegration, but Saint-Domingue was distinguished by its drastic metamorphosis from star colony to precocious postcolony, like a rare astronomical event.

The question of whether we can read history as trauma, despite the individual arena of the psychoanalytic paradigm of trauma, has been explored in considerable detail in recent years. Philosophies of history often employ rhetoric suggestive of a link between the undefended experience of historical change and trauma, experience exemplified by accounts of the shock of the Haitian Revolution. As Joseph Flanagan notes, the momentous upheavals that make up history have been equated by Walter Benjamin with memory "as it flashes up in a moment of danger" and by Fredric Jameson with "whatever hurts."[60] The shocks that "make history" but threaten to undo its narration parallel the temporary disabling or splintering of the traumatized subject's cognitive apparatus, in which the formation of memory is damaged. In post-traumatic stress disorder, the traumatic experience manifests itself not through the hindsight of a coherent recollection but through dissociated flashbacks, hypervigilence, and other symptoms. This symptomatic rather than narrative revisiting of the past has been seized by critics, according to Flanagan, "as a means of understanding the elusiveness of historical knowledge more generally."[61]

History denotes an extrasubjective, extraindividual domain, despite the inextricability of subjective individual experience from it. The critical analogy between trauma and history rests partly on the hypothesis that through the breaching of defenses in the trauma, the "otherness" of the historical real intrudes without being thoroughly filtered by cognition and subjectivity. The traumatized subject is a broken vessel into which the real spills. "The outside has gone inside," as Cathy Caruth states, "without any mediation."[62]

For Caruth, this triumph of the referential, admittedly in aporetic form, can be transmitted socially. It can even be transmitted transgenerationally, to the point that it cannot be pinned down as the issue of a given individual's psychic processing. Instead, it circulates more broadly, as dissociated historical residue, and comes to function as historical legacy. In this paradigm, trauma is in a genetic relation to history and its unstable narratives; one could also say that traumatic memory, rather than memory *tout court*, provides an alternative epistemological model to history. Yet, a psychoanalytic paradigm of social history is paradoxical, as Sibylle Fischer reminds us, because the psychic effects associated with history by trauma theorists are also present in the conventional constitution of the neurotic: "Surely, shock, trauma, and neurotic fantasies are not the exclusive domain of the victims of history . . . many critics who claim to have successfully developed the relation between psychoanalysis and social history run into serious difficulties in this regard." Reading history as trauma can become tautological, Fischer cautions, if trauma in turn is seen as giving rise to history.[63]

A French writer who, as a teenager, experienced the upheavals of the revolutionary Caribbean in 1802, Marceline Desbordes-Valmore described witnessing the yellow fever epidemic, in which her own mother died, and insurrection and reprisals by blacks and colonists—" blacks locked in iron cages"[64]—in terms of the instability of an earthquake: "Terror chased me from this moving island. An earthquake a few days earlier had thrown me onto the bed while I was standing before a little mirror, braiding my hair. I feared the walls, the sounds of the leaves, the air."[65] Once on board a ship, sun, fog, and phantoms clouded her consciousness of the difference between the real and the imaginary: "Later, beset during the long crossing by an ardent sun one moment and cold fog the next, I could do nothing but listen to the voices of the new phantoms that passed before my eyes. Were they real or imaginary? Who knows?" The unfiltered intrusion of revolutionary reality leaves her permanently distrustful of history, which had impacted her but was inaccessible precisely to the degree of its impact: "Are we truly certain of what is real when we believe we are writing history?"[66]

The traumatic destabilization of historical subjectivity in France in relation to the Haitian Revolution in effect provides a continuum of locations of the unconscious in relation to slavery, and then represses its traces.

Hypnotic Imperialism

The destabilized real of traumatic history puts hypnotic identification—identification with the power of the rebellious slave on the one hand and with the power of Napoleon on the other, with the power of Napoleon against the slave and the power of the slave against Napoleon—at the center of the postcolonial conditioning of French and Haitian historical subjectivities in the era of the nineteenth-century "invention" of a certain culturally recognized discourse of imperialism.

As the subject of hypnotic identifications and projections, it is worth noting that Napoleon, who came to stand as the human symbol of the imperial, was born on the wrong side of imperial power. He was a native of Corsica, annexed in 1768 as a kind of consolation prize after the consecration—through the 1763 Treaty of Paris—of the loss of many of the French colonies. The autarchic island resisted its French nationality but was conquered militarily in 1769. Napoleon was an independence fighter prior to his rupture with the independence leader Paoli. After this falling out, he went on to suppress (in 1796) the independence movement in what Eugen Weber has called "the colonial wilds of Corsica."[67] But at the start of his military career, Napoleon had been bitterly critical of the

French annexation of Corsica. François-René de Chateaubriand documented written testimonials of the young Napoleon's anger at the French subjugation of his people: "I was born while my fatherland perished. Thirty thousand Frenchmen were vomited onto our coasts, drowning the throne of liberty in pools of blood."[68] During the months in which French revolutionary ideology fomented in 1789, Napoleon was still militating against France in terms not inconsistent with Fanon's psychology of militant anticolonialism: "While France is being reborn, what will we become, poor unfortunate Corsicans? Ever servile and debased, will we continue to kiss the insolent hand that holds us down?"[69] It is a productive enigma that it would be this resistant colonized subject of France who would attempt not only to reverse revolutionary abolition but also to colonize the colonizers in a vast European conquest; mastering the masters without freeing the unfree.

Napoleon is indelibly associated with the meaning and history of imperialism as it was recognized by the European public long after the demise of Napoleon's own empire, specifically at the time of the greatest European imperial expansion, in the second half of the nineteenth century. Robert Young argues that when the term "imperialism" came into common usage in political speech in England, it was, like the related term "Caesarism," "a derogatory term to describe the political system of the Second French Empire under Napoleon III."[70] It apparently had first been used by Karl Marx to describe the mimetic continuum of bellicose nationalism from the empire of Napoleon Bonaparte to the Second Empire, under Louis-Napoleon. It was supplemented by the term "Soulouquerie," which critiqued Napoleonic ideology in relation to the much-caricatured second Haitian emperor, Faustin Soulouque I, who ruled from 1849 to 1858.[71]

How had Napoleon's Haitian defeat affected the evolution of Napoleonic imperialism? There seems to be little doubt that the victory of the slaves in Haiti quickly became a taboo in representations of the French state. In French historical consciousness, as Francis Arzalier notes, "The hyperbolic image of a victorious Napoleon became, over the course of the nineteenth and twentieth centuries, one of the foundational myths of French nationalism. Anything having to do with the problematic expedition [to Haiti] was suppressed, because it utterly contradicted this myth."[72] Christopher Miller, in "Forget Haiti," queries, "Cultural memory is a topic that has been much discussed in recent years, but what about forgetting?"[73] The forgetting of French participation in the slave trade in general has recently become a public political issue through the media interventions of Patrick Chamoiseau and other francophone and French scholars and activists, but Françoise Vergès suggests that the Haitian Revolution had a special role in what Miller calls French postcolonial "mnemopsychosis": "The Haitian Revolution, its violence, and its excesses allow Europe to justify its role as ruler of the world."[74] In the realm not of state history but of colonial memoirs, however, Miller demonstrates that in the first part of the nineteenth century, "France was having a hard time forgetting its former colony and letting it go," as evidenced by a flood of "narratives of the 'crime, tortures, and devastations' of the revolution [which] perpetuated a one-sided view of France as purely a victim in the Haitian Revolution."[75]

In the same nineteenth-century postrevolutionary era in which a process of traumatic rememoration and postcolonial forgetting was being elaborated between Haiti and France, the colonial power subverted in Saint-Domingue was being replaced with an ideology of imperial power initially redirected against the other European powers themselves. After the final defeat of Napoleon at Waterloo and his imprisonment and death on the island of St. Helena, the next major French imperial venture was the conquest of Algeria, beginning in 1830 and culminating in 1847, characterized by an ideology of metropolitan expansion in regions defined by cultural otherness. Although smaller colonial/imperialist ventures occurred throughout the nineteenth century, including some failed ventures, such as Louis Napoleon's investment in Mexico, a new era of overwhelming French imperialist expansion began after the 1870 defeat of the French (involving the traumatic breaching of boundaries and actual invasion of France) in the Franco-Prussian war. The 1880s were the scene of a larger and more generalized European "scramble for Africa," accompanied by an elaborate discourse of the "civilizing mission" in the colonies and tied in France to the psychology of territorial violation. Throughout nineteenth-century France, national defeat and the rise of imperial ambition are peculiarly dialectical, a cycle unleashed in Saint-Domingue. Traumatic imperialism in the context of nineteenth-century France thus denotes an imperialism born of trauma as well as the trauma born of imperialism.

Traumatic Mimesis

The genealogy of psychoanalytic trauma in the late nineteenth century begins with hypnosis, as Ruth Leys has noted: "Hypnosis, or hypnotic suggestion, was the means by which Charcot legitimated the concept of trauma by proposing that the hysterical crises that he suggestively induced in his patients were reproductions of traumatic scenes." Not only did Charcot rely on the suggestive induction of crises meant to mimic patients' traumatic experiences, but Charcot also saw a basic hypnotic suggestivity in traumatized patients. "The tendency of hypnotized persons to imitate or repeat whatever they were told to say or do," explains Leys, "provided a basic model for the traumatic experience."[76] As we know, the debts of trauma to hypnosis also go further back in history to Mesmer, and thus, by extension, to Saint-Domingue: "At the end of the eighteenth century, what we now call hypnosis was named 'animal magnetism,' a term created by Franz Anton Mesmer . . . both hypnosis and magnetism have had troubled relations with scientific reason."[77]

The applicability of trauma theory to historical inquiry is especially complicated, according to Leys, by a fundamental tension in the history of its definition that is inseparable from hypnosis: the question of whether trauma has an imitative or mimetic character. Mesmerism also has a longstanding relationship with imitation; Chertok and Stengers point out that Antoine Lavoisier's scientific commission to investigate mesmerism at the behest of Louis XVI concluded that mesmerism operated via "the combined action of imitation, imagination, and touch."[78] Allan Young, in Laurence J. Kirmayer, Robert Lemelson, and Mark Barad's *Understanding Trauma*, casts the relation of both trauma and hypnosis to mimesis as an abandonment or loss of autonomy: "There are instances of mimesis— clinical suggestion, hypnosis, and possession, for instance—in which a performer abandons his autonomy and submits himself to someone else's design. The phenomenon of clinical transference, as it is described by psychoanalysts, is likewise a mimetic performance."[79]

Virtually all definitions of trauma concur that it represents what Leys calls an "originary invasion" that lets the other—the aggressor, or simply the radically unexpected—past protective barriers.[80] But is the postinvasion relationship with this traumatic otherness governed by the pull of imitation, internalization, and extreme openness, or by rejection, antimimeticism, and quasi-autistic hermeticism? For Leys, the question of mimesis arises in relation to the potentially hypnotic experience of this invaded relationship. Hypnosis frames this unconscious mimetic turn within trauma: "Trauma was defined as a situation of dissociation or 'absence' from the self in which the victim unconsciously imitated, or identified with, the aggressor or traumatic scene in a condition that was likened to a state of heightened suggestibility or hypnotic trance."[81] (Throughout Leys's work, imitation and identification are presented as essentially equivalent, but imitation seems to be a more performative, actional dimension of identification.) Trauma described an experience of abject and unconscious—even disabled—identification: "Trauma was therefore understood as an experience of hypnotic imitation or identification . . . an experience that, because it appeared to shatter the victim's cognitive-perceptual capacities, made the traumatic scene unavailable for a certain kind of recollection."[82] Leys, following the work of Philippe Lacoue-Labarthe[83] and Jean-Luc Nancy[84] on abject and "bad" mimesis, coined the expression "traumatic mimesis" (which I had simultaneously coined to describe a "politics of likeness" that "has come to function instead as a social wound"[85]) to describe the unconscious and traumatic identification with violence.

Conceptualizations of trauma as a mimetic dynamic threaten idealizations of the dichotomy between "the autonomous subject and the external trauma" that underpin many readings of historical trauma.[86] (This idealization of trauma's externality was exemplified in the controversy over Freud's interpretation of sexual abuse memories as fantasy, which many critics perceived as a form of blaming the victim of universally real abuses.) In the mental health fields, competing antimimetic theories evolved, framing trauma as an external event "coming to a sovereign if passive victim" and privileging "individual autonomy and responsibility."[87] In literature, narratives of trauma that specifically valorize trauma, such as what the twentieth-century subgenre Naomi Morgenstern calls the "neoslave narrative," have tended to repress the mimetic dynamics of trauma in favor of a clear delineation of the politics of victimization.[88]

According to Leys, antimimeticism within the mimetic paradigm traditionally has informed discontinuities of therapeutic treatment: "The therapist's demand that the patient *be a subject* capable of distancing herself from the traumatic scene—is simultaneously the moment when the emphasis tends to shift from the notion of trauma as involving a mimetic yielding of identity to identification to a notion of trauma as a purely external cause or event."[89] She does not contest this discontinuity, however, concluding that "intelligent, humane, and resourceful pragmatism" is justified in therapeutic response to the controversies in trauma theory.[90] Elsewhere, Leys implies that the poles of mimesis and antimimesis in the genealogy of trauma theory legitimately arise within the individual subject as well. In some cases of post-traumatic stress disorder after military combat, for example, "the asocial traumatized soldier who is so antimimetically withdrawn from the world that he is completely numb to it is simultaneously so socially identified with it that the boundaries between himself and others are completely effaced." Traumatic reaction involves both "binding" and "unbinding," "the success of protection and the breaching of the protective shield—antimimesis and mimesis."[91]

Transgenerational transmissibility and extraindividual historical circulation have been privileged within antimimetic conceptualizations of trauma, even though logically, that free-floating quality, as Leys points out, could just as well blur the externality of traumatic events and the absoluteness of victim/aggressor historical distinctions. In effect, whereas antimimetic theories of trauma have an implicit vocation of discerning historical responsibility and fighting impunity, they also have the potential to turn the "'cries' of the Jews into testimony to the trauma suffered by the Nazis."[92] By contrast, mimetic theories of trauma lay the groundwork for studying victim and aggressor as different historical moments—or more often, as imbricated historical moments—of an unfolding continuum of traumatic causality and effect within which, like the question of which came first, the chicken or the egg, origins migrate. As such, the idea of traumatic mimesis is especially useful in analyzing the messy "hurtfulness" of history, the repetitions of violence in which hypnotic identifications come to bind aggressors and victims, even as it raises the specter of relativism in assessing historical responsibility.

Leys's paradigm of trauma as a field inevitably constructed around irreducible tension between mimetic and nonmimetic identification is particularly applicable to theorization of nineteenth-century postcoloniality, in which victims (Napoleon as colonized subaltern) and abusers (Napoleon as determined suppressor of a movement of decolonization) often overlap. (Another example is the "neocolonial" perpetuation of race-based hierarchies by former revolutionary leaders in independent Haiti.) This contrasts with the dynamics of twentieth-century postcolonial theory, which, like feminism and other identity-politics-based movements, arguably was identified with straightforwardly antimimetic ideologies of historical trauma. As Tejumola Olaniyan has summarized, at its height, postcolonialism functioned almost "as an open warrant to rifle through the history of Empire—before, during, and after—*from the perspective of the victims."*[93] Nineteenth-century postcoloniality was the legacy of a single historical rupture within the global fabric of conscious and unconscious dominions. It did not entail a system of generally privileged identifications of those oppressed by empire, although it did open new possibilities of European identification with its cultural others. Within nineteenth-century postcoloniality, imperialism, as a hegemonic machine, was not yet fully conceptualized as an "external" cause of trauma, to the point that abolitionists such as Lamartine, who represented slavery as a prototraumatic experience, were often in favor of colonialism without slavery. Nineteenth-century identifications and counter-identifications with colonial power and with revolt on the part of the colonized had a political as well as a traumatic fluidity.

Traumatic mimesis is useful in reading nineteenth-century postcoloniality in Saint-Domingue as inextricable from episodes of extraordinary violence against virtually all involved parties, from the burning and pillaging by slaves beginning on August 22, 1791, to the execution of blacks by man-eating dogs under the rule of French General Rochambeau. Joan Dayan comments, "The last years of the revolution in Saint-Domingue are recognized by most historians, no matter their bias, as unparalleled in brutality."[94] For the colonists, who represent the traumatizing aggressors in their role as slaveholders, violent decolonization was no doubt all the more shocking because of the agency seized by persons who had been treated as, and traded as, things. As Dayan notes, slaves were "legally divested of their selfhood," and "legally, their being was a 'being for others.'"[95] The "unthinkable" quality of the defeat not only of the French metropole but also of Napoleon, by a population previously defined only by its use value to the French, was sufficiently overwhelming to create disturbances of memory and identification on the part of the French. The lack of a reality principle in the compulsive imperialism developed by Napoleon was an index of this intrusion of a traumatic reality in Saint-Domingue—a replacement of the memory of defeat with ever-escalating aggression against the state life of other collectivities.

Black and White Napoleons

A paradigmatic example of the identificatory confusion—the mimetic binding and unbinding of the French with the revolutionary leaders of Saint-Domingue—is Chateaubriand's contextualization in *Memoirs from Beyond the Tomb* of Toussaint Louverture as the object of a fatal mimetic cathexis on the part of Napoleon: Toussaint is "the black Napoleon, imitated and killed by the white Napoleon."[96] The trope of the black Napoleon, which had been suggested, if not spelled out, as early as 1803 in anti-Napoleonic media, contains a simple analogy: Toussaint Louverture is like Napoleon.[97] But in 1848, Chateaubriand gave it an additional half twist, making Napoleon, in the light of the existence of the black Napoleon, into the white Napoleon. The white Napoleon is the murderous imitator of the man who is ostensibly his derivative double.

The trope of the black Napoleon suggests that Napoleon as an identity is already in place, allowing secondary identifications with that preexisting Napoleonic identity, or Napoleonism. But if being the white Napoleon is an effect of murderous imitation, white Napoleonism suddenly becomes secondary to the already-secondary identification of black Napoleonism. Somewhere in the discursive construction of the analogy between Toussaint and Napoleon, Chateaubriand seems to have come to view Napoleonism as a secondary effect of the analogical identification rather than the point of departure for it. Chateaubriand's establishment of a circular identification and counteridentification of Napoleon and Toussaint creates a space of irremediable invasion of identity.

Elsewhere in *Memoirs*, Chateaubriand applies the same construct of invaded identity to his own experience of the imperial fluctuation of geopolitical boundaries under Napoleon. Chateaubriand describes imperialism as a structure resembling Nelson Goodman's paradigm of mimetic worldmaking,[98] with new imperialist worlds inevitably made over existing worlds, beginning with Columbus. (As Chateaubriand writes, "Columbus created a world."[99]) In the case of Napoleon's worldmaking, Chateaubriand is obsessed with how the people already inhabiting the worlds he remakes are then caught up in the phenomenology of Napoleon's existential manipulations. "Napoleon shakes up empires," Chateaubriand writes. "The whole world was mixed up with him." Napoleon is "universal" here, in the sense that as the agitator of empires, all the earth is mixed up with him, not *like* him, but forcibly drawn into the same Napoleon-controlled text. The borders of the Napoleonic world change constantly and literally: "The Napoleonic world wasn't yet set; its limits changed with the rising and ebbing tides of our victories."[100]

Not only do people inhabit the worlds of Napoleon's remaking, but he also inhabits them: "He began to grow into our very flesh; he broke our bones."[101] In this formulation, Chateaubriand indicates that as the leader

of unceasing waves of imperialist military ventures, Napoleon lived symbi-
otically or parasitically in the flesh of a nation of soldiers whose bodies
he would break in the expansion of his empire. Through his mobiliza-
tion of "great movements," his stirring the pot of the Western world,
Napoleon made the displacement of immigration and exile a "universal"
condition.[102] His tyranny was literally overwhelming; it "enveloped" Chateaubriand like "another solitude," creating a subjectivity of imperialist
melancholy, an inner empire to which not only Chateaubriand but a generation of romantics would be subjected. Above all, Napoleon, however
mysteriously, was "the executor of the social intelligence all around him:
an intelligence that unheard of events, extraordinary perils, had developed."[103] Napoleon imitates existing models of power into new existence,
appropriating them as appendages of his imperial identity. He grossly
forges a real world of imperial dreams, as in Jorge Luis Borges's parable of
the colonial map that actually materializes the territory it charts.

The ultimate effect of Napoleon's making of new historical worlds for
Chateaubriand is a stunning inability to tell oneself apart from the world
of contemporary history. "Did you hear the Empire fall?" asks Chateaubriand, hauntingly, when he picks up in book three some years after where
he had left off book two in January 1814. No, he reflects; its fall would have
been silent for the reader who had not lived these events, even though the
empire collapsed with a great crash of historical stone and dust into Chateaubriand's personal life: "But the Empire did collapse; its immense ruins
crumbled into my life."[104] Having been made into the New World of the
Napoleonic Empire, his own world had become a *mise en abyme* of that
worldmaking.

For Chateaubriand, the trauma of empire binds subjects into its drastic
reconfigurations, shattering individual autonomy. Empire is associated
with a shocking and traumatic mimesis, a mimesis in which the subjects of
the emperor lose themselves to identification with his expansions. The
emperor himself becomes emblematic of that mimesis, an alter ego of the
rivals who have been oppressed by his power but who, through their
mimetic identifications with him, can successfully appropriate his mimetic power.

Traumatic mimesis in the nineteenth-century Haitian/French postcolonial domain shows the degree to which colonial trauma becomes
internalized both as damage and as creation identification and counter
identification. Postcolonies such as Haiti are left in the vulnerable position

of having to unlearn not only the hypnotic patterns of racist authoritarian abuse, but also the very ways they have learned to learn. It is a motif by which we can ponder the psychoanalytic paradox of the postscript scrawled by the former slave and revolutionary leader Toussaint Louverture—the black Napoleon—in his 1802 prison memoir, addressed to the French leader who had imprisoned him, Napoleon Bonaparte (the white Napoleon): "Gairice mes plai illé tre profound, vous seul pouvé porter les remède saluter et lanpéché de ne jamai ouvrir, vous sète médecin" (Heal my wounds [sic], it is very deep, only you can apply the healthful remedies and prevent it from ever reopening, you are a doctor).[105]

Literature from the romantic era in France presented history in Saint-Domingue as something that needed to be "cured." In Claire de Duras's 1823 novella *Ourika*, the young Senegalese-born heroine learns of the "massacres in Saint-Domingue" with what is described as a new and searing sensation of pain, and she suddenly has a sense of "belonging to a race of barbarous murderers." Shortly afterward, an acquaintance's racist sneer imprints itself in her psyche to the point that "it stood before me like my own reflection."[106] She internalizes this racist gaze and becomes phobic about her own skin. After taking the veil in a convent, she falls into a state of mortal languor. When the young doctor who comes to treat her comments that "it's the past we must cure," it is not clear whether this refers to Ourika's own past or the historical past of the Haitian Revolution and its metropolitan reception.

In Alphonse de Lamartine's 1851 work "Toussaint Louverture," Albert, one of Toussaint's sons, virtually a political hostage of the French government during his metropolitan "education," paradoxically develops a passionate filial attachment to Napoleon Bonaparte. At the same time that his father is developing an ever-stronger rivalry with Napoleon, Albert is developing an impassioned colonial family romance, coming to see Napoleon as "father, mother, race, and nation."[107]

For Hugo, Duras, Lamartine, and Chateaubriand, Haiti represented a field of conflictual identifications in which imitative cathexis and benumbed asociality mutually dominated traumatic subjectivity. The contribution of colonial culture in Saint-Domingue to European developments in hypnotic therapeutic techniques and subsequently to hypnosis-influenced psychoanalytic constructs of trauma arguably manifests a creolization of the unconscious that is simultaneously the unconscious of creolization—a lack of European consciousness of the influence of African diasporan

practices and colonial interculturation. The Haitian Revolution, representing the first major reversal of an established modern colonial power,
yielded literary discourses that prefigured psychoanalytic ideas of trauma
against the backdrop not of childhood development and familial neurosis
but of colonial relations. A (post)colonial concept of traumatic mimesis
helps to situate Haiti in geopsychoanalytic time and space, not only far
from, and before, nineteenth-century *fin-de-siècle* Vienna and Paris, but
also omnipresent as the specter of the return not of the repressed but of
the oppressed.

Freud's Haiti

Freud did refer, once, to Saint-Domingue in the context of his theorization
of hypnosis and hysteria. This quintessentially enigmatic allusion epito-
mizes the oblique presence of the colonies in Freudian thought. Describing his treatment of his patient Fanny Moser, who contended that she became depressed after taking physician-prescribed baths, Freud recorded
the following dialogue:

> Afterwards I asked her in her hypnosis, "Was it really the cool bath that
> depressed you so much?" "Oh," was her answer, "the cool bath had
> nothing to do with it. But I read in the paper this morning that a
> revolution had broken out in San Domingo. Whenever there is any
> unrest there the whites are always the sufferers; and I have a brother in
> San Domingo who has already caused us a lot of concern, and I am
> worried now in case something happens to him."[108]

As Filip Geerardyn and Gertrudis van de Vijver note, this reference
refers not to the Dominican Republic (sometimes called Santo Domingo)
but to Haiti, where Moser's brother lived during the civil conflict between
two presidential aspirants in 1888 and 1889.[109] The notion of a revolution
in Saint-Domingue quite directly, but erroneously, evokes the Haitian
Revolution from a century earlier, particularly through the allusion to
the sufferings of whites, who in fact barely were represented in the post-
revolutionary Haitian population. Freud, as the representative of Moser's
words, seems to engage the psychological terrors for whites of Haiti's
decolonization, even as he dismisses Moser's concern as a symptom of patients' tendencies to blame doctors' prescriptions—in this case, the oddly
mesmerist baths—rather than their real-world anxieties. Freud's San Domingo reference fits with Harrington's observation that in psychoanalysis

and "a new kind of medical narrative," the doctor would now be the only expert reader of the "body that speaks":[110] "It will be agreed that this instance is typical also of the behaviour of a large number of neuropaths in regard to the therapeutic procedures recommended by their physicians. The patient who develops a symptom on a particular day—whether owing to unrest in San Domingo or elsewhere—is always inclined to attribute it to his doctor's advice."[111]

If "unrest in San Domingo or elsewhere" is the true cause of the symptoms patients attribute to their doctors' advice, did Freud mean to magnify the importance of the colonies in patients' psychic experience—not banal political turbulence in late nineteenth-century Haiti, but the suffering of whites in events cast so as to recall the Haitian Revolution? Or was the "unrest in San Domingo" simply a trivial cause, similar to the triviality of baths, in the phenomenon of patients' inability to read their unconscious minds?

Haiti's decolonization, and the specter it raised of further violence against the European colonial metropoles, not only anticipated the terms of psychoanalytic trauma as articulated on the scale of the individual but also haunted the essential psychoanalytic location of the psychic within the individual rather than the collectivity. Slavery was a repressed trauma in a human rather than European bourgeois "family," and the hypnotic repeatability of that trauma, that "bad mimesis,"[112] is at the heart of the tension between psychoanalytic sovereignties and the vulnerable sovereignty of the first postcolony of former slaves.

Notes

1. This slogan is featured in calling-card format within the flyleaves of the first issue (1924) of *Révolution surréaliste*.
2. Chakrabarty, *Provincializing Europe*, 70.
3. Derrida, "Geopsychoanalysis 'and the Rest of the World,'" 322.
4. Hartnack, "British Psychoanalysts in Colonial India," 233.
5. Freud, as cited in Hartnack, *Psychoanalysis in Colonial India*, 1.
6. See Ben Plotkin, "Psychoanalysis, Transnationalism, and National Habitus."
7. Anderson, *Imagined Communities*, 47.
8. See Palmié, "Creolization and Its Discontents."
9. Brathwaite, "Creolization in Jamaica," 152.
10. Ibid., 154, 153.
11. Beecroft, "Edward Kamau Brathwaite," 71.
12. Derrida, *Resistances of Psychoanalysis*, 113.
13. Harrington, *Cure Within*, 68.

14. Freud, "Moses and Monotheism," 50.

15. Gary Wilder suggests that this Freudian roving through time influenced the processes of temporal and spatial condensation in the Negritude movement, although this feature was certainly present in oneiric texts preceding Freud's writings, such as Rimbaud's "Mauvais sang": "I am referring here to the process of condensation that Freud identified in dreams, in which a multiplicity of times and spaces become identical, unconstrained by the coordinates of empirical reality." Wilder, *French Imperial Nation-State*, 268.

16. Khanna, *Dark Continents*, 93.

17. Moreau de Saint-Méry, *Description topographique, physique, civile, politique et historique de la partie française de l'isle Saint-Domingue*, 1:529, 1:531. Unless otherwise noted in bibliography entries, all translations from French to English in this chapter are my own.

18. Meusnier de Querlon et al., *Histoire générale des voyages*, 23:84.

19. Chevalier, *Lettres à M. de Jean*, 32.

20. Thibaut de Chanvalon, *Voyage à la Martinique*, 85.

21. Dazille, *Observations sur les maladies des nègres*, 108.

22. Ibid., 94.

23. Rush, "Account of the Diseases Peculiar to the Negroes in the West-Indies," 82.

24. Ibid.

25. Ibid.

26. Cartwright, "Diseases and Peculiarities of the Negro Race," 331–33, as cited in Franklin and Schweninger, *Runaway Slaves*, 275.

27. Beard and Findlay, *Drapetomania*.

28. Nicolas, "De la maladie du sommeil," 670.

29. Anonymous review of "Du Sommeil non-naturel" in *Encéphale* (1886): 223.

30. Chertok and Stengers, *Critique of Psychoanalytic Reason*, 281.

31. Ibid., 280.

32. Anonymous, "La Maladie du sommeil" in *L'Année scientifique et industrielle*, vol. 7 (1863): 360.

33. Desportes, *Histoire des maladies de Saint-Domingue*, was published decades after the physician's death in Saint-Domingue in 1748.

34. Reynaud, "Epidémiologie de la maladie du sommeil." Reynaud, a retired colonial physician, gave among the synonyms for "maladie du sommeil" not only hypnosis but also "négro-léthargie" (309): "A côté de la théorie de la nostalgie, qui avait été émise par les observateurs des Antilles, prennent place celles de l'hypnose causé par des piqûres de raie . . . [et] par les maléfices des sorciers administrant des poisons" (322).

35. Buret, "La Maladie du sommeil," 608.

36. The term *hypnosis* itself emerged to denote trance states, without the element of "trauma"-like affect and the relationship to colonial slavery that interests me here, in earlier times and various language environments.

37. Chertok and Stengers, *Critique of Psychoanalytic Reason*, ix.

38. Ellenberger, *Discovery of the Unconscious*, vii, 53.

39. See Weaver, *Medical Revolutionaries*, 100–101.

40. Ellenberger, *Discovery of the Unconscious*, 53.

41. Delbourgo and Dew, *Science and Empire in the Atlantic World*, 23, 311.

42. Ellenberger, *Discovery of the Unconscious*, 73.

43. Weaver, *Medical Revolutionaries*, 101, 103, 105.

44. Moreau de Saint-Méry, *Description topographique, physique, civile, politique et historique de la partie française de l'isle Saint-Domingue*, 1:50.

45. Ranse, Baudoin, and Guerin, *Gazette médicale de Paris*, 185.

46. Chakrabarty, *Provincializing Europe*, 130.

47. Von Hartmann, *Philosophie de l'inconscient*. See Rand, "Hidden Soul."

48. Palente, *Pessimisme et individualisme*, 18.

49. Von Hartmann, *Philosophie de l'inconscient*, 153, 154.

50. Lanessan's work was discussed in an anonymous "Causerie bibliographique" in the *Revue rose*, 246.

51. Corre, *L'Ethnographie criminelle d'après les observations et les statistiques judiciaries recueillies dans les colonies françaises*, 496.

52. See Burke, *Reflections on the Revolution in France*.

53. Lachance emphasizes the importance of the Haitian defeat in the sale of Louisiana. See his "Repercussions of the Haitian Revolution in Louisiana." Geggus presents a more divided view of the factors influencing Napoleon's decision in "French Imperialism and the Louisiana Purchase."

54. Loomba, *Colonialism/Postcolonialism*, 7–8.

55. Nesbitt, "Idea of 1804," 6.

56. Fanon, *Peaux noire, masques blancs*, 183; emphasis added.

57. Hugo, *Bug-Jargal*, 262–63.

58. Loomba, *Colonialism/Postcolonialism*, 57.

59. See Crone, "Imperial Trauma."

60. Flanagan, "Seduction of History," 387.

61. Ibid., 388.

62. Caruth, *Unclaimed Experience*, 59.

63. Fischer, *Modernity Disavowed*, 138, 140.

64. Desbordes-Valmore, introduction to *Sarah*, xvi.

65. Desbordes-Valmore, *Sarah*, 4.

66. Ibid., 6.

67. Weber, *Peasants into Frenchmen*, 199.

68. De Chateaubriand, *Mémoires d'outre-tombe*, 1:676.

69. Ibid., 1:677.

70. Young, "Bruno and the Holy Fool," 29.

71. On the history of "Soulouquerie," see Dayan, *Haiti, History, and the Gods*, 10–11.

72. Arzalier, "La Révolution française dans l'imaginaire française," 350.

73. Miller, "Forget Haiti," 39.

74. On French participation in the slave trade as a political issue, see Stéphanie Binet, "Grande gueule noire," *Libération*, June 20, 2005. Vergès, as quoted in Miller, "Forget Haiti," 40.

75. Miller, "Forget Haiti," 39.

76. Leys, *Trauma*, 8.

77. Chertok and Stengers, *Critique of Psychoanalytic Reason*, x.

78. Ibid.

79. Young, "Bruno and the Holy Fool," as quoted in Kirmayer, Lemelson, and Barad, *Understanding Trauma*, 346. Young sees only mimetic forms of trauma, divided into fictitious and factitious post-traumatic stress disorder (PTSD). In fictitious PTSD, "the individual self-consciously tells a lie about his past in order to assume an altered and advantageous identity." In the factitious variety, "a person appropriates autobiographical memory and altered identity from someone, real or fictional, and pushes the origins of the memory out of awareness." The two forms of traumatic mimesis are often "parts of a single process, in which a mimesis transmutes itself from a self-conscious and self-observed condition into a transformed condition and inner identity" (346).

80. Leys, *Trauma*, 32.

81. Ibid., 8.

82. Ibid., 8–9.

83. Lacoue-Labarthe notes that "mimesis has no 'proper' to it"; that it is "the very lapse 'itself' of essence." *Typography*, 116.

84. See, for example, Nancy on "bad mimesis," or "a *mimesis* that dissimulates it [logic] according to its invested simulacrum, the self-consuming 'spectacle.'" *Being Singular Plural*, 72.

85. Jenson, *Trauma and Its Representations*, 14.

86. Leys, *Trauma*, 9.

87. Ibid., 10, 9.

88. Morgenstern, "Mother's Milk and Sister's Blood."

89. Leys, *Trauma*, 37.

90. Ibid., 307.

91. Ibid., 35.

92. Ibid., 297.

93. Olaniyan, "'Post-Colonial Discourse,'" 744.

94. Dayan, *Haiti, History, and the Gods*, 152.

95. Ibid., 203.

96. Chateaubriand, *Mémoires d'outre-tombe*, 2:764.

97. The first book title to have suggested the black Napoleon trope was probably Stephen's 1804 *Buonaparte in the West Indies*. This work, addressed to an abolitionist and anti-Napoleonic English readership, was more intent on deconstructing than constructing any resemblance between the two leaders but was arguably playing with the stakes of a comparative epistemology.

98. See Goodman, *Ways of Worldmaking*.

99. Chateaubriand, *Mémoires d'outre-tombe*, 1:202.

100. Ibid., 1:746.

101. Ibid., 1:692.

102. Ibid., 1:490.

103. Ibid., 1:672.

104. Ibid., 1:75.

105. Toussaint, as quoted in Roussier, *Lettres du général Leclerc*, 349.

106. Duras, *Ourika*, 20, 29.

107. Lamartine, "Toussaint Louverture," 1274.

108. Freud and Breuer, *Studies on Hysteria*, 68.

109. "This dating is confirmed by the following fact: Freud reports that, during the first course of the treatment, Fanny Moser read about the outbreak of a revolution in San Domingo, and was very concerned because one of her brothers lived there. However, Fanny Moser's brother did not emigrate to San Domingo (as Freud states) but to Haiti. Therefore the revolution in question took place not in San Domingo, but in Haiti. In actual fact: 'Civil war was waged in 1888–89 between Generals Légitime and Hippolyte, and the latter succeeded in obtaining the vacant presidency.'" Geerardyn and van de Vijver, *Pre-Psychoanalytic Writings*, 151.

110. Harrington, *Cure Within*, 76.

111. Freud and Breuer, *Studies on Hysteria*, 68.

112. Nancy, *Being Singular Plural*, 72.

Colonial Madness and the Poetics of Suffering
Structural Violence and Kateb Yacine

We most often imagine medicine as a healing art, a means of alleviating pain. And yet, what of a scenario in which medicine is a primary source of—or is at least as coextensive with—suffering and trauma? Since Michel Foucault's critical framings of clinical knowledge and medical power, social scientists and humanists have exhaustively explored the production of biopolitical knowledge and its implications for modernity.[1] Yet, a concern for exposing the operation of medical power has produced fewer examinations of medicine as an explicit source of suffering. This chapter explores iatrogenic forms of suffering by examining the complicity of medicine in the structural violence of the colonial situation, one in which medicine cannot be imagined as anything other than a force of oppression.

Such a perspective illuminates the overlapping of layers of suffering and violence under colonialism, a scenario in which the clinic is often a literal theater for colonial conflict. For Algerian author Kateb Yacine, the intersection of sickness and healing outlines an encounter marked by overdetermined forms of physical, emotional, and psychological trauma. Kateb's poetry, his dramatic works, and his enigmatic novel *Nedjma* provide crucial sources for exploring the clinic as a space of colonial violence and literature as a site of resistance against both imperialism and the sickness it generates. For Kateb, as for Frantz Fanon, madness in particular is the paradigmatic sickness of colonialism, while psychiatry operates as a biopolitical machine for the regulation of colonial order. Yet Kateb's examination of colonial madness and medicine departs significantly from standard twentieth-century critiques of psychiatry, such as those of figures as diverse as André Breton and Ronald Laing.[2] Psychiatry, like other forms of colonial medicine, is a policing force in Kateb's view. Yet, the madness it constrains behind asylum walls is not, as for Breton or Laing, the bedrock of artistic creation. It is instead the crucible of suffering and trauma and a highly specific form of acute anguish, both born of and producing colonial violence.

I use Kateb's works here as a source for extracting key meanings of the violence and suffering at the heart of madness and medicine in French Algeria. As will be obvious from what follows, I read these texts not through the eyes of a literary critic attuned to the subtleties of form and representation but instead through those of a social historian of medicine with an interest in how Kateb's drama and fiction render the experience of colonial violence and suffering in a medicalized language. The intention is twofold: to demonstrate the uses of literature for historians of medicine and to explore the possibilities of applying methodologies borrowed from the social history of medicine and medical anthropology to literary works with the goal of shedding new light on the political dynamics of sickness and healing. By reading Kateb's work alongside critical documents in the history of colonial madness and psychiatry—including Fanon's contemporary articulation of violence and pathology in Algeria—this chapter points to the multiple axes of oppression that shape suffering and preclude healing under colonialism. The chapter also draws on recent anthropological work on suffering and structural violence to explore Kateb's uses of medical language for the reinscription of social experience. Framing these works in this manner exposes layers of suffering and violence that characterized local imaginings of colonial circumstance in French Algeria—imaginings that played deep roles in informing Kateb's experience as a colonial *évolué* and author.

Experiencing Madness and Violence in the Maghreb: Kateb, Fanon, and Porot

Kateb Yacine was born in Constantine, Algeria, in 1929, the son of a lawyer, who received a Qur'anic education until age seven, when he entered the French colonial education system. As a student in French schools and a child of relative privilege, Kateb was a member of the paradoxical group of the colonized elite—or *évolués*, in the brutal language of the French civilizing mission. In contrast to what Frantz Fanon called the colonial "lumpenproletariat"—the disenfranchised population of broken masses who sought not to compete with the colonizer but to replace him—the colonized elite, destined for frustration, sought the improvement of its own condition through compromise with the French and the rejection of "native" values, producing powerful forms of alienation and self-hatred.[3]

The *évolués* occupied an uncomfortable middle ground as those who rejected their own cultures while facing an equally adamant rejection from the colonizer. As figures who transgressed colonialism's most rigid boundaries, the *évolués* upset assumptions that supported French hegemony in the Maghreb in profoundly threatening ways.[4] For sociologist Stéphane Bernard, European settlers in Algeria, Tunisia, and Morocco found psychological "shelter in the caste barriers separating" the French and Muslim populations. These caste barriers were crucial to "European psychology," as "the inferiority imposed on the Muslims" appeared "to the colonizer as the justification of his presence in the colony, as the condition of his settlement in the country, and as the safeguard of the privileges attached to his social condition."[5] Given the psychological importance of maintaining the façade of inherent difference that supported the hierarchy of colonial power, Muslims who claimed membership in French civilization inexcusably rent the thin fabric that veiled colonial hypocrisy. As a European teacher admonishes the protagonist in Moroccan author Driss Chraïbi's autobiographical novel *Le passé simple*, "We, the French, are in the process of civilizing you, the Arabs. Badly, in bad faith, and with no pleasure. Because, if by chance you come to be our equals, I ask you: in relation to whom or to what will *we* be civilized?"[6]

At the heart of these assumptions are the subjective and epistemic violences of everyday life that marked the experience of the *évolué* and whose implications for Kateb were profound. Faced with a choice between Qur'anic schools rendered illegitimate through colonial occupation or a French education, Kateb's father insisted on the latter for his son, despite the admission of defeat entailed by his enrollment.[7] The French school brought Kateb what "the Qur'anic school could not": a passion for literature and writing.[8] Yet, this came at the cost of alienation. In a frequently cited passage from *Le Polygone étoilé*, one of his later novels, Kateb compares the trauma of his entry into French schools to being thrown "into the lion's den" (*dans la gueule du loup*): an exposure to a harsh world of violent rejection.[9] Indeed, as many of his biographers have noted, his name itself reflects an ironic appropriation of the lycée's assault on the subjectivity of the colonized: born Yacine Kateb, the author adopted the reversed given and surnames characteristic of roll calls in French schools, reflecting the inversion of identity forced upon the *évolué*.[10] Yet, beyond the ritualized dehumanization of colonial schooling, it was also as a lycéen that Kateb first experienced two interlocking and catastrophic phenomena that shaped several of the most pervasive themes in his literary works: Algerian nationalism and the failure of his mother's sanity.

At only fifteen, Kateb was directly exposed to the horrific violence of the Algerian liberation struggle. His initiation into the nationalist cause came inadvertently with his participation in the bloody uprising at Sétif on May 8, 1945, when rioting Algerian military veterans killed some one hundred Europeans. Kateb wrote that at the time, "I had no consciousness of what was happening in our country . . . Then, I remember, there was a demonstration in the streets; and simply because there were classmates who found themselves caught up in this demonstration, as a student, I wanted to be with them, just like one wants to be with students who are horsing around."[11] The retaliation against Algerians reached well into the thousands.[12] Kateb was relatively fortunate: imprisoned and threatened with execution, he was later freed.

Historians have long recognized Sétif as the opening salvo in the brutal struggle for Algerian independence. As for a number of future revolutionaries, Sétif was formative for Kateb in terms of its violence. But its significance was exacerbated for Kateb, as it also introduced him to the powerful tension between the dual sufferings of madness and psychiatric confinement, both of which he came to attribute to the inherent violence and impossibility of real subjectivity of the colonial situation. Where for many, the experience of incarceration was the primary incitement to radicalism —writing of the Algerian revolution, historian Alastair Horne describes French prisons as the revolutionary's "university"—Kateb dismissed it as "nothing, I was thrown in jail." For his mother, however, "it was more serious. She lost her mind."[13] Yasmina Kateb had long suffered from periodic breakdowns. Yet upon hearing rumors of the execution of her only living son (her first son, Belghith, had died at age two), she reached a crisis stage and spent the next few years in and out of hospitalization at the Dispensaire Psychiatrique de Constantine. After her husband's death from tuberculosis in 1950, Yasmina's sister-in-law committed her to the Hôpital

Psychiatrique de Blida-Joinville, near Algiers, where she spent at least several years.[14]

Yasmina's story is one of the intersection of violence and madness in the context of anticolonial revolution. In the Algerian case, such a formulation was central to the thought of Frantz Fanon. Although highly controversial, his framing of colonialism's Manichean world—a world of lightness, whiteness, and wealth that is the European world and one of darkness, crime, and misery that is the Casbah or the Medina—remains powerfully influential in readings of the pathology of colonial society. Likewise, Fanon's conceptualization of violence as crucial to both revolutionary nationalism and the formation of the revolutionary subject is essential to understanding the forces that shaped and constrained the possibilities for action—or at least the experience of agency—in colonial Algeria. Reading Fanon's work in light of his experience as a psychiatrist practicing in the colonial context, in particular, provides an essential background for exploring the intersections of violence, madness, and suffering in Algeria as well as in Kateb's fiction and drama.

A Martiniquais psychiatrist who had studied at Lyon in the 1940s and 1950s, Fanon took a position as a ward director at the Hôpital Psychiatrique de Blida-Joinville in 1953.[15] Blida was immensely overcrowded upon his arrival, and some of his earliest psychiatric publications condemned the institution's egregious conditions.[16] Yet, just as much to blame for the impossibility of mental healing in the colony was a psychiatric paradigm that dehumanized North African Muslims as criminally impulsive and irremediably primitive beings. Instead of the reintegration of patients into society that Fanon had sought to achieve in his earlier psychiatric work, French psychiatrists in Algeria sought merely to confine dangerous social elements for the preservation of public order. Based on his experience with the institutionalized racism of the psychiatric staff, as well as his politicization at the outbreak of the liberation struggle in 1954, Fanon sided with the National Liberation Front (FLN) and eventually resigned both his post at Blida and his French citizenship. Fanon then moved to Tunisia, where he continued both his psychiatric work and his political activities on behalf of the FLN.

Fanon's experience at Blida is crucial for understanding his conceptualization of the brutality of colonial racism. Psychiatry at Blida bore the stamp of the Algiers School of French psychiatry, a group whose history is tightly bound to the history of colonial violence. From its outset, French colonial psychiatry was a military organism. Orientalist writers and isolated medical travelers had noted curiosities about madness and the treatment of the insane in North Africa since the French conquest of Algiers, but the creation of an organized school of colonial psychiatric thought was a product of the First World War.[17] Antoine Porot, a French physician who had initially settled in Tunis in the early twentieth century, began treating shell-shocked European and Muslim soldiers in an Algerian military hospital during the First World War. From his earliest publications until the 1960s, Porot and his students at the Algiers Faculté de Médecine labeled North African Muslims inherently puerile, mentally deficient, and incapable of coping with the realities of modern civilization.[18] These works merged nineteenth-century paradigms of degeneration and criminality with new ethnological ideas about "primitive mentalities," and by 1939, Porot proposed that North African fatalism and criminal aggression resulted from a combination of Islamic cultural traditions and physical anomalies in the cerebral cortex of North Africans' brains.[19] Muslims were inherently dangerous to the social order and required intense policing and punishment rather than rehabilitation: "It is above all through . . . sanctions that we teach these thwarted and overly instinctive beings that human life must be respected . . . a thankless, but necessary task in the general work of civilization."[20]

Fanon responded with a scathing criticism of both colonial logic and its scientific basis. He denounced the colonial Manichean world that policed, oppressed, and dehumanized the colonized population in the interests of European exploitation, and he argued that psychiatry operated as a regulatory arm of state power. Colonial psychiatric theories about the inherent and overdetermined inferiority of the colonized precluded any claims on their part for political or cultural legitimacy and therefore bombarded North Africans with messages of their primitive nature. Fanon claimed that colonial psychiatry, with its understanding of Algerians as "born slackers, born liars, born robbers, and born criminals," brutally assaulted the very subjectivity of the colonized.[21]

To counter this attack, Fanon located the origins of Algerian violence in the mechanics of colonial society and in the psychological formation of the revolutionary subject. Popular and scientific imaginings of Algerian impulsivity justified police repression, perpetuating an endless cycle of violence. For Fanon, colonial society was a malfunctioning organism that engendered madness and savagery in the dominated population. It was the colonialist's aggression that bred concomitant behavior in the individual. Algerians *were* unnaturally violent, he conceded, but such outbursts constituted a response to pathological violence rather than a reliable measure of the Algerian's "primitive" or "criminal" nature.[22]

Fanon also insisted on violent action as a necessary step in the development of revolutionary consciousness. Such action was essential to the revolution on a series of levels. It exposed the inherent violence of colonial society through the reprisal it engendered from the settler. It committed the revolutionary: it was an articulation that he or she had reached a point of no return and had forsaken the civilizing mission. It was an appropriation of the violence of the settler, turned toward the end of liberation and the creation of new revolutionary subjects. A mind and a society shattered by violence could only find their salvation in an equal and opposite violence, one directed at the cleansing liberation of a colonial society.

Fanon's advocacy of violence has elicited fierce debate among scholarly critics. Some, such as Ranjana Khanna, have found Fanon's response to Porot to be restrained, given the virulence of the Algiers School's pronouncements.[23] Others, such as Robert Berthelier and Jock McCulloch, have argued that Fanon was merely the obverse of Porot—that his formulation of the Algerian's violence effectively embraced Porot's description but provided an account of the stimulus that inspired the inevitable response of brutal criminal passion. Yet despite valid criticisms of the mechanistic nature of Fanon's theory of Algerian violence, it is clear that colonialism, for Fanon, operated in a logic analogous to that recently outlined by anthropologists Arthur Kleinman and Veena Das in their trenchant analysis of violence and subjectivity. In their account, the experience of the "violence of everyday life" produces specific forms of subjectivity as state and global forces distort local moral orders that normally preserve social integrity. Violence shapes identity as it becomes the subject's principal register for framing the local social world and, in turn, individual and collective action.[24] French colonialism fractured community in Algeria. When faced with the overwhelming repressive force of the colonizer, the colonized (male) subject internalized and redirected his anguish and aggression toward other Algerians as the only possible outlet. Under colonialism, Fanon argued, "Algerian criminality takes place in a closed circle. Algerians rob each other, cut each other up, and kill each other."[25] Yet, the liberation struggle offered a new channel for this violence and a means for deploying that rage in the creation of a new Algeria.

"The Rose of Blida": Madness, Suffering, and Forms of Colonial Violence

These formulations offer a key chart on which to map the patterns of violence and insanity that appear in the texts of Kateb Yacine, especially those concerning the figure of the suffering mother. This figure, wracked with insanity, is a recurring theme in Kateb's work. "La femme sauvage" ("The Wild Woman") of 1959, for example, presents a wandering and unstable yet fascinating figure who surfaces again and again in his oeuvre. "Mourning or ordinary abandonment, the nature of her illness didn't matter, since she had decided to personify in herself its indignity . . . summarized in the grotesque imagery of her mania . . . Her gaze ran up and down the walls, then became absolutely fixed, and the shape of her mouth indicated nothing more than bitterness: a sardonic suffering deprived of its object."[26] The connection to Yasmina is more explicit in his 1963 poem, "La Rose de Blida."[27] In dedicating the poem to the "memory of the one who gave me life / The black rose of the hospital," Kateb invokes both the asylum and the rose that is closely tied to the maternal figure in a number of his texts. (That Blida was known colloquially as the "City of Roses" adds a further level of irony to this framing.[28]) Yet, the mother's beauty is offset by instability: she is a "rose that fell from its rosebush / And took flight."

The identical theme appears in his first novel and masterwork *Nedjma*. Set in 1945, and composed between the riots at Sétif and the brutal massacres at Philippeville in 1956, *Nedjma* draws on Kateb's experiences to present the enigmatic story of four young men—Mustapha, Lakhdar, Rachid, and Mourad—who are both united and torn by their love for Nedjma. The novel orbits around omnipresent themes of violence and retribution. The character Nedjma, who appears in a number of Kateb's works, herself originated in an act of horrific violence. She was conceived during the rape of a French-Jewish woman by four Algerians, including Rachid's father and another character named Si Mokhtar, an attack that also led to the former's death by an unexplained murder. Nedjma stands in for a new Algeria, forged in a crucible of brutality and seized from the colonizer.

Like Kateb's mother in "La Rose," the mother of the character Mustapha (named Ouarda, or "rose") is tormented by the violence that surrounds her, manifesting her anguish in insanity. Arriving home to care for his tubercular father, Mustapha laments that "our courtyard is empty. No one to meet me. Mother has let the rosebush die." She is a "prone shape," a "tangle of white hair" inside the house. As he escorts his father to the hospital, Mustapha relates a song that his youngest sister is singing: "My brother's in prison, / My mother's going crazy / And my father's on his deathbed."[29] As the rose's madness and eventual death in the poem are prefigured by its uprootedness—the mad "rose that fell from its rosebush / And takes flight"—pervasive and maleficent birds in *Nedjma* reinforce the theme of flight into madness while providing a vehicle for imagining the mother's delusions.[30] As Mustapha complains, "Mother can't talk anymore without tearing at her face, lifting her dry eyes toward the sky. She talks to the birds and curses her children."[31] Kateb's language mirrors the breakdown of her mind as he represents her in fragmented descriptions (a tangle of hair, a prone shape), impossible imaginings (a dead rose that takes flight), and an oxymoron (the black rose that merges death and emptiness with life and beauty).

The character appears again in Kateb's play *Le Cadavre encerclé*, the first installment of Kateb's 1959 cycle *Le Cercle de représailles*. The play first appeared in *L'Esprit* in 1954 and was staged several times: first in Tunis in 1958, then later that year in Brussels, and eventually (but clandestinely) in Paris. *Le Cadavre* includes several of the prominent characters from *Nedjma*, including Nedjma and Lakhdar, and is set explicitly during the Sétif massacres and reprisals. Like all of Kateb's works on Algeria, in lieu of a straightforward narrative, the play revolves around central themes: colonial authority and resistance, imprisonment and death, and love and the condition of women in Algerian society. Fatally stabbed by his stepfather, who was an Algerian collaborator with the French, Lakhdar had already been rendered mad through his imprisonment and torture. His madness, a reflection of colonial violence, is mirrored in that of an escaped mental patient whom he encounters—Mustapha's mother. Stage directions specify that she appears wearing "the blue gown of psychiatric hospitals," her "barely graying hair stands up on her head," and "her gaze of searing intensity fixes on nothing, and neither her broken silhouette nor her gestures of distress are remotely feminine." The character speaks in verse: "And the daughters shave their heads / In memory of their demented mother / And as the birds leap, they mock / They mock me."[32]

The aetiology of the mother's madness crosses textual boundaries of genre, appearing in the poem, the novel, and the play in identical forms. Her unreason stems from what Jacqueline Arnaud calls an "accumulation of suffering" through the imagination of her son's death—or her prescient mourning of his certain death in the nationalist cause. In "La Rose," she is "the *femme sauvage* sacrificing her only son / Watching him take up the knife." This presaging of death appears in other works, as in *Le Cadavre*, when the mother keens over the "dissipating image of her son," or in *Nedjma*, as Mustapha complains, "For a long time she's been singing the prayer of the dead for me. Despair followed melancholy, then torpor."[33] Yet, there is also a cyclical aspect to this nexus of violence and suffering. In *Nedjma*, Mustapha, drunk with wine and rage, contemplates the murder of his father's friend, a fritter vendor. Describing his father's sickness and especially his mother's madness as a gross "injustice," he is driven to re-demptive violence himself. His homicidal furor is a means of wreaking vengeance on a landscape of suffering, the vendor a bystander to Mus-tapha's misery:

> I think of my sisters, between the madwoman and their tubercular father. He might be dying at this very moment. In the back of the shop there's a razor; with a little effort, the vendor's head could be rolling at my feet . . . Can a murder by itself assassinate injustice? Mother, I'm dehumanized, I'm turning myself into a leper-house, a slaughterhouse! What can I do with your blood, madwoman, and on whom can I avenge you? It's the idea of blood that drives me to the wine.[34]

Through his analysis of mother-son alliances in francophone Maghre-bian writing, Hédi Abdel-Jaouad provides a useful starting point for inter-preting Kateb's link between mourning and unmooring, between the loss of the son and the descent into madness.[35] For the Maghrebi woman who faces immediate repudiation by her husband at every turn, identification with the son is a strategy for physical and emotional survival. As a "custo-dian" of Maghrebian patriarchy, the mother's delivery of a son confers legitimacy and ensures her continued social survival. Yet, in Kateb's work, a series of reflexive turns complicates this relationship. First, there is an important narcissistic component to the mother's overwhelming suffering in Kateb's work. The mourning mother's recognition of her loss stems from a loss of recognition. As a subject dependent upon the son for her continued legitimacy as a subject, the maternal self is constituted through recognition by the son. Both Yasmina's world and her ego have become empty and meaningless. Thus, in the guise of the mother in *Le Cadavre* who repeatedly calls her son's name, she clings to his image "through the medium of a hallucinatory wishful psychosis" that preserves his (and therefore her own) existence.[36] Although the relationship with the son is always ambivalent, it contains at least an implicit defense against repudiation, as her only source of subjective legitimacy rests in her perpetuation of a patriarchal lineage. The only son's death—even if merely fantasized—deals an equally mortal blow to the ego.

To push Abdel-Jaouad's analysis further, there is a second turn that complicates Kateb's relationship with the mother figure in these texts. The mother's madness resonates beyond psychoanalytic dimensions, operating as a powerful signal of the disruption of Algerian society by colonial violence. Abdel-Jaouad argues convincingly that the place of the mother in Maghrebian texts is often invoked as a defense against the onslaught of colonial modernity, a grounding of the francophone son in the mythic past through identification with the mother as a source of "immutable" and unspoiled "authenticity."[37] Indeed, in colonial psychiatric discourse, female insanity evoked a mirror image of such immutability. As psychiatrist Suzanne Taïeb argued in a 1939 thesis, Algerian women were far less touched by the forces of "civilization" than Algerian men and thus constituted a reservoir of unmediated primitivism and superstition.[38] Yet, for Kateb, this identification of the mother figure with unspoiled tradition highlights a further trauma. The son's effort to find permanence in his mother's image is foiled by her insanity, which is an insistent reminder of colonial violence. That her mourning and insanity cannot end results from the endless cycle of rebellion and reprisal that mark the modern history of Algeria. Whereas Freud sees mourning as characterized by "grave departures from the normal attitude to life," the pathologies of colonial society preclude a return to normalcy.[39]

Recent work in medical anthropology on suffering and structural violence illuminates the layers of meaning in Yasmina's madness. As Arthur and Joan Kleinman have argued, the imagery of suffering often serves as a repository for condensing social, economic, and political experience. A narrative of survival of unspeakable violence becomes rewritten as a trauma story, highlighting the horrors of victimization.[40] By this reading, Yasmina's madness serves Kateb as a source of symbolic capital: the story of her breakdown draws on a medicalized language to communicate the experience of the structural violence of colonial Algeria. As anthropologist Paul Farmer conceives it, structural violence is produced in scenarios in which overwhelming social, political, and economic forces combine to limit the subject's potential agency.[41] Such forces organize a (mostly) unidirectional flow of violence down what Farmer calls "steep gradients of power" and thereby structure risk for victimized populations.[42] In this calculus, sickness and suffering connect closely to the operational forces of structural violence. Sicknesses—including mental illnesses such as Yasmina's pathological mourning—are barometers of social inequality, what Farmer describes as "biological reflections of social fault lines" in which multiple forms of oppression constrain possibilities of action and shape the violent expression of communal discord.[43]

The notion of structural violence offers a useful field for exploring how the colonial predicament informs the layers of suffering in Kateb's works. Yasmina's madness, by this reading, is a response to identifiable human actions rather than a neurological malfunction. While it is Kateb's imagined death that appears as the primary cause of her breakdown, the son's execution—indeed, even his participation in the Sétif riots, along with the riots themselves—resulted from the scenario of colonial oppression. Yasmina's madness was constituted in the field of colonial power and resistance, one that shaped all possible responses to the French colonial presence and its brutalities. As Kateb notes in his conclusion to "La Rose," it is a mother's ability to witness the violence of anticolonial revolution and reprisal through the privileged lens of intuition that allows her special insight into revolution's circumstances but that also determines her madness: "Fountain of blood, of milk, of tears, she knew from instinct how they were born, how they fell to the ground, and how they fell again, from a brutal conscience, without a parachute, burst like bombs, burned one against another, then cooled in the ashes of the birth pyre, without flame or heat, expatriated."[44]

Yasmina's breakdown is simultaneously a reflection of subjective fragmentation and an instantiation of resistance. The inherent violence of both the colonial state and patriarchal domination have inscribed Yasmina in the domain of what the philosopher Giorgio Agamben has called "bare life," a bestialized existence removed from the order of human and divine law. She remains unmoored, existing in a space of emotional discord and potentially in a form of what anthropologist João Biehl, writing of the disenfranchised homeless and insane populations in Brazil, has called a "zone of social abandonment," as she is menaced with potential repudiation on the grounds of her childlessness and her insanity.[45] This position shapes Yasmina's field of action, limiting her possibilities of resistance to expression through emotional collapse. She is subject to multiple orders of marginalization by virtue of her social position: as Kateb perceives the situation, she is tangled in a web of power relations in which her agency is tightly constrained. "Multiaxial" forms of oppression inform her risk for breakdown. Axes of race and gender inform the nature of her illness and suffering at every turn. As an Algerian, the fact of difference precludes her political engagement on equal terms with the colonizer. As a woman in a rigidly patriarchal society, her self-definition through motherhood predisposes her to subjective annihilation when that which shapes her social position is taken from her—a brutal repetition of the loss of her first son in infancy, but a loss now attributable to the actions of the colonizer.

Psychiatry's Violence: Failures of Healing and the Persistence of Suffering

Yet, despite Yasmina/Ouarda's suffering, to seek comfort in psychiatric treatment is to perpetuate the cycle of traumatic violence. In *A Dying Colonialism* and *The Wretched of the Earth*, Fanon presents medicine and psychiatry as ideological instruments of colonial power. Psychiatrists, by this account, see their Muslim patients as a data set for testing the limits of invasive therapies, as in the case where a French psychiatrist subjected a pregnant Tunisian woman to electroshock until she spontaneously delivered.[46] They appear in the interrogation room both to administer shock treatments as a tool for interrogation as well as to assess the validity of a torture victim's testimony, while their physician colleagues assess the body's ability to withstand pain and punishment. The doctor exploits the native's credulity—itself an invention of colonial psychiatric discourse— by selling useless medicines and performing x-rays with a vacuum canister. During the war, the physician refuses to treat Algerians with suspicious wounds or even inflicts further pain on the wounded. Medicine constitutes a site of colonial surveillance and the clinic a means of amassing useful data in the assistance of domination.[47] Even the objective truth of an accurate diagnosis is rejected by the colonized, Fanon notes, as it is always "vitiated by the lie of the colonial situation."[48]

As with Fanon, psychiatry and medicine are forces of violent social control in Kateb's work. *Le Cadavre* provides the clearest example, as it is the presence of psychiatry itself that situates the text in the realm of madness. The cue that exposes the insanity of Mustapha's mother is her patient's gown; it is psychiatry's trappings as much as her pathological appearance (her erratic "gaze of searing intensity," her "hair stand[ing] up on her head") that diagnose her condition for the audience.

Far from comforting, the hospital is a malicious force. The patient describes herself as "the escaped madwoman," reinforcing the perception of the institution as a carceral rather than a therapeutic site. In the background, a loudspeaker confirms the hospital's menacing presence: "Electroshock! Electroshock! Electroshock!" Like Oedipus, the madwoman is a social pariah who bears responsibility for her transgressions through her blindness. She is "a widow in reprieve," but at the same time a "mother in quarantine," and a chorus chants in the background, "Night falls, and our entire Universe leans out the window of nothingness! Do not throw stones at the madwoman, she has arisen to close the window, and that is why her eyes are ruined." With allusions to scripture and Greek tragedy as well as the Algerian revolution, her escape is a form of deliverance from domination. As the patient "leaps out of the scene," the choir seizes on her escape from Blida as a microcosm of the entrapment of Algerians in the discourses of colonial psychiatry as well as their imprisonment in the colonial system. Pinning Ouarda's escape to the national liberation struggle, the chorus narrates her exit from the scene by calling out, "Nothing resists the exodus."[49]

Central to this representation are the multiple forms of psychiatric confinement in Algeria. The psychiatric hospital in this scenario is less a mechanism of healing than one of powerful repression. It is a factory for the production of knowledge about the mentality of the *indigène*, manufacturing and processing clinical presentations like the savage impulsivity of the Arab criminal and the primitive superstitions of the sequestered Muslim woman. Such clinical types, in the language of the Algiers School, informed increasingly fixed ideas about the modal personality of the colonized in administrative, judicial, and medical circles, constituting a form of judgment that entrapped the Algerian in the bonds of psychological alterity.[50] Yet, it is also a site of literal imprisonment and surveillance. Associations of psychiatric confinement with imprisonment were frequent in colonial Algeria. Patients regularly complained of neglect and of the punishing aspects of internment. For M. O., an Algerian male hospitalized at Blida in the 1930s who wrote in his journal, "If [my confinement] continues, I might lose my sanity or die," or for D. D., an Algerian woman at Blida who complained that physicians were "letting [her] die," confinement was incongruous with healing, operating instead as a mechanism for policing deviance.[51]

Le Cadavre's theme of psychiatric punition carries over into Nedjma. In the middle of the novel, Rachid, one of the four protagonists, arrives in Constantine and begins wandering through the city. As he stops at a smoking den, he is torn about whether to enter, when he spots an acquaintance: "The man holding the sachets was sitting there, an Olympian of twenty with a bulging forehead [le front accidenté]. Rachid had thought he was in the psychiatric hospital. 'You got away from them again, brother Abdallah!' "[52]

Through a range of cues, Kateb offers a searing indictment of psychiatry as a force of imperial incomprehension. It is Abdallah's physiognomy and his occupation that brand him as an ideal Algerian clinical type. His "bulging forehead" signals his deviance, rendering him the target of an outdated psychiatric paradigm with roots in Cesare Lombroso's criminal anthropology.[53] Far from a raving lunatic, Abdallah is merely a social reprobate, an addict and proprietor of an illegal hash bar populated by a coterie of degenerates. After Rachid, a lycée dropout, later joins Abdallah as an employee, he "no longer left the savage collective, the Divan, the intimate reverie of the horde: ten or twenty men of all ages—silent dreamers who scarcely knew each other—dispersed along the balcony, deep in their intoxication, on the edge of the cliff . . . he would probably die on this balcony, in a cloud of the forbidden herb." Rachid "had long known about the fondouk of which he had just become the master": "He knew, like every child, that the music-lovers at the fondouk smoked something other than tobacco—something that made them madmen, but not like drunkards." This group is Rachid's new cohort in Constantine—these "known criminals, the unemployed, the homeless, the sans-papiers, the demi-fous like this Abdallah, always just out of the asylum." For Kateb, psychiatry's function was the regulation of social deviance through the surveillance of this drug-addled "horde," this "savage collective" of "troglodytes."[54]

This version of colonial psychiatry as a disciplinary force is important in Nedjma because the novel is also the site of a range of powerful expressions of mad violence. Here, Kateb appropriates and reverses the Algiers School's stereotypes of the Algerian's impulsively violent character. Violence is omnipresent in the novel. Nedjma herself, of course—this figure of the new Algeria—is produced through successive rape in the womb of a

Frenchwoman: she is born of violence and seized from the colonizer. Other instances of violence are linked to this rape—Si Mokhtar's murder of Rachid's father, for example—or, more often, to the instigation of the *pieds-noirs*. Yet, such actions are specifically gendered in *Nedjma*: clear patterns dictate why Yasmina/Ouarda's experience of colonial domination drives her to insanity, while the life-world of the Algerian men in *Nedjma* leads inevitably to murderous outcomes. Just as the structural violence of the colonial situation shapes Yasmina's insanity, the forces of poverty, brutal labor, and the colonizer's aggression inform the possibilities of action for male Algerians. As Fanon insisted, it is these forces that "canalize" the Algerians' rage toward the colonial aggressor, a global force that deranges local social worlds.

The first of these scenes of masculine violence involves Lakhdar—one of the four young men infatuated with Nedjma—as well as Monsieur Ernest, a French construction foreman, and Suzy, Ernest's daughter.[55] Other day laborers warn Lakhdar on his first day of work about Ernest's temper: "Ameziane unties the string he's using in place of a belt and shows a festering scrape on his lower back: 'There's M. Ernest's character.'" Ernest demands to know what the workers are talking about. Without waiting for an answer, he strikes Lakhdar in the head with a stick. Lakhdar watches his own blood flowing as Ernest's daughter Suzy tells her father, "He hasn't had enough, that one . . . *He hasn't gotten what he deserves.*" Ernest moves closer to Lakhdar to continue the beating, "his daughter's heckling having raised him to the peak of heroism." But Lakhdar strikes first, knocking Ernest unconscious with a single blow.[56]

Ernest's violence is a pose, a ritual of the colonizer's masculinity, like George Orwell's in "Shooting an Elephant."[57] Driven on by his daughter, Ernest plays a role of domination. He is at center stage in a drama of colonial violence; he must act decisively or lose face in front of both his daughter and his workers. It is less Lakhdar's insubordination than the colonial situation itself that shapes this interaction: it is a scenario in which the agency of the central actors is decided in advance. Ernest's actions and Suzy's "heckling" are mandatory reiterations of domination, an ordering of the colonial world played out in microcosm. Lakhdar's preventive strike, although understood as an impulsive criminal violence, is a refusal of submission and a rejection of the violences of everyday colonial life: the poverty, marginalization, and coercive labor forced upon a disenfranchised population.

A second and more disturbing scene between Suzy and the character Mourad captures the dynamics of a bloodthirsty and "dying" colonialism lashing out in its death throes. When Mourad sees Suzy on the street and tries to talk to her, we see how the constraints of a discourse of colonial violence inform Mourad's identity and motivate his subsequent actions. "Leave me alone," Suzy tells him.

> "And that's that," thinks Mourad, "the honeymoon's over, I'm just her father's workman again, she's going to walk back across that empty lot . . . as if I'm committing a crime just by walking in the same place as she, as if we should never find ourselves in the same world, other than as a result of violence or rape. And that's that. Already she's *tutoie*-ing me, and she tells me to leave her, as if I had grabbed her shockingly and violently . . ." Then he thought of nothing else but striking her, seeing her on the ground, maybe picking her up and throwing her down again.[58]

Mourad's desires stem from Suzy's perceptions of him as violent and impulsive. His imaginary violation is realized on the night of Suzy's wedding to Monsieur Ricard, a contractor. Ricard is the archetypal *pied-noir*: a self-made broussard, a rough-and-tumble, hard-drinking settler with no patience for polite society. Kateb establishes Ricard's character from the outset in an altercation between Ricard and his Algerian maid: "He grabbed her by the throat. 'Have you been stealing the coffee?' "[59] The wedding night, a travesty from the outset, degenerates into a mêlée as Ricard and the guests become violently drunk. As the crowd tries to force Ricard and Suzy into bed to consummate the marriage, the maid intervenes. The "orgy" of violence quickly turns on her. The guests seize the maid and force a bottle of rum down her throat. As the maid retches, Ricard begins to beat her senselessly: "The blows rained down. M. Ricard beat her with an expression of indignant stupidity . . . he knew now, in his fading drunkenness, that he couldn't stop beating her or finish off his staggering prey without turning against the partiers who squeezed around him in a circle." Like Ernest, Ricard explodes in incomprehensible violence as a means of saving face among the *pieds-noirs* who surrounded him. Yet, at this point, Mourad, who has witnessed the orgy from outside, creeps into the room: "A blow from his knee doubled the contractor's body over, just when Suzy was pulling him back, and now Mourad pummeled him fiercely and unrelentingly, could not restrain his blows."[60] Before the crowd is able to pull Mourad off the contractor's body, Mourad beats him to death.

Suzy rejects Mourad as a criminal, "as if we should never find ourselves in the same world, other than as a result of violence or rape." In response, he becomes one: he saves the maid's life as he erupts into uncontrollable rage, beating Ricard to death. But Kateb reveals that Mourad's violence, like Lakhdar's, is a response to a more brutal violence: the maddening aggression of the colonizer. Kateb, like Fanon, never refutes the stereotype of the Algerian's violent impulses. Instead, he places Algerian violence in context. The revolution opens what Fanon called the "closed circle" of Algerian violence: "There are no more disputes and no longer any insignificant details which entail the death of a man. There are no longer explosive outbursts of rage because my wife's forehead or her left shoulder were seen by my neighbor."[61] In *Nedjma*, Algerian rage seeks its outlet in response to the physical and psychological violence inflicted by the settler. Ernest's beating of Lakhdar, Suzy's recognition of Mourad as nothing but a host of sexual impulses, Ricard's suspicion and brutality: each of these acts of violence merits an Algerian response. In these moments, Kateb co-opts the Algiers School's portrait of the Algerian to reveal the origins of violence in Algerians' articulation of their subjectivity. Like the "exodus" in *Le Cadavre*, like the rose's flight from the rosebush, this appropriation is also a form of deliverance that reveals the suffering at the heart of psychiatric discourses of Algerian violence and insanity.

Conclusions: "Satan in a White Coat" and Medicine as an Agent of Suffering

Colonial medicine is fascinating because of its multiple resonances.[62] It is the most frequently invoked defense of the civilizing mission, as in the famous dictum attributed to Hubert Lyautey, the French field marshal who led the conquest of Morocco and who served as the first resident-general of the Moroccan protectorate: "Medicine is the only excuse for colonization." Yet, in his address to a psychiatric congress in 1933, Lyautey also pointed to medicine's uses as a tool of colonial domination. "The physician," he argued, "if he understands his role, is the primary and most effective of our agents of pacification and penetration." Where the soldier is ambushed, the physician finds a receptive audience; where the policeman is rejected, the vaccination team finds eager families with their children, anxiously awaiting salvation from the certainty of sickness.[63] Medicine is an efficient means of establishing control precisely because of its seductive power. The physician's exclusive knowledge grants a specific authority, one that can belittle the patient because of its monopoly status. It can amass data about the population because it can demand any form of information in exchange for its services. It can establish truth about patients because it exploits their vulnerability. It is a unique form of totalitarian power because it is one to which we willingly submit. We grant medicine's authority in domains we cannot understand; this is the bargain we enter when we seek a cure.

Yet colonial medicine, Fanon and Kateb argue, does not meet its end of the compromise. When colonized patients sacrifice their authority to the doctor, the doctor sees only gratitude for the colonial presence—an exercise that transforms the clinical visit into a ritual of domination. This is the framework for Kateb's 1963 meditation on colonial medicine titled "Ce pays est un grand hôpital." The sketch—only six pages long—is a fragmentary continuation of the farcical drama *La Poudre d'intelligence*, the centerpiece in the cycle *Le Cercle des représailles*. Jacqueline Arnaud has characterized the piece as situated "between the pamphlet and the theater," which accounts for its hyperbolic tone.[64] Set in Morocco, the sketch explores the reciprocal relationship between clinical and colonial domination. The sultan, suffering from a fever, summons a doctor: enter Dr. Paul Chatinières, a colonial physician who assisted Lyautey's "pacification" efforts during the Moroccan conquest. The doctor's soliloquy as he enters the scene consumes most of the play. He announces that colonialism introduced doctors to "an entirely new role whose existence and utility we had not suspected." While armed force initiated conquest, "military leaders . . . facilitated our medical action and used our moral influence to consolidate French authority. The doctor became an agent of pacific penetration" as "France endeavored to attenuate this brutal manifestation of the right of the strongest, the right of the conqueror, with a bit of humanity." The doctor proved useful in this "moral conquest": "Better than the priest, [the doctor] can lay bare the human soul with its hidden faults, its unavowed miseries. His practiced eye, which scrutinizes and which weighs heavily, quickly pierces the pride and the mistrust that opposes it: because the man who has stripped off his shirt is less hesitant to reveal his soul, and the notation of lesions and symptoms that cannot be denied forces the patient's sincerity."[65] Remarkably, this passage is a direct quotation from Chatinières himself; taken verbatim from his memoirs, it betrays an awareness of both the seductive force and the political uses of colonial medicine.[66] Although the sultan is fascinated by the doctor's power and requests his diagnosis, the character Nuage de Fumée (Puff of Smoke) sees through the ulterior motives of colonial medicine. A complex figure who stands at once as the colonized intellectual and the Muslim revolutionary struggling in frustration against the obsolescence of the sultanate and the abuses of colonialism, Nuage de Fumée rejects Chatinières as a "heathen" whose "science" is still in its infancy, then pleads, "Help, Muslim brothers! Satan in a white coat claims to take me in his arms."[67]

The sketch, admittedly a minor piece in Kateb's oeuvre, appears to have little direction outside of indicting colonial medicine as an abuse of power and pointing out the fragmentation of colonial society. When read alongside a range of Kateb's other works (as well as Fanon's), however, it becomes clear that for Kateb, colonial medicine is a political force that strips the Maghreb of its traditions as it divides its populations. As such, it is complicit in colonial violence, serving as a means of "pacific penetration" and as an agent of colonial suffering. Yet, its seductive power renders it difficult to resist and to conquer. More than a form of social control, it is a factor that shapes the structural violence of the colonial situation. By insinuating itself into the deeply personal space of health and illness, through its prescriptive and proscribing powers of language and discourse, medicine is a crucial instrument in the establishment of colonial hegemony; the physician, in turn, is the architect of a colonial social and political order and a catalyst for the breakdown of local social worlds.

Historian of medicine David Arnold has argued that all medicine is at least implicitly colonial in its assertion of monopolistic control over the body and its annexation and destruction of alternative forms of healing.[68] While this may be an exaggeration, it remains clear that the extremities of colonial rule magnify the operations of power at work in the clinical space. It is clear, as well, that this mechanism of domination was profoundly disconcerting for Kateb, many of whose texts reveal the complicated intersection of medical violence and social suffering that, for him, was a primary site for interrogating colonial marginalization.

What Kateb's works convey with respect to medicine, violence, and suffering is the articulation of a possible experience under colonialism. As such, his works are a sort of fragment that complicates the "official" history of colonial medicine—a history that often still sees biomedicine through a lens focused on its triumphs, yet remains blind to its violences.[69] The deeply personal glimpses of madness and violence provided within Kateb's texts are both powerfully revelatory and drastically limiting. As a narrative of lived experience, they condense the pathological insanity of the colonial social order into the madness of the mother and the rage of young men. Yet precisely because this poetics of violence and suffering is so personal, because it encapsulates one author's vision by bearing witness to his past, it reveals the limits of historical knowledge. Ironically, even as the "*Nedjma* complex" of texts offers a testament of colonial experience, the entirety of such suffering remains ungraspable in the untold stories of countless other Katebs—and countless other Yasminas—out of the reach of medical, ethnographic, or historiographical discourse.

Notes

This chapter is a slightly revised version of "Violence, Resistance, and the Poetics of Suffering," which was originally published in *Colonial Madness: Psychiatry in French North Africa*. Chicago: University of Chicago Press, 2007. © 2007 by The University of Chicago. Reprinted by permission.

1. Foucault, *Birth of the Clinic*. A small sampling of works informed by Foucauldian understandings of biopower include those by philosopher Agamben, *Homo Sacer*; historian Stoler, *Race and the Education of Desire*; sociologist Donzelot, *Policing of Families*; and anthropologist Rabinow, *French Modern*.

2. See Breton, *Nadja*; Laing, *Divided Self*; and also Castel, *L'ordre psychiatrique*. For an early analysis of French antipsychiatry, see Meyer, "L'antipsychiatrie."

3. Fanon, *Wretched of the Earth*, 59–62.

4. On colonial "middle figures" in a different context, see Hunt, *Colonial Lexicon of Birth Ritual, Medicalization, and Mobility in the Congo*.

5. Bernard, *Le conflit franco-marocain*, 135.

6. Chraïbi, *Le passé simple*, 208.

7. On the struggles between French and Qur'anic education in Algeria, see Turin, *Affrontements culturels dans l'Algérie coloniale*. On the dilemma faced by the *évolués* and their families, see Arnaud, *Recherches sur la littérature maghrébine de langue française*, 31.

8. Kateb, *Le Poète comme un boxeur*, 14.

9. Kateb, *Le Polygone étoilé*, 182.

10. See, for example, Bernard Aresu's introduction to Kateb, *Nedjma*, xiv.

11. Kateb, "Poésie et vérité de la femme sauvage," 39.

12. Estimates range between 1,000 and 45,000 victims in the reprisals; see Horne, *Savage War of Peace*, 27.

13. Horne, *Savage War of Peace*, 27; *Kateb*, "Poésie et verité," 39.

14. Arnaud, *Recherches sur la littérature maghrébine de langue française*, 493–94; also M. la Bardonnie, "Un tramway nommé Yacine," *Libération*, October 21, 1999.

15. See Macey, *Frantz Fanon*.

16. See esp. Dequeker et al., "Aspects actuels de l'assistance mentale en Algérie."

17. See, for example, Flaubert, *Première éducation sentimentale*, 242; de Nerval, "Aurélia," 758; de Lamartine, "Voyage en Orient," 230; and du Camp, *Le Nil, Egypte, et Nubie*, 39. For more explicitly medical accounts, see Moreau, *Du haschish et de l'aliénation mentale*; Moreau, "Recherches sur les aliénés, en Orient"; and also Jacob, "La psychiatrie française face au monde colonial au XIXe siècle."

18. Porot, "Notes de psychiatrie musulmane."

19. Porot and Sutter, "Le 'primitivisme' des indigènes Nord-Africains."

20. Porot and Arrii, "L'impulsivité criminelle chez l'indigène algérien."

21. Fanon, *Wretched of the Earth*, 296.

22. Ibid., 309.

23. Khanna, *Dark Continents*, 150.

24. See the introduction by Das and Kleinman, as well as the chapter by Mamphela Ramphele, in Das et al., *Violence and Subjectivity*.

25. Fanon, *Wretched of the Earth*, 305−6.

26. Kateb, "La femme sauvage/1," 164.

27. Kateb, "La Rose de Blida," 4.

28. See, for example, coverage of the celebration of the Blida hospital's inauguration in *La Dépêche algérienne* (Algiers), "L'hôpital psychiatrique de Blida a été inauguré hier par M. le Gouverneur Général Le Beau," April 9, 1938.

29. Kateb, *Nedjma*, 225−26.

30. An aspect at which Jacqueline Arnaud has hinted; see her *Recherches sur la littérature maghrébine de langue française*, 415−16.

31. Kateb, *Nedjma*, 226.

32. Kateb, "Le Cadavre encerclé," 62−63.

33. Kateb, "Le Cadavre encerclé," 62; Kateb, *Nedjma*, 226.

34. Kateb, *Nedjma*, 77.

35. Abdel-Jaouad, "'Too Much in the Sun.'"

36. Freud, "Mourning and Melancholia," 246, 244.

37. Abdel-Jaouad, "'Too Much in the Sun,'" 24.

38. Taïeb, *Les idées d'influence dans la pathologie mentale de l'Indigène Nord-Africain*, 78.

39. Freud, "Mourning and Melancholia," 243.

40. Kleinman and Kleinman, "Appeal of Experience."

41. Farmer, "Suffering and Structural Violence"; also Farmer, *Pathologies of Power*, 29−50, passim.

42. Farmer, *Infections and Inequalities*, esp. 76−82.

43. Farmer, *Infections and Inequalities*, 5; also Farmer, "Suffering and Structural Violence," 273−76.

44. Kateb, "La Rose de Blida," 4.

45. Agamben, *Homo Sacer*. See also Biehl's analysis of this operation in "Vita."

46. Maréchal, Soltane, and Corcos, "Résultats du traitement par l'électro-choc appliqué à 340 malades à l'Hôpital psychiatique de La Manouba (Tunisie)."

47. Fanon, *Dying Colonialism*, 120−45.

48. Ibid., 128.

49. Kateb, *Le Cadavre encerclé*, 62–64.

50. See, for example, the effects of psychiatric language on evolving ideas about Maghrebian immigration into France in Hirsch, "La Criminalité des nord-africains en France est-elle une criminalité par défaut d'adaptation?"

51. Taïeb, *Les idées d'influence dans la pathologie mentale de l'Indigène Nord-Africain*, cases 24 and 39.

52. Kateb, *Nedjma*, 151.

53. See Pick, *Faces of Degeneration*.

54. Kateb, *Nedjma*, 159–60.

55. This is the first violent scene *chronologically*, although it appears twenty pages after the second in the text.

56. Kateb, *Nedjma*, 41–46.

57. Orwell, "Shooting an Elephant."

58. Kateb, *Nedjma*, 17.

59. Ibid., 16.

60. Kateb, *Nedjma*, 24–25.

61. Fanon, *Wretched of the Earth*, 305–6.

62. These dimensions of colonial medicine have attracted significant scholarly attention. See, for example, Anderson, " 'Where Every Prospect Pleases and Only Man is Vile' "; Prakash, *Another Reason*; Comaroff, " 'Diseased Heart of Africa' "; and Katz, "The 1907 Mauchamp Affair and the French Civilising Mission in Morocco." For a review of the literature on psychiatry in particular, see Keller, "Madness and Colonization."

63. Lyautey to Georges Guillain, 17 March 1933. Printed in *Comptes-rendus du Congrès des médecins aliénistes et neurologistes de France et des pays de langue française, XXXVIIe Session—Rabat* (Paris: Masson, 1933), 73–74. On this aspect of colonial medicine in Morocco, see Micouleau-Sicault, *Les médecins français au Maroc*.

64. The Arnaud quote appears in Kateb, *L'Oeuvre en fragments*, 440n10.

65. Kateb, "Ce pays est un grand hôpital," 391–93.

66. See Chatinières, *Dans le Grand Atlas marocain*; the volume includes an introduction by Lyautey.

67. Kateb, "Ce pays est un grand hôpital," 394–96.

68. Arnold, *Colonizing the Body*, 9.

69. I draw here on the notion of the evidentiary "fragment" employed by Pandey, "In Defense of the Fragment," esp. 28–30.

Ethnopsychiatry and the Postcolonial Encounter
A French Psychopolitics of Otherness

> For the orientalist's construct, by focusing on a particular image of the Islamic tradition, and for the anthropologist's, by focusing on a particular image of the African tradition, both helped to justify colonial domination at particular moments in the power encounter between the West and the Third World. No doubt, this ideological role was performed largely unwittingly.
>
> —Talal Asad, *Anthropology and the Colonial Encounter*

A few years ago, a West African woman was brought to an ethnopsychiatric clinic at the university hospital where I was working, in the poor outskirts northeast of Paris, known worldwide since the 2005 riots under their French name, *banlieues* (suburbs). She did not suffer from any particular psychological symptom—at least, she had no specific complaint of this kind. But she had been forced by the local juvenile court to go to this particular clinic and receive specific treatment—otherwise, she was told, her children would be taken away from her. Her "problem," as seen by the judge, was the following. She was a Muslim Soninke woman from Mali who had arrived in France more than ten years before and was then living in a small apartment in Seine-Saint-Denis. Divorced from her husband, she was raising alone eight children, from fourteen years to three months old, with the welfare grants and the meager salary of her part-time domestic work. One of her children, a three-and-a-half-year-old boy, was in preschool. His teacher noticed he was hyperactive and complained about him disturbing the rest of the class. In particular, she was concerned with his conduct toward little girls of his age, whose skirts he would lift up, trying to touch their buttocks. Worried about what she saw as a precocious form of sexual abuse, she reported the case to the local social services. In the administrative file that was opened, the little boy was described as a *violeur* (rapist). A social investigation of the family was conducted. Doubts were expressed about the fact that a woman alone could get enough financial resources to raise eight children. As the mother was good-looking and elegantly dressed— and on top of that, African—she was immediately suspected of bringing men home and having commercial sex with them, probably even, someone added, in the same bedroom where her children were sleeping as that was indeed the only room in the apartment. Although no evidence of it was given, this intuition was satisfactory both to explain the mother's supposedly excessive income and to account for the child's stigmatized sexuality.

The case was presented to the juvenile court. Before taking her child from her, the judge said he would give her a last chance. She received a "therapeutic injunction," just as drug addicts get when they are caught for the first time, meaning that she would avoid repressive consequences by consulting a psychologist. Being an African, she was sent without hesitation to the ethnopsychiatry clinic. So she went. In the hospital, she had to tell her story in front of an assembly of ten so-called co-therapists from different origins and cultures, some trained, others still students. She refused the interpreter, considering she did not need him to express herself. However, visibly embarrassed by the uncomfortable public confession she was supposed to make, she seemed reluctant to talk. She was asked about her marriage and said her husband was a cousin. She was asked about her dreams and said she sometimes dreamt of gold. Every phrase she uttered became a sign worth being interpreted. The co-therapists commented on all her answers, especially the fact that the problematic child had a twin brother. They discussed in front of her the West African traditional beliefs concerning twins about which they had read. They became extremely interested after learning that all the children had been named after "Muslim saints." They considered the fact that while she was speaking the child had peacefully sat on her lap as a sort of "reconciliation ritual." Finally, the ethnopsychiatrist who was leading the group concluded the session by explaining sententiously to her younger colleagues that this therapeutic scene was generally beneficial for patients because they appreciated being in a place where they were not judged but listened to. The mother, however, did not seem to share this view: she did not understand why she was there and only said she was afraid that her children would be taken away from her.

This anecdote could be read as a mere variation on the theme of Ken Loach's *Ladybird*—the story of a British working-class woman fighting administrations and prejudices to get her four children back from the social services who accuse her of being incapable of taking care of them. But this French variation has a distinct melody: it is postcolonial—not simply because the woman happens to be from a former French colony but because her coming from this former French colony is embedded in a larger historical picture that represents Africans and Muslims as exoticizable others. The two ascribed identities are narrowly linked in this story, as they are in many similar situations where immigrants and their descendants are concerned. When Achille Mbembe writes that "it is in relation to Africa that the notion of 'absolute otherness' has been taken farthest" and that "Africa as an idea, a concept, has historically served, and continues to serve, as a polemical argument for the West's desperate desire to assert its difference from the rest of the world," the argument can be extended to Islam, particularly in the present French context.[1] The background of this permanent ideological reinvention of Africa and Islam is political in the sense that it involves power relations, and the phrase about domination in the epigraph of this chapter may undoubtedly be reformulated from the colonial to the postcolonial encounter.[2] The social condition of foreigners of African origin or Islamic religion, the prejudices from which they suffer, and the discrimination and stigmatization with which they are confronted are inscribed in the long-term history of labor migration (even if their legitimacy as a workforce has been challenged since the mid-1970s) and in the more recent developments of scapegoating immigrants (as was demonstrated most notably during the 2005 riots). The call for ethnopsychiatrists to deal with situations like the one evoked here and the legitimization of this marginal sector of the mental health system through its collaboration with state institutions in charge of regulating immigrant populations may thus be seen as part of a psychopolitics of otherness—that is, adapting Foucault's biopolitics, a technology that normalizes through psychiatry and psychology those who are constructed and governed as radical others.[3]

Whereas a French child belonging to the middle class would have been sent with his mother to the psychologist, could have been diagnosed as having attention-deficit hyperactivity disorder, and may have received Ritalin for treatment, the African boy here was sent with his mother to the social worker and the juvenile judge and from there to the ethnopsychiatrist because they were Africans and Muslims and therefore presumed to need specific consideration and care: the interpretation appeared as cultural rather than psychopathological, obscure beliefs about twins were preferred to a clinical diagnosis, and instead of being offered support or medication for her child, the woman was confronted with the alternative of choosing between the institutional sanction (having her little boy taken away from her) and the exotic ascription (being qualified and treated as different). The fact that she is African and Muslim thus becomes the clue for the interpretation of her case, an interpretation that draws on mundane prejudices (the child is seen as a rapist, the mother is suspected of being a prostitute) and supposedly learned knowledge (ethnological vulgate revisited by psychological culturalism). Probably, it is even more than this: culture, here, appears as a mask for race; the difference is racialized before being culturalized. The color of the skin becomes an insurmountable line that separates distinct groups—equal but different; that is, formally equal but treated differently. In her historical exploration of colonial desire, Ann Stoler explains how "the quest to define moral predicates and invisible essences tied the bourgeois discourses of sexuality, racism, and nationalism in fundamental ways."[4] Seeing a black male as a potential sexual abuser and suspecting a black woman of reprehensible lasciviousness belongs to a long tradition of racializing Africa through moral predicates about invisible essences.[5] In the case of France, a sexual genealogy of the nation has even been traced through the colonial and even precolonial discourse.[6] But the issue does not simply concern African or black populations, because a series of events in recent years, from the "affair of the veil" to the "scandal of the gang rapes," have revealed similar prejudices, both cultural and racial, about Muslims and Arabs.[7] Sending the Malian woman and her son to the ethnopsychiatric clinic is thus part of a postcolonial scene, which singularizes—probably with the best intentions on the part of the judge and later the therapists—the administration of migrant populations.[8]

Certainly, the continuity between colonial and postcolonial should not be taken for granted, and it would be incorrect to infer a linear, univocal, and deterministic relation between past and present. In particular, as we will see, there is, strictly speaking, no historical link between colonial psychiatry and postcolonial ethnopsychiatry. However, there is clearly a genealogy in the construction and government of others—colonized yesterday, immigrants today—through the radicalization of their difference. And in this genealogy, psychiatric knowledge has sometimes played a significant role by essentializing psychic identities and justifying specific policies, including discriminatory or even repressive measures. The paradox is that the French state that claims the republican values of universalism provides not only derogatory but also explicitly differentialist services to its migrant population. In this chapter, I will first contextualize the emergence of ethnopsychiatry in the longer history of the approach of otherness in mental health. I will then analyze the singularity of its development in the recent years. Finally, I will discuss the political meaning of its extension in the public services far beyond the realm of psychopathology as a mode of administration of social problems involving African and Muslim immigrants and, even more specifically, their children. Interestingly, neither colonial nor postcolonial ethnopsychiatry claimed a psychoanalytical legacy—mostly by ignorance in the case of the colonial psychiatrists, such as Antoine Porot in Algiers, and principally by rejection for postcolonial psychologists, like Tobie Nathan near Paris.

French Ethnopsychiatry in Perspective

Until recently, French psychiatry had hardly been concerned with otherness—or rather, it had been concerned for the last two centuries with a different kind of otherness, that of mental illness. After the Second World War, the profession was deeply affected by the discovery of the complete abandonment of the patients in asylums under the Vichy government and the Nazi regime, which had caused the death of forty percent of their population due to lack of care and even of food. For the progressive psychiatrists François Tosquelles, Lucien Bonnafé, and Georges Daumezon, the rehumanization of the mental health system was the political priority and the claim for universalism an ethical necessity. The reform of what Erving Goffman later called "total institutions" was on their agenda, certainly with special consideration for the social inequalities that underlay them (because most patients in asylums belonged to the lower class), but no specific measures were envisaged for the colonial subjects who were still called *indigènes* (natives): in spite of their increasing number, these *citoyens de seconde zone* (second-level citizens), as they were described, were hardly visible in the French society. Many lived in workers' hostels or overcrowded slums in the outskirts of the largest cities; when they were sick, they theoretically had access to the public health system, but in fact, many were treated in separate facilities such as the Avicenna Hospital in northern Paris, which had been exclusively dedicated to natives until 1945, or in special wards such as the tropical diseases unit at the Claude Bernard Hospital.[9]

Nevertheless, the situation was different in the colonies and particularly in Algeria, where medical doctors had built their careers since the late 1910s on the invention of a "colonial psychiatry."[10] The Algiers School became, for almost half a century, a reference for experimentation and innovation in the exploration of psychic otherness. Antoine Porot, with his accounts of "Muslim psychiatry," anticipated by several decades the "discoveries" by John Colin Carothers about the "African mind," both theories mixing ordinary prejudices and pseudoscientific evidence on what they reified, clinically and anatomically, as ontological—not only cultural—differences.[11] The French psychiatrist thus described the "mental puerilism" of North Africans: "The intellectual reduction associating credulity and stubbornness makes the Muslim native's psychic pattern close to that of the child," adding, however, that the latter had the curiosity about the world in which the former seemed so deficient; even their "psychopathies" have "simple patterns: a few confusions almost always in the form of stupidity."[12] In a similar vein, the British physician later wrote, "The African has been described as conventional; highly dependent upon physical and emotional stimulation; lacking in spontaneity, foresight, tenacity, judgment and humility; inapt for sound abstraction and for logic; given to phantasy and fabrication; and in general unstable, impulsive, unreliable, irresponsible and living in the present without reflection or ambition or regard for the rights of people outside his own circle."[13] But this psychiatry in Algeria, just as its sister discipline in Kenya, was not only the reflection of colonial ideologies. It also served the political project of the colonizer. Porot's writings contributed to the stigmatization of "Muslim natives" and more broadly to the diffusion of racist views of North Africans, to the legitimization of colonization as a civilizing process and of punishments against so-called impulsive criminals, and to the justification for the lack of reparation of traumatized soldiers combating during the two world wars and for warfare programs against insurgents during the liberation struggle, just as Carothers's books participated in the interpretation of the revolt of the Mau Mau as a pathologic reaction rather than a protest against land dispossession and more generally supported discrimination and repression against the colonized.[14] Less prestigious than their metropolitan colleagues (although a few of them had their hour of glory), and not exempt from ideals about their mission on the African continent (to which they thought they could bring the benefits of Enlightenment), the colonial psychiatrists, particularly those involved in the Algiers School, did play a significant part in the colonial enterprise. Remarkably, however, this historical dimension of the colonial encounter was absent from their analyses, and it was only through the works of Octave Mannoni in Madagascar and of Frantz Fanon in Algeria that the psychic processes were critically analyzed in terms of the interaction between colonizers and colonized.[15]

After decolonization, several of Porot's students, such as Jean Sutter and Henri Aubin, reintegrated the metropolitan mental health system but with relatively marginal academic positions, except for Yves Pélicier, who nevertheless distanced himself from the founding father by developing an "acculturation" model. Certainly, the influence of the Algiers School did not disappear, particularly because of Porot's *Manuel alphabétique de psychiatrie*, which remains at present a major reference in the training of psychiatrists: in the entry dedicated to the "Noirs," it is noted that "natives of Black Africa are close to the primitive mentality," that "among them physical needs (nutrition, sexuality) are at the forefront," and that "the liveliness of their emotions and the indigence of their intellectual activity make them experience mostly the present, like children."[16] But from the 1950s on, a series of deep transformations occurred in the practice of psychiatry in France: with the introduction of psychotropic drugs, the discipline entered its medical modernity, and with the critique of the confinement system, it claimed its social concern. Later, with the antipsychiatric movement, it affirmed its political dimension. In this context, the prejudices held by colonial ethnopsychiatry about African and Muslim "primitivism" became out of place. In fact, the only space where they could still be found was in occupational medicine, which adapted the nosographical category of "sinistrosis," invented for injured workers at the beginning of the twentieth century, to the case of migrant workers. Qualifying a presumably neurotic condition characterized by the existence of symptoms of pain and fatigue without organic substratum after an accident at work, the diagnosis found its justification in psychopathological features supposedly specific to North Africans—in particular, their tendency to simulation, vindication, and even persecution.[17] Once more, the ideological construction of otherness by psychiatrists was inseparable from their political use, and sinistrosis permitted social security experts to contest the claim for reparation of injured workers.

Besides this limited legacy of colonial psychiatry, the landscape of mental health institutions for immigrants remained largely inscribed in a universalistic approach.[18] Certainly, specific structures were created at the margins of the public health system, which was hardly interested in the problems of this population; thus, the Minkowska Center was opened in 1951, initially for Eastern European refugees and later for Asian and African immigrants. But their theoretical claim was that the singularity of subjective experiences prevailed over the specificity of cultural features: each individual case had to be understood within its unique configuration; adaptation of the therapy for these patients was necessary, indeed, but mainly in linguistic terms with the systematic use of interpreters. In the 1970s, in the context of post-1968 protest, the health problems of migrants began to be analyzed within a political economy perspective: the Medico-Social Committee for the Health of Migrants contested the psychopathological models inherited from the colonial psychiatrists and focused on the deleterious consequences of the living conditions of immigrants. In the 1980s, as increasingly restrictive policies were implemented toward foreign populations, the issue of rights became crucial: the Comede, Medical Committee for the Exiles, and, later, Doctors of the World and Doctors Without Borders developed programs articulating health care and social claims, especially for undocumented immigrants. Finally, in the 1990s, with the rise of asylum seekers and the parallel decline of the legitimacy of the refugees, a new orientation coalesced around the issue of torture and political violence: the Association for the Victims of Repression in Exile and its dissident Primo Levi Center developed specific psychotherapeutic programs. Although the sedimentation of these different generations of psychiatrists and psychologists presents a complex configuration, a common thread is recognizable: it focuses on the shared experience of exile more than on the intrinsic characteristics of the immigrant.[19] Ethnopsychiatry, as developed at the Georges Devereux Center, thus appears as a discordant voice.

Curiously, there seems to be no link between the Fann School in Dakar and the Georges Devereux Center in Saint-Denis, which represent the two main postcolonial attempts to create an ethnopsychiatric clinic—or rather, one should say that psychologist Tobie Nathan never claimed any influence from psychiatrist Henri Collomb.[20] The neuropsychiatry department at the Fann Hospital was opened in 1956, but its major innovation was the creation of a pluridisciplinary group in 1962. Philosopher Edmond Ortigues, psychoanalyst Marie-Cécile Ortigues, psychologist— and later ethnologist—Andràs Zempléni, and specialists of child psychology Simone Valantin and Jacqueline Rabain developed with Henri Collomb a series of collective research on the psychopathology of the Senegalese.[21] Interested in the cultural expressions but also interpretations of mental health problems, the group published numerous studies on traditional syndromes such as the *nit ku bon* and rituals such as the *ndëpp*. However, the boundary seemed clearly drawn between research that attempted to articulate anthropological and psychoanalytical knowledge and practice that was based on a tolerant adaptation of the psychiatric institution to local modes of life. The ambitious theories of Edmond and Marie-Cécile Ortigues in *Oedipe Africain* coexisted with classical descriptions in the journal *Médecine d'Afrique Noire*. Traditional healers were accepted to a certain extent, but the health professionals did not transform themselves into witch doctors. More than anything else, priority was given to the quality of the care delivered to the patients in respect of their habits and families. The large influence of the Dakar experiment in Africa and in spite of the vitality of the journal *Psychopathologie Africaine*, the Fann School, which had been particularly active during the 1960s and 1970s, seems to have had little impact on the later development of the psychiatry of immigration in France and even less on its ethnopsychiatric branch, which began its expansion in the 1980s around the figure of Tobie Nathan.

French postcolonial "ethnopsychiatry"—as it is usually called, although its founder was neither an ethnologist nor a psychiatrist but a psychologist, like most of his followers—is inscribed in another intellectual tradition: that of "ethnopsychoanalysis," developed at the École des hautes études en sciences sociales by Georges Devereux, who was himself a psychoanalyst and an ethnologist.[22] In a conference he held in 1998 in homage to the author of the book *Reality and Dream: Psychotherapy of a Plains Indian*, Nathan, who describes himself as Devereux's favorite student, relates that his professor broke with him the very day he opened his own ethnopsychiatric clinic in 1981, a decision that the young psychologist interpreted as a way to gain his freedom. Beyond this anecdote, it is clear that Nathan's theory and practice proposed a radical rupture with Devereux's paradigm and ethics. Contrary to his master, the disciple violently rejected psychoanalysis, just as he rebuffed anthropology, and developed a radical theory reifying cultures—and ascribing all individuals to their origins.[23] Thus, his ethnopsychiatry had nothing to do with ethnopsychoanalysis—no more than it had to do with psychoanalytical anthropology. For Devereux, "the psychoanalyst must understand the nature and function of culture considered per se—beyond any particular culture—not only because it is a universal phenomenon, an exclusive characteristic of mankind, but also because the general categories of culture—which must not be confused with the content of these categories in a given culture—are universal phenomena."[24] For Nathan, conversely, "a culture is constituted by all individuals culturally similar, who have in common characters which distinguish them from other human beings, themselves members of a culture and capable of engendering individuals culturally similar," and consequently, "a functional culture ensures the closure of the group and gives a consciousness of its identity (we are Bambara and not Soninke)."[25] The radically differentialist perspective in Nathan's paradigm was therefore the opposite of the universalist view in Devereux's theory of culture with a capital *C* as contrasted with the singularity of each culture. Moreover, whereas the latter had dedicated his two famous books *Essai d'ethnopsychiatrie générale* and *Ethnopsychanalyse complémentariste* to Marcel Mauss and Claude Lévi-Strauss, respectively, the former stigmatized ethnology as "novelist work without the courage of its imagination."[26] Finally, while Devereux had a high opinion of psychoanalysis, even considering it an "instrument of ethnological investigation," Nathan became increasingly ironical about and critical of his first psychoanalytic skill pleading a "scientific psychopathology" strictly based on the description of therapeutic techniques.[27]

This opposition between the professor and his rebellious disciple even took a personal turn when Nathan accused Devereux of being a closet Jew: "Psychoanalysts from Eastern Europe told me that they had known him in the United States where he was known to be Jewish. When I asked him he denied the evidence: 'If I were Jewish, why would I hide it?' But he was hiding it! He was hiding it but simultaneously exposed it, just like the minister was hiding the letter in Edgar Poe's short story."[28] Conversely, Nathan proclaimed his own "being Jewish," going as far as to ask, "Is not the Jew an individual who, when he or she is treated *à la Juive* [in the

Jewish mode], the most likely to be healed?"[29] This is the principle he applied to his practice at the Georges Devereux Center when he founded it in 1993 at the University of Paris 8. As he wrote, by treating a Soninke patient according to his own culture, "I allow him to be above all a Soninke —which is the only way to be human for a Soninke, I believe" (in fact, the careful reader of this case study may notice that the proverb he uses to interpret the illness is Bambara).[30] Thus, Nathan developed in Saint-Denis a practice that was radically new in the French context of mental health. He influenced a generation of psychologists, medical doctors, and social workers interested in other cultures. But by essentializing otherness in his theories as well as in his practice, he was actually reinventing, probably without knowing it, a vision of humanity that had been dominant under the colony.[31] In the Algiers School, it was for the sake of colonization. In the Saint-Denis School, it was meant to be for the good of the immigrants. Whereas Porot was presenting an overtly racist theory of the Muslim patient corresponding to the virulent political discourse of the empire, Nathan gave it an apparently benign culturalist and ethnicist turn, which encountered both the rising influence of the themes of identity from the right and the ambiguous desire to respect differences from the left. In both cases, this psychopolitics of otherness received encouragement and support from public authorities.

French Ethnopsychiatry as a Clinical Practice

Clinical situation. Bintou, a splendid Malian, age nineteen. Dressed like a French youth, with fashionable jeans and shirt—gorgeous! She is sent by doctors and social workers because of permanent complaints: she feels that she is becoming blind, faints without reason, wanders about like a lost soul from her aunt's to her elder sister's, from a youth hostel to an insalubrious squat—the case is worrying . . . Bintou, pregnant at the age of fourteen, hid her condition from her family. She gave birth in the toilets alone and left the baby on the window ledge of the second floor. The child fell, miraculously survived, but was left heavily handicapped, blind, deaf, and mute, and was placed in a special institution since then and probably also autistic. Bintou was first charged with infanticide and later considered by the judge as victim of an indecent assault.

Fragments of a therapeutic dialogue. Clinician: "When she was a child, Bintou played with elder persons. She even looked at adults in the eyes. (Turning to her) It is for this reason that your Mum sent you to France—because you were different?" Bintou: "I don't know. One day I heard her talk with somebody about my departure, that's all." Clinician: "At one year old, when her father died, Bintou fell sick. (Turning to her) You fell sick at that moment?" Bintou: "I don't know, I was one year old." Clinician: "Your mother did not tell you?" Bintou: "No. She doesn't tell me these things. She just sends me things to wash myself." Clinician: "I even know that you have marks on your body, scars on both sides of your belly, I know." Bintou (Smiling, with astonished eyes): "Yes, I have marks there (Showing her belly)." Clinician (to the group): "When her father died, she was sick for three months." Another clinician: "She almost died." Clinician (to Bintou): "You look very much like your father, right? I mean: physically." Bintou: "I don't know." Clinician: "You don't even have pictures of your father?" Bintou: "My mother does not want me to look at them." Clinician (to the group): "Bintou thinks a lot about her father." Bintou: "Yes, I think a lot about him, every day and I am afraid of it." Clinician: "And when you were a child, you hurt yourself quite often. You came back home with bleeding knees." Bintou: "Yes, my mother says that I got her very tired." Then she started to smile staring at the floor. One felt that her mind was working at full speed . . . making thoughts, establishing links, elaborating meanings.

An hour and a half later in the same consultation. Clinician: "When you will talk to your mother on the phone, tell her that you saw me. Also tell her that I have seen in the cauris that she must bury alive a big animal and a small one—a cow and her calf . . . or maybe simply a ewe and her lamb. She'll understand, for sure."

Interrogation: Answer briefly and precisely the following questions: 1. How do you comprehend the suffering of this patient? 2. Try to reconstitute the clinician's thought.[32]

This text was given in an exam that sanctioned the psychopathology course at the University of Paris 8 several years ago. Students had two hours to interpret the story on the sole basis of this brief reconstitution. However, the exegete of Nathan's writings has today a few more indications because the case study was published with some comments in a booklet that the famous ethnopsychiatrist published as a "manifesto for a scientific psychopathology": actually, he is the clinician in the story.[33] One learns that in the "very large room with a very high ceiling," there were "at least ten, psychologists and psychoanalysts of course, but also doctors and anthropologists, all with diplomas from French universities," and that the professor "introduced all of them, giving his or her cultural origin and academic title each time."[34] It is no surprise that the young woman felt both impressed and uncomfortable, as the author notices. About Bintou's life, there are not many more details, except that she was born after twins and that she was later accused of being responsible for her father's death, but the ethnopsychiatrist's interpretation that the students were supposed to reconstitute is presented as "evident although implicit": the young woman had a "probable supernatural husband" and was considered as "her father's twin," hence her suffering.[35] The diagnostic procedure had been conducted by a psychologist at the center who was "a Fulani from Senegal" and had "thrown the cauris" using a traditional divination method with shells, revealing that an "offering of two things which look the same" was necessary.[36] As the author explains to us, the translation of this prescription into the sacrifice of two animals was simply the result of the adaptation by Nathan himself of Henri Hubert's and Marcel Mauss's *Essai sur la nature et la fonction du sacrifice* (*Essay on the Nature and Function of Sacrifice*) to Bintou's case: the animals were to be buried alive so that their breath could be enclosed, thus allowing the patient to get "extra vitality." Nathan concludes, "Bintou, not so long ago lonely, will henceforth find herself, thanks to this consultation, surrounded by her mother, aunts and uncles, a marabout or two or three . . . QED." At least, this is what the ethnopsychiatrist asserts, but the reader is left with the sole information that immediately after the consultation, Bintou looks "radiant with happiness" and "does not want to leave the room."[37] What happens next, no one knows. In fact, even therapists usually have no follow-up on the clinical and social outcome. It is only assumed—without evaluation—that the patients get better. However, the mental health professionals who see them afterward may have different stories, as some of them confided to me.

This case study is paradigmatic of Nathan's practice—and used by him as such. It is paradigmatic of the final period of his institutional activity in ethnopsychiatry. It reveals a radicalization of his practice, which is reflected in his last books. In his first writings, he discusses psychoanalysts, particularly Freud, and anthropologists, notably Lévi-Strauss. From the mid-1990s, he denounces them. Psychoanalysts are accused of obscurantist dogmatism: "They decree the existence of an object they are the only ones to perceive; they make instruments to describe this object and make it opaque to all strangers; and they validate themselves the adequacy of their instruments. Thus they have come full circle. The chain of reasoning is locked."[38] The critique extends to psychiatrists: "So-called 'scientific discoveries' by Professors Charcot and Freud condemning witches, sybils and prophetesses to hysterical misery, are only the official registration and the death certificates of the disappearing of the multiplicity of universes."[39] According to Nathan, all psychopathological theories are doctrines merely focused on individuals and dishonestly guided by self-interest: "The goal of the 'scientific psychotherapists' is always to cut the subject from his universes. And why is it so? Exclusively to increase the number of their patients. Because, as far as psychopathology is concerned, medicine and its by-products, wherever they install their soldiers (doctors), their supply corps (pharmaceutical companies), their judges (the scientists who decide the true from the false), always have for consequences to dismantle belongings."[40] Anthropologists are not better treated by him. With his colleague Lucien Hounkpatin, he asserts in clear hostile reference to Lévi-Strauss, "We are neither ethnologists nor anthropologists, thank God! To imagine ourselves in the kitchen of strangers studying their manners of preparing the cooked and—who knows?—in their bed at night to explore their passion for the raw, no, certainly not! This ethnology that comprehends, explains, interprets, narrates and, from this long fermentation, draws enunciations about persons who will not have access to them, we refute it in its very principle!"[41] In fact, to Nathan and Hounkpatin, of all the characters with which traditional societies have been confronted, from the priest to the journalist, the anthropologist is by far the most obnoxious and dangerous: "Even a slave trader or a colonial administrator can be welcomed because one can understand their intentions. But an ethnologist! He goes there just to search material for the progression of his career in the CNRS [National Center for Scientific Research] or the Collège de France. It is his genuine interest—everyone knows it! Is it therefore acceptable to be just material for ethnologists?"[42] Thus, in spite of its name, ethnopsychiatry has nothing to do with either psychiatrists or ethnologists—an assertion that disqualifies in advance the critiques coming from two disciplines in which Nathan has no training and little knowledge but from which he draws much of his self-proclaimed expertise on a clientele composed of exotic patients. This strategy, however, does not prevent psychoanalyst and ethnologist Yannick Jaffré from proposing a subtle analysis of the misinterpretations of the case studies presented by Nathan—a "savage interpretation," as he ironically writes.[43]

The main consequence of this systematic denunciation of psychic and social sciences is that it gives Nathan the opportunity to claim the foundation of something radically new. The scorched earth policy makes possible an intellectual tabula rasa (hence, the manifesto) and a ritual academic rebirth (from Paris 13 to Paris 8). The psychotherapist—admirer of Mauss, follower of Devereux, colleague of psychiatrist and psychoanalyst Serge Lebovici, friend of psychologist and ethnologist Andràs Zempléni—breaks with his intellectual and institutional affiliations and becomes a diviner who diagnoses with cauris, a traditional healer who calls for the sacrifice of animals, and, as we will see, even a political prophet who announces dangerous times. Certainly, Nathan is playing with his public—for instance, when he comments on how he guessed that Bintou had scarifications on her abdomen: "The point is not what I see, but that I see," he says, leaving his imaginary interlocutor convinced of his gifts and ignoring the fact that all the details have been given to him in advance. Like an illusionist, he does not reveal his tricks and prefers to let the magic of the performance work.[44]

"The first reason for my disagreement with him is ethical," writes the scholar Aboubacar Barry. "I am a psychologist and not a marabout, and nothing in my training confers upon me the competences that are necessary to formulate therapeutic injunctions. I think that if a psychologist considers that his patient requires the expertise of a 'tradipractitioner', the best advice he may give him or her is to consult one."[45] Nathan and his cotherapists have a different view of their role: they precisely turn themselves into "tradipractitioners," improvising techniques of divination and healing from heterogeneous fragments of knowledge gleaned according to readings and encounters. The choice of this designation is not innocent: since the 1980s, the policy of the World Health Organization has been to "rehabilitate" traditional medicines, especially on the African continent, by creating organizations of so-called tradipractitioners. The result of this policy has been the multiplication of self-proclaimed healers and the development of hybrid knowledge.[46] Certainly, Nathan's innovative enterprise is inscribed in the same logic of self-recognition, as we have seen, but also of hybridity, somewhat contradictorily with the claim of cultural purity. A little-noticed element of this hybrid configuration resides in the ethnopsychiatric consultation itself borrowing from the classical nineteenth-century presentation (which may still be observed nowadays) of the "case" in neuropsychiatric wards, where the powerless patient was confronted with a group of specialists and students examining and commenting on his or her case.

The clinical practice of ethnopsychiatry thus exerts a complex form of violence on those it is supposed to help.[47] The patients are denied access to common law: not only do they have no choice of the care from which they may benefit (they are ascribed to their supposed cultural institution), but they also have no possibility of having their voice heard (they are confined in a restrictive cultural interpretation). This was the case for Bintou, who was obviously scared and reluctant during the consultation and whose words were hardly heard and were not taken into consideration: the ethnopsychiatrist knows better and talks on her behalf. But the reproduction of the ethnopsychiatric scene is not limited to the consultation at the Georges Devereux Center, where it is permanently reinvented. It is also exported to various worlds such as hospitals and clinics, social services and educational structures, and sometimes, even more unexpectedly, judicial courts.

French Ethnopsychiatry as a Cultural Practice

Teo, the panther-child. 19 September 1994: I find in my mail a petition from the state prosecutor for a measure of protection. Teo, a thirteen-year-old Cameroonian, is endangering himself. The social services note that the living conditions of his family are extremely precarious. The adolescent is in permanent conflict with his mother, commits delinquent acts, encounters school difficulties and often runs away from home. As I read the file, the following alternative is offered to me.

I may analyze the situation according to my own cultural representations. A child raised by his maternal grandmother in Africa is suddenly reunited at the age of twelve at his mother, whom he has not seen for six years. She lives in France with four children of a different father, whom Teo does not even know. Is it for this reason that the boy steals, runs away, does not study and permanently changes from aggressiveness to depression? The mother seems psychologically fragile. Often sick, she looks powerless in front of this child, unwelcomed by his stepfather who is himself experiencing a difficult situation as an undocumented immigrant.

Or I can try to understand the case by entering the system of values and representations of the family. How do they analyze Teo's problems? And first of all, who is he? Why did he rejoin his mother? Trained to the approach of traditional interpretations, I wonder about this "strange child." Several elements of the description by social services support this hypothesis: he had a twin brother who died when he arrived in France; one aunt also deceased in the same period; his behavior is peculiar with regards to his family's customs, notably his night wanderings and his attitudes towards adults.

I summon Teo, Mela Kodonu, the mother, and Makome Kodonu, the stepfather, for a first hearing. Mrs. Kodonu comes alone. She explains that her husband cannot be present for obscure reasons—probably because he fears the court, since he is a clandestine—and that her son simply refused to come. Mrs. Kodonu looks very disappointed when I tell her I must see Teo before "judging." I have the impression she expected that I would decide to admit him in an institution. I propose to ask the assistance of an ethnoclinician mediator who has an anthropological training, belongs to her culture and speaks Lingala. I assume that he is thus aware of traditional etiologies. Initially surprised, Mela Kodonu accepts but remarks that it is not necessary since she understands French perfectly well. I explain to her that actually this hearing of intercultural transmission is a means to make compatible two universes of significations, by nature different.[48]

This story is told by the judge of a juvenile court in Paris, Thierry Baranger, who became a student of Tobie Nathan at the University of Paris 8 in the 1990s and who wrote a book on his experience along with Martine de Maximy, a colleague from Bobigny, and Hubert de Maximy, a film director. For Baranger, a parallel may be seen between a witchcraft ordeal and a judicial trial: "Whereas in the West the judge sees 'problems,' his African colleague sees 'signs'; the judge of the juvenile court tries to solve the 'problems' to allow the child to return to normality; the traditional judge, conversely, does not attempt to suppress the 'signs' but to produce an alchemy which goes beyond and gives a positive value to the singularity of the child by transforming them into a 'good' witchcraft." In the case of Teo, he finally decides simultaneously on an "admission in a hostel for adolescents" and an "ethnopsychoanalytic expertise." Tobie Nathan is invited as "justice auxiliary." After having talked with Teo, Baranger hypothesizes that the child is a witch because he dreams of dogs; the judge comments that in a Wolof tale, it is said that "dogs see everything that comes out at night." As the mother mentions that the child is "a lamb at home and a panther outside," again, the judge evokes traditional beliefs about which he has read, this time from Guinea and Liberia about panther-men. At the end of the hearing, the ethnopsychiatrist asks the mother to give Teo a new name, Tatavutukidi, which means "daddy came back." In conclusion of this case study of the "witch-child between his two judges," which gives the exotic title of his book, Baranger notes, "This respect of the person confronted to justice induces the judge into a function similar to that of the shaman who shows the way to the patient and accompanies him in a process of restoration."[49] However, just as previously for Bintou, the reader will not have access to the final outcome of this case study: what happened afterward to Teo and his family remains unknown, but this is probably not the crucial issue.

The judge is actually more interested in the solution of the intellectual puzzle (the supposed case of witchcraft, with its world of chimera, both humans and animals) than in resolving the practical problem (the social difficulties encountered by the family): in fact, his ethnopsychiatric expertise helps him to realize that there is precisely no sense in thinking in terms of "problems" and that he should rather try to recognize "signs." Of course, the judge knows that he must decide about the admission of the adolescent into a hostel to alleviate the mother's anxiety and fatigue, but he considers also that his role goes beyond this judicial routine and implies shamanistic functions. For him, even the absence of the undocumented father at the first hearing is justified by "obscure reasons"—in spite of what is known about irregular immigrants being arrested by the administration when they are summoned under an apparently unrelated pretext. The "invisible," as Nathan says, is everywhere. This is what Baranger presents as the final lesson of the mediation: the recognition of a difference and the reconciliation between two worlds. Notwithstanding the reluctance of the mother (considered as a symptom of her Westernization), the interpretative approximations of the case (the Cameroonian story read through Senegalese or Guinean theories), the naïve idealization of healers (with the improbable positivization of witchcraft), the frailty of the final hypothesis (unveiling the witch-child), the oddness of the treatment (giving him a new name), and the lack of evidence of its efficacy, the judge is taken by the performance: he is a believer.

"The only discipline scientifically defensible would be—if you forgive this barbarism—an influenceology, that would have for its object to analyze the different procedures of transformation of the other," writes Nathan.[50] Influence—another word for power, which is, from an anthropological perspective, the capacity to act on others to transform the course of events: this is precisely what characterizes Nathan's own enterprise.[51] In only a few years, he has extended his influence well beyond the realm of mental health and academic psychology. Surrounded by students and disciples, he has received visits and support from many social scientists, the most faithful being Isabelle Stengers and Bruno Latour, who themselves are influential.[52] The media have been keen to open their pages or their channels to this original thinker who likes to shake up academic and medical authorities, from the newspaper *Le Monde* to the radio network France Culture. Public sponsors of scientific research have abundantly funded his programs, which are always presented at the interface of action and science. Public services and administrations, from the national to the local level, have brought him cases so that he could perform his psychotherapy; social workers, medical doctors, and judges have come to his consultations, sometimes follow his classes, and often become his spokespersons. Not only has he himself been an excellent pedagogue, but his disciples have served as his best messengers: each year, hundreds of sessions are held all over the country, and occasionally abroad, to disseminate his word to professionals of all kinds and to nongovernmental organizations. At a certain point, the state itself was delegating part of its prerogatives on immigrant populations to Nathan and his school—not only for psychotherapy but also social policies, health, and justice. In the country of the self-proclaimed universalist republicanism, the ethnopsychiatrist of Saint-Denis had succeeded in making a radical form of cultural differentialism reign.

The most troubling fact, indeed, is that the discourse held by the then director of the Georges Devereux Center could be so contradictory with the official position of French public authorities from which he was receiving his subsidies and support. There was actually no ambiguity in Nathan's statements: "I affirm it very clearly: the children of Soninke, Bambara, Fulani, Dyula, Ewondo—who else?—belong to their ancestors. To brainwash them in order to change them into Whites, Republicans, atheists, is purely a declaration of war."[53] Calling for "ghettos in order not to oblige a family to abandon their cultural system," he denounced "janissaries whitened in republican schools who will come back one day to colonize their people for the benefit of the victor" and predicted that "once they will have grown up, these black children raised in the French way will be the most insipid of all Whites."[54] Justifying by anticipation the failures of the French policies of integration not on a social but on a cultural basis, he asserted, "To put brutally at school a three-year-old Soninke child born in France and breastfed according to the Soninke usage and to expect that he will adapt to it is to know nothing of psychic functioning. And it is a shame!"[55] Considering Nathan's thought as a whole, there is certainly a profound coherence between the ideological system based on the essentialization of culture and the radicalization of difference, on the one hand, and the political system based on a racialized vision of the world and pleading for spatial segregation of immigrants, on the other hand. More unexpected is the rallying of intellectuals, journalists, professionals, bureaucrats, and politicians to his cause. It is remarkable that this convergence took place in a period when immigration became the "problem" of France, or, better said, it was "problematized" as the major issue by French society under the ideological and political pressure of the extreme right.[56] As a distant echo to Socialist Prime Minister Laurent Fabius, declaring in 1984 that "Mr. Le Pen asks good questions but gives false answers," social scientist Bruno Latour wrote an opinion piece provocatively asserting that the National Front leader "was the only man in France who knew how to do politics" and that "through the last political discourse left to them, that of immigration, French people rejected the obligation imposed on them to take for granted the acceptation of aliens, to consider it as a definitive fact, a natural fact, an inescapable fact."[57] A few days later, Nathan answered a journalist who asked him what he thought of the growing influence of Jean-Marie Le Pen's ideas: "I think the left has done a very big mistake by forgetting to think the difference."[58] Finally, the next year, Latour wrote another article, this time in defense of the ethnopsychiatrist who had been under attack for his extreme statements, with the ironic title, "Why So Much Hatred?"[59] Underlining these postcolonial dangerous liaisons is not suggesting an extreme-right connection including radical ethnopsychiatry and ultrarelativist anthropology. It is only illustrating the degree of political confusion to which reification of culture and fascination with difference may give rise.

Epilogue

At the moment I am writing these lines, the world in which ethnopsychiatry is embedded has profoundly changed. During the past decade, Tobie Nathan, the principal character of my narrative, has completely disappeared from the French intellectual landscape. In 2003, he became delegate for the Agence universitaire de la francophonie (French-speaking universities network) in Burundi, and in 2004, he was recruited as the conseiller culturel (cultural counselor) at the French embassy in Israel. He is henceforth absent from the media and bookstores; no more controversial statements and public scandals. Certainly, the Georges Devereux Center is still active, but its members keep out of the limelight. They clearly avoid their spiritual master's excesses. Françoise Sironi, who is probably Nathan's most faithful follower in this university group and who became director after the professor left, recently asserted in a conference, "Migrant populations who consult in our center today do not come any more from the depth of the bush. Arriving from third world metropolis or villages, they live in the era of mobile phones and television networks."[60] Exit exoticism. Marie-Rose Moro, a former student of Nathan who created the main hospital ethnopsychiatry unit in France, pleads for a soft version of diversity that she proposes "to think, almost to sublimate, in order to anticipate a mixed-race society," adding nevertheless that "the first condition not to do violence to mixed-race children is not to ask them to look like us."[61] End of the racial episode. One could thus think that the Nathan parenthesis, with its excesses and provocations, is now closed. In a sense, that is true. Ethnopsychiatry is pacified.

But this only indicates that, to paraphrase de Gaulle's famous sentence, if Nathan has lost a battle, he may have won the war—precisely the one he had predicted and of which the 2005 riots could be the peak.[62] Ethnopsychiatry is no longer polemical: it has become ordinary practice. Dozens of consultation facilities exist all over the country. Their specialists serve as mediators in social services, hospitals, and courts. In many institutions in charge of "social problems," it is now a reflex to call for an ethnopsychiatrist whenever immigrants or youth of immigrant descent—that is, in fact, Africans or of African origin—are concerned. Certainly, this is a soft version of what the master of Saint-Denis had imagined. The performance is less spectacular but structurally unchanged, as seen in the case presented in the introduction to this chapter. The psychopolitics of otherness has become a normalized way of governing postcolonial immigrants under the auspices of the republic.

Notes

This chapter has little in common with the paper presented in Madison, Wisconsin, at the conference organized by Warwick Anderson and Richard C. Keller, to whom I am deeply grateful for their invitation to reconsider my previous research on ethnopsychiatry. It has been prepared benefiting from a grant from the French ANR (National Agency for Research) and from discussions with colleagues in the program Frontières.

1. Mbembe, *On the Postcolony*, 2.
2. Asad, *Anthropology and the Colonial Encounter*.
3. Foucault, *History of Sexuality*.
4. Stoler, *Carnal Knowledge and Imperial Power*, 154.
5. Gilman, *Difference and Pathology*.
6. Dorlin, *La matrice de la race*.
7. Bowen, *Why the French Don't Like Headscarves*; Muchielli, *Le scandale des tournantes*.
8. Beneduce, *Etnopsichiatria*, 27.
9. Goffman, *Asylums*.
10. Berthelier, *L'homme maghrébin dans la littérature psychiatrique*.
11. Porot, "Notes de psychiatrie musulmane"; Carothers, *African Mind in Health and Disease*.
12. Porot, "Notes de psychiatrie musulmane," 382.
13. Carothers, *African Mind in Health and Disease*, 87.
14. Keller, *Colonial Madness*; McCulloch, *Colonial Psychiatry and the 'African Mind.'*
15. Mannoni, *Prospero and Caliban*; Fanon, *Black Skin, White Masks*.
16. Porot, *Manuel alphabétique de psychiatrie*. The last edition was released in 1996; these excerpts are from the 1952 edition, which was republished in 1969. Unless otherwise noted, all translations are my own.
17. Sayad, "Santé et équilibre social chez les immigrés."
18. Fassin and Rechtman, "Anthropological Hybrid."
19. Fassin and Rechtman, *Empire of Trauma*.
20. Corin, "Playing with Limits."
21. Collignon, "Vingt ans de travaux à la clinique psychiatrique de Fann-Dakar."
22. Devereux, *Ethnopsychanalyse complémentariste*.
23. Nathan, "Manifeste pour une psychopathologie scientifique."
24. Devereux, *Essais d'ethnopsychiatrie générale*, 337.
25. Nathan, *L'influence qui guérit*, 179, 213.
26. Nathan, "Etre juif?" 9; Devereux, *Essais d'ethnopsychiatrie générale*; and Devereux, *Ethnopsychanalyse complémentariste*.

27. Devereux, *Essais d'ethnopsychiatrie générale*, 354; Nathan, "Manifeste pour une psychopathologie scientifique," 106.

28. Nathan, "Etre juif?" 12.

29. Ibid., 11.

30. Nathan, *L'influence qui guérit*, 23.

31. Fassin, "Les politiques de l'ethnopsychiatrie."

32. *Examen de psychopathologie*, Université Paris VIII (undated, non-paginated typescript); a different version of the case study was published later in Nathan and Stengers, *Médecins et Sorciers*.

33. Nathan, "Manifeste pour une psychopathologie scientifique," 29–40.

34. Nathan and Stengers, *Médecins et Sorciers*.

35. Ibid.

36. Ibid.

37. Ibid.

38. Nathan, "Manifeste pour une psychopathologie scientifique," 24.

39. Ibid., 16.

40. Ibid., 20.

41. Nathan and Hounkpatin, *La parole de la forêt initiale*, 9.

42. Ibid., 67.

43. Jaffré, "L'interprétation sauvage."

44. Fethi Benslama, "L'illusion ethnopsychiatrique," *Le Monde*, December 4, 1996.

45. Barry, "Psy d'étrangers."

46. Fassin, *Pouvoir et maladie en Afrique.*

47. Fassin, "Les politiques de l'ethnopsychiatrie."

48. De Maximy, Baranger, and de Maximy, *L'enfant sorcier africain entre ses deux juges.*

49. Ibid., 121.

50. Nathan, *L'influence qui guérit*, 25.

51. Fassin, "L'ethnopsychiatrie et ses réseaux."

52. Stengers, "Le médecin et le charlatan"; Latour, *Petite réflexion sur le culte moderne des dieux faitiches.*

53. Nathan, *L'influence qui guérit*, 331.

54. Ibid., 216, 330–31.

55. Ibid., 217.

56. Silverman, *Deconstructing the Nation.*

57. Latour, "Un nouveau délit d'opinion: Faire de la politique," *Le Monde*, October 4, 1996.

58. Dhombres, "Freud ressemblait à un guérisseur africain," *Le Monde*, October 22, 1996.

59. Latour, "Pourquoi tant de haine?" *Le Monde*, June 20, 1997.

60. Sironi, "Comment inventer des pratiques cliniques adaptées."

61. Moro, *Enfants d'ici venus d'ailleurs*, 13, 182.

62. Fassin and Fassin, *De la question sociale à la question raciale?*

RANJANA KHANNA

Concluding Remarks | **Hope, Demand, and the Perpetual**

The ambition of psychoanalysis, not of Freud alone, has been internationalist. The *International Journal of Psychoanalysis* was not named thus in order to assume that the globe extended only through Europe but saw the reach of the profession as extending to the far regions of the planet. As Mariano Plotkin notes in chapter 5 of this volume, it is, with Marxism, one of the two defining discourses of the twentieth century. Like Marxism, it had an internationalist impulse, and, also like Marxism, it required many versions of internationalism in order to take the changing world order into account. Although Freud was dismissive of some international psychoanalysts, who wrote, for example, in South Africa or India— such as Wulf Sachs, Frederick S. Perls, or Grindeshekar Bose— nevertheless, he did correspond with them with some interest, even as he resisted any claims of fundamental difference in psyche. At the same time, some of the anthropological texts Freud chose to read and cite were naturally imperialist in their endeavors. And yet, to say so is to say very little. Inevitably, they were at a time of such European global power. Some anthropologists were attractive to Freud because they took the then quite bold position of assuming the same degree of humanity in all parts of the world—whether in Europe, the Dark Continent, Asia, or even Australia. This volume demonstrates in many chapters (such as Alice Bullard's chapter 2 and Joy Damousi's chapter 3) that it is impossible to think of the internationalist scope of psychoanalysis without addressing its various anthropological investments and afterlife.

The modern psyche Freud tried to understand (or perhaps partly created) was marked by disappointment and loss. Loss is a common enough indication of internationalist modernism, and indeed, many thought him to be echoing and analyzing that. But the loss theorized by Freud and by many of his followers—critics such as Melanie Klein—was of war and in a time of war and therefore perhaps inevitably articulated itself in terms both of actual loss of life and also of political ideals—a rethinking of ideas of sovereignty (see John Cash's chapter 1 for more on this)—and ways of being in the world. Not insignificantly for us today, the forms of loss he theorized in relation to the First World War and understood differently as he approached the Second World War also coincided with decolonization movements and independence struggles. In the context of postwar displacement, we might ask what forms of nation could generate hostility and hospitality in peace time and how that displacement was shaped by different understandings of imperial nation-building, modernist decolonizations, sovereignty, and, indeed, comparative colonialisms. Loss, in the context of colonialism, is usefully analyzed psychoanalytically in relation to the concept of melancholia, which was theorized by Freud as the loss of an ideal—for example, the ideal of the nation as it figures into the work of decolonization. The many ideals that constituted the colonial impulse as well as organized resistance to it had a psychic life that included unconscious dominions. International psychoanalysis is usefully framed through melancholia, which Freud ultimately failed to theorize adequately. However, it is perhaps this failure that is most compelling for international psychoanalysis.

In *Cultures of the Death Drive: Melanie Klein and Modernist Melancholia*, Esther Sanchez-Pardo presents a monumental study of melancholia rivaling Robert Burton's in length, which came many centuries before.[1] She discusses the importance of the interwar period as the moment of modernist melancholia. For Sanchez-Pardo, Melanie Klein's highly developed and highly influential notion of melancholia as an interwar phenomenon is one of the most important developments in modernism. Drawing on Wolf Lepenies's book *Melancholy and Society*[2]—which itself traces the development of melancholy beyond and before psychoanalysis, from Burton and the fictional utopian societies of the Renaissance, to the ennui of the French aristocracy in the seventeenth century, to the cult of inwardness and escapism among the middle class in eighteenth-century Germany, and through romanticism and modernism—she concludes that melancholia emerges in moments in which there are repressive sociohistorical factors. She is particularly invested in issues of sexual difference and desire, which is perhaps why she, like Judith Butler (less explicitly), turns to Klein for her theorization of melancholia as a known loss of polysexuality in the advent of a kind of compulsory heterosexuality. It is also—not coincidentally, I will suggest—the moment in which there is a massive generation of displaced peoples. Hannah Arendt famously ends her section on imperialism in *The Origins of Totalitarianism* with a discussion of the major changes wrought by the First World War—which "exploded the European comity of nations beyond repair" and created massive inflation and unemployment while engendering civil wars and a mass migration of people.[3] Refugees and stateless peoples were, for her, the most symptomatic of the time.

I want to put these products of interwar peace time—melancholia and displacement—together to attempt to understand the phenomenon of postcolonial melancholia. What does the international modernism of psychoanalysis do to the shape of melancholia? And is the current interest in melancholia one that marks postcolonialism's modernist impulses and aspirations? To echo Raymond Williams (and later Geeta Kapur), one might ask, when was modernism?[4] This begs a question concerning the temporality of melancholia, but also the temporality of postcoloniality, and the theory of temporality in psychoanalysis. I am particularly interested in whether psychoanalysis has a theory of the present, and if so, whether that theory of the present is complicated when one puts psychoanalysis in an international context. The international framing of the talking cure complicates the question of whether the symptom, affect (with its own confused temporality and its imbrication in transference), and demand could be thought of as psychoanalytic theories of the present; and whether the more political terms of hope, demand, and the perpetual are formed by the same sense of temporality. All three terms are shaped in my analysis by the messiness of international modernity and the concept of melancholia and are in some ways curtailed by the more streamlined notion of the superego.

Freud never completed his theorization of melancholia, perhaps because he began to see this affect as more generally a part of modern life rather than as the "diseased critical agency" he named it in 1915/1917.[5] By 1923, in his second topology, the idea of a critical agency would be transferred from its initial theorization in the concept of melancholia to that of the critical moralizing, sovereign, and conservative function of the superego.[6] So how could this idea of critical agency—once diseased—become normative of the controlling apparatus of the modern subject and its imperial dominion? Why would it move from an unhealthy, wretched, and impoverished status to a healthy, controlling one? How did this change relate to the distinctive moment of the world wars in which melancholia was most fully theorized to its transferred status to health in a time of peace? And how do we understand the departure from the idea of perpetual melancholia in a time of war to health in a moment of apparent perpetual peace?

Comparative Colonialisms

In "The Accumulation of Capital," Rosa Luxemburg famously delineated the manner in which capitalism needed an international arena and explained how both colonialism and imperialism, however justified, were centered in "the rule of the capitalist bourgeoisie and its institutions of ownership."[7] While acknowledging the historical facts of cultural and political differentiation—for example, the manner in which the French in Algeria were different from the empire that preceded them (the Ottomans) and also the overt reasons given for their rule (the *mission civilisatrice* and the betterment of the Algerian people, apparently ruined for traditional existence from precolonial times and unready for French-style modern life)—Luxemburg sees these factors as superstructural rationalizations and outcomes of a fundamental base. When she described the French insistence on breaking up the Arab family structure as a way of destroying and disrupting communal property, something already disrupted among the Kabyles by the presence of the Turks in Algeria, she supplied the (somewhat simplistic and romanticized) anthropological detail only in order to make the general point more convincing. In no uncertain terms, however, she refused any sort of understanding of the national or even continental economic and cultural formations that ignored the colonial relation and its later manifestation as imperialism. In order to make her point, her comparative work consistently returned to the same vision, and comparison became analogy. She acknowledged the different strategies of the British in India from the French in Algeria, explaining how they artificially created "a landed aristocracy at the expense of" (the again romanticized) "ancient property-rights of the peasant communities, and then proceeded to 'protect' the peasants against these alleged oppressors, and to bring this illegally usurped land into the possession of

British capitalists."[8] And yet, even though in this example she explained the substantial difference between direct and indirect rule in the histories of French and British colonial practices, her tracing of comparative genealogies of colonialism through the lens of imperialism ultimately considered the commonalities more important. She wrote, "Just as the English had done in British India, so Louis-Philippe's governors in Algeria declared the existence of communal property of the clan to be 'impossible.' This fiction served as an excuse to claim for the state most of the uncultivated areas, and especially the commons, woods and meadows, and to use them for purposes of colonization."[9]

She argued that the status of the economic and the anthropological are implicated in the consideration of genealogies of comparative colonialisms, partly because of the manner in which they were overshadowed by the imperial. It is not simply that there were different economic, political, cultural, or philosophical differences locally in play with the comparative, but that the very status of these factors came into question. Luxemburg was the most important of political theorists for insisting on the imbrications of nation-states and capital with the colonial project and effectively on the impossibility of thinking of capitalism, nation-statehood, or, indeed, the political itself outside the international realm. And this is true also of the few moments when she overtly addressed questions around the status of women, particularly proletarian women internationally, from what she called "the horrors of capitalist domination."[10]

When Hannah Arendt took up the question of imperialism in *The Origins of Totalitarianism*, she similarly traced the differences between imperialism (following John A. Hobson, manifest in the three decades from 1884 to 1914) and colonialism that preceded this. While the period of imperialism was characterized by her as a "stagnant quiet in Europe and breath-taking developments in Asia and Africa," the differences between the political philosophies differentiating French and British colonialism are important to her, and they do have an impact also on the later development of imperialism.[11] Arendt understood the fundamental difference to be the manner in which the British, through Edmund Burke, conceived of the inherited rights of Englishmen in contrast to the French model of abstract concepts of rights, which existed prior to national membership. For Arendt, this led to a fundamental difference in the way expansion— the keystone of imperialism and the fundamental difference between imperialism and the conquests of colonial ventures—was to be perceived and also how successful it could be. The British ruled indirectly, maintaining a sharp sense of distinction between themselves—conceived as a higher race of people—and the people of the empire. Indirect rule also meant that many local practices were maintained as intact. France went about maintaining power through a more intense relationship. Arendt underscores the importance of the *mission civilisatrice*, which caused France to absorb Algeria into itself, making it into three departments—or counties—of France. Even though some Arab forms of law were maintained—or rather, reconstituted—Algeria was governed by France as if a part of itself, but the inhabitants were given few rather complicated paths to citizenship. One could also add to Arendt's point that a whole set of laws, known as the Code de l'Indigénat, was put into place, which meant that Algerians had legal codes that applied to them but not to any Europeans. In addition, the differences Arendt pointed out also had huge consequences for the different education systems in British and French colonies. As a result, Arendt saw a far more brutal treatment of the inhabitants of French colonies than of the British, for they came to constitute a literal reserve army, brought in to fight at any moment.

Arendt saw imperialism less as the last moment of capitalism—or its culmination in the necessary accumulation of capital through consumers and workers in the global periphery—than as the first empowerment and emancipation of the bourgeoisie, who played an important role in expansion. And this is where tension appeared. Imperialism could not be a political concept for her, because it went against the limits of the nation-state as the primary unit. It could be only an economic concept. Businessmen, rather than the national elite, had to promote it. The European bourgeoisie had more in common then with each other than the French businessman did with the French aristocracy or peasant.

But Arendt, in spite of her criticisms of Edmund Burke, saw the possibility of survival for the British nation as opposed to the French, whose efforts to take their laws everywhere, in an *ius imperium*, made them vulnerable and less able to maintain a strong sense of the nation-state other than through power or assimilation. The British could maintain their idea of protection for the Englishman and could not absorb countries—for example, the metropolitan colony of Ireland—into themselves. She was cognizant of the fact that this protection could be maintained only through Darwinian-inspired racism and the creation of a different set of overseas subjects. If Luxemburg was tracing a genealogy that would lead up to the imperial expansion as being the epitome of capitalist venture in the hope of a different Marxist future, Arendt understood imperialism as the path toward totalitarianism. She also saw the manifestation of racism not only in the European imperial ventures but also in the continental pan-movements that she included in her discussion of imperialism: the tribalism of the Russian pan-Slavs and the Austrian pan-Germans in Russia and Austria-Hungary was to manifest itself in Europe because there was no chance of overseas expansion. As a result of this, the decline of the nation-state for Central and East European countries occurred very visibly within Europe—not as a result of overseas expansion. Psychologically, she claimed, it was more introverted, which also meant that it was more prone to identifying its neighbors as the enemy. "Natural sovereignty," she claimed, had therefore "lost its original connotation of freedom of the people and was being surrounded by a pseudomystical arbitrariness."[12] This resulted also in hostility toward the state and a rampant hostility toward Jews, particularly Zionist ones, who, she thought, embodied for the pan-movements the threat that God may have chosen them rather than the pure figures of the pan-tribal nationalists. Lawlessness reigned, political parties became irrelevant, and the imperialist-inspired pan-movements became the inspiration for a Nazism that, through force, allowed for the onslaught of totalitarianism. The threat to what she called the anachronistic concept of asylum was a threat to humanity as we—or rather, she—knew it.

The comparative genealogy of imperialism traced was ingenious, and the picture drawn was extremely bleak. She famously discussed her idea of the surplus, or superfluous population (which is also analyzed in *The Human Condition*), and related it to surplus wealth. The stateless seemed to be part of this vision of superfluity. And yet, even though she was insistent that Nazism and Bolshevism (the two kinds of totalitarianism she rather problematically glued together) had their roots in pan-Germanism and pan-Slavism, which in turn had their roots in imperialism, when she came to compare the two, there was an unmistakable idealizing of overseas imperialism: "Their [pan-Slavism's and pan-Germanism's] chief difference from the more respectable imperialism of Western nations was the lack of capitalist support; their attempts to expand were not and could not be preceded by export of superfluous money and superfluous men, because Europe did not offer colonial opportunities for either . . . While overseas imperialism, its antinational tendencies notwithstanding, succeeded in giving a new lease on life to the antiquated institutions of the nation-state, continental imperialism was and remained unequivocally hostile to all existing political bodies."[13]

Ultimately, when Arendt discussed the bleak outcomes of the First World War and its creation of stateless peoples, she seemed rather nostalgic for the national institutions of British imperialism and the Burkean strain she had somewhat guardedly criticized. She discussed the "Anglo-Saxon party," explaining, through Burke, that the importance of the two-party system in Britain meant that "the peculiar fanaticism of Continental party strife, which springs not so much from conflicting interests as antagonistic ideologies, is completely absent."[14] When she discussed, quite brilliantly, the plight of the stateless, her conclusions seemed out of step with herself. She wrote,

> The danger in the existence of such people [who are unable to participate in the human artifice and are without rights, opinion, citizenship, profession, identity] is twofold: first and more obviously they threaten our political life, our human artifice, the world which is the result of our common and coordinated effort . . . The danger is that a global, universally interrelated civilization may produce barbarians from its own midst by forcing millions of people into conditions which, despite all appearances, are the conditions of savages.[15]

In other words, as a member herself, it was this very British-style polity that she sought to protect as ideal. Even though she acknowledged the threat of imperialism, she held on to the notion of the nation-state she saw emerging with the colonial British paradigm. Even in her own anxiety concerning the status of the refugee, she embraced a violent ideal of the nation-state.

Reading this today, when many asylum seekers and refugees are precisely not those refugees of continental imperialism but rather of British and French imperialism, it reads as retrograde, to say the least, and highly Eurocentric in its understanding of colonialism and imperialism and of the anthropologies, as Julia Kristeva puts it, she wishes to draw of them.[16] Many of these contemporary refugees are denied the role of being even politically persecuted, and their claims are made often as cultural claims, albeit often reinforcing the sense of a barbarian or even diseased pa-triarchal culture—protection against a culture or a practice, particularly for women. The major issue of economics is persistently set aside, or if it does appear, it is as criticism. Even if the accumulation of capital in the West occurred through imperialism, economic asylum is, of course, en-tirely disallowed and vehemently criticized by protectionists.

As a conservative historian of British imperialism, Niall Ferguson has very different aims from Arendt and from the British anti-immigrant sen-timent.[17] While Ferguson suggests nostalgically that British imperialism brought modernity to its colonies and the gifts of the English language, English forms of land tenure, Scottish and English banking, the common law, Protestantism, team sports, the limited or night watchman state, representative assemblies, and the idea of liberty, Arendt at times sounds rather like him. Ferguson's idea was to show the genealogy of the gift to the United States of modernity and global capitalism that originates in British colonialism and then imperialism, and in some ways, Arendt does the same. It is true that Ferguson began his book *Empire: The Rise and Demise of the British World Order and the Lessons for Global Power* with a nostal-gic reflection of a child brought up in the colonies and with stories of adventure and moral uprightness that stand in quite shocking contrast to Hazel Carby's recent work on children of empire.[18] Arendt does not have this and rather likens herself to a dog with a name—recognized by virtue of her genius—who therefore received asylum. You have to be a genius or a criminal to warrant such recognition, she suggested.

Ferguson's book came at a time of deep hysteria in Britain surrounding asylum seekers and immigration that was more generally spawned by European Union migration and the desire for barriers against Mediterra-nean crossing. And while there are certainly some interesting things to be said about the book, it has been voraciously criticized, sometimes in a rather knee-jerk fashion. But this is partly because he began the book with nostalgia and by rejecting the many criticisms of Britain's colonial and then imperial period. In 2005, French conservatives similarly attempted to curb such criticisms by instituting a law, which ultimately did not pass, that legislated the teaching of positive views of colonialism in schools.[19] The desire to put this in place emerges from what France sees as its "immigrant problem"; its desired genealogy of empire comes from that starting point.

Melancholia, the Superego, and the Perpetual

> Let us dwell for a moment on the view which the melancholic's disorder affords of the constitution of the human ego. We see how in him one part of the ego sets itself over against the other, judges it critically, and, as it were, takes it as its object. Our suspicion that the critical agency which is here split from the ego might also show its independence in other circumstances will be confirmed by every other observation. We shall really find grounds for distinguishing this agency from the rest of the ego. What we are here becoming acquainted with is the agency commonly called "conscience"; we shall count it, along with the censorship of consciousness and reality-testing, among the major institutions of the ego, and we shall come upon evidence to show that it can be diseased on its own account.
>
> —Sigmund Freud, "Mourning and Melancholia"

Melancholia, for Freud, is an affect and not an affectation—in this sense, the psychoanalytic term is quite distinct from the romantic feeling or emotion. It is also quite distinct from the traditions that come to mark representational genres—such as laments, eulogies, or ghazals—even as it may insinuate itself into them, creating a new archival configuration of temporality. It cannot be chosen, and, at least to the one who endures it, it cannot really be known. Those who suffer from it have no access to its source. Even if they have the sense that they have lost something, they cannot know what loss or part of that loss is the cause of the melancholia. As theorized in relation to coloniality, it does not appear as a cultural loss, nor could it assume any authentic precolonial nature or culture destroyed by the colonizing power. In fact, the loss is the kind of political loss described in Gayatri Spivak's double negative of deconstruction concerning the critique of what one cannot not want.[20] It related to the extraordinary hope of decolonization akin to the modernist utopian drive in relation to internationalism and the force of the sense of futurity encapsulated within that idea of hope. It was not hope related to an identity category, and it was not the loss of one, either. It took from Freud the idea that melancholia could very likely be about the loss of an ideal—such as a nation, for example. It may have resulted in extraordinary self-berating, a split, or a diseased critical agency. It was not, however, about a lost idea of self. Manifestations of nativism—a factor in most decolonization movements, theorized extensively by Frantz Fanon in *Wretched of the Earth*— seem barely melancholic at all.

Melancholia cannot be seen as good or bad, because affect is not about judgment, even if it is about a form of demand for justice. Indeed, the demand of the melancholic is that it could be for rogues with a good cause. It is not, in patronizing and condescending terms, invested in an idea of difference that insists on understanding the oppressed subject as morally good. Difference in itself is not necessarily politically subversive in an actively moral sense, and Didier Fassin's chapter 9 in this volume, which criticizes Tobie Nathan's recent work, is testament to this. Following Nicolas Abraham and Maria Torok, as well as Jacques Derrida's reading of them, the loss one takes in and is inhabited by initiates a critical agency in relation to an unknown and perpetual alterity.[21] If melancholia has a "work" in the way that mourning does, it is actually mourning's inverse; it is not to know and assimilate this alterity but rather to be undone (in Freud's language, "impoverished") by it and to maintain that process of undoing. An internal antagonism or even civil war is formed. Melancholia is not just about coming undone, of course; it is always about the critical relation outside of the moralism of the superego.

Claims have been made (by myself, among others) of the political potential—or rather, the political demand—made in the state of melancholia. I would like to spend some time clarifying that in relation to these questions about war and peace, the demand and the perpetual, and hope's relation to the loss of an ideal. One of the reasons psychoanalytically conceived melancholia is a compelling rubric for an analysis of postcoloniality is that it is anti-identitarian while compelled by a situation and is affective without sentimentality. It is also highly self-critical without, in the Freudian sense, a discourse of authenticity, nativism, or originality, unlike that we often see in the language of mourning, or of trauma, or in the reification of cultural difference.

The anti-identitarian mode of postcolonial thought is important to retain and can be theorized through melancholia. Melancholia's theoretical complexity should not be reduced to an identity category. Its force does not lie in the absence of some kernel so much as in the symptoms emerging from it. To imagine it otherwise would be to believe in an attachment to which the melancholic has no access, even as he or she may suffer the consequences of the attachment.

The superego in Freudian theory, by contrast, constitutes a regulatory mechanism through which "conscience" violently imposes itself on the ego. The ego's relation to reality-testing, when hindered by melancholia, can challenge the notion of sovereignty and selfhood that relies on the moral violence of perpetual peace. The moral violence of the superego has been analyzed extensively, of course, by Leo Bersani in the development of psychoanalytically informed queer studies.[22] Freud theorized the superego only in 1923. While it is true that Freud refashioned his notion of "critical agency" as the "conscience" of the morally regulating and normalizing superego, this critical agency was no longer melancholic. His concept of melancholia remained unresolved, but the critical agency of melancholia was understood as "diseased" because of an ambivalence felt toward the thing lost. Ambivalent rather than judgmental, the ego is undone by melancholia, not reaffirmed in its sovereignty through compliance to the demands of the superego.[23]

The temporal demand of melancholia has, of course, been analyzed in Derrida's *Specters of Marx* in terms of Hamlet's ghost, who makes demands in the present on Hamlet—demands that come as form rather than identity from the future.[24] In the moment of apprehension of the implications of loss, when, in Abraham and Torok's terms, the phantom may appear and threaten to reveal a secret well repressed, the demand is made. Demand in Lacanian terms carries within it need (articulated in terms of an infant's needs for food, etc.), whereas demand carries that need coupled with its surplus desire. Need is immediate, demand is psychoanalytically undertheorized, and desire is entirely future oriented and attached to hope. The attention of psychoanalysis to sexual difference and the development of the infant has meant that temporal focus has turned to the past and the future. Melancholia's formal demand may constitute a theory of the present in the dissolution it articulates.

The moralizing conscience of the superego developed in peace time conceals its own violence and externalizes loss so that impoverishment and dissolution may occur elsewhere, such as in the fantasy life of the Rat Man in Cash's chapter 1 or in the establishment notion of Nathan's cultural difference in the attempt to absorb the other into state control in Fassin's chapter 9.

Disposability, or Perpetual Peace

Theoretically, in the sphere of international law, it has always been true that sovereignty is nowhere more absolute than in matters of "emigration, naturalization, nationality and expulsion" . . . But one should bear in mind that . . . there was hardly a country left on the Continent that did not pass between the two wars some new legislation which, even if it did not use this right extensively, was always phrased to allow for getting rid of a great number of its inhabitants at any opportune moment.

—Hannah Arendt, *The Origins of Totalitarianism*

No independent nation, be it large or small, may be acquired by another nation by inheritance, exchange, purchase, or gift . . . A nation is not (like the ground on which it is located) a possession (patrimonium). It is a society of men whom no other than the nation itself can command or dispose of.

—Immanuel Kant, *Perpetual Peace*

In the preceding two quotations, both Kant and Arendt appear to be arguing against the disposability of some nations—for Arendt as a way to mark totalitarianism, and for Kant as a way to write against the overt forms of colonial and non-republican citizenry: "Where subjects are not citizens, the easiest thing in the world is to declare war."[25] And yet, through an act of disavowal, both assert the national right to defeat the internal barbarian, in the case of Arendt, or, as in the case of Kant, to dispose of citizens.

The disposability of people and the threat of disposability that puts us all at risk—some, of course, more than others—has been recently discussed widely by Françoise Vergès, Bertrand Oglivie, and Giorgio Agamben.[26] This is the demand of postcolonial melancholia—the recognition that one's entire society, polity, and culture was disposable and that one's hope for a form of nation-statehood reinscribed the right of disposability. This is not to analogize disposability (a throwing) and melancholia (an impossible holding).

Freud suffered deeply from the melancholia that marked him as vulnerable to disposability. It was perhaps that personal manifestation of disposability that led to the European formulation of the superego as healthy while concealing within it a stagnation, akin to that of imperialism described by Arendt, and the capability of disposing of large sectors of the population in times of peace. Displaced exilic figures in Arendt's time and the moment she described are more easily understood today as asylum seekers with perpetual demands quite distinct from those of the moralizing superego of perpetual peace.

The exilic framework of European modernism—of Arendt and of Freud —can be more usefully understood today in terms of a modernism of asylum. What it means to arrive and to receive hospitality in a hostile nation marked by the threat of the sovereign decision concerning life or death—and indeed, forms of bare life and sacral death—is something distinct from living away from one's country, whether chosen or commanded. Without analogizing the melancholic "non-subject of the political" (to use Alberto Moreiras's phrase)[27] and the modern nation-state that is inhabited by an unknown barbarian, the rejuvenated concept of asylum may offer a way of understanding what the extraordinary moralizing violence of perpetual peace threatens.

I would like to close with a discussion of how a rejuvenated concept of asylum can be the critical counterpoint to the brutal facts of disposability and to the melancholic affect that generalized disposability creates. Asylum has everything to do with the establishment of city-states and borders and with the division of land, the institution of law, and the hierarchies that follow from this. The thinking of asylum is part of the critical agency of melancholia.

This journey into asylum through the lens of disposability helps to understand the extraordinary violence of contemporary hospitality in which life is made expendable as hostis or sacrificial victim or is made disposable through the loss or absence of citizenship—the reification of difference as cultural difference—or through the threat of that loss. One can think of the disposability of the human waste products of modern capital who, as Bertrand Oglivie describes, do not attain the status of the oppressed but are simply swept away from the genocidal bulldozers of modern capital in times of peace with its superegoic moralizing force.

What might the migrant melancholic form mean through the lens of asylum at different historical junctures? What might it mean to ask us to consider once again, as Raymond Williams asks, when was modernism? For Williams, that question addressed how man's relationship with enclosure and city changed notions of community—and perhaps implicitly, for example, of who could seek refuge where and in what capacity—and of whose work and concept would go into the structures and definitions of modernism. He wrote, "If we have to break out of the non-historical fixity of post-modernism, then we must search out and counterpose an alternative tradition taken from the neglected works left in the wide margin of the century, a tradition that may address itself not to this by now exploitable because inhuman rewriting of the past but, for all our sakes, to a modern future in which community may be imagined again."[28]

The future-oriented search for community in Williams's work emerges from the model of exile he formulates and from exilic modernist writing and experimentation as occurring within the "general processes of mobility, dislocation and para-national communication."[29] Melancholic form understood as the formal element that demonstrates the impossibility of assimilation is perhaps closer to an asylum formation, an impoverishment, and, indeed, an unworking, inoperable labor that cannot articulate a community but is rather the site of a critique of it.

The exilic model favored by Williams paradoxically leaves out the manner in which stasis (stillness) as opposed to mobility shapes relations on land. The promise of asylum as a political concept rests in the observation that nations, and indeed other communities, provide hospitality only with hostility, or at least the threat of it. Nicole Loraux, discussing the post-Homeric period during which time Athens established itself as a city, explains what she sees as the divisions at the heart of democracy that began to reveal themselves. In *The Divided City: On Memory and Forgetting in Ancient Athens,* Loraux explains how at the end of the oligarchic dictatorship of the Thirty, the democrats return to the city victorious. The citizens (not the slaves, not the women, and not the disposable) invent amnesty through an act of willed (disavowed) amnesia. They agree to forget the unforgettable. Loraux looks at the formal emergence of the discord affecting the entire city: doomed to divide itself, it remains agonistic—indeed, antagonistic. The emergence of the formal eruption goes against the state's willed superegoic amnesty to the emergent melancholic forms. Loraux dwells on the term "stasis." The extraordinary somersaults of Franco-Algerian amnesty laws at the approach and aftermath of Algerian independence, or the study of the Weimar Constitution by the postcolonial Indian state at the time of creating their own constitution, speak to this violent state enforcement of amnesty. Stasis, she reminds us, does not refer only to a lack of mobility—a stagnation or stoppage in the Greek case—but also to faction and discord and, indeed, to civil war. Through Loraux, we recognize how the structure of conscious dominion creates a stasis through which we understand assimilation and inclusion as the end of politics. But this is actually the very location in which civil war is announced, struggle becomes necessary, and politics becomes available as formal perpetual melancholic demand. The wide margin of the century might then look different when we look to the asylum and to refuge as conditions that are political rather than pre- or postpolitical. This best contextualizes the disposable who may rise up to defy a violent nationalist force at the very site in which they have supposedly been given refuge or made disposable. These disposable melancholics may break out of the stasis (or stillness) through a loss of superegoic peaceful memorializing teleology. In the concept of the melancholia of disposability, we find elements of political discord and permanent struggle as opposed to permanent war and therefore a way in which the disposable may seek a fully political asylum in a world and present and future to come.

Conclusion

There are various images in this collection that are particularly suggestive of what happens when the unconscious moves through different domains: the simple folding chair of Bose (as discussed in Christine Hartnack's chapter 4), which takes the place of Freud's couch, adorned in its luxurious Turkish rug;[30] Freud's hysterical patient who imagines that it is white people who suffer most when there is a revolt in Saint-Domingue (as discussed in Deborah Jenson's chapter 7); and the various women who, under the guise of a misshapen psychoanalysis, are patronized when their various economic and mental conditions are labeled cultural difference, without a thought for the deep imbrication of colonialism's impact on mental life and on the whole constitution of difference. Indeed, difference is banalized unless the various concepts of the unconscious are provincialized and parochialized in their local settings that are nonetheless globally constituted and interrelated.

That psychoanalysis is international in its ambition and its constitution has been well documented.[31] And yet, the facts of its international impact, its reconfiguration, its differential relations with the psychiatric and psychological fields to which it relates, and its reshaping of notions of the unconscious that predate and outlive it are often overlooked by those, such as by Freud himself, who sought a sovereign referent of psychoanalysis. It was inevitable, however, that its move to international dominions would trouble the distinctions between psychoanalysis and anthropology that need some maintenance, as Róheim suggested (see Joy Damousi's chapter 3 in this volume). Didier Fassin produces a fascinating sketch of the impact of an idea of cultural difference quite distinct from the melancholic and nonidentitarian impossibility of assimilation. His rendering of Tobie Nathan as someone who confuses the role of anthropologist and psychoanalyst demonstrates the banalization of notions of the primitive in Freud by paradoxically refusing psychoanalysis in the guise of complicating it.

The international demands of psychoanalysis a new version of itself, as it did of Marxism some time earlier. It is perhaps melancholia that paradoxically impoverishes the unconscious dominion of psychoanalysis without banalizing it as the reification of cultural difference and without rendering it disposable. Like Luxemburg's revolutions and Loraux's stasis, it struggles with psychoanalysis from within, resisting the dominion of the superego, to reach for a different possibility to come.

Notes

1. Sánchez-Pardo, *Cultures of the Death Drive*. See also Burton, *Anatomy of Melancholy*, first published in 1621.
2. Lepenies, *Melancholy and Society*.
3. Arendt, *Origins of Totalitarianism*, 267–302.
4. Williams, "When Was Modernism?" in *The Politics of Modernism*, 31–35; Kapur, *When Was Modernism*.
5. The concept of a diseased critical agency can be found in Freud, "Mourning and Melancholia," 256–57. See also Freud, "Remembering, Repeating, and Working Through," as well as the section titled "Modifications of Earlier Views" in "Inhibitions, Symptoms, and Anxiety," 159, and the full "Mourning and Melancholia."
6. Freud, "Ego and the Id," 3–66.
7. Luxemburg, "Accumulation of Capital," 70.
8. Ibid., 66.
9. Ibid., 70.
10. Luxemburg, "Proletarian Woman," 245.
11. Arendt, *Origins of Totalitarianism*, 123.
12. Ibid., 231.
13. Ibid., 224–25.
14. Ibid., 254.
15. Ibid., 302.
16. Julia Kristeva, starting from the point of discussing Arendt's focus on natality in her doctoral thesis, which was later published as *Love and Saint Augustine*, chooses to read this as an opening for a kind of transparency in Arendt's life. She also discusses the peculiarly anthropological mode of *Origins of Totalitarianism*. See Kristeva, *Hannah Arendt*.
17. Ferguson, *Empire*.
18. See, for example, Carby, "Postcolonial Translations."
19. See *LOI n°2005–158 du 23 février 2005 portant reconnaissance de la Nation et contribution nationale en faveur des Français rapatriés*. This law demanded that school teachers present a positive view of French colonialism. The law was extremely controversial and was ultimately repealed by President Jacques Chirac. See "Les principales prises de position (concernant la loi du 23 février 2005)," *Le Nouvel Observateur* (Paris), January 26, 2006; "French Revisionism: Case of Positive Role of

French Colonisation," *Cameroun Post*, December 18, 2005; "France under Pressure to Defend Its Colonial Past,." *Agence France*, December 8, 2005; and "Chirac revient sur le 'rôle positif' de la colonisation," *Radio France Internationale*, January 26, 2006.

20. See, for example, Spivak, "Subaltern Studies."

21. Derrida, "Fors."

22. See, for example, Bersani, "Is the Rectum a Grave?" 3–30.

23. In "Signatures of the Impossible," I have described the importance of the diseased critical agency and melancholia as follows: "Quite different from disavowal, in which the subject *knows very well*, melancholia embraces the unknown and undoes the ego in the process. Therefore there is no real possibility of identification with the thing lost, even though there is a 'diseased' embrace between the disintegrating ego and the inassimilable remainder. Through disintegration, the question of value itself is somewhat un-dermined. The 'disidentification' with the ego controlled by the super-ego cannot simply lead to the valuation of the subordinated. It is indeed the very structure undone that is Bersani's focus of interest. This is not the valuing of an object. It is the refusal of the ego because of the problematic relation to the abject, inassimilable, lost and possibly repudiated object. Judith Butler's *Psychic Life of Power* has explored this form of disidentification extensively. For her, the unknown lost object is homosexual desire, which threatens 'the gendered character of the ego.' If gender and heterosexuality are built on the repudiation of the homosexual, then one would have to acknowledge also the refusal of the feminine which accompanies heterosexuality in the male. The girl child comes into womanhood also through the repudiation of the feminine as first love object, hence leading to the very problematic identification with the mother. Perhaps, however, the term disidenitification already suggests an ego and active resistance from it, rather than the dissolution I favor" (81).

24. Derrida, *Specters of Marx*.

25. Kant, *Perpetual Peace*, 113.

26. Agamben, *Homo Sacer*; Oglivie, "Violence et représentation"; and Vergès, "Age of Love." See also Khanna, "Disposability."

27. Moreiras, *Línea de sombra*, unpublished manuscript.

28. Williams, "When Was Modernism?" 35.

29. Ibid.

30. See also Hartnack, *Psychoanalysis in Colonial India*.

31. See, for example, Damousi, *Freud in the Antipodes*; Keller, *Colonial Madness*; Khanna, *Dark Continents*; and Plotkin, *Freud in the Pampas*.

Abdel-Jaouad, Hédi. " 'Too Much in the Sun': Sons, Mothers, and Impossible Alliances in Francophone Maghrebian Writing." *Research in African Literatures* 27, no. 3 (1996): 15–33.

Afrique occidentale française. *La justice indigène en Afrique occidentale française.* Rufisque, Senegal: Imprimerie du Haut Commissariat, 1941.

Agamben, Giorgio. *Homo Sacer: Sovereign Power and Bare Life.* Stanford, Calif.: Stanford University Press, 1998.

Alatas, Syed Hussein. *The Myth of the Lazy Native: A Study of the Image of the Malays, Filipinos and Javanese from the 16th to the 20th Century and Its Function in the Ideology of Colonial Capitalism.* London: Frank Cass, 1977.

Allier, Raoul. *La psychologie de la conversion chez les peuples non-civilisés.* Paris: Payot, 1925.

———. *Le non-civilisé et nous, différence irréductible ou identité foncière?* Paris: Payot, 1927.

American Psychiatric Association. *Diagnostic and Statistical Manual of Mental Disorders–IV*, text rev. Washington, D.C.: American Psychiatric Association, 1994.

Ames, David. "Belief in 'Witches' among the Rural Wolof of the Gambia." *Africa* 29, no. 3 (1959): 263–73.

Anderson, Benedict Richard O'Gorman. "The Idea of Power in Javanese Culture." In *Culture and Politics in Indonesia*, edited by Claire Holt, 1–69. Ithaca, N.Y.: Cornell University Press, 1972.

———. *Imagined Communities: Reflections on the Origins and Spread of Nationalism.* London: Verso, 1983.

———. *Java in a Time of Revolution: Occupation and Resistance, 1944–1946.* Jakarta: Equinox, 2006. First published in 1972.

Anderson, Warwick. *The Cultivation of Whiteness: Science, Health and Racial Destiny in Australia.* New York: Basic Books, 2003.

———. "Postcolonial Histories of Medicine." In *Locating Medical History: The Stories and Their Meanings*, edited by Frank Huisman and John Harley Warner, 285–306. Baltimore, Md.: Johns Hopkins University Press, 2004.

———. "The Trespass Speaks: White Masculinity and Colonial Breakdown." *American Historical Review* 102, no. 5 (1997): 1343–70.

———. " 'Where Every Prospect Pleases and Only Man is Vile': Laboratory Medicine as Colonial Discourse." *Critical Inquiry* 18 (1992): 506–29.

Anon. "Causerie bibliographique." *Revue scientifique* 10 (July 1886–January 1887).

Anon. "Dr. Girindrasekhar Bose (Obituary)." *Manas: A Journal of Scientific Psychology* 1 (1954): 63–64.

Arendt, Hannah. *The Human Condition.* 2nd edn. Chicago: University of Chicago Press, 1998.

——. *Love and Saint Augustine.* Translated by J. V. Scott and J. C. Stark. Chicago: University of Chicago Press, 1996.

——. *The Origins of Totalitarianism.* New York: Harcourt, 1994. First published in 1951.

Arnaud, Jacqueline, ed. *L'Oeuvre en fragments.* Paris: Sindbad, 1986.

——. *Recherches sur la littérature maghrébine de langue française: Le cas de Kateb Yacine.* Paris: L'Harmattan, 1982.

Arnold, David. *Colonizing the Body: State Medicine and Epidemic Disease in Nineteenth-Century India.* Berkeley: University of California Press, 1993.

Arzalier, Francis. "La Révolution française dans l'imaginaire française." In *La Révolution française et Haïti: Filiations, Ruptures, Nouvelles Dimensions*, edited by Michel Hector, 348–57. Port-au-Prince, Haiti: Henri Deschamps, 1995.

Asad, Talal, ed. *Anthropology and the Colonial Encounter.* London: Ithaca Press, 1973.

Aubin, Henry. "A Propos de l'ouvrage de Maude Mannoni." *L'Evolution psychiatrique* 1 (1968).

——. "Conceptions phénoménologiques et psychothérapie institutionnelle d'après l'oeuvre de Hesnard." *L'Evolution psychiatrique* 2 (1971): 309–19.

——. "Conduites de refus et psychothérapie." *L'Évolution psychiatrique* 15, no. 4 (1950): 565–91.

——. "Deux ouvrages de psychiatrie transculturelle." *L'Evolution psychiatrique* 33, no. 1 (1968): 181–87.

——. "Foucault et sa conception idéologique de l'histoire de la folie." *L'Evolution psychiatrique* 2 (1971).

——. "Introduction à l'étude de la psychiatrie chez les Noirs." *Annales Médico-Psychologiques* 1, nos. 1–2 (1939): 1–29, 181–213.

——. *La guérison par l'art.* Conférence Académie du Var, 1965.

——. "La magie éternelle." *Bulletin des Amis de Solliès–Ville*, 1966.

——. "L'Assistance psychiatrique indigène aux colonies." In *Congrès des Médecins Aliénistes et neurologistes de France et des pays de langue française XLIIᵉ session, Alger, 6–11 avril 1938*, edited by P. Combemale, 147–76, 196–97. Paris: Impr. Coueslant Masson, 1939.

——. *L'Homme et la magie, bibliothèque neuro-psychiatrique de langue française.* Paris: Desclée, De Brouwer and Cie, 1952.

——. "Médecine magique et arts sculpturaux de l'Afrique." *Société de Psychiatrie de Marseille*, 1963.

——. "Pensée magique et psychiatrie." *L'Evolution psychiatrique* 20, no. 2 (1955): 399–404.

——. "Refus, Reniement, Repression." *L'Évolution psychiatrique* 1 (1951): 31–40.

Babou, Cheikk Anta. "Amadu Bamba and the Founding of the Muridiyya: The History of a Muslim Brotherhood in Senegal, 1853–1913." Ph.D diss., Michigan State University, 2002.

Barry, Aboubacar. "Psy d'étrangers: Le risque de l'exotisme à deux sous." *Hommes et migrations* 1233 (2001): 92–99.

Bastide, Roger. "Matériaux pour une sociologie du rêve." *Revue Internationale de Sociologie* 41 (1933): 11–12.

———. "Psicanálise do cafuné." In *Sociologia do folclore brasileiro*. São Paulo, Brazil: Editôra Anhambi, 1959. First published in 1941.

———. "Psychiatrie, ethnographie et sociologie: Les maladies mentales et le Noir brésilien." In *Désordres mentaux et santé mentale en Afrique au sud du Sahara*, 223–30. London: Commission for Technical Cooperation in Africa South of the Sahara (CCTA), 1960.

———. *Sociologia do folclore brasileiro*. São Paulo, Brazil: Editôra Anhambi, 1959.

———. *Sociologie et psychanalyse*. Paris: Presses Universitaires de France, 1950.

Bataille, Georges. "L'Amérique disparue." In *L'art précolombien*, edited by J. Babelon and Georges Bataille, 5–14. Paris: Les Beaux Arts, 1930.

———. *La part maudite, essai d'économie générale*. Paris: Éditions de Minuit, 1949.

Baum, Robert Martin. "Crimes of the Dream World: French Trials of Diola Witches in Colonial Senegal." *International Journal of African Historical Studies* 37, no. 2 (2004): 201–28.

Beard, Derrick Joshua, and James A. Findlay. *Drapetomania, a Disease Called Freedom: An Exhibition of 18th-, 19th- and Early 20th-Century Material Culture of the African Experience in the Americas from the Collection of Derrick Joshua Beard*. Ft. Lauderdale, Fla.: Bienes Center for the Literary Arts, 2000.

Beecroft, Simon. "Edward Kamau Brathwaite." In *Encyclopedia of Postcolonial Studies*, edited by John C. Hawley, 69–71. New York: Greenwood Publishing Group, 2001.

Beller, Steven. *Vienna and the Jews, 1867–1938: A Cultural History*. New York: Cambridge University Press, 1989.

Bendick, C. *Emil Kraepelins Forschungsreise nach Java 1904: Ein Beitrag Zur Geschichte der Ethnopsychiatrie*, vol. 49, *Kölner Medizinhistorische Beiträge*. Köln: Institut für Geschichte der Medizin der Universität Köln, 1989.

Beneduce, Roberto. *Ethnopsichiatria: Sofferenza Mentale e Alterita Fra Storia, Dominio e Cultura*. Milano: Carocci, 2007.

Benslama, Fethi. *La psychanalyse à l'épreuve de l'Islam*. Paris: Aubier, 2002.

Berkeley-Hill, Owen. "The Anal-Erotic Factor in the Religion, Philosophy and Character of Hindus." *International Journal of Psychoanalysis* 2 (1921): 306–38.

———. "The 'Color Question' from a Psychoanalytic Viewpoint." *Psychoanalytic Review* 11 (1924): 246–53.

Bernard, Stéphane. *Le conflit franco-marocain, 1943–1956*. Brussels: Editions de l'Institut de Sociologie de l'Université Libre de Bruxelles, 1963.

Bersani, Leo. "Is the Rectum a Grave?" In *Is the Rectum a Grave? and Other Essays*, 3–30. Chicago: University of Chicago Press, 2009.

Berthelier, Robert. *L'homme maghrébin dans la littérature psychiatrique*. Paris: L'Harmattan, 1994.

Bhabha, Homi K. *The Location of Culture*. New York: Routledge, 1994.

———. "Remembering Fanon: Self, Psyche and the Colonial Condition." In *Colonial Discourse and Post-Colonial Theory: A Reader*, edited by P. Williams and L. Christman, 112–23. New York: Colombia University Press, 1994.

Bhattacharyya, Deborah P. *Pagalami: Ethnopsychiatric Knowledge in Bengal*. Syracuse, N.Y.: Maxwell School of Citizenship and Public Affairs, 1986.

Biehl, João. "Vita: Life in a Zone of Social Abandonment." *Social Text* 68 (2001): 131–49.

Black, Isabella. "Race and Unreason: Anti-Negro Opinion in Professional and Scientific Literature since 1945." *Phylon* 26 (1965): 65–79.

Boilat, Père David. *Esquisses sénégalaises: physionomie du pays, peuplades, commerce, religions, passé et avenir, récits et légendes*. Paris: P. Bertrand, 1853.

Bois, Jules. "Étude documentaire sur l'auteur." In *La sorcellerie au Maróc*, edited by Émile Mauchamp, 11–67. Paris: Dorbon-Aîné, 1911.

Bonaparte, Marie. "A Lion Hunter's Dreams." *Psychoanalytic Review* 16 (1947): 1–10.

Bondurant, Joan. V. *Conquest of Violence: The Gandhian Philosophy of Conflict*. Princeton, N.J.: Princeton University Press, 1988. First published in 1958.

Borges, Dain. "Puffy, Ugly, Slothful and Inert: Degeneration in Brazilian Social Thought, 1880–1940." *Journal of Latin American Studies* 25, no. 2 (1993): 235–56.

Bose, D. M. "Asutosh Mukherjee." *Science and Culture* 30 (1964): 299–311.

Bose, Girindrasekhar. "Analysis of Wish." *Samiksa* 6 (1952): 1–11.

———. "The Concept of Repression." Ph.D diss. University of Calcutta. 1921.

———. "Dream." *Indian Journal of Psychology* 5 (1930): 37–86.

———. "The Duration of Coitus." *International Journal of Psychoanalysis* 18 (1937): 235–55.

———. *Everyday Psychoanalysis*. Calcutta: Mis Susil Gupta Publishing, 1945.

———. "The Genesis and Adjustment of the Oedipus Wish." *Samiksa* 3 (1949): 222–40. Reprinted in *Vishnu on Freud's Desk: A Reader in Psychoanalysis and Hinduism*, edited by T. G. Vaidyanathan and J. J. Kripal, 21–38. Delhi: Oxford University Press, 1999.

———. "Is Perception an Illusion?" *Indian Journal of Psychology* 1 (1926): 135–52.

———. "A New Theory of Mental Life." *Indian Journal of Psychology* 8 (1933): 37–157.

———. "Opposite Fantasies in the Release of Repression." *Indian Journal of Psychology* 10 (1935): 29–41.

———. "Progress of Psychology in India during the Past Twenty-Five Years." In *The Progress of Science in India during the Past Twenty-Five Years*, edited by B. Prasad, 336–52. Calcutta: Indian Science Congress Association, 1938.

———. "Psychological Outlook of Hindu Philosophy." *Indian Journal of Psychology* 5 (1930): 119–46. Reprinted in *Modern Review*, 1931, 14–25.

———. "Psychology and Psychiatry." *Indian Journal of Psychology* 6 (1931): 143–46.

———. "The Reliability of Psychoanalytic Findings." *British Journal of Medical Psychology* 3 (1923): 105–15.

———. "Yoga Sutras." *Samiksa* 11 (1957): 44–63, 157–85, 217–37.

Bose, S. C. *An Indian Pilgrim: An Unfinished Autobiography and Collected Letters.* New York: Asia Publishing House, 1965.

Bowen, John R. *Why the French Don't Like Headscarves: Islam, the State, and Public Space.* Princeton, N.J.: Princeton University Press, 2007.

Brathwaite, Edward Kamau. "Creolization in Jamaica." In *The Post-Colonial Studies Reader*, 2nd edn., edited by Bill Ashcroft, Gareth Griffiths, and Helen Tiffin, 152–54. London: Taylor and Francis, 2006.

Breman, Jan, ed. *Imperial Monkey Business: Racial Supremacy in Social Darwinist Theory and Colonial Practice.* Amsterdam: VU University Press, 1990.

Breton, André. *Nadja.* Paris: Gallimard, 1964. First published in 1929.

Bulhan, Hussein Abdilahi. *Frantz Fanon and the Psychology of Oppression.* New York: Plenum Press, 1985.

Bullard, Alice. "The Critical Impact of Frantz Fanon and Henri Collomb: Race, Gender and Personality Testing of North and West Africans." *Journal for the History of Behavioral Sciences* 41, no. 3 (2005): 225–48.

———. *Exile to Paradise: Savagery and Civilization in Paris and the South Pacific, 1790–1900.* Stanford, Calif.: Stanford University Press, 2000.

———. "Imperial Networks and Postcolonial Independence: The Transition from Colonial to Transcultural Psychiatry." In *Psychiatry and Empire*, edited by Megan Vaughan and Sloane Mahone, 119–97. London: Palgrave Macmillan, 2007.

———. "L'Oedipe Africain: A Retrospective." *Transcultural Psychiatry* 42, no. 2 (2005): 171–203.

Burack, Cynthia. *Healing Identities: Black Feminist Thought and the Politics of Groups.* Ithaca, N.Y.: Cornell University Press, 2004.

Buret, Maurice. "La Maladie du sommeil." *Questions diplomatiques et coloniales* 16 (1903): 605–12.

Burke, Edmund. *Reflections on the Revolution in France.* Edited by F. M. Turner. New Haven, Conn.: Yale University Press, 2003.

Burton, Robert. *The Anatomy of Melancholy.* Edited by T. C. Faulkner, N. K. Kiessling, and R. L. Blair. Oxford: Clarendon Press, 1989.

Bussemaker, H. T. *Bersiap! Opstand in het Paradijs: De Bersiap-Periode Op Java en Sumatra, 1945–1946.* Zutphen, Netherlands: Walbug Pers, 2005.

Butler, Judith. *The Psychic Life of Power: Theories in Subjection.* Stanford, Calif.: Stanford University Press, 1997.

Cândido, Antonio. "A Recolucão de 1930 e a Cultura." *Novos Estudos Cebrap* 2, no. 4 (1984).

Cândido, Antonio, and José Aderaldo Castello. *Presenca da literatura brasileira: Modernismo/História e antologia.* Rio de Janeiro: Bertrand Brasil, 2001.

Carby, Hazel. "Postcolonial Translations." *Ethnic and Racial Studies* 30, no. 2 (2007): 213–34.

Carothers, John Colin. *The African Mind in Health and Disease: A Study in Ethnopsychiatry*. Geneva: World Health Organization, 1953.

——. *The Psychology of Mau Mau*. Nairobi, Kenya: Government Printer, 1955.

Cartwright, Samuel. "Diseases and Peculiarities of the Negro Race." *De Bow's Southern and Western Review* 11 (1851): 331–36.

Caruth, Cathy. *Unclaimed Experience: Trauma, Narrative, and History*. Baltimore, Md.: Johns Hopkins University Press, 1996.

Cash, John D. "Conclusion: Politics, History and the Unconscious." In *History on the Couch*, edited by Joy Damousi and R. Reynolds, 188–98. Melbourne: Melbourne University Press, 2003.

——. *Identity, Ideology and Conflict: The Structuration of Politics in Northern Ireland*. New York: Cambridge University Press, 1996.

——. "Troubled Times: Changing the Political Subject in Northern Ireland." In *Challenging Subjects: Critical Psychology for a New Millennium*, edited by Valerie Walkerdine, 88–100. Basingstoke, U.K.: Palgrave Macmillan, 2002.

Castel, Robert. *L'ordre psychiatrique: L'âge d'or de l'aliénisme*. Paris: Minuit, 1976.

Cazanove, Frank. "Les conceptions magico-religieuses des indigènes de l'Afrique occidentale française." *Les Grandes Endémies Tropicales* 5 (1933): 38–48.

——. "Memento de psychiatrie coloniale africaine." *Bulletin du comité d'études historiques et scientifiques de l'AOF* 10, no. 1 (1927): 133–77.

Chakrabarty, Dipesh. "Postcoloniality and the Artifice of History: Who Speaks for Indian Pasts?" *Representations* 37 (1992): 1–26.

——. *Provincializing Europe: Postcolonial Thought and Historical Difference*. Princeton, N.J.: Princeton University Press, 2000.

Charcot, Jean Martin, and Paul Richer. *Démoniaques dans l'art*. Paris: Delahayes et Lecrosnier, 1887.

Chatinières, Paul. *Dans le Grand Atlas marocain: Extraits du carnet de route d'un médecin d'assistance médicale indigène, 1912–1916*. Paris: Plon-Nourrit, 1919.

Chatterjee, Partha. *The Nation and Its Fragments: Colonial and Postcolonial Histories*. Princeton, N.J.: Princeton University Press, 1993.

Chertok, Leon, and Isabelle Stengers. *A Critique of Psychoanalytic Reason: Hypnosis as a Scientific Problem from Lavoisier to Lacan*. Stanford, Calif.: Stanford University Press, 1992.

Chesterman, John, and Brian Galligan. *Citizens without Rights: Aborigines and Australian Citizenship*. New York: Cambridge University Press, 1997.

Chevalier, Jean Damien, *Lettres à M. de Jean, Docteur-Régent de la faculté de médecine, en l'université de Paris, sur les maladies de St. Domingue*. Paris: Chez Durand, 1752.

Chraïbi, Driss. *Le passé simple*. Paris: Denoël, 1954.

Clifford, James. *The Predicament of Culture: Twentieth-Century Ethnography, Literature, and Art*. Cambridge, Mass.: Harvard University Press, 1988.

Codrington, Robert Henry. *The Melanesians: Studies in Their Anthropology and Folk-Lore*. Oxford: Clarendon Press, 1891.

Coetzee, J. M. *Disgrace*. London: Secker and Warburg, 1999.

Cohn, Bernard S. *Colonialism and Its Forms of Knowledge: The British in India.* Princeton, N.J.: Princeton University Press, 1996.

Collignon, René. "Vingt ans de travaux à la clinique psychiatrique de Fann-Dakar." *Psychopathologie africaine* 14, nos. 2–3 (1978): 133–324.

Colombijn, Freek "What Is So Indonesian about Violence?" In *Violence in Indonesia*, edited by Ingrid Wessel and Georgia Wimhöfer, 25–46. Hamburg: Abera, 2001.

Colombijn, Freek, and J. Thomas Lindblad. Introduction to *Roots of Violence in Indonesia: Contemporary Violence in Historical Perspective*, edited by Freek Colombijn and J. Thomas Lindblad, 1–31. Leiden, Netherlands: KITLV Press, 2002.

Comaroff, Jean. " 'The Diseased Heart of Africa': Medicine, Colonialism, and the Black Body." In *Knowledge, Power, and Practice: The Anthropology of Medicine and Everyday Life*, edited by Shirley Lindenbaum and Margaret M. Lock, 305–29. Berkeley: University of California Press, 1993.

Comptes-rendus du Congrès des médecins aliénistes et neurologistes de France et des pays de langue française, XXXVIIᵉ Sesion--Rabat (Paris: Masson, 1933), 73–74.

Conklin, Alice L. *A Mission to Civilize: The Republican Idea of Empire in France and West Africa, 1895–1930.* Stanford, Calif.: Stanford University Press, 1997.

Cooper, Frederick. *Colonialism in Question: Theory, Knowledge, History.* Berkeley: University of California Press, 2005.

Corin, Ellen. "Playing with Limits: Tobie Nathan's Evolving Paradigm in Ethnopsychiatry." *Transcultural Psychiatry* 34 (1997): 345–58.

Corre, Armand. *L'Ethnographie criminelle d'après les observation et les statistiques judiciaries recueillies dans les colonies françaises.* Paris: C. Reinwald et Cie, 1894.

Couperus, Louis. *The Hidden Force* [De Stille Kracht]. Translated by E. M. Beekman. Amherst: University of Massachusetts Press, 1985. First published in 1900.

Coward, Harold G. *Jung and Eastern Thought.* Albany: State University of New York (SUNY) Press, 1985.

Cribb, Robert B. "From Total People's Defence to Massacre: Explaining Indonesian Military Violence in East Timor." In *Roots of Violence in Indonesia: Contemporary Violence in Historical Perspective*, edited by Freek Colombijn and J. Thomas Lindblad, 227–41. Leiden, Netherlands: KITLV Press, 2002.

———. *Gangsters and Revolutionaries: The Jakarta People's Militia and the Indonesian Revolution, 1945–1949.* Honolulu: University of Hawaii Press, 1991.

———. "Misdaad, Geweld en Uitsluiting in Indonesië." In *Van Indië tot Indonesië*, edited by E. Bogaerts and R. Raben, 31–48. Amsterdam: Boom, 2007.

———. *Modern Indonesia: A History since 1945.* London: Longman, 1995.

Crone, Patricia. "Imperial Trauma: The Case of the Arabs." *Common Knowledge* 12, no. 1 (winter 2006): 107–16.

da Costa, Emilia Viotti. "The Myth of Brazilian Racial Democracy." In *The Brazilian Empire, Myths and History*. Chicago: University of Chicago Press, 1985.

da Rocha, Franco. *A doutrina de Freud*. 2nd edn. São Paulo, Brazil: Companhia Nacional, 1930.

———. "Do delírio em geral." Opening lecture, course on Clinical Psychiatry of 1919, Medical School of São Paulo, Brazil, March 20, 1919. Reproduced in "A psicologia de Freud," *Revista Brasileira de Psicanálise* 1, no. 1 (1967): 127–42.

———. *O Pansexualismo na doutrina de Freud*. São Paulo, Brazil: Tyographia Brasil de Rothschild Cia, 1920.

———. "A psicologia de Freud." *Revista Brasileira de Psicanálise* 1, no. 1 (1967): 127–42.

Damousi, Joy. *Freud in the Antipodes: A Cultural History of Psychoanalysis in Australia*. Sydney: University of New South Wales (UNSW) Press, 2005.

Damousi, Joy, and Mariano Ben Plotkin, eds. *The Transnational Unconscious: Essays in the History of Psychoanalysis and Transnationalism*. New York: Palgrave Macmillan, 2009.

Das, Veena, Arthur Kleinman, Mamphela Ramphele, and Pamela Reynolds, eds. *Violence and Subjectivity*. Berkeley: University of California Press, 2000.

Dayan, Joan. *Haiti, History, and the Gods*. Berkeley: University of California Press, 1998.

Dazille, Jean Barthélemy. *Observations sur les maladies des nègres, leurs causes, leurs traitements, et les moyens de les prévenir*. Paris: Chez Didot le Jeune, 1776.

de Almeida Prado Galvão, L. "Notas para a história da psicanálise em São Paulo." *Revista Brasileira de Psicanálise* 1 (1967): 46–68.

de Andrade, Mário. "Prefácio Interessantíssimo." In *Paulicéa Devairada*. São Paulo, Brazil: Casa Mayença, 1922.

———. "A Escrava que não é Isaura (discurso sobre algumas tendéncias da poesis modernista)." São Paulo, Brazil: Livraria Lealdade, 1925.

de Andrade, Oswald. *Estética e política, ensaios e crítica*. São Paulo, Brazil: Editora Globo, 1991. First published in 1929.

———. "Manifesto Antropófago." In *Vanguardas latino-americanas: Polêmicas, manifestos e textos críticos*, edited by Jorge Schwartz, 142–47. São Paulo, Brazil: EDUSP, 1995. First published in 1926.

———. "Retoques ao retrato do Brasil." In *Retrato do Brasil*, 9th edn., edited by Paulo Prado, 212–32. São Paulo, Brazil: Companhia das letras, 2001. First published in 1929.

de Chateaubriand, François-René. *Mémoires d'outre-tombe*. 42 vols. Paris: Editions Gallimard, 1951.

de Duras, Claire. *Ourika: An English Translation*. Translated by John Fowles. New York: MLA Editions, 1994.

de Knecht-van Eekelen, A. "Tropische Geneeskunde in Nederland en Koloniale Geneeskunde in Nederland-Indië." *Tijdschrift voor Geschiedenis* 105, no. 3 (1992): 407–28.

de Lamartine, Alphonse. "Toussaint Louverture." In *Oeuvres poétiques completes*, edited by Marius-François Guyard. Paris: Gallimard, 1963.

——. "Voyage en Orient." In *Oeuvres poétiques complètes*, edited by Marius-François Guyard, vols. 6–8. Paris: Gallimard, 1963.

de Lanessan, Jean Marie Antoine. *L'Expansion coloniale de la France*. Paris: Félix Alcan, 1886.

de Langen, C. D. "Bij het 25-jarig Hoogleraarschap in de Psychiatrie en Neurologie van Prof. Dr. P. M. van Wulfften Palthe." *Folia Psychiatrica, Neurologica et Neurochirirurgica Neerlandica* 58, no. 4 (1955): 212–16.

de Maximy, Martine, Thierry Baranger, and Hubert de Maximy. *L'enfant sorcier africain entre ses deux juges*. Saint-Germain-en Laye, France: Odin, 2000.

de Moraes, Pedro Deodato. *A Psicanálise na educação*. Rio de Janeiro: Machado S. C., 1927.

de Nerval, Gérard. "Aurélia." In *Oeuvres*, edited by H. Lemaître. Paris: Garnier, 1958. First published in 1855.

Dean, Carolyn J. *The Self and Its Pleasures: Bataille, Lacan, and the History of the Decentered Subject*. Ithaca, N.Y.: Cornell University Press, 1992.

Delbourgo, James, and Nicholas Dew. *Science and Empire in the Atlantic World*. London: Taylor and Francis, 2007.

Deodato de Moraes, Pedro. *A Psicanálise na Educação*. Rio de Janeiro: Machado S. C., 1927.

Dequeker, J., Frantz Fanon, R. Lacaton, M. Micucci, and F. Ramée. "Aspects actuels de l'assistance mentale en Algérie." *Information Psychiatrique* 31, no. 4 (January 1955): 11–18.

Derrida, Jacques. *The Beast and the Sovereign*. Chicago: University of Chicago Press, 2009.

——. "*Fors*: The Anglish Words of Nicolas Abraham and Maria Torok." Translated by Barbara Johnson. Foreword to *The Wolf Man's Magic Word: A Cryptonymy*, by Nicolas Abraham and Maria Torok, xi–xlviii. Minneapolis: University of Minnesota Press, 1986.

——. "Geopsychoanalysis 'and the Rest of the World.'" In *Psyche: Inventions of the Other*, edited by P. Kamuf and E. Rottenberg, 318–43. Stanford, Calif.: Stanford University Press, 2007.

——. *Margins of Philosophy*. Chicago: University of Chicago Press, 1982.

——. *On Cosmopolitanism and Forgiveness*. New York: Routledge, 2001.

——. *Politics of Friendship*. New York: Verso, 1997.

——. *Resistances of Psychoanalysis*. Translated by Peggy Kamuf, Pascale-Anne Brault, and Michael Nass. Stanford, Calif.: Stanford University Press, 1998.

——. *Rogues: Two Essays on Reason*. Stanford, Calif.: Stanford University Press, 2005.

——. *Specters of Marx: The State of the Debt, the Work of Mourning, and the New International*. Translated by Peggy Kamuf. New York: Routledge, 1994.

——. "The Transcendental 'Stupidity' ('Bêtise') of Man and the Becoming-Animal According to Deleuze." In *Derrida, Deleuze, Psychoanalysis*, edited by G. Schwab, 35–60. New York: Columbia University Press, 2007.

Desbordes-Valmore, Marceline. *Sarah: An English Translation*. Translated by Deborah Jenson and Doris Kadish. New York: MLA Editions, 2008.

Deshpande, Govind Purushottam. "Dialectics of Defeat." *Political and Economic Weekly* 12 (1987): 2170–76.

Desportes, J.-B.-R. P. *Histoire des maladies de Saint-Domingue*. Paris: Chez Lejay, 1770.

Devereux, George. *Essais d'ethnopsychiatrie générale*. Translated by T. Jolas and H. Gobard. Paris: Gallimard, 1977. First published in 1970.

———. *Ethnopsychanalyse complémentariste*. Paris: Flammarion, 1972.

———. *Reality and Dream: Psychotherapy of a Plains Indian*. New York: New York University Press, 1969.

Dias Duarte, Luiz Fernando. "Em busca do castelo interior: Roger Bastide e a psicologização no Brasil." In *Psicologização no Brasil: Atores e autores*, edited by Luiz Fernando Dias Duarte, Jane Russo, and Ana Teresa Venancio, 167–82. Rio de Janeiro: Contra Capa Livraria, 2005.

Dias Duarte, Luiz Fernando, Jane Russo, and Ana Teresa Venancio, eds. *Psicologização no Brasil: Atores e autores*. Rio de Janeiro: Contra Capa Livraria, 2005.

Diriwachter, Rainer. "Völkerpsychologie: The Synthesis That Never Was." *Culture and Psychology* 10, no. 1 (2004): 85–109.

Dirlik, Arif. "The Postcolonial Aura: Third World Criticism in the Age of Global Capitalism." *Critical Inquiry* 20 (1994): 329–56.

Donnadieu, A. "Psychose de civilisation." *Anneles Médico-Psychologiques* 97, no. 1 (1939): 30–37.

Donzelot, Jacques. *The Policing of Families*. New York: Pantheon Books, 1979.

Dorlin, Elisabeth. *La matrice de la race: Généalogie sexuelle et coloniale de la nation française*. Paris: La Découverte, 2006.

Dozon, Jean-Pierre, and Didier Fassin. *Critique de la santé publique: Une approche anthropologique*. Paris: Balland, 2001.

du Camp, Maxime. *Le Nil, Egypte, et Nubie*. Paris: Hachette, 1877.

Echenberg, Myron. *Colonial Conscripts: The Tiralleurs Sénégalais in French West Africa*. Portsmith, N.H.: Heinemann, 1991.

Edwards, J. "In Memoriam." *Indian Journal of Psychology* 28 (1953): 126–27.

Elfakir, A. *Oedipe et personnalité au Maghreb: Eléments d'une ethnopsychologie clinique*. Paris: L'Harmattan, 1995.

Elias, Norbert. *The Germans: Power Struggle and the Development of Habitus in the Nineteenth and Twentieth Centuries*. New York: Columbia University Press, 1996.

Elkin, Adolphus Peter. "Notes on the Psychic Life of the Australian Aborigines." *Mankind* 2, no. 3 (1937): 49–56.

Ellenberger, Henri F. *The Discovery of the Unconscious*. New York: Basic Books, 1981.

Engelen, O. E., Aboe Bkar Loebis, Abdullah Ciptoprawiro, Soejono Joedodibroto, Oetarjo, and Idris Siregar. *Lahirnya Satu Bangsa dan Negara*. Jakarta: Penerbit Universitas Indonesia, 1997.

Etkind, Alexander. *Eros of the Impossible: The History of Psychoanalysis in Russia.* Boulder, Colo.: Westview Press, 1997.

Facchinetti, Cristiana. *Deglutindo Freud: Histórias da digestão do discurso psicanalítico no Brasil.* Rio de Janeiro: Universidade Federal do Rio de Janeiro, 2001.

Fanon, Frantz. *Black Skin, White Masks.* New York: Grove Press, 1967.

———. *A Dying Colonialism.* Translated by H. Chevalier. New York: Grove Press, 1967.

———. "Le Syndrome nord-africain." *L'Esprit* 20, no. 2 (1952): 237–51.

———. *Peau noire, masques blancs.* Paris: Éditions du Seuil, 1952.

———. *Studies in a Dying Colonialism, with an Introduction by Adolfo Gilly.* New York: Monthly Review Press, 1965.

———. *Toward the African Revolution: Political Essays.* New York: Monthly Review Press, 1967.

———. *The Wretched of the Earth.* Translated by C. Farrington. New York: Grove Press, 1963.

Fanon, Frantz, and René Lacaton. "Conduites d'aveu en Afrique du Nord" *Congrès des médecins aliénistes et neurologistes de France et des pays de langue française* 53 (1955): 657–60.

Farmer, Paul. *Infections and Inequalities: The Modern Plagues.* Berkeley: University of California Press, 1999.

———. "On Suffering and Structural Violence: A View from Below." *Daedalus* 125, no. 1 (1996): 261–83.

———. *Pathologies of Power: Health, Human Rights, and the New War on the Poor.* Berkeley: University of California Press, 2003.

Fassin, Didier. "Culturalism as Ideology." In *Cultural Perspectives on Reproductive Health*, edited by Carla Makhlouf Obermeyer, 300–317. Oxford: Oxford University Press, 1999.

———. "Les politiques de l'ethnopsychiatrie: La psyché africaine, des colonies britanniques aux banlieues parisiennes." *L'Homme: Revue française d'anthropologie* 153 (2000): 231–50.

———. "L'ethnopsychiatrie et ses réseaux: Une influence qui grandit." *Genèses: Sciences sociales et histoire* 35 (1999): 146–71.

———. *Pouvoir et maladie en Afrique: Anthropologie de la banlieue de Dakar.* Paris: Presses Universitaires de France, 1992.

———. *When Bodies Remember: Experiences and Politics of AIDS in South Africa.* Berkeley: University of California Press, 2007.

Fassin, Didier, and Eric Fassin. *De la question sociale à la question raciale? Représenter la société française.* Paris: La Découverte, 2006.

Fassin, Didier, and Richard Rechtman. "An Anthropological Hybrid: The Pragmatic Arrangement of Universalism and Culturalism in French Mental Health." *Transcultural Psychiatry* 42, no. 3 (2005): 347–66.

———. *The Empire of Trauma: An Inquiry into the Condition of Victimhood.* Princeton, N.J.: Princeton University Press, 2009.

Ferguson, Niall. *Empire: The Rise and Demise of the British World Order and the Lessons for Global Power.* New York: Basic Books, 2004.

Fischer, Sibylle. *Modernity Disavowed: Haiti and the Cultures of Slavery in the Age of Revolution.* Durham, N.C.: Duke University Press, 2004.

Fisher, David James. "Sigmund Freud and Romain Rolland: The Terrestrial Animal and His Great Oceanic Friend." *American Imago* 33 (1976): 1–59.

Flanagan, Joseph. "The Seduction of History: Trauma, Re-Memory, and the Ethics of the Real." *Clio* 31, no. 4 (summer 2002): 387–402.

Flaubert, Gustave. *Première éducation sentimentale.* Paris: Seuil, 1963. First published in 1845.

Forrester, John. *Dispatches from the Freud Wars: Psychoanalysis and Its Passions.* Cambridge, Mass.: Harvard University Press, 1997.

Foucault, Michel. *The Birth of the Clinic: An Archaeology of Medical Perception.* Translated by A. M. Sheridan Smith. New York: Vintage Books, 1973.

——. *Histoire de la folie à l'âge classique.* Paris: Gallimard, 1961.

——. *The History of Sexuality: An Introduction.* New York: Vintage Books, 1990. First published in 1976.

Franklin, John Hope, and Loren Schweninger. *Runaway Slaves: Rebels on the Plantation.* Oxford: Oxford University Press, 2000.

Freud, Sigmund. "Beyond the Pleasure Principle." In *The Standard Edition of the Complete Psychological Works of Sigmund Freud,* vol. 18, edited by James Strachey, in collaboration with Anna Freud, assisted by Alix Strachey and Alan Tyson, 7–64. London: Hogarth Press, 1959. First published in 1922.

——. *Civilization and Its Discontents.* Translated by Joan Riviere. London: Hogarth Press, 1973.

——. *The Complete Letters of Sigmund Freud to Wilhelm Fliess, 1877–1904.* Translated by Jeffrey Moussaieff Masson. Cambridge, Mass.: Belknap Press, 1985.

——. *The Diary of Sigmund Freud, 1929–1939: A Record of the Final Decade.* Translated by Michael Molnar. London: Hogarth Press, 1992.

——. "A Difficulty in the Path of Psycho-Analysis." In *The Standard Edition of the Complete Psychological Works of Sigmund Freud,* vol. 17, edited by James Strachey, in collaboration with Anna Freud, assisted by Alix Strachey and Alan Tyson, 136–44. London: Hogarth Press, 1953. First published in 1917.

——. "The Ego and the Id." In *The Standard Edition of the Complete Psychological Works of Sigmund Freud,* vol. 19, edited by James Strachey, in collaboration with Anna Freud, assisted by Alix Strachey and Alan Tyson, 3–66. London: Hogarth Press, 1961. First published in 1923.

——. "Fetishism." In *The Standard Edition of the Complete Psychological Works of Sigmund Freud,* vol. 21, edited by James Strachey, in collaboration with Anna Freud, assisted by Alix Strachey and Alan Tyson, 149–57. London: Hogarth Press, 1961. First published in 1927.

——. "The Future of an Illusion." In *The Standard Edition of the Complete Psychological Works of Sigmund Freud,* vol. 21, edited by James Strachey, in collaboration with Anna Freud, assisted by Alix Strachey and Alan Tyson, 3–56. London: Hogarth Press, 1961. First published 1927.

———. "Group Psychology and the Analysis of Ego." In *The Standard Edition of the Complete Psychological Works of Sigmund Freud*, vol. 18, edited by James Strachey, in collaboration with Anna Freud, assisted by Alix Strachey and Alan Tyson, 67–143. London: Hogarth Press, 1959. First published in 1922.

———. "Inhibitions, Symptoms, and Anxiety." In *The Standard Edition of the Complete Psychological Works of Sigmund Freud*, vol. 20, edited by James Strachey, in collaboration with Anna Freud, assisted by Alix Strachey and Alan Tyson, 87–175. London: Hogarth Press, 1981. First published in 1926.

———. "Moses and Monotheism." In *The Standard Edition of the Complete Psychological Works of Sigmund Freud*, vol. 23, edited by James Strachey, in collaboration with Anna Freud, assisted by Alix Strachey and Alan Tyson, 3–137. London: Hogarth Press, 1968. First published in 1939.

———. "Mourning and Melancholia." Translated by James Strachey. In *The Standard Edition of the Complete Psychological Works of Sigmund Freud*, vol. 14, edited by James Strachey, in collaboration with Anna Freud, assisted by Alix Strachey and Alan Tyson, 243–60. London: Hogarth Press, 1953. First published in 1914.

———. "Notes upon a Case of Obsessional Neurosis." In *Sigmund Freud: Case Histories*, vol. 2. London: Penguin Books, 1987.

———. "Presentation: Beginning of a Case History." In *Minutes of the Vienna Psychoanalytic Society, 1906–1908*, vol. 1, edited by Herman Nunberg and Ernest Federn. New York: International Universities Press, 1962.

———. "Remembering, Repeating, and Working Through." In *The Standard Edition of the Complete Psychological Works of Sigmund Freud*, vol. 12, edited by James Strachey, in collaboration with Anna Freud, assisted by Alix Strachey and Alan Tyson, 147–56. London: Hogarth Press, 1981. First published in 1914.

———. "Three Essays on Sexuality." In *The Standard Edition of the Complete Psychological Works of Sigmund Freud*, vol. 7, edited by James Strachey, in collaboration with Anna Freud, assisted by Alix Strachey and Alan Tyson, 125–245. London: Hogarth Press, 1961. First published in 1905.

———. "Sigmund Freud to Lou Andreas-Salomé, 13 March 1922." In *Sigmund Freud and Lou Andreas-Salomé Letters*, edited by Ernst Pfeiffer, 114. New York: Harcourt Brace and Jovanovich, 1972.

———. "Totem and Taboo: Some Points of Agreement between the Mental Lives of Savages and Neurotics." In *The Standard Edition of the Complete Psychological Works of Sigmund Freud*, vol. 13, edited by James Strachey, in collaboration with Anna Freud, assisted by Alix Strachey and Alan Tyson, 1–161. London: Hogarth Press, 1955. First published in 1913.

———. The "Uncanny." In *The Standard Edition of the Complete Psychological Works of Sigmund Freud*, vol. 17, edited by James Strachey, in collaboration with Anna Freud, assisted by Alix Strachey and Alan Tyson, 219–52. London: Hogarth Press, 1953. First published in 1919.

Freud, Sigmund, and Josef Breuer. *Studies on Hysteria*. Translated by James Strachey. New York: Basic Books, 1957.

Freyre, Gilberto. *Casa-grande e senzala. Formação da família Brasileira sob o regime de economia patriarcal*. Rio de Janeiro: Jose Olympio, 1958. First published in 1933.

Frosh, Stephen. *For and Against Psychoanalysis*. New York: Routledge, 1997.

Gaines, Atwood. *Ethnopsychiatry: The Cultural Construction of Professional and Folk Psychiatries*. Albany: State University of New York (SUNY) Press, 1992.

Gandhi, Mohandas Karamchand. "Interview to Indian Psycho-Analytical Society." In *The Collected Works of Mahatma Gandhi*, vol. 28, 109–10. Delhi: Publications Division, Ministry of Information and Broadcasting, Government of India, 1958.

Gates, Henry Louis, Jr. "Critical Fanonism." *Critical Inquiry* 17 (1991): 457–70.

Gates, Henry Louis, Jr., and Kwame Anthony Appiah, eds. *"Race," Writing and Difference*. Chicago: University of Chicago Press, 1992.

Gay, Peter. *Freud: A Life for Our Time*. New York: Norton, 1988.

——. *Freud for Historians*. New York: Oxford University Press, 1985.

Geerardyn, Filip, and Gertrudis van de Vijver. *The Pre-Psychoanalytic Writings of Sigmund Freud*. London: Karnac Books, 2002.

Geggus, David P. "French Imperialism and the Louisiana Purchase." In *The Louisiana Purchase and Its Peoples: Perspectives from the New Orleans Conference*, edited by Paul E. Hoffman, 25–34. Lafayette: University of Louisiana at Lafayette, 2004.

Gelder, Ken, and Jane M. Jacobs. "The Postcolonial Uncanny: On Reconciliation, (Dis)possession and Ghost Stories." In *Uncanny Australia: Sacredness and Identity in a Postcolonial Nation*, 23–42. Melbourne: Melbourne University Press, 1998.

Ghosal, Srimati Svarna Kumari Devi. *An Unfinished Song*. New York: Macmillan, 1913.

Gilman, Sander L. *Difference and Pathology: Stereotypes of Sexuality, Race, and Madness*. Ithaca, N.Y.: Cornell University Press, 1985.

Goffman, Erving. *Asylums: Essays on the Social Situation of Mental Patients and Other Inmates*. New York: Anchor, 1961.

Goldstein, Jan. *Console and Classify: The French Psychiatric Profession in the Nineteenth Century*. Chicago: University of Chicago Press, 2001. First published in 1989.

Good, Byron. "Culture and DSM-IV: Diagnosis, Knowledge and Power." *Culture, Medicine and Psychiatry* 20 (1996): 127–32.

Goodman, Nelson. *Ways of Worldmaking*. Indianapolis: Hackett, 1978.

Gouda, Frances. *Dutch Culture Overseas: Colonial Practice in the Netherlands Indies, 1900–1942*. Amsterdam: Amsterdam University Press.

——. "Gender and 'Hyper-Masculinity' as Post-Colonial Modernity during Indonesia's Struggle for Independence, 1945 to 1949." In *Gender, Sexuality and Colonial Modernities*, edited by Antoinette Burton, 163–76. London: Routledge, 1999.

——. "Languages of Gender and Neurosis in the Indonesian Struggle for Independence, 1945–1949." *Indonesia* 64 (1997): 45–76.

——. *What's to Be Done with Gender and Post-Colonial Studies?* Amsterdam: Vossiuspers UVA, 2001.

Griaule, Marcel. *Conseiller de l'Union Française.* Paris: Nouvelles Éditions latines, 1957.

Guha, Ranajit, ed. *A Subaltern Studies Reader, 1986–1995.* Minneapolis: University of Minnesota Press, 1997.

Hacking, Ian. *Rewriting the Soul: Multiple Personality and the Sciences of Memory.* Princeton, N.J.: Princeton University Press, 1995.

Haebich, A. *Broken Circles: Fragmenting Indigenous Families, 1800–2000.* Fremantle, Australia: Fremantle Arts Centre Press, 2000.

Hale, Nathan G. *Freud and the Americans: The Beginning of Psychoanalysis in the United States, 1876–1917.* New York: Oxford University Press, 1971.

——. *The Rise and Crisis of Psychoanalysis in United States: Freud and the Americans, 1917–1985.* New York: Oxford University Press, 1995.

Harrington, Anne. *The Cure Within: A History of Mind-Body Medicine.* New York: W.W. Norton, 2008.

Hartnack, Christiane. "British Psychoanalysts in Colonial India." In *Psychology in Twentieth-Century Thought and Society*, edited by Mitchell G. Ash and William R. Woodward, 233–52. Cambridge: Cambridge University Press, 1989.

——. *Psychoanalysis in Colonial India.* New York: Oxford University Press, 2001.

——. "Vishnu on Freud's Desk: Psychoanalysis in Colonial India." *Social Research* 57 (1990): 921–49.

Hesnard, Angelo. "Discussion du rapport d'assistance psychiatrique." In *Congrès des Médecins Aliénistes et neurologistes de France et des pays de langue françaises XLIIe session, Alger, 6–11 avril 1938*, edited by P. Combemale, 182–84. Paris: Impr. Coueslant Masson, 1939.

Hirsch, Charles A. "La Criminalité des nord-africains en France est-elle une criminalité par défaut d'adaptation?" Paper presented to the Société Internationale de Prophylaxie Sociale, Paris, March 27, 1959. Archives of the Centre Henri Ellenberger, Centre Hospitalier Sainte-Anne, VI 2, Ethnopsychiatrie III: Criminalité chez certains peuples, Paris.

Hobsbawm, Eric J. *Bandits.* 2nd edn. London: Penguin, 1985.

Holmes, D. E. "Race and Transference in Psychoanalysis and Psychotherapy." *International Journal of Psychoanalysis* 73 (1992): 1–11.

Horne, Alastair. *A Savage War of Peace: Algeria, 1954–1962.* London: Macmillan, 1977.

Hubert, Henri, and Marcel Mauss. *Esquisse d'une théorie générale de la magie.* Vol. 7. Paris: F. Alcan, 1904.

Hudis, Peter, and Kevin B. Anderson, eds. *The Rosa Luxemburg Reader.* New York: Monthly Review Press, 2004.

Hugo, Victor. *Bug-Jargal / Tamango.* Paris: Urbain Canel, 1826.

Hunt, Nancy Rose. *A Colonial Lexicon of Birth Ritual, Medicalization, and Mobility in the Congo*. Durham, N.C.: Duke University Press, 1999.

Huémavo-Griamud, Aimée. *Les Médecins Africains en AOF: Etude Socio-historique sur la formation d'une elite coloniale*. Masters thesis, University of Dakar, 1979.

Indian Psychoanalytical Society. Annual Report, 1923. *International Journal of Psychoanalysis* 5 (1924): 121–22, 256, 507.

———. Annual Report, 1926. *International Journal of Psychoanalysis* 8 (1927).

———. Annual Report, 1928. *International Journal of Psychoanalysis* 9 (1928): 391–93.

———. Report. *International Journal of Psychoanalysis* 10 (1929): 39–41.

———. Report. *International Journal of Psychoanalysis* 11 (1930): 354–55.

———. Report. *International Journal of Psychoanalysis* 14 (1933): 456–57.

———. Report. *International Journal of Psychoanalysis* 16 (1935): 259–61.

Jackson, John P. *Social Scientists for Social Justice: Making the Case against Segregation*. New York: New York University Press, 2001.

Jacob, Françoise. "La psychiatrie française face au monde colonial au XIXe siècle." In *Découvertes et explorateurs: Actes du Colloque International, Bordeaux 12–14 Juin 1992; VIIe Colloque d'Histoire au Présent*, 365–73. Paris: L'Harmattan, 1994.

Jaffré, Yannick. "L'interprétation sauvage." *Enquête* 3 (1996): 177–90.

Jenson, Deborah. *Trauma and Its Representations: The Social Life of Mimesis in Post-Revolutionary France*. Baltimore, Md.: Johns Hopkins University Press, 2001.

Jones, Ernest. "Psycho-Analysis and Anthropology." In *Essays in Applied Psychoanalysis*, vol. 2, *Essays in Folklore, Anthropology and Religion*, 114–44. London: Hogarth Press, 1951.

Kafka, Franz. *The Trial*. New York: Schocken Books, 1999.

Kakar, Sudhir. *Culture and Psyche: Selected Essays*. Delhi: Oxford University Press, 1997.

Kant, Immanuel. *Perpetual Peace, and Other Essays on Politics, History, and Morals*. Translated by T. Humphrey. Indianapolis: Hackett, 1983.

Kapila, Shruti. "Freud and His Indian Friends: Religion, Psychoanalysis and Selfhood in Late Colonial India." In *Psychiatry and Empire*, edited by Megan Vaughan and Sloane Mahone, 125–52. London: Palgrave Macmillan, 2007.

Kapur, Geeta. *When Was Modernism: Essays on Contemporary Cultural Practice in India*. New Delhi: Tulika, 2000.

Kateb, Yacine. "Ce pays est un grand hôpital." In *L'Oeuvre en fragments*, edited by Jacqueline Arnaud. Paris: Sindbad, 1986.

———. "La femme sauvage / 1." In *L'Oeuvre en fragments*, edited by Jacqueline Arnaud. Paris: Sindbad, 1986.

———. "La Rose de Blida." *Les Lettres françaises*, February 7–14 (1963): 4.

———. "Le Cadavre encerclé." In *Le Cercle des représailles*. Paris: Seuil, 1959.

———. *Le Poète comme un boxeur: Entretiens, 1958–1989*. Paris: Seuil, 1994.

———. *Le Polygone étoilé*. Paris: Seuil, 1966.

———. *Nedjma*. Paris: Seuil, 1956.

——. "Poésie et vérité de la femme sauvage." In *Kateb Yacine, éclats de mémoire*, edited by Olivier Corpet and Albert Dichy. Paris: IMEC Editions, 1994.

Katz, Jonathan G. "The 1907 Mauchamp Affair and the French Civilising Mission in Morocco." In *North Africa, Islam, and the Mediterranean World: From the Almoravids to the Algerian War*, edited by Julia Clancy-Smith, 143–66. London: Frank Cass, 2001.

Keller, Richard C. *Colonial Madness: Psychiatry in French North Africa*. Chicago: University of Chicago Press, 2007.

——. "Madness and Colonization: Psychiatry in the British and French Empires, 1800–1962." *Journal of Social History* 35, no. 2 (2001): 295–326.

Kemperman, Jeroen. *De Japanse Bezetting in Dagboeken: Tjideng*. Amsterdam: Bert Bakker, 2002.

Khanna, Ranjana. *Dark Continents: Psychoanalysis and Colonialism*. Durham, N.C.: Duke University Press, 2003.

——. "Disposability." *Differences* 20, no. 1 (spring 2009): 181–98.

——. "Signatures of the Impossible." *Duke Journal of Gender, Law and Policy* 11 (spring 2004): 69–91.

Kirmayer, Laurence J., and H. Minas. "The Future of Cultural Psychiatry: An International Perspective." *Canadian Journal of Psychiatry* 45 (2000): 438–46.

Kirmayer, Laurence J., Robert Lemelson, and Mark Barad, eds. *Understanding Trauma: Integrating Biological, Clinical, and Cultural Perspectives*. Cambridge: Cambridge University Press, 2007.

Klein, Melanie. *Envy and Gratitude, and Other Works, 1946–1963*. Free Press edn. London: Virago, 1988.

Kleinman, Arthur. "Anthropology and Psychiatry: The Role of Culture in Cross-Cultural Psychiatric Research on Illness." *British Journal of Psychiatry* 151 (1987): 447–54.

——. *Patients and Healers in the Context of Culture: An Exploration of the Borderland between Anthropology, Medicine, and Psychiatry*. Berkeley: University of California Press, 1980.

Kleinman, Arthur, and Joan Kleinman. "The Appeal of Experience, the Dismay of Images: Cultural Appropriations of Suffering in Our Times." *Daedalus* 125, no. 1 (1996): 1–23.

Kluckhohn, Clyde, and Henry Alexander Murray. *Personality in Nature, Society, and Culture*. New York: A. A. Knopf, 1948.

Kohlbrugge, Jacob Herman Frederik. *Blikken in het Zieleleven van den Javaan en Zijner Overheerschers*. Leiden, Netherlands: E.J. Brill, 1907.

——. "Psychologische Koloniale Politiek." *Vereeniging Moederland en Koloniën* 8, no. 2 (1997): 1–44.

Kristeva, Julia. *Hannah Arendt*. Translated by R. Guberman. New York: Columbia University Press, 2001.

——. *Melanie Klein*. New York: Columbia University Press, 2001.

——. *Nations without Nationalism*. New York: Columbia University Press, 1993.

——. *Strangers to Ourselves*. New York: Columbia University Press, 1991.

Kroeber, Alfred L. "Totem and Taboo: An Ethnologic Psychoanalysis." *American Anthropologist* 22 (1920): 48–55.

Kua, Ee Hoek. "Amok in Nineteenth-Century British Malaya History." *History of Psychiatry* 3 (1991): 429–36.

Kuklick, Henrika. *The Savage Within: The Social History of British Anthropology, 1885–1945*. Cambridge: Cambridge University Press, 1991.

Lacan, Jacques. *The Ego in Freud's Theory and in the Techniques of Psychoanalysis, 1954–55*. Translated by Sylvana Tomaselli. Book II, *The Seminar of Jacques Lacan*, edited by Jacques-Alain Miller. New York: W. W. Norton, 1988.

Lachance, Paul. "Repercussions of the Haitian Revolution in Louisiana." In *The Impact of the Haitian Revolution in the Atlantic World*, edited by D. P. Geggus, 209–30. Columbia: University of South Carolina Press, 2001.

Lacoue-Labarthe, Philippe. *Typography*. Translated by C. Fynsk. Stanford, Calif.: Stanford University Press, 1998.

Laing, Ronald D. *The Divided Self: A Study of Sanity and Madness*. Chicago: Quadrangle, 1960.

Lane, Christopher, ed. *The Psychoanalysis of Race*. New York: Columbia University Press, 1998.

Latour, Bruno. *Petite réflexion sur le culte moderne des dieux faitiches*. Paris: Synthélabo, 1996.

Le Bon, Gustave. *The Crowd: A Study of the Popular Mind*. New York: MacMillan, 1938. First published in 1895.

——. *Psychologie des Foules*. Paris: Felix Alcan, 1905. First published in 1895.

Leiris, Michel. *L'Afrique fantôme*. Paris: Gallimard, 1951. First published in 1934.

Lepenies, Wolf. *Melancholy and Society*. Cambridge, Mass.: Harvard University Press, 1992.

Lévy-Bruhl, Lucien. *Les Fonctions mentales dans les sociétés inférieures*. 9th ed. Paris: Alcan, 1928.

——. *Primitive Mentality*. New York: Macmillan, 1923.

Leys, Ruth. *Trauma: A Genealogy*. Chicago: University of Chicago Press, 2000.

Li, Victor. "Marshall Sahlins and the Apotheosis of Culture." *New Centennial Review* 1, no. 3 (2001): 201–88.

Littlewood, Roland, and Maurice Lipsedge, eds. *Aliens and Alienists: Ethnic Minorities and Psychiatry*. 3rd edn. London: Routledge, 1997.

Loomba, Ania. *Colonialism/Postcolonialism*. 2nd edn. New York: Routledge, 1998.

Loraux, Nicole. *The Divided City: On Memory and Forgetting in Ancient Athens*. New York: Zone Books, 2002.

Luxemburg, Rosa. "The Historical Conditions of Accumulation." In *The Rosa Luxemburg Reader*, edited by Peter Hudis and Kevin Anderson, 32–70. New York: Monthly Review Press, 2004.

——. "The Proletarian Woman." In *The Rosa Luxemburg Reader*, edited by Peter Hudis and Kevin Anderson, 242–45. New York: Monthly Review Press, 2004.

Luyendijk-Elshout, Antonie M., ed. *Dutch Medicine in the Malay Archipelago, 1816–1942.* Amsterdam: Rodopi, 1989.

Ly, Madeleine. *Introduction à une psychoanalyse africaine.* Paris: Le François, 1948.

Macey, David. *Frantz Fanon: A Life.* London: Granta, 2000.

Majumdar, R. C. *History of Modern Bengal.* Calcutta: G. Bharadwaj, 1978.

Malinowski, Bronislaw. *Sex and Repression in Savage Society.* New York: Harcourt Brace, 1927.

Manfredi, Victor. "Ìgbo Initiation: Phallus or Umbilicus?" *Cahiers d'Études Africaines* 37, no. 145 (1997): 157–211.

Mann, Gregory. "Fetishizing Religion: Allah Koura and French 'Islamic Policy' in Late Colonial French Soudan." *Journal of African History* 44, no. 2 (2003): 263–83.

Mannoni, Octave. *Prospero and Caliban: The Psychology of Colonization.* 2nd edn. New York: Friedrick Praeger, 1964. First published in 1950.

Maran, René. *Batoula, veritable roman nègre.* Paris: Albin Michel, 1921.

Marcondes, Durval. "O simbolismo estético na literatura: Ensaio de uma orientação para a crítica literária baseada nos conhecimentos fornecidos pela psicanálise" Thesis presented to obtain the chair in literature at the Ginásio do Estado, n.d.

Marcus, Julie. *The Indomitable Miss Pink: A Life in Anthropology.* Sydney: University of New South Wales Press, 2001.

Maréschal, P., T. B. Soltane, and V. Corcos. "Résultats du traitement par l'électro-choc appliqué à 340 malades à l'Hôpital psychiatique de La Manouba (Tunisie)." In *Comptes Rendus du Congrès des médecins aliénistes et neurologistes de France et des pays de langue française—Montpellier 1942,* 341–46. Paris: Masson, 1942.

Markus, Andrew. *Governing Savages.* Boston: Unwing Hyman, 1990.

Mauchamp, Émile, ed. *La sorcellerie au Maroc.* Paris: Dorbon-Aîné, 1911.

Mauchamp, P. "Lettre de M. P. Mauchamp à J. Bois." In *La sorcellerie au Maroc,* edited by Émile Mauchamp, 1–3. Paris: Dorbon-Aîné, 1911.

Mbembe, Achille. *On the Postcolony.* Berkeley: University of California Press, 2001.

McClintock, Anne. *Imperial Leather: Race, Gender and Sexuality in the Colonial Contest.* New York: Routledge, 1995.

McCulloch, Jock. *Black Soul, White Artifact: Fanon's Clinical Psychology and Social Theory.* Cambridge: Cambridge University Press, 1983.

——. *Colonial Psychiatry and "the African Mind."* New York: Cambridge University Press, 1995.

McGregor, Russell. *Imagined Destinies: Aboriginal Australians and the Doomed Race Theory, 1880–1939.* Melbourne: Melbourne University Press, 1997.

Mehta, Uday Singh. "Liberal Strategies of Exclusion." In *Tensions of Empire: Colonial Cultures in a Bourgeois World,* edited by Frederick Cooper and Ann Laura Stoler, 59–86. Berkeley: University of California Press, 1997.

Meijer, D. H. "Over het Bendewezen op Java." *Indonesië* 3 (1949–50): 178–89.

Memmi, Albert. *The Colonizer and the Colonized.* New York: Orion Press, 1965.

Menzies-Lyth, I. *Containing Anxiety in Institutions.* London: Free Association Books, 1988.

Meszaros, Judet. "The Tragic Success of European Psychoanalysis: 'The Budapest School.'" *International Forum of Psychoanalysis* 7, no. 4 (1998): 207–14.

Meusnier de Querlon, Anne-Gabriel, A. Deleyre., J.-P. Rousselot de Surgy, P. J. Du Bois, J. Green, and T. Astley, eds. *Histoire générale des voyages, ou nouvelle collection de toutes les relations de voyage par mer et par terre.* Amsterdam: Van Harrevelt and D. Changuion, 1777.

Meyer, P. "L'antipsychiatrie." *L'Esprit* (1971): 207–25.

Miceli, Sergio. *Intelectuais e classe dirigente no Brasil (1920–1945).* São Paulo, Brazil: DIFEL, 1979.

Micouleau-Sicault, M.-C. *Les médecins français au Maroc (1912–1956): Combats en urgences.* Paris: L'Harmattan, 2000.

Miller, Christopher L. "Forget Haiti: Baron Roger and the New Africa." In "The Haiti Issue: 1804 and Nineteenth-Century French Studies," edited by Deborah Jenson, special issue, *Yale French Studies* 107 (spring 2005): 39–69.

Miller, Martin A. *Freud and the Bolsheviks: Psychoanalysis in Imperial Russia and the Soviet Union.* New Haven, Conn.: Yale University Press, 1998.

Mills, James H. *Madness, Cannabis and Colonialism: The "Native Only" Lunatic Asylums of British India, 1857–1900.* New York: St. Martin's Press, 2000.

Mitra, S. C. "Prof. Girindrasekhar Bose: An Appreciation." *Science and Culture* 19 (1953): 141–43.

Mokrejs, E. *A Psicanálise no Brasil: As Origens do Pensamento Psicanalítico.* Petrópolis, Brazil: Vozes, 1993.

Monteil, Charles. "La Divination chez les noirs de l'Afrique occidentale française." *Bulletin du comité des études historiques et scientifiques* 14, no. 1 (1931): 27–136.

Monteschi Valladares de Oliveira, Carmen Lucia. "Os primeiros tempos da psicanálise no Brasil es as teses pansexualistas na educação." *Agora. estudos em teoria psicanalítica* 5, no. 1 (Jan.–June, 2002): 133–54.

Moreau, Jacques Joseph. *Du haschish et de l'aliénation mentale: Etudes psychologiques.* Paris: Masson, 1845.

———. "Recherches sur les aliénés, en Orient." *Annales médico-psychologiques* 1 (1843): 103–32.

Moreau de Saint-Méry, Médéric Louis Elie. *Description topographique, physique, civile, politique et historique de la partie française de l'isle Saint-Domingue.* Philadelphia: Chez l'auteur, 1797.

Moreira-Almeida, Alexander, Angélica A. Silva de Almeida, and Fransico Lotufo Neto. "History of 'Spiritist Madness' in Brazil." *History of Psychiatry* 16, no. 1 (2005): 5–25.

Morgenstern, Naomi. "Mother's Milk and Sister's Blood: Trauma and the Neoslave Narrative." *Differences* 8, no. 2 (summer 1996): 101–26.

Moro, Marie-Rose. *Enfants d'ici venus d'ailleurs: Naître et grandir en France.* Paris: La Découverte, 2002.

Morse, Richard M. "The Multiverse of Latin American Identity, c. 1920–c. 1970." In *Ideas and Ideologies in Twentieth Century Latin America,* edited by Leslie Bethell, 3–129. New York: Cambridge University Press, 1996.

Mrázek, Rudolf. *Sjahrir: Politics and Exile in Indonesia*. Ithaca, N.Y.: Southeast Asia Program, Cornell University, 1994.

Muchielli, Laurent. *Le scandale des tournantes: Dérive médiatique, contre-enquête sociologique*. Paris: La Découverte, 2006.

Nancy, Jean-Luc. *Being Singular Plural*. Translated by R. Richardson. Stanford, Calif.: Stanford University Press, 2000.

Nandy, Ashis. *Alternative Sciences: Creativity and Authenticity in Two Indian Scientists*. New Delhi: Allied Publishers, 1980.

——. *Bonfire of Creeds*. New Delhi: Oxford University Press, 1983.

——. *The Intimate Enemy: Loss and Recovery of Self under Colonialism*. Delhi: Oxford University Press, 1974.

——. "The Psychology of Colonialism." *Psychiatry* 45 (1982): 197–218.

——. *The Savage Freud, and Other Essays on Possible and Retrievable Selves*. Princeton, N.J.: Princeton University Press, 1995.

——. "The Savage Freud: The First Non-Western Psychoanalyst and the Politics of Secret Selves in Colonial India." In *Decolonizing Knowledge: From Develpment to Dialogue*, edited by Frédérique Apffel-Marglin and Stephan A. Marglin, 340–88. Oxford: Clarendon Press, 1996.

Nathan, Tobie. "Etre juif?" *Nouvelle Revue d'Ethnopsychiatrie* 31 (1996): 7–12.

——. *La folie des autres: Traité d'ethnopsychiatrie clinique*. Paris: Dunod, 2001.

——. "Le rôle de Georges Devereux dans la naissance de l'ethnopsychiatrie clinique en France." *Ethnopsy: Les mondes contemporains de la guérison* 1 (February 2000): 197–226.

——. *L'influence qui guérit*. Paris: Odile Jacob, 1994.

——. "Manifeste pour une psychopathologie scientifique." In *Médecins et sorciers*, edited by Tobie Nathan and Isabelle Stengers, 9–113. Paris: Synthélabo, 1995.

——. "Préface, Devereux, un hébreu anarchiste." In *Ethnopsychiatrie des Indiens Mohaves*, 11–18. Paris: Synthélabo, 1996.

Nathan, Tobie, and Lucien Hounkpatin. *La parole de la forêt initiale*. Paris: Odile Jacob, 1996.

Nathan, Tobie, and Isabelle Stengers. *Médecins et Sorciers*. Paris: Les Empêcheurs de Penser en Rond, 2004.

Nesbitt, Nick. "The Idea of 1804." In "The Haiti Issue: 1804 and Nineteenth-Century French Studies," edited by Deborah Jenson, special issue, *Yale French Studies* 107 (spring 2005): 6–38.

Nicolas [Dr.]. "De la maladie du sommeil." In *Gazette Hebdomadaire de médecine et de chirurgie*, vol. 8 (1861): 670–73.

Nieuwenhuis, G. J. *Opvoeding tot Autonomie: Een Sociaal-Paedagogische Studie van het Philippijnsche Onderwijsstelsel, Vergeleken met het Nederl.-Indische*. Groningen en Weltevreden: J. B. Wolters, 1923.

Nordholt, Henke Schulte. "A Genealogy of Violence." In *Roots of Violence in Indonesia: Contemporary Violence in Historical Perspective*, edited by F. Colombijn and J. T. Lindblad, 81–103. Leiden, Netherlands: KITLV Press, 2002.

Nordholt, Henke Schulte, and Margreet van Till. "Colonial Criminals in Java, 1870–1910." In *Figures of Criminality in Indonesia, the Philippines, and Colonial Vietnam*, edited by V. L. Rafael, 47–69. Ithaca, N.Y.: Southeast Asia Program Publications, Cornell University, 1999.

Nunberg, Herman, and Ernst Federn, eds. *Minutes of the Vienna Psychoanalytic Society, 1906–1908*, vol 1. New York: International Universities Press, 1962.

Nunes, Silvia Alexim. "Da Medicina Social à Psicanálise." In *Percursos na história da psicanálise*, edited by Joel Birman, 61–122. Rio de Janeiro: Livraria Taurus Editora, 1988.

Nye, L. J. "Blood Pressure in the Australian Aboriginal, with a Consideration of Possible Aetiological Factors in Hyperpiesia and Its Relation to Civilisation." *Australian Medical Journal* 2 (1937): 1000–1001.

Nye, Robert A. *Masculinity and Male Codes of Honor in Modern France*. New York: Oxford University Press, 1993.

———. *The Origins of Crowd Psychology: Gustave Le Bon and the Crisis of Mass Democracy in the Third Republic*. Beverly Hills, Calif.: Sage Publications, 1975.

Obeyesekere, Gananath. "Further Steps in Relativization: The Indian Oedipus Revisited." In *Vishnu on Freud's Desk: A Reader in Psychoanalysis and Hinduism*, edited by T. G. Vaidyanathan and Jeffrey J. Kripal, 147–62. Delhi: Oxford University Press, 1999.

———. *The Work of Culture: Symbolic Transformation in Psychoanalysis and Anthropology*. Chicago: University of Chicago Press, 1990.

Oglivie, Bertrand. "Violence et représentation: La production de l'homme jetable." *Lignes* 26 (October 1995): 113–41.

Ohayon, Annick. *L'Impossible rencontre: Psychologie et psychanalyse en France, 1919–1969*. Paris: La Decouverte, 1999.

Olaniyan, Tejumola. " 'Post-Colonial Discourse': An Introduction." *Callaloo* 16, no. 4 (autumn 1993): 743–49.

Orgão da Sociedade Brasileira de Psychanalyse. *Revista Brasileira de Psicanálise* 1, no. 1 (1967): 34–70.

Ortigues, Marie-Cécile, and Edmond Ortigues. *Oedipe Africain*. Paris: Plon, 1966.

Orwell, George. "Shooting an Elephant." In *Shooting an Elephant, and Other Essays*. New York: Harcourt Brace, 1950.

Otis, Laura. *Membranes: Metaphors of Invasion in Nineteenth-Century Literature, Science, and Politics*. Baltimore, Md.: Johns Hopkins University Press, 1999.

Palente, Georges. *Pessimisme et individualisme*. Paris: F. Alcan, 1914.

Palmié, Stephan. "Creolization and Its Discontents." *Annual Review of Anthropology* 35 (2006): 433–56.

Pandey, Gyanendra. "In Defense of the Fragment: Writing about Hindu-Muslim Riots in India Today." In *A Subaltern Studies Reader, 1986–1995*, edited by R. Guha, 1–33. Minneapolis: University of Minnesota Press, 1997.

Pandolfo, Stefania. *Impasse of the Angels: Scenes from a Moroccan Space of Memory*. Chicago: University of Chicago Press, 1997.

Parin, Paul, Fritz Morgenthaler, and Goldy Parin-Matthey. *The Whites Think Too Much*. Zurich: Atlantis Verlag, 1963.

Patel, Geeta. *Literary Movements, Historical Hauntings: Gender, Colonialism and Desire in Miraji's Urdu Poetry*. Stanford, Calif.: Stanford University Press, 2002.

Pautrat, R. *La justice locale et la musulmane en A.O.F.* Rufisque, Senegal: Imprimerie du Haut Commissariat, 1957.

Pécaut, D. *Entre le peuple et la nation: Les intellectuels et la politique au Brésil*. Paris: Editions de la Maison des Sciences de l'Homme, 1989.

Peixoto, Fernanda Arêas. *Diálogos Brasileiros: Uma análise da obra de Roger Bastide*. São Paulo, Brazil: Edusp, 2000.

Perestrello, Marialzira. "Primeiros econtros com a psicanálise: Os precursores no Brasil, 1899–1937." In *Efeito psi: A influência da psicanálise*, edited by Sérvulo Figueira, 151–81. Rio de Janeiro: Campus, 1988.

Pfeiffer, Ernst, ed. *Sigmund Freud and Lou Andreas-Salomé Letters*. New York: Harcourt Brace and Jovanovich, 1972.

Pick, Daniel. *Faces of Degeneration: A European Disorder, c. 1848–c. 1918*. Cambridge: Cambridge University Press, 1989.

Pietz, William. "The Problem of the Fetish." Pt. 1. *Res* 9 (1985): 5–15.

———. "The Problem of the Fetish," pt. 3a, "Bosman's Guinea and the Enlightenment Theory of Fetishism." *Res* 16 (1988): 105–23.

Plotkin, Mariano Ben, ed. *Argentines on the Couch: Psychiatry, Society and the State in Argentina, 1880–1970*. Albuquerque: University of New Mexico Press, 2003.

———. *Freud in the Pampas: The Formation of a Psychoanalytic Culture in Argentina, 1910–1983*. Stanford, Calif.: Stanford University Press, 2001.

———. "Psychoanalysis, Transnationalism, and National Habitus." In *The Transnational Unconscious: Essays in the History of Psychoanalysis and Transnationalism*, ed. Joy Damousi and Mariano Ben Plotkin, 145–78. New York: Palgrave Macmillan, 2009

Pols, Hans. "Divergences in American Psychiatry during the Depression: Somatic Psychiatry, Community Mental Hygiene, and Social Reconstruction." *Journal of the History of the Behavioral Sciences* 37, no. 4 (2001): 369–88.

———. "The Nature of the Native Mind: Contested Views of Dutch Colonial Psychiatrists in the Former Dutch East Indies." In *Psychiatry and Empire*, edited by Megan Vaughan and Sloane Mahone, 119–97. London: Palgrave MacMillan, 2007.

———. "Psychological Knowledge in a Colonial Context: Theories on the Nature of the 'Native' Mind in the Former Dutch East Indies." *History of Psychology* 10, no. 2 (2007): 111–31.

Porot, Antoine. "Discussion du rapport d'assistance psychiatrique." In *Congrès des Médecins Aliénistes et neurologistes de France et des pays de langue françaises XLIIe session, Alger, 6–11 avril 1938*, edited by P. Combemale, 177–80. Paris: Impr. Coueslant Masson, 1939.

———. *Manuel alphabétique de psychiatrie*. Paris: Presses Universitaires de France, 1952.

———. "Notes de psychiatrie musulmane." *Anneles Médico-Psychologiques* 76 (May 1918): 377–84.

Porot, Antoine, and Don Côme Arrii. "L'impulsivité criminelle chez l'indigène algérien: Ses facteurs." *Annales Médico-Psychologiques* 90, no. 2 (1932): 588–611.

Porot, Antoine, and Jean Sutter. "Le 'primitivisme' des indigènes Nord-Africains. Ses incidences en pathologie mentale." *Sud médical et chirurgical* (15 April 1939): 226–41.

Porteus, Stanley D. *The Psychology of a Primitive People: A Study of the Australian Aborigine.* London: Edward Arnold, 1931.

Porto-Carrero, Júlio Pires. "Aspectos clinicos da psychanalyse." In *Ensaios de psychanalyse*. Rio de Janeiro: Flores and Mano, 1929.

———. "Bases da educação moral do brasileiro." In *Ensaios de psychanalyse*. Rio de Janeiro: Flores and Mano, 1929.

———. "Conceito psychanalytico da pena." In *Ensaios de psychanalyse*. Rio de Janeiro: Flores and Mano, 1929.

———. *Criminologia e psicanálise*. Rio de Janeiro: Flores and Mano, 1932.

———. *Ensaios de psychanalyse*. Rio de Janeiro: Flores and Mano, 1929.

———. "O carácter do escolar, segundo a psychanalyse." Paper presented at the First National Conference on Education, Curitiba, Brazil, 1927.

———. *Psicanálise de uma civilizacão*. Rio de Janeiro: Editora Guanabara, 1935.

Povinelli, Elizabeth A. *The Cunning of Recognition: Indigenous Alterities and the Making of Australian Multiculturalism*. Durham, N.C.: Duke University Press, 2002.

———. "The State of Shame: Australian Multiculturalism and the Crisis of Indigenous Citizenship." *Critical Inquiry* 24 (1998): 575–610.

Prado, Paulo. *Retrato do Brasil: Ensaio sobre a tristeza brasileira*. São Paulo, Brazil: Companhia das Letras, 1997. First published 1928.

Prakash, Gyan. *After Colonialism: Imperial Histories and Postcolonial Displacements*. Princeton, N.J.: Princeton University Press, 1995.

———. *Another Reason: Science and the Imagination of Modern India*. Princeton, N.J.: Princeton University Press, 1999.

———. "Science Between the Lines." In *Subaltern Studies*, vol. 9, *Writings on South Asian History and Society*, edited by Shahid Amin and Dipesh Chakrabarty, 49–82. Delhi: Oxford University Press, 1996.

Pritchard, E. E. "Levy-Bruhl's Theory of Primitive Mentality." *Faculty of Arts Bulletin* 2, no. 1 (1934).

Rabinow, Paul. *French Modern: Norms and Forms of the Social Environment*. Cambridge, Mass.: MIT Press.

Rafael, Vicente L., ed. *Figures of Criminality in Indonesia, the Philippines, and Colonial Vietnam*. Ithaca, N.Y.: Southeast Asia Program Publications, Cornell University, 1999.

——. "Mimetic Subjects: Engendering Race at the End of Empire." *Differences* 7, no. 2 (1995): 127–49.

Ramana, C. V. "On the Early History and Development of Psychoanalysis in India." *Journal of the American Psychoanalytic Association* 12 (1964): 110–34.

Ramanujan, A. K. "The Indian Oedipus." In *Vishnu on Freud's Desk: A Reader in Psychoanalysis and Hinduism*, edited by T. G. Vaidyanathan and Jeffrey J. Kripal, 109–36. Delhi: Oxford University Press, 1999.

Ramos, Artur. *Educação e Psychanalyse*. São Paulo, Brazil: Companhia Editora Nacional, 1934.

——. *Estudos de Psychanalyse*. Bahia, Brazil: Casa editora-Livraria Scientifica Argeu Costa, 1931.

——. *O negro brasileiro: Ethnographia, religiosa e psychanalyse*. Recife, Brazil: Massangana, 1988. First published in 1934.

——. *O negro brasileiro*. Vol. 1. 5th edn. Rio de Janeiro: Graphia editorial, 2003.

Rand, Nicholas. "The Hidden Soul: The Growth of the Unconscious in Philosophy, Psychology, Medicine, and Literature, 1750–1900." *American Imago* 61, no. 3 (2004): 257–89.

Ranse, Felix Henri, Marcel Baudoin, and Jules René Guérin, eds. *Gazette médicale de Paris* 6 (1877).

Reboul, Henry, and Emmanuel Régis, eds. "L'Assistance des aliénés aux colonies." In *Rapport au Congrès des médecins aliénistes et neurologistes de France et des pays de langue française, XXII session, Tunis, 1–7 avril 1912*. Paris: Masson, 1912.

La Révolution surréaliste. Paris: Gallimard, 1930.

Reynaud, G. "Epidémiologie de la maladie du sommeil." *Annales d'hygiène publique et de médecine légale* 4 (1905): 309–49.

Rimbaud, Arthur. "Mauvais sang." In *A Season in Hell and Other Works / Une Saison en enfer et oeuvres diverses*. Minneola, N.Y.: Dover, 2003.

Rivers, W. H. R. *Conflict and Dream*. New York: Harcourt Brace, 1923.

Robinson, David. *Paths of Accommodation: Muslim Societies and French Colonial Authorities in Senegal and Maurania, 1880–1920*. Athens: Ohio University Press, 2000.

Robinson, Paul A. *The Freudian Left: Wilhelm Reich, Géza Róheim, Herbert Marcuse*. New York: Harper and Row, 1969.

Róheim, Géza. *Australian Totemism: A Psycho-Analytic Study in Anthropology*. With an introduction by Montague David Eder. New York: Humanities Press, 1972. First published in 1926.

——. *Children of the Desert*. Vol. 1. New York: Basic Books, 1974.

——. "La psychologie raciale et les origines du capitalisme chez les primitifs." *Revue française de psychanalyse* 2, no. 1 (1928): 173–74.

——. "Psychoanalysis of Primitive Cultural Types." *International Journal of Psychoanalysis* 13 (1932): 1–224.

——. *The Riddle of the Sphinx*. London: Hogarth Press, 1934.

Roland, Alan. *Cultural Pluralism and Psychoanalysis: The Asian and North American Experience*. New York: Routledge, 1996.

Rose, Jacqueline. *On Not Being Able to Sleep: Psychoanalysis and the Modern World*. Princeton, N.J.: Princeton University Press, 2003.

Roudinesco, Elizabeth. *Jacques Lacan*. Translated by B. Bray. New York: Columbia University Press, 1997.

———. *La bataille de cent ans: Histoire de la psychanalyse en France*. Paris: Editions Ramsay, 1982.

———. *Pourquoi la psychanalyse?* Paris: Flammarion, 2001.

Roudinesco, Elisabeth, and Michel Plon. *Dictionnaire de la psychanalyse*. Paris: Fayard, 1997.

Roussier, Paul, ed. *Lettres du général Leclerc, commandant en chef de l'armée de Saint-Domingue en 1802*. Paris: Société de l'histoire des colonies françaises et Librairie Ernest Leroux, 1937.

Rush, Benjamin. "An Account of the Diseases Peculiar to the Negroes in the West-Indies, and Which Are Produced by Their Slavery." *American Museum; or, Repository of Ancient and Modern Fugitive Pieces, Prose and Poetical* 4, no. 1 (1788): 82.

Russo, Jane. "A Difusão da Psicanálise no Brasil na Primeira Metade do Século XX-Da Vanguarda Modernista à Radio-Novela." *Estudos e Pesquisas em Psicologia* 2, no. 1 (2002): 53–64. www.cocsite.coc.fiocruz.br/.

———. "A Psicanálise no Brasil-Institucionalizacão e Difusão entre o Público Leigo." Paper presented at the annual meeting of the Latin American Studies Association, Puerto Rico, March 15–18, 2006.

———. "Júlio Porto-Carrero: A psicanálise como instrumento civilizador." In *Psicologizacão no Brasil: Atores e autores*, edited by Luiz Fernando Dias Duarte, Jane Russo, and Ana Teresa Venancio, 127–49. Rio de Janeiro: Contra Capa Livraria, 2005.

Rutherford, Jennifer. *The Gauche Intruder: Freud, Lacan and the White Australian Fantasy*. Melbourne: Melbourne University Press, 2000.

Sachs, Wulf. *Black Hamlet: The Mind of an African Negro Revealed by Psychoanalysis*. Baltimore, Md.: Johns Hopkins University Press, 1996. First published in 1947.

Sadowsky, Jonathan H. *Imperial Bedlam: Institutions of Madness in Colonial Southwest Nigeria*. Berkeley: University of California Press, 1999.

Sagawa, Roberto Yutaka. "A psicanálise pioneira es os pioneiros da psicanálise em São Paulo." In *Cultura da Psicanálise*, edited by Sévulo Figueira, 15–34. São Paulo, Brazil: Brasiliense, 1985.

Said, Edward W. *Culture and Imperialism*. New York: Knopf, 1993.

———. *Freud and the Non-European*. London: Verso, 2003.

———. *Joseph Conrad and the Fiction of Autobiography*. Cambridge, Mass.: Harvard University Press, 1966.

Sánchez-Pardo, Esther. *Cultures of the Death Drive: Melanie Klein and Modernist Melancholia*. Durham, N.C.: Duke University Press, 2003.

Sayad, Abdelmalek. "Santé et équilibre social chez les immigrés." *Psychologie médicale* 13, no. 11 (1981): 1747–75.

Schmitt, Carl. *The Concept of the Political.* Chicago: University of Chicago Press, 1996.

Schorske, Carl E. *Fin-de-siècle Vienna: Politics and Culture.* New York: Vintage Books, 1981.

Schreiner, Alexandre. "Uma aventura para amanhã: Arthur Ramos e a neuro-higiene infantil na década de 1930." In *Psicologizacão no Brasil: Atores e autores,* edited by Luiz Fernando Dias Duarte, Jane Russo, and Ana Teresa Venancio, 151–66. Rio de Janeiro: Contra Capa Livraria, 2005.

Schwab, Gabriele. *Derrida, Deleuze, Psychoanalysis.* New York: Columbia University Press, 2007.

Schwarz, Roberto. "Las ideas fuera de lugar." In *Absurdo Brasil: Polémicas en la cultura brasileña,* edited by Adriana Amante and Florencia Garramuño, 45–60. Buenos Aires: Biblos, 2000.

Schwarcz, Lilia Moritz. *As barbas do imperador: D. Pedro II, um monarca nos trópicos.* São Paulo, Brazil: Companhia das Letras, 1998.

Scott, Daryl Michael. *Contempt and Pity: Social Policy and the Image of the Damaged Black Psyche, 1880–1996.* Chapel Hill: University of North Carolina Press, 1997.

Scott, David. "Colonial Governmentality." *Social Text* 43 (1995): 191–220.

Sears, Laurie J. *Shadows of Empire: Colonial Discourse and Javanese Tales.* Durham, N.C.: Duke University Press, 1996.

Seshadri-Crooks, Kalpana. *Desiring Whiteness: A Lacanian Analysis of Race.* New York: Routledge, 2000.

Shore, Bradd. *Culture in Mind: Cognition, Culture, and the Problem of Meaning.* New York: Oxford University Press, 1996.

Silverman, Maxim. *Deconstructing the Nation: Immigration, Racism, and Citizenship in Modern France.* London: Routledge, 1992.

Simmons, William S. *Eyes of the Night: Witchcraft among a Senegalese People.* Boston: Little, Brown, 1971.

Sinha, Tarun Chandra. "Development of Psychoanalysis in India." *International Journal of Psychoanalysis* 47 (1966): 427–39.

———. "A Short Life Sketch of Girindrasekhar Bose." In "Special Issue on Bose," edited by Nagendranath Dey, special issue, *Samiksa* (1954): 62–74.

Sironi, Françoise. "Comment inventer des pratiques cliniques adaptées aux mondes contemporains." Lecture given for the "Portes ouvertes" series of the Centre Georges Devereux in Paris, University of Paris 8, May 29, 2001. Available at http://www.ethnopsychiatrie.net/.

Skidmore, Thomas E. *Black into White: Race and Nationality in Brazilian Thought.* 2nd edn. Durham, N.C.: Duke University Press, 1993.

Spillers, Hortense J. "All the Things You Could Be by Now if Sigmund Freud's Wife Was Your Mother." *Critical Inquiry* 22 (1996): 710–34.

Spivak, Gayatri Chakravorty. "Subaltern Studies: Deconstructing Historiography." In *Selected Subaltern Studies,* edited by Ranajit Guha and Gayatri Chakravorty Spivak, 3–32. Oxford: Oxford University Press, 1988.

Stengers, Isabelle. "Le médecin et le charlatan." In *Médecins et sorciers*, edited by Tobie Nathan and Isabelle Stengers, 115–61. Paris: Synthélabo, 1995.

Stephen, J. *Buonaparte in the West Indies; or, the History of Toussaint Louverture, the African Hero.* London: J. Hatchard, 1803.

Stiglitz, Joseph. *Globalization and its Discontents.* New York: W. W. Norton, 2002.

Stoler, Ann Laura. *Carnal Knowledge and Imperial Power: Race and the Intimate in Colonial Rule.* Berkeley: University of California Press, 2002.

———. *Race and the Education of Desire: Foucault's History of Sexuality and the Colonial Order of Things.* Durham, N.C.: Duke University Press, 1995.

Storper-Perez, Danielle S. *La folie colonisé.* Paris: François Maspero, 1974.

Strachey, James, Anna Freud, and Carrie Lee Rothgeb, eds. *The Standard Edition of the Complete Psychological Works of Sigmund Freud.* 24 vols. London: Hogarth Press, 1943–74.

Sulloway, Frank J. *Freud, Biologist of the Mind: Beyond the Psychoanalytic Legend.* Cambridge, Mass.: Harvard University Press, 1992.

Taïeb, Suzanne. *Les idées d'influence dans la pathologie mentale de l'Indigène Nord-Africain: Le Rôle des superstitions.* Algiers: Imprimerie Victor Heintz, 1939.

Taussig, Michael. *Mimesis and Alterity: A Particular History of the Senses.* New York: Routledge, 1993.

———. *The Nervous System.* New York: Routledge, 1992.

Teixeira, B. A. *Educacão e Psychanalyse.* São Paulo, Brazil: Companhia Editora Nacional, 1934.

Thomas, Nicholas. *Colonialism's Culture: Anthropology, Travel, and Government.* Princeton, N.J.: Princeton University Press, 1994.

Thibaut de Chanvalon, Jean Baptiste. *Voyage à la Martinique, contenant diverses observations sur la physique, l'histoire naturelle, l'agriculture, les moeurs, et les usages de cette isle, faites en 1751 et les années suivantes.* Paris: Chez J. B. Bauche, 1763.

Thompson, J. C. "Tropical Neurasthenia: A Deprivation Psychoneurosis." *Military Surgeon* 54 (1924): 319–27.

Tlatli, Soraya. *Le psychiatre et ses poètes: Essai sur le jeune Lacan.* Paris: TCHOU, 2002.

Torgovnick, Marianna. *Gone Primitive: Savage Intellects, Modern Lives.* Chicago: University of Chicago Press, 1990.

Travaglino, P. H. M. "Politiek en Psychologie." *PEB: Orgaan van den Nederlandsch-Indischen Politiek-Economischen Bond* 5, no. 8 (1924): 86–93.

Turin, Yvonne. *Affrontements culturels dans l'Algérie coloniale: Ecoles, médecine, religion, 1830–1880.* Paris: Maspero, 1971.

Turkle, Sherry. *Psychoanalytic Politics: Jacques Lacan and Freud's French Revolution.* 2nd edn. New York: Guilford Press, 1992.

van Ginneken, Jaap. *Crowds, Psychology, and Politics, 1871–1899.* Cambridge: Cambridge University Press, 1992.

van Loon, F. H. "Acute Verwardheidstoestanden in Nederlands-Indië." *Geneeskundig Tijdschrift voor Nederlandsch-Indië* 62 (1922): 658–90.

——. "Amok and Lattah." *Journal of Abnormal and Social Psychology* 4 (1927): 434–44.

van Till, Margreet. *Batavia bij Nacht: Bloei en Ondergang van het Indonesisch Roverswezen in Batavia en de Ommelanden, 1869–1942*. Amsterdam: Aksant, 2006.

van Wulfften Palthe, Pieter Mattheus. "Forensische Psychiatrie in Nederlandsch-Indië." *Psychiatrisch-Juridisch Gezelschap, Verslagen* 13 (1936): 1–28.

——. "Geestesstoornis en Gemeenschapsstructuur." *Geneeskundig Tijdschrift voor Nederlands Indië* 33, no. 76 (1936): 2050–67.

——. "Koro: Eine Merkwürdige Angsthysterie." *Internationale Zeitschrift für Psychoanalyse* 21, no. 2 (1935): 248–57.

——. *Neurologie en Psychiatrie*. Amsterdam: Wetenschappelijke Uitgeverij, 1948.

——. *Over het Bendewezen op Java*. Amsterdam: Van Rossen, 1949.

——. *Psychological Aspects of the Indonesian Problem*. Leiden, Netherlands: Brill, 1949.

——. "Psychological Aspects of the Indonesian Problem." (Letter to the Editor). *Nederlandsch Tijdschrift voor Geneeskunde* 93, no. 49 (1949): 418–19.

——. "Psychologische Beschouwing omtrent den Huidigen Toestand op Java." *Nederlands Tijdschrift voor Geneeskunde* 90, no. 18 (1946): 425–30.

——. *Zintuigelijke en Psychische Functies Tijdens het Vliegen*. Leiden, Netherlands: Doesburgh, 1921.

van Wulfften Palthe, Pieter Mattheus, and P. A. Kerstens. *Opening Nood-Universiteit: Redevoeringen Uitgesproken door Prof. Dr. P.M. van Wulfften Palthe, President der Nood-Universiteit en P.A. Kerstens, wd. Directeur van Onderwijs & Eeredienst te Batavia op 21 Januari 1946*. Groningen en Batavia: J. B. Wolters, 1946.

Vaughan, Megan. *Curing Their Ills: Colonial Power and African Illness*. Cambridge: Polity Press, 1991.

Venancio, Ana Teresa, and Lázara Carvalhal. "Juliano Moreira: A psiquiatria científica no processo civilizador brasileiro." In *Psicologizacão no Brasil: Atores e autores*, edited by Luiz Fernando Dias Durate, Jane Russo, Ana Teresa Venancio, 65–83. Rio de Janeiro: Contra Capa Livraria, 2005.

Vergès, Françoise. "The Age of Love." *Transformation* 47 (2001): 1–17.

——. "Chains of Madness, Chains of Colonialism: Fanon and Freedom." In *The Fact of Blackness: Frantz Fanon and Visual Representation*, edited by Alan Read, 47–75. Seattle: Bay Press, 1996.

——. *Monsters and Revolutionaries: Colonial Family Romance and Métissage*. Durham, N.C.: Duke University Press, 1999.

Vezzetti, Hugo. *Aventuras de Freud en el país de los Argentinos*. Buenos Aires: Paidós, 1996.

Vickers, Adrian. *A History of Modern Indonesia*. Cambridge: Cambridge University Press, 2005.

Vikár, G. "The Budapest School of Psychoanalysis." In *Ferenczi's Turn in Psychoanalysis*, edited by Peter L. Rudnytsky, Antal Bókay, and Patrizia

Giampieri-Deutsch, 60–76. New York: New York University Press, 1996.

von Hartmann, Eduard. *Philosophie de l'inconscient.* Translated by D. Nolen. Paris: G. Baillière et Cie, 1877.

Weaver, Karol Kimberlee. *Medical Revolutionaries: The Enslaved Healers of Eighteenth-Century Saint Domingue.* Urbana: University of Illinois Press, 2006.

Weber, Eugen. *Peasants into Frenchmen: The Modernization of Rural France, 1870–1914.* Stanford, Calif.: Stanford University Press, 1976.

Wiener, Margaret J. "Dangerous Liaisons, and Other Tales from the Twilight Zone: Sex, Race, and Sorcery in Colonial Java." *Comparative Studies in Society and History* 49, no. 3 (2007): 495–526.

Wilder, Gary. *The French Imperial Nation-State: Negritude and Colonial Humanism between the Two World Wars.* Chicago: University of Chicago Press, 2005.

Williams, Raymond. *The Politics of Modernism: Against the New Conformists.* London: Verso, 2007. First published in 1989.

Wrong, Dennis H. *Skeptical Sociology.* New York: Columbia University Press, 1976.

Young, Allan. "Bruno and the Holy Fool: Myth, Mimesis, and the Transmission of Traumatic Memories." In *Understanding Trauma: Integrating Biological, Clinical, and Cultural Perspectives,* edited by Laurence J. Kirmayer, Robert Lemelson, and Mark Barad, 339–62. Cambridge: Cambridge University Press, 2007.

Young, Robert J. C. *Postcolonialism: An Historical Introduction.* Oxford: Blackwell, 2001.

Zempléni, Andràs. "From Symptom to Sacrifice: The Story of Khady Fall." In *Case Studies in Spirit Possession,* edited by Vincent Crapanzano and Vivian Garrison, 87–139. New York: Wiley, 1977.

CONTRIBUTORS

WARWICK ANDERSON is a research professor in the Department of History and the Centre for Values, Ethics and the Law in Medicine at the University of Sydney, as well as a professorial fellow at the Centre for Health and Society at the University of Melbourne. Until recently, he was Robert Turell Professor of Medical History and Population Health and chair of the Department of Medical History and Bioethics at the University of Wisconsin, Madison. He is the author of *The Cultivation of Whiteness: Science, Health, and Racial Destiny in Australia* (2002), *Colonial Pathologies: American Tropical Medicine, Race, and Hygiene in the Philippines* (2006), and *The Collectors of Lost Souls: Turning Kuru Scientists into Whitemen* (2008).

ALICE BULLARD, formerly associate professor of history at Georgia Tech University, is currently a juris doctor candidate at Georgetown Law School and an independent historian. A scholar of the intellectual culture of French colonialism, she is currently researching the histories of psychiatry and psychoanalysis in French West Africa. She is the author of *Exile to Paradise: Savagery and Civilization in Paris and the South Pacific, 1790–1900* (2000) and has recently published two articles on the emergence of transcultural psychiatry: "L'Oedipe Africain: A Retrospective" (2005) and "The Critical Impact of Franz Fanon and Henri Collomb: Race, Gender and Personality Testing of North and West Africans" (2005).

JOHN CASH is currently teaching at the University of Melbourne. His research interests are in the fields of social and political theory, psychoanalytic studies, the politics of identity, and the analysis of contemporary subjectivities. He is particularly interested in the study of conflict in Northern Ireland and other divided societies. His publications include *Identity, Ideology and Conflict: The Structuration of Politics in Northern Ireland* (1996) and a series of articles that draws critically on contemporary social and psychoanalytic theory in an attempt to develop novel approaches to the study of entrenched ethnic conflict.

JOY DAMOUSI is professor of history in the School of Historical Studies at the University of Melbourne. She has published widely in the fields of cultural history, feminist history, the history of emotions, war and memory, and the history of psychoanalysis. She is the author of numerous books and articles, including *The Labour of Loss: Mourning, Memory and Wartime Bereavement in Australia* (1999), *Living with the Aftermath: Trauma, Nostalgia and Grief in Post-war Australia* (2001), and *Freud in the Antipodes: A Cultural History of Psychoanalysis in Australia* (2005). She is also the coeditor of *History on the Couch: Essays in History and Psychoanalysis* (with Robert Reynolds, 2003) and *The Transnational Unconscious: Essays in the History of Psychoanalysis and Transnationalism* (with Mariano Plotkin, 2008).

DIDIER FASSIN, an anthropologist, sociologist, and medical doctor, is James D. Wolfensohn Professor of Social Science at the Institute for Advanced Study, Princeton, and director of studies at the Ecole des Hautes Etudes en Sciences Sociales in Paris. His teaching and research interests include the social dimensions of medicine and public health, and he has recently developed a new field of research in critical moral anthropology. He is the author or coauthor of several works, including *The Empire of Trauma: An Inquiry into the Condition of Victimhood* (with R. Rechtman; 2009) and *When Bodies Remember: Experiences and Politics of AIDS in South Africa* (2007). He is also the editor or coeditor of various books, including *Contemporary States of Emergency: The Politics of Military and Humanitarian Interventions* (with M. Pandolfi, 2010) and *Les Nouvelles Frontières de la Société Française* (2010).

CHRISTIANE HARTNACK is deputy head of the Department of Cultural Studies at the Donau Universitat Krems in Austria. A clinical psychologist by training, she has published widely on the history of psychoanalysis in India, including the book *Psychoanalysis in Colonial India* (2001).

DEBORAH JENSON is professor of romance studies and a faculty affiliate of the Duke Global Health Institute at Duke University, where she co-directs the Franklin Humanities Institute "Haiti" humanities laboratory. She was, until recently, professor of French and director of the Center for the Humanities at the University of Wisconsin, Madison. Her most recent monograph, *Beyond the Slave Narrative: Politics, Sex, and Manuscripts in the Haitian Revolution* assesses the international literary and philosophical impact of Haiti's first leaders. Jenson's work on trauma ranges from a PTSD research project in Haiti to her book *Trauma and Its Representations* (2001). She is also active in "neurohumanities" research and has co-authored an article on mirror neurons and mimesis with neuropsychiatrist Marco Iacoboni.

RICHARD C. KELLER is associate professor of medical history and the history of science at the University of Wisconsin, Madison. He is the author of *Colonial Madness: Psychiatry in French North Africa* (2007), as well as numerous articles on colonial psychiatry. Currently, he is writing a book on the deadly Paris heat wave of 2003.

RANJANA KHANNA is professor of English and Margaret Taylor Smith Director of Women's Studies at Duke University. She is the author of *Dark Continents: Psychoanalysis and Colonialism* (2003) and *Algeria Cuts: Women and Representation, 1830 to the Present* (2007), as well as articles related to postcoloniality, feminism, and psychoanalysis.

MARIANO PLOTKIN is a researcher at the Instituto de Desarrollo Economico y Social in Buenos Aires, Argentina, and professor at the Universidad Nacional de Tres de Febrero. He was visiting professor at Harvard University and at the Universidad de Salamanca. He is the author of *Manana es San Peron: A Cultural History of Peron's Argentina* (2003) and *Freud in the Pampas* (2001) and is coeditor of *The Transnational Unconscious* (with Joy Damousi, 2008).

HANS POLS is the director and a senior lecturer in the Unit for History and Philosophy of Science at the University of Sydney. A scholar of the history of psychiatry and psychology, the history of medicine, and the history of human sciences, he is currently at work on a study of Dutch colonial psychiatry in the East Indies.

Brazilian Communist Party, 125
Brazilian Educational Association, 123, 135 n. 23
Brazilian League of Mental Hygiene, 121, 124
Brazilian Psychoanalytic Association, 119, 121, 124–25, 128
Breton, André, 11, 127, 200
Breuer, Joseph, 24, 39 n. 15
Brill, Abraham Arden, 124
Buddhism, 156
Bullard, Alice, 6, 247
Buret, Maurice, 175
Burke, Edmund, 179, 251–52, 254
Burton, Robert, 248
Bush, George W., 36
Butler, Judith, 21–22, 249, 264 n. 23

Caeté Indians, 127
cafuné, 130–31
Calcutta University, 99–101, 103
Cândido, Antonio, 126
candomblé, 56, 132
cannibalism, 52–53
capitalism, 47, 250–53, 255, 260
Carby, Hazel, 255
Carles, Dr., 175
Carmarans, Father, 59–60
Carmichael Medical College and Hospital, 101
Carothers, John Colin, 13, 70 n. 27, 151–52, 228–29
Cartwright, Samuel, 173
Caruth, Cathy, 182
Cash, John D., 5–6, 248, 258
castration, 47, 106
cathexis, 68, 190, 192
Catholicism, 51, 57–61, 116, 123, 125, 127
Cazanove, Frank, 47–49, 61
Cendrars, Blaise, 137 n. 59
Centre National de Recherche Scientifique (CNRS), 236
Centro Dom Vital, 125

Chakrabarty, Dipesh, 167, 177
Chamoiseau, Patrick, 185
Charcot, Jean-Martin, 61, 70 n. 22, 175, 176, 186, 236
charlatanism, 51
Chateaubriand, François-René de, 184, 189–92
Chatinières, Paul, 217–18
Chatterji, Suniti Kumar, 107
Chertok, Leon, 174–75, 186
Chesterman, John, 82
Chevalier, Jean Damien, 171, 173
child psychology, 86–87, 121, 193, 223, 225–27, 231, 238–40
children, as compared to "primitives": by Algiers School, 228–29; in Australia, 83, 93; in British Empire, 80–81; by Freud, 32, 79; in Indonesia, 144–45, 147, 151–52, 154, 157; by Jones, 78; in West Africa, 50, 74 n. 98
Chirac, Jacques, 263 n. 19
Chraïbi, Driss, 201
Christison, Lieutenant-General Sir Philip, 150
citizenship, 2, 7, 9, 14–15, 82, 108, 203, 227, 251–52, 254, 259, 261
civilization: Arendt on, 254; Christian, 57; culture versus, 2, 156; hierarchies of, 4, 26, 74 n. 96, 90, 125, 144, 147–48, 201, 204; pathologies of, 92–93, 132, 171, 177; "primitives" as antithesis of, 11, 13, 62, 76, 80–85, 127, 129, 160, 209; "primitives" as harboring, 7, 120, processes of, 6, 31–32, 48, 64–68, 228; race and, 23, 74 n. 105
Civilization and Its Discontents (Freud), 1, 22, 81, 85
civilizing mission, 185, 201, 250, 252
Claude Bernard Hospital, 228
Clérambault, Gaëtan Gatian de, 47
climate, 171
Code de l'Indigénat, 252
Codrington, Robert Henry, 66, 74 n. 100

Farmer, Paul, 210
fascism, 116, 123
Fassin, Didier, 15, 257–58, 262
Faustin Soulouque I, 184
fauvism, 126
Federn, Paul, 38
feminism, 84, 188
Ferenczi, Sandor, 76, 136 n. 24, 168
Ferguson, Niall, 255
fetishism: Bhabha on, 22, 25; in Brazil, 122; McClintock on, 43; in "modern" populations, 11; Pietz on, 16; in West Africa, 50–51, 53, 60, 66
First World War: Arendt on, 254; Brazil's role in, 125; civilization disrupted by, 11; Freud on, 248–50; Rat Man's death in, 38, treatment of colonial soldiers during, 54, 204, 228; van Wulfften Palthe's experience in, 146
Fischer, Sybille, 182
Flanagan, Joseph, 181–82
Fliess, Wilhelm, 107
folklore, 77, 79, 103, 131
folkloric unconscious, 121
Forrester, John, 113
Foucault, Michel, 48, 199, 225
free association, 88, 90–91, 102, 104
French Equatorial Africa, 63
French Revolution, 179–80
Freud, Sigmund: anthropology and, 84, 247; as archaeologist, 105; archives of, 111 n. 39; Brazilian reception of, 114, 118–20, 125, 127–28, 131, 133, 134 n. 5, 136 n. 24, 137 n. 59; Breuer and, 24; on civilization, 171; colonial challenges to, 8; on condensation, 195 n. 15; French reception of, 46–47; on Haiti, 167, 193–94, 198 n. 109, 262; on hypnosis, 174; Indian reception of, 101–3, 106–8, 111 nn. 38–39, 168; influence on Géza Róheim, 86–88, 92–93; internationalism of, 262; lectures at Clark University by, 39 n. 15; on loss, 248; on melancholia,

16, 249, 256–57, 259, 263 n. 5; on mind/body connection, 170; on mourning, 209; Nandy on, 22, 25; on narcissism, 32; Nathan on, 235–36; on "oceanic self," 2; on the pleasure principle, 104; on "primitives," 3, 4; psychoanalysis and, 113, 134 n. 4; on repression, 56; on seduction theory, 187; on the superego, 258; translations of, 84, 121; on the uncanny, 5, 6, 28, 33–34; on the unconscious, 10. See also Oedipal complex; specific cases and works
Freud Prize, 77
Freyre, Gilberto, 133
Front de Libération Nationale (FLN, Algeria), 109, 203
Frosh, Stephen, 80
Future of an Illusion, The (Freud), 122
futurism, 126

Galligan, Brian, 82
Gandhi, Mohandas K., 40 n. 24, 99, 105
Gassner, Johann Joseph, 175
Geerardyn, Filip, 193, 198 n. 109
Gelder, Ken, 7
gender: in Australian Aboriginals, 86–87; colonial models of, 97, 147; in India, 26–27, 36; Islam and, 214; in psychoanalytic theory, 258, 264 n. 23; slavery in Brazil and, 130–31
genocide, 260
geopsychoanalytic space, 13–14, 167–98
Georges Devereux Center, 230, 233, 238, 241–42
Ghosal, Srimati Svarna Kumari Devi, 99
globalization: capitalism and, 255; fragmentation of self by, 36–37; Kristeva on, 34; of unconscious, 1–17, 43, 50, 52, 54, 109, 167, 171
Gobineau, Arthur de, 117
God, 61, 253
Goetz, Bruno, 107

Islam: in Algeria, 108, 201, 203–4, 211, 218; ethnopsychiatry and, 223–45; in Indonesia, 145, 156; in West Africa, 50–51, 61, 67, 71 n. 32
ius imperium, 252

Jacobs, Jane M., 7
Jaffré, Yannick, 236
jagos, 159–60, 165 n. 62
Jamaica, 169
Jameson, Fredric, 182
Janet, Pierre, 46, 55–56, 71 n. 43, 72 n. 53
Japan, occupation of Indonesia, 141–65
Java Institute, 154
Jenson, Deborah, 13, 262
Jesus Christ, 58–59, 61
Jews, 188, 232–33, 253
João VI, 116
Jones, Ernest, 38, 78–80, 101, 168
Journal of the American Psychoanalytical Association, 111 n. 39
Jumu, 86
Jung, Carl, 46, 107, 121
justice, 66, 257

Kabyles, 250
Kakar, Sudhir, 8
Kama Sutra, 103
Kant, Immanuel, 259
Kapur, Geeta, 249
Kateb, Yacine, 14–15, 199–221
Kateb, Yasmina, 202–3, 206–11, 214, 219
Keller, Richard C., 14–15
Kenya, 13, 151, 228–29
Khanna, Ranjana, 4, 16, 80, 171, 205
Kikuyu, 151–52
Kipling, Rudyard, 13
Kirmayer, Laurence J., 186
Klaxon, 128
Klein, Melanie, 25, 36, 76, 86, 248–49
Kleinman, Arthur, 205, 209
Kleinman, Joan, 209

Koch, Adelaide, 125
koro, 146
Kraepelin, Emil, 135 n. 13, 148
Kristeva, Julia, 25, 34, 36–37, 254, 263 n. 16

Lacan, Jacques, 4, 11–12, 24–25, 39 n. 19, 45, 133, 258
Lacoue-Labarthe, Philippe, 187
Laforgue, René, 47
Lagache, Daniel, 73 n. 95
Laing, Ronald, 200
Lamarck, Jean-Baptiste, 120, 135 n. 13
Lamartine, Alphonse de, 189, 192
Lanessan, Jean Marie Antoine de, 178
Lanzer, Ernst. *See* Rat Man
lata, 146–47
Latour, Bruno, 241–42
Lavoisier, Antoine, 186
Le Bon, Gustave, 155, 161
Lebou, 50, 53–54
Lebovici, Serge, 237
Leclerc, Charles-Emmanuel, 179
Leiris, Michel, 5, 11
Lemelson, Robert, 186
Le Pen, Jean-Marie, 242
Lepenies, Wolf, 248
leprosy, 48, 173
Lévi-Strauss, Claude, 4, 129, 232, 235–36
Lévy-Bruhl, Lucien, 11, 45–46, 69 n. 5, 121, 130
Leys, Ruth, 14, 185–89
liberalism, 3, 4, 7, 9, 10
libido, 89–90, 137 n. 50
Lipsedge, Maurice, 81
Littlewood, Roland, 80–81
Loach, Ken, 225
Lombroso, Cesare, 213
Loomba, Ania, 180
Loraux, Nicole, 261, 263
Loritja, 86
loss, 248, 256, 258
Louis XVI, 186
Louisiana Purchase, 179, 196 n. 53

Louis-Philippe, 251
Louverture, Toussaint, 179, 189–90, 192
Luxemburg, Rosa, 250–51, 253, 263
Ly, Madeleine, 48, 63
Lyautey, Hubert, 216–17
lying, 62–63, 68, 197 n. 79

Macandal, François, 176
Madagascar, 11–12, 229
magic, 10, 43–74, 121, 152, 155, 159–60, 174
Magnan, Valentin, 119
magnetism, 14, 176–77, 186
Mahdi, 156
Malagasy, 11–12
malaria, 48, 147
mal d'estomac, 171–73
Malfatti, Anita, 126
mana, 43, 46, 65–68
Manicheanism, 12, 22, 25, 109, 203–4
Mannoni, Maud, 48
Mannoni, Octave, 4, 11–12, 229
Manuel alphabétique de psychiatrie (Porot), 45, 229
marabouts, 15, 51, 57–58, 71 n. 32, 237
Maran, René, 63–64
Marcondes, Durval, 119, 123–25, 128–29, 136 n. 33
Marcus, Julie, 83
marriage, 15, 83
Marx, Karl, 22, 127, 184
Marxism, 12, 16, 113, 247, 253, 263
Mauchamp, Emile, 49
Maudsley, Henry, 81
Mau Mau, 13, 151–52, 228–29
Mauss, Marcel, 46, 74 n. 100, 232, 235, 237
Maximy, Hubert de, 239
Maximy, Martine de, 239
May, Karl, 155
Mbembe, Achille, 225
McClintock, Anne, 43
McCulloch, Jock, 205

McWatters, R. C., 101
Medical Committee for the Exiles, 230
Medico-Social Committee for the Health of Migrants, 230
melancholy, 4, 16, 137, 170, 172–73, 175, 248–50, 256–264
Melanesia, 79
Memmi, Albert, 12
memory, 33, 182, 197 n. 79
mental hygiene, 119, 121, 123–24
Menzies-Lyth, I., 40 n. 48
Mesmer, Franz Anton, 175–76, 186
mesmerism, 14, 170, 175–77, 186, 193
mestizos, 127
metempsychosis, 172
metropole, 168–69, 178
Miceli, Sergio, 124
Michel-Lévy Hospital, Marseilles, 46, 54
Middle Passage, 171–72, 174
Miller, Christopher, 184–85
Millet, Madame, 176
mimesis, 2, 14, 169, 170, 176, 192. *See also* traumatic mimesis
mimicry, 24
Ministry of Education and Health (Brazil), 123
Minkowska Center, 230
missionaries, 53, 56–63, 83
mnemopsychosis, 185
modal personality, 6, 8, 11–12, 21, 119, 212
Modern Art Week (São Paulo, 1922), 126, 128
modernism: in Brazil, 115, 126–28, 130, 132–33, 136 n. 39; exile and, 259–60; melancholia and, 248–49, 256; psychoanalysis and, 1, 10, 167
modernity: Anderson on, 168; biopolitical dimensions of, 199; imperialism and, 10, 57, 180, 255; internationalism and, 249; melancholia and, 4; primitivism versus, 7, 11, 21, 68–69, 77, 81, 83, 132, 204; as setting for psychoanalysis, 3

modernization, 117, 124

monarchy, in Brazil, 116, 118, 124, 134 n. 7

monotheism, 171

Monteil, Charles, 49

Montessori, Maria, 122

moralism, 257

Moreau de Saint-Méry, M. L. E., 171, 177

Moreira, Juliano, 118–19, 124, 135 nn. 12–13

Moreiras, Alberto, 260

Morel, Bénédict-Augustin, 119

Moreno, Jacob Levi, 132

Morgenstern, Naomi, 187

Morgenthaler, Fritz, 48

Moro, Marie-Rose, 243

Morocco, 49, 201, 216–17

Moser, Fanny, 193, 198 n. 109

mourning, 208–10, 257

"mulatto," 119, 122, 132, 134 n. 12

multiculturalism, 7, 15–16, 84

Musée de l'Homme, 73 n. 95

mysticism, 156

myth, 26, 46, 77–78, 85–87, 92–93, 131, 137 n. 50, 184, 209

Nancy, Jean-Luc, 187, 197 n. 84

Nandy, Ashis, 8, 13, 21–27, 35–37, 40 n. 24, 80, 171

Napoleon III, 184–85

narcissism, 12–13, 27, 29, 32, 36–37, 158

natality, 263 n. 16

Nathan, Tobie, 231–45, 257–58, 262

nation, 2, 7, 248, 251–56, 259–60

national identity, 10; in Brazil, 113–37

nationalism: Algerian, 199–221; Arendt on, 253; codependence with psychoanalysis, 2, 7; Fanon on, 12; Indian, 99; Indonesian, 8, 13, 143–65; Kristeva on, 36; modernism and, in Brazil, 126; Stoler on, 226; violence and, 34, 261

Native Union, 83

nativism, 256–57

Nazism, 125, 188, 227, 253

ndëpp, 231

necroanthropophagy, 52

Negritude, 195 n. 15

"Negro," 8, 61, 119

Negrophobia, 68–69

neocolonialism, 187–88

Nesbitt, Nick, 180

neurasthenia, 70 n. 22

neurology, 47, 173, 181

neurosis, 79, 104, 157, 182, 193–94

New Guinea, 77

Nicolas, Dr., 173–74

Nietzsche, Friedrich, 127

nit ku bon, 231

Nones, 60

North Africa, 9, 65, 168, 199–221, 228–29

"North African Syndrome" (Fanon), 67

nostalgia, 14, 174–75, 177

nyai, 160

objectivity, 44

obsession, 60, 67

Oedipal complex: Bose on, 106–8; in Brazil, 123, 131, 137 n. 50; in Indonesia, 149–50, 156; in "primitives," 78–79; reversal in colonial context, 8; Róheim on, 85–87, 92; universal nature of, 69 n. 2

Oedipe Africain, 45, 48, 70 n. 8, 231

Ogilvie, Bertrand, 259–60

Olaniyan, Tejumola, 188

Old Republic (Brazil), 116

Ombrédane, André, 73 n. 91

ontogenesis, 120

Organization of African Unity, 109

orientalism, 5, 29, 146, 204, 223

Ortigues, Edmond, 45, 48, 70 n. 8, 231

Ortigues, Marie-Cécile, 45, 48, 70 n. 8, 231

Orwell, George, 214

psychodrama, 132
Psychopathologie Africaine, 231
psychosis, 54–55, 64, 71 n. 46, 209
psychosomatic disorders, 175
psychotropic drugs, 229
public health, 118, 230
Puységur, Antoine-Hyacinthe, 176

queer studies, 258
Qur'an, 60, 200–201

Rabain, Jacqueline, 231
racial decline, 81–84, 86
racial purity, 83
Radcliffe-Brown, Alfred, 84
Ramos, Arthur, 115, 120–21, 123, 129–31, 137 n. 50
rampok, 156, 165 n. 63
Ranchi Mental Hospital (India), 8, 98, 101
Rand, Nicholas, 177
Rank, Otto, 38
rationalism, 2, 10, 44, 65–66, 81–84, 90, 147, 153
Rat Man, 5, 25, 28–41, 258
reality principle, 189
reason, 62, 66
Reboul, Henri, 48
recognition, 208
Reform Party of Bengal, 99
refugees, 16, 230, 249, 253–54, 260. *See also* asylum; exile
Régis, Emmanuel, 47–49
relativism, 188, 242
religion: authority over mental illness based in, 49; fetishism and, 43, 50, 53; as marker of primitivism in Brazil, 119, 122, 130–32, 137 n. 50; missionary practices in West Africa and, 57–63, 69; Nandy on, 26; psychoanalytic influence on, 84; the uncanny and, 33; violence in Indonesia and, 156
Renaissance, 248
repetition, 14, 24, 31
repression: concealment of human nature by, 65–66; as constitutive of subject, 22, 31, 33–34, 177; Derrida on, 168; Freud on, 79, 85; as function of civilization, 93; as function of colonialism, 160; gender and, 89; Haitian revolution and, 183, 193; means of coping with, in the West, 148; mind-body connection and, 170; as pathogenic, 104
republicanism: citizenship and, 259; incompatibility with slavery, 116; independence in Indonesia and, 143, 150, 152; paradoxes of cultural particularism in, 15–16, 227, 241–43; universal subject as prerequisite for, 2
repudiation, 33, 208–9, 211
resistance: anticolonial, 25, 27, 37, 142, 157, 159, 207, 210; to psychoanalysis, 91–92; subjectivity and, 22, 170
Revue française de psychanalyse, 47
Revue rose, 178
Reynaud, Gustave, 174–75, 195 n. 34
Ribo, Théodule-Armand, 128
Richer, Paul, 70 n. 22
rights, 66, 153, 251; human, 82–83, 230, 254; land, 7, 250
Rimbaud, Arthur, 48, 195 n. 15
Ritalin, 226
Rivers, W. H. R., 4, 6
Robinson, David, 71 n. 32
Robinson, Paul, 84–85, 93
Rochambeau, Comte de, 189
Rodrigues, Raymundo Nina, 119–20, 135 n. 12
Róheim, Géza, 6–7, 47, 75–95, 137 n. 47, 262
Roland, Alan, 84, 88
Rolland, Romain, 107, 111 n. 38
romanticism, 117, 191–92, 248
Roudinesco, Elisabeth, 45, 114, 125
Royal Anthropological Institute, 77
Rush, Benjamin, 170, 172–73
Russo, Jane, 120, 136 n. 24
Rutherford, Jennifer, 7

Sachs, Wulf, 4, 70 n. 8, 247
sacrifice, 56, 234–35, 237
sadism, 122
Sadowsky, Jonathan, 80
Saint-Domingue. *See* Haiti
Salazar, Oliveira, 116
Sanchez-Pardo, Esther, 248–49
Sardinha, Bishop, 127
Satan, 61
Satyagraha, 99
savagery: as function of colonial domi-
    nation, 205, 212; race and, in Brazil,
    122, 125; Róheim on, 76, 78–80, 82,
    86, 90–91; subjectivity and, 25
scarification, 237
Schopenhauer, Arthur, 177
Schwarcz, Lilia Moritz, 134 n. 7
scientific racism, 117
scramble for Africa, 185
secondary processes, 147
Second World War, 21, 142–43, 158,
    227–28, 248, 250
see-saw method, 104
Segal, Lasar, 126
seizures, 60
self: distinction from environment, 66;
    epistemologies of, 9; fragmentation
    of, 5, 33, 186, 208; indigenous, 75, 86;
    as modern and rational, 80, 82;
    Nandy on, 22, 25–27, 30, 35–37; psy-
    choanalysis as constitutive of, 2, 113,
    127, 177, 258; repudiation of, 68;
    slavery and, 189; universal nature of,
    76, 88, 93
Senegal, 43–74
Serer, 53–54, 60
Sétif, massacres at, 202, 206–7, 210
settler colonialism, 7, 14, 143, 178, 201,
    205, 214–16
sex education, 120–22
sexual abuse, 187, 224, 226
sexuality: Bose on, 103; in Brazil, 119–
    21, 130–31, 133; Butler on, 264 n. 23;
    fetishism as component of, 43; Freud

on, 3, 32, 35; influence of psycho-
    analysis on, 7, 84, 113; Klein on, 249;
    regulation of, in France, 226, 229;
    repression of, 30; Rivers on, 4;
    Róheim on, 87, 89, 91; van Wulfften
    Palthe on, 160, 165 n. 64
sex work, 224, 226
shamanism, 240
shell-shock, 204
shock, 14, 182
simulation, 230
sinistrosis, 229–30
Sironi, Françoise, 243
Siva, 103
slavery, 10, 115–18, 130–31, 133, 169–
    98, 261
social contract, 30–31
social Darwinism, 117
social hygiene, 118
social sciences, 4, 115, 125, 128–33
social workers, 233, 241, 243
somatoform disorders, 172–73, 177
Soninke, 223, 232–33, 241–42
sovereignty: melancholia and, 248–49;
    political, 253; psychoanalysis as tool
    for conceptualizing, 2–6, 9, 17, 194;
    subjectivity and, 16, 21–41, 258–59;
    trauma and, 10, 14
Spencer, Baldwin, 91
spirits, 48, 51, 53–54, 57, 60–61, 68–
    69, 78
spiritualism, 145, 178
Spivak, Gayatri, 167, 256
splitting, 22, 31, 33–37, 39 n. 18
state, 2, 7, 9, 10, 12, 16, 124, 205, 210,
    261
Stengers, Isabelle, 174–75, 186, 241
Stiglitz, Joseph, 1
Stoler, Ann, 226
STOVIA. *See* Batavia Faculty of
    Medicine
Strehlow, Carl, 91
structural violence, 6, 14–15, 199–221,
    238, 243

resistance and, 160–61; creolization of, in Haiti, 169, 175, 178–80, 183, 192; criminality as function of, 122–23; globalization of, 1–17, 76, 110, 113–14, 167–68, 189, 262–63; hypnosis as revelatory of, 174, 186; prepsychoanalytic concept of, 177; "primitives" and, 78–80, 129; race and, 24, 39 n. 18, 40 n. 19, 132–33; repression and, 29–32, 194; Róheim on, in Australians, 85–90, 93; subconscious versus, 136 n. 42; trauma and, 187; in West Africa, 43–74

United Aborigines Mission, 83
United East Indies Company, 154
United Nations, 141
universalism: Aubin on assimilation of difference and, 44, 46, 53, 56–57, 60–69, 69 n. 2, 73 n. 96; cultural particularism versus, 90; French republicanism and, 227, 230, 232, 241; Napoleonic empire as emblematic of, 190–91; psychoanalytic pretentions to, 1–7, 11, 14–16, 22, 107; of psychopathology, 80; of religion, 171; of self, 88, 93; of unconscious, 76, 167
University of Paris 8, 233–34, 239
University of São Paulo, 129, 131
Upanishads, 102
urbanization, 118
Utkendra Samiti, 100
utopianism, 248, 256

Valantin, Simone, 231
van de Vijver, Gertrudis, 193, 198 n. 109
van Loon, Feico Herman Glastra, 146–47
van Till, Margreet, 159
van Wulfften Palthe, Pieter Mattheus, 13, 141–65
Vargas, Getulio, 116–17, 123–24
Vergès, Françoise, 185, 259
Vichy France, 227
Vienna Psychoanalytic Society, 38
Vienna University, 107

Vietnam, 21
Vila-Lobos, Heitor, 126
violence: Algerian independence struggle and 199–221; colonial, 6, 15, 37; French Revolution and, 184; Haitian revolution and, 181, 185, 189, 192, 194; Indonesian independence struggle and, 141–42, 150–53, 155–61, 164 n. 58; moral, 258, 260; nation-state and, 254, 260–61; subjectivity and, 22, 25–26, 30, 34–35; in *tirailleurs Sénégalais*, 50, 64; trauma and, 188; unconscious and, 2, 3. *See also* structural violence
Virgin Mary, 59–61
Vishnu, 108
Vodou, 175–77
Völkerpsychologie, 148
Volksraad, 145
von Hartmann, Eduard, 177–78

Waterloo, 185
wayang kulit, 145
Weaver, Karol Kimberlee, 175–76
Weber, Eugen, 183
Weimar Constitution, 261
welfare state, 15
West Africa, 43–74, 223–45
West Indies, 170
West Papua (Irian), 141
whiteness, 83, 117, 131–32
Wilder, Gary, 195 n. 15
Wilhelmina, 143
Williams, Raymond, 249, 260–61
wishes, 6, 13, 78–79, 103–4, 106–7, 150, 153, 161, 209
witchcraft: in Australia, 78, 91–92; in Indonesia, 152, 160; as pathogenic, 174, 236; as postcolonial pathology, 15, 239; therapeutic dimensions of, 231, 240; in West Africa, 48–74
Wolof, 53–54, 57, 60, 240
World Health Organization, 56, 70 n. 27, 237

WARWICK ANDERSON is Professor of History at the University of Sydney and the author of *The Collectors of Lost Souls: Turning Kuru Scientists into White Men* (2008) and *Colonial Pathologies: American Tropical Medicine, Race, and Hygiene in the Philippines* (2006).

DEBORAH JENSON is Professor of Romance Studies, a faculty affiliate in Global Health, and codirector of the Franklin Humanities Institute "Haiti" humanities laboratory at Duke University. She is the author of *Beyond the Slave Narrative: Politics, Sex, and Manuscripts in the Haitian Revolution* (2011) and *Trauma and Its Representations: The Social Life of Mimesis in Post-Revolutionary France* (2001).

RICHARD C. KELLER is Associate Professor of Medical History and Bioethics at the University of Wisconsin, Madison and the author of *Colonial Madness: Psychiatry in French North Africa* (2007).

Library of Congress Cataloging-in-Publication Data
Unconscious dominions : psychoanalysis, colonial trauma, and global sovereignties / edited by Warwick Anderson, Deborah Jenson, and Richard C. Keller.
p. cm.
Includes bibliographical references and index.
ISBN 978-0-8223-4964-8 (cloth : alk. paper)
ISBN 978-0-8223-4979-2 (pbk. : alk. paper)
1. Psychiatry, Transcultural—History.
2. Ethnopsychology—History. I. Anderson, Warwick, 1958– II. Jenson, Deborah. III. Keller, Richard C. (Richard Charles), 1969–
RC455.4.E8U536 2011
155.8—dc22   2011015527